ANSI vs. UNICODE string functions

When developing for Windows CE, you need to use the UNICODE string manipulation functions, rather than the ANSI ones. The following table shows you the ANSI functions and their UNICODE equivalent:

ANSI FUNCTION	UNICODE FUNCTION	ANSI FUNCTION	UNICODE FUNCTION
strtod	_tcstod	strncmp	_tcsncmp
strtol	_tcstol	strncpy	_tcsncpy
strtoul	_tcstoul	strncpy	_tcsnccpy
_itoa	_itot	strpbrk	_tcspbrk
_ltoa	_ltot	strrchr	_tcsrchr
_ultoa	_ultot	strspn	_tcsspn
atoi	_ttoi	strstr	_tcsstr
atol	_ttol	strtok	_tcstok
strcat	_tcscat	_strdup	_tcsdup
strchr	_tcschr	_stricmp	_tcsicmp
strcmp	_tcscmp	_strnicmp	_tcsnicimp
strcpy	_tcscpy	_strnicmp	_tcsnicmp
strcspn	_tcscspn	_strnset	_tcsnset
strlen	_tcslen	_strnset	_tcsncset
strlen	_tcsclen	_strrev	_tcsrev
strncat	_tcsncat	_strset	_tcsset
strncat	_tcsnccat	_strlwr	_tcslwr
strncmp	_tcsnccmp	_strupr	_tcsupr

UNICODE and TCHAR equivalents of common string functions

CHAR	WCHAR	TCHAR
strcpy	wcscpy	_tcscpy
strstr	wcsstr	_tcsstr
strcat	wcscat	_tcscat
strcmp	wcscmp	_tcscmp
strchr	wcschr	_tcschr
strlen	wcslen	_tcslen
strtok	wcstok	_tcstok
strrev	wcsrev	_tcsrev
toupper	towupper	_totupper
tolower	towlower	_totlower

MFC Classes Not Supported

The following is a list of MFC Classes that are not supported on Windows CE:

All COle*Dialog classes	CFileFind	COleDataObject
CAnimateCtrl	CFontDialog	COleDataSource
CasyncMonikerFile	CFtpConnection	COleDocument
CCachedDataPath-Property	CFtpFileFind	COleDropSource
CCheckListBox	CGopherConnection	COleDropTarget
CDaoDatabase	CGopherFile	COleIPFrameWnd
CDaoException	CGopherFileFind	COleLinkingDoc
CDaoFieldExchange	CGopherLocator	COleMessageFilter
CDaoQueryDef	CHotKeyCtrl	COleServerDoc
CDaoRecordset	CHtmlStream	COleServerItem
CDaoRecordView	CHttpFilter	COleStreamFile
CDaoTableDef	CHttpFilterContext	COleTemplateServer
CDaoWorkspace	CHttpServer	CPageSetupDialog
Cdatabase	CHttpServerContext	CPictureHolder
CDataPathProperty	CMDIChildWnd	Crecordset
CDBException	CMDIFrameWnd	CRecordView
CDBVariant	CMetaFileDC	CRichEditCntrl
CDocItem	CMiniFrameWnd	CRichEditCntrlItem
CDockState	CMonikerFile	CRichEditDoc
CDocObjectServer	CMultiDocTemplate	CRichEditView
CDocObjectServerItem	CMultiLock	Csemaphore
CDragListBox	Cmutex	CSharedFile
CFieldExchange	COleClientItem	CToolTipCtrl
	COleCmdUI	

Jason P. Nottingham
Steven Makofsky
Andrew Tucker

SAMS
Teach Yourself

Windows® CE
Programming
in 24 Hours

SAMS

A Division of Macmillan USA
201 West 103rd St., Indianapolis, Indiana, 46290 USA

Sams Teach Yourself Windows® CE Programming in 24 Hours

Copyright © 1999 by Sams Publishing

International Standard Book Number: 0-672-31658-7

Library of Congress Catalog Card Number: 99-60834

Printed in the United States of America

First Printing: August 1999

01   00   99   4   3   2   1

Trademarks

Warning and Disclaimer

ASSOCIATE PUBLISHER
Brad Jones

ACQUISITIONS EDITOR
Chris Webb

DEVELOPMENT EDITOR
Matt Purcell

MANAGING EDITOR
Jodi Jensen

PROJECT EDITOR
Dawn Pearson

COPY EDITOR
Kate Talbot

INDEXER
William Meyers

PROOFREADER
Megan Wade

TECHNICAL EDITOR
Jon Sturgeon

TEAM COORDINATOR
Meggo Barthlow

SOFTWARE DEVELOPMENT SPECIALIST
Dan Scherf

INTERIOR DESIGN
Gary Adair

COVER DESIGN
Aren Howell

COPY WRITER
Eric Bogert

LAYOUT TECHNICIAN
Louis Porter, Jr.

Overview

Contents

Foreword

We are in the midst of a revolution in computing. With the growing acceptance of the Internet and the current state of the art in 32-bit microprocessors, there will be a rapid, nonlinear growth in Internet appliances. According to many market researchers, the sales volume of Internet appliances will exceed the sales volume of personal computers early in the next decade. Although PCs will still fill a major role in home and business computing, these new Internet appliances will increasingly assume specialized functions that have been fulfilled by PCs until now.

In late 1994, BSQUARE Corporation began developing the low-level development tools for an operating system that has come to be known as *Windows CE*. A product of Microsoft, Windows CE is an embedded operating system developed specifically for non-PC form factor devices. The first such product developed using Windows CE is the Handheld PC (H/PC), initially released in 1996. Companies such as Hewlett Packard, Hitachi, LG, Casio, and many more have manufactured this device. In two short years, the H/PC has become the market share leader in the clam-shell form factor device category.

Since then, Microsoft and its partners have developed a multitude of novel, non-PC devices—all with the capability to access the Internet. To many, the battle line is drawn between Java and Windows CE. Although design trade-offs tend to be involved, they are not between Java and Windows CE. Rather, the trade-offs are between programming in Windows CE's native language, Visual C++, or Java, because Windows CE supports Java as well as any embedded operating system.

One major benefit of using Windows CE as a platform is that you can elect to use the right programming tool for the job. A task might best be solved with Java, Visual C++, Visual Basic, or a combination of some or all of them. By using Windows CE, you are not locked into any one programming paradigm.

Another nice aspect of selecting Windows CE as the embedded operating system for your platform is the leverage you acquire across the many devices developed using Windows CE. Your software, if properly architected, is highly portable between devices, minimizing the incremental development effort required to migrate between devices. This maximizes your greatest asset—you!

This book was written to quickly bring you to the point where you can be productive programming for the Windows CE operating system. You will be guided through this process by three of the best Windows CE developers on the planet.

Jason Nottingham architected and implemented the first Windows CE product to carry the official Microsoft *Made for Windows CE* logo. This product, bFAX Professional, has been ported to every H/PC and Palm-size PC (P/PC).

Steve Makofsky came to BSQUARE to develop Internet applications such as bMOBILE News. Steve served as the architect and lead developer of the bUSEFUL Utilities Suite. This product was nominated the Best Utility Suite in the Fall 1998 Comdex computer trade show—an amazing honor for a product designed for a non-PC operating system.

Andrew Tucker is a lead developer of some of the most important programming tools that affect all Windows CE developers. He has served as a key developer for Visual C++ for Windows CE, working in conjunction with Microsoft. To that end, Andrew has been instrumental in creating the robust tools on which Windows CE is predicated.

If you embrace and become proficient in developing software for Windows CE, you will have an opportunity to target the new generation of mobile computing appliances, set-top boxes, and in-car navigation and entertainment systems, to name just a few. We hope that you enjoy reading this book as much as the authors enjoyed writing it.

William Baxter
President and CEO
BSQUARE Corporation

About the Authors

STEVEN MAKOFSKY is a senior software engineer for the commercial applications division of BSQUARE Corporation. Since 1995, he has been writing programs targeting Windows CE platforms, including BSQUARE's bUSEFUL Backup, bMOBILE News, bUSEFUL FindSpace, and bTASK. Besides programming, he enjoys hiking and lots of coffee.

JASON P. NOTTINGHAM is the director of application products for the commercial applications division of BSQUARE Corporation. He has a bachelors of science degree in electrical engineering from the University of Connecticut. Since 1994, he has been writing programs targeting Windows CE platforms, including BSQUARE's award-winning bFAX and several of the bUSEFUL utility applications.

ANDREW TUCKER works on developer tools for Windows CE at BSQUARE Corporation. He has been writing Windows code since 1991 and has published technical articles in *C/C++ Users Journal*, *Dr. Dobbs Journal*, and *Windows Developer Journal*. He recently gave a presentation on debugging at the 1999 Windows CE Developers Conference. Andrew has a bachelor of science degree in computer science from Seattle Pacific University and is working on a master of science degree in computer science at the University of Washington.

Dedication

To my family for their support and encouragement. Without them, I would not be who I am today.

—Steven Makofsky

To Cynthia Lee Nottingham and Reed Fletcher Nottingham, for their patience while I worked on this book.

—Jason Nottingham

To my beautiful and wonderful wife, Victoria Mathew. You are a constant inspiration, and being partners with you makes me the luckiest man alive.

—Andrew Tucker

Acknowledgments

First and foremost, I'd like to thank the excellent staff at Macmillan USA, including Chris Webb, Matt Purcell, Kate Talbot, and Dawn Pearson. I'd also like to thank Jon Sturgeon for his excellent technical editing of the book.

Special thanks to my colleagues who, through their humor, enabled me to complete this book without losing my sanity: Jason for making sure that I was on schedule; Sam for his clear-cut, no-nonsense attitude; Jeremy for his calm demeanor and the morning coffee; Chris for breaking my software; and Diane for the movies (good times!).

I am grateful to Randy and Fred, who always seem to get themselves in some predicament, creating much humor for those around them.

Finally, I would like to thank Lisa for many years of friendship, through good times and bad.

—Steven Makofsky

I would like to thank the other people involved with creating this book: Steve Makofsky (BSQUARE), Andrew Tucker (BSQUARE), Matt Purcell, Chris Webb, Dawn Pearson, (all three Macmillan), and Jon Sturgeon (FutureSoft). I'd also like to thank the BSQUARE founders and early employees: Bill Baxter, Al Dosser, Peter Gregory, John Hatch, Chris McGregor, Edit Markinchec, and Tor Trygstad.

I'd also like to thank my coworkers: Martin Susser, Peter Eberhardy, Diane Allerdice, Chris Petersen (and the rest of our application QA group), Meiyu Lin, Andy Harding, David Brownell, Ken McCaw, Clemens Butz, Jeff McLeman, Joe Notarangelo, David Bialer, John Simmons, Craig Hummel, Suzanne Kass, Bravo Lee (who also delivered devices and materials to my home while I wrote on paternity leave), and Yen Lee (for technical assistance for the ActiveSync hour).

Finally, I'd like to thank John Utz, James Utz, and Aaron Diesen for "musical therapy," and Cynthia and Reed for tolerating it.

—Jason Nottingham

First of all, thanks to all the people at Sams Publishing. Chris Webb and Matt Purcell always kept the project on track, and Kate Talbot did a great job of improving the text from the initial first drafts. Major kudos also go to our technical editor, Jon Sturgeon, for checking the accuracy of the code and text and raising a red flag when necessary.

—Andrew Tucker

Tell Us What You Think!

As the reader of this book, *you* are our most important critic and commentator. We value your opinion and want to know what we're doing right, what we could do better, what areas you'd like to see us publish in, and any other words of wisdom you're willing to pass our way.

As an associate publisher for Sams Publishing, I welcome your comments. You can fax, email, or write me directly to let me know what you did or didn't like about this book— as well as what we can do to make our books stronger.

Please note that I cannot help you with technical problems related to the topic of this book, and that due to the high volume of mail I receive, I might not be able to reply to every message.

When you write, please be sure to include this book's title and author as well as your name and phone or fax number. I will carefully review your comments and share them with the authors and editors who worked on the book.

Fax: 317-581-4770.

Email: opsys@mcp.com

Mail: Brad Jones
           AssociatePublisher
           Sams Publishing
           201 West 103rd Street
           Indianapolis, IN 46290 USA

If you have a technical question about this book, call the technical support line at (317) 581-3833 or send email to support@mcp.com.

Introduction

This book is written for beginning to advanced Win32 developers who are new to Windows CE. We won't teach you how to write programs with the Win32 API. Instead, we'll guide you down the winding path of porting code and show you the features and tricks that are unique to Windows CE devices.

How This Book Is Structured

This book is divided into four sections, each of which corresponds to an area of Windows CE development.

Part I, "Getting Started," is an overview of how to get up and running with the Windows CE Toolkit for Visual C++ 6 and what's different about writing code for Windows CE compared to Windows NT or 98.

Part II, "User Interfaces," delves into the details of how to use the standard controls and dialogs in your Windows CE applications.

Part III, "Tap in to the System," covers how to get the most out of the Windows CE system resources, such as the object store, threads, Winsock, and printing.

Part IV, "Advanced Windows CE Programming," includes important topics such as communicating with the desktop, mail-enabling your application, and power management.

Each lesson in the book is designed to take you about an hour to complete. It begins with a list of teaching objectives and then dives right in to the first topic. In each hour, discussions are intertwined with hands-on examples that show you real-world applications for the features you're learning. The end of the hour contains a Q&A section, a quiz, and exercises designed to test your knowledge and understanding of the hour's material. The answers to the quiz are in Appendix A, "Answers."

What You Will Need

To compile the code, you must install Visual C++ 6 and the Windows CE Toolkit for Visual C++ 6 on your desktop machine, running Windows NT or 98.

To run the code, you have two options. Although some projects will run on the desktop with the Windows CE emulator, it's recommended that you use a Windows CE H/PC, H/PC Professional Edition, or P/PC device for the best results.

PART I
Getting Started

Hour

HOUR 1

Getting Started with Visual C++ for Windows CE

Welcome to Hour 1 of *Sams Teach Yourself Windows CE Programming in 24 Hours*! This first hour will get you well on your way towards using Visual C++ 6.0 to quickly develop applications for Windows CE, an exciting new version of Windows.

In this hour, you will learn

- How to install the Visual C++ 6.0 for Windows CE toolkits
- How to create a Hello World! application and build and run it under the Windows CE emulator on the desktop, as well as on actual Windows CE devices
- How to start porting your existing desktop Win32 applications to Windows CE
- How to use the remote software tools included with the Visual C++ 6.0 Windows CE toolkits

Installing Visual C++ for Windows CE

The first step in developing for Windows CE is to get the Windows CE toolkits installed and up-and-running on your development computer.

The Windows CE toolkits integrate with your existing installation of Visual C++ 6.0. If you do not have Visual C++ 6.0 installed on your desktop machine, you should install it and run it once (to initialize Registry settings) before proceeding with installing the Windows CE toolkits.

> You can develop for Windows CE devices using a desktop computer running Windows 95, Windows 98, or Windows NT. The Windows CE desktop emulators (used for running and debugging Windows CE applications on your desktop machine instead of actual devices) require a desktop operating system that supports Unicode, so these emulators will work only if you are using Windows NT for your development computer.

Developing applications for Windows CE requires that you have the Windows CE Toolkit for Visual C++ 6.0 and one or more Windows CE Platform SDKs installed on your development machine. Installing these components is discussed in the next sections.

Installing the Windows CE Toolkit for Visual C++ 6.0

When you insert the Windows CE Toolkit for Visual C++ 6.0 installation CD-ROM in your desktop computer, it will automatically launch the setup program. The Windows CE toolkit will be successfully installed after you

1. Enter a valid registration key.
2. Select a destination directory (typically C:\Windows CE Tools or D:\Windows CE Tools).
3. Select your installation options (it is recommended that you choose the default installation options).

This setup program installs the cross compilers, linkers, and other tools (such as a remote Registry editor and a remote spy utility) used for working with Windows CE. The *cross compilers* are optimizing compilers that run on desktop X86 Windows machines, but that produce executable code that runs on the range of CPUs that support Windows CE. Table 1.1 lists the compilers and the CPUs they support. This is useful to know if you prefer to build from the command line rather than from within the Visual C++ IDE.

TABLE 1.1 The Windows CE Cross Compilers

Compiler	Target CPU
SHCL.EXE	SH3 and SH4 processors
CLMIPS.EXE	MIPS processors
CLARM.EXE	StrongARM processor
CLPPC.EXE	Power PC processor

The headers and libraries required to build for specific Windows CE platforms are installed by the Windows CE Platform SDK setup programs that are automatically launched after this first setup program completes successfully.

The Windows CE help files are installed in this step. They are in compiled HTML format and are located in the \Windows CE Tools\HTMLHELP directory. The software required to view compiled HTML files is also installed, if it is not already present on the system.

When the setup for the Windows CE Toolkit for Visual C++ 6.0 completes, it will automatically launch the setup for the Windows CE Platform SDK for the Handheld PC.

Installing the Windows CE Platform SDK for the Handheld PC

The setup program for the Windows CE Platform SDK for the Handheld PC installs the components required to build and debug applications for the Handheld PC (H/PC) platform. These components include the Win32, MFC, and ATL header files, libraries, and samples. They are installed under the \Windows CE Tools\WCE200\MS HPC directory. This setup program also installs the H/PC desktop emulator on your computer. The README file is in HTML format and is installed to \Windows CE Tools\hpcreadme.htm on your hard drive.

When the setup for the Windows CE Platform SDK for the Handheld PC completes, it will automatically launch the setup for the Windows CE Platform SDK for the Palm-Size PC.

Installing the Windows CE Platform SDK for the Palm-Size PC

The setup program for the Windows CE Platform SDK for the Palm-Size PC installs the Win32 and MFC header files and libraries necessary to build and debug applications for the Palm-Size PC (PsPC) platform. This setup program also installs the PsPC desktop emulator on your development machine. All PsPC components are installed under the

\Windows CE Tools\WCE201\MS PALM SIZE PC directory. The README file for the PsPC Platform SDK is in HTML format and is installed to \Windows CE Tools\ ppcreadme.htm on your hard drive.

> The Windows CE Platform SDK for the Handheld PC Professional Edition is not included on the installation CD-ROM for Windows CE Toolkit for Visual C++ 6.0. You can download the H/PC Professional Edition Platform SDK for free from the Microsoft Web site from the following URL:
>
> http://msdn.microsoft.com/cetools/platform/hpcprofeatures.asp

Congratulations! You have successfully installed the Windows CE toolkits. The next step is to make sure that Windows CE Services is installed on your desktop computer.

Installing Windows CE Services

Windows CE Services is the desktop software component that enables your desktop computer to communicate with a Windows CE device. If you have previously purchased a Windows CE device and connected it to your desktop computer, its likely that you have already installed Windows CE Services (it is included on the CD-ROM with every Windows CE device sold).

If you are not sure whether it is installed, you can quickly check by clicking the Start button on your desktop version of Windows and selecting Programs. If Microsoft Windows CE Services is listed in the pop-up Programs menu, it is installed on your desktop computer.

If Windows CE Services is not already installed on your desktop computer, you must install it from the Windows CE Services CD-ROM that came with your Windows CE device.

Performing a Clean Reinstall to Fix Installation Issues

If you encounter recurring issues with the Visual C++ toolkits for Windows CE, the quickest way to fix them is to perform a clean reinstall. Some of these issues can include difficulty with copying your application to the emulation environment or to Windows CE devices, or the Visual C++ IDE crashing when you attempt to rebuild your application after a debug session. These types of issues don't happen with most installations, but knowing how to proceed can help save you valuable time.

A clean reinstall involves uninstalling the Windows CE Platform SDKs, the Windows CE toolkit, and Visual C++ 6.0 and then reinstalling them.

You initiate the uninstall process by running the Add/Remove Programs Control Panel applet on your desktop computer. From within the applet, you uninstall any of the following that are installed on your desktop computer:

- Windows CE Platform SDK (H/PC Professional Edition)
- Windows CE Platform SDK (H/PC)
- Windows CE Platform SDK (PsPC)
- Microsoft Windows CE Toolkit for Visual C++ 6.0
- Microsoft Visual Studio 6.0

Depending on the type of problem you are attempting to resolve, it can also be important to delete the following desktop Registry entries before reinstalling:

```
HKEY_CURRENT_USER\Software\Microsoft\DevStudio
HKEY_LOCAL_MACHINE\Software\Microsoft\DevStudio
```

> You can edit the Registry on a Windows 95 or Windows 98 machine by running the REGEDIT.EXE tool. On Windows NT, you can edit the Registry by using the REGEDT32.EXE tool.

The first program to reinstall is Visual C++ 6.0. Do not forget to run it at least once (to initialize Registry settings) before continuing on to install the Windows CE toolkits. After Visual C++ 6.0 has been successfully reinstalled, you can install the Windows CE toolkits in the manner discussed earlier this hour.

Creating Your First Windows CE Application: Hello World!

For your first Windows CE application, you will create a Windows program with a menu and an About dialog that displays Hello World! in its main window. This is a quick first application to create because the Visual C++ wizards will author the application source code for you.

The first step you must take is to select New from the File menu within the Visual C++ IDE. This will display the New dialog displayed in Figure 1.1. If it does not default to the Projects tab, select it yourself. Note that in addition to all the project choices you had before you installed the Windows CE toolkits, you now have the option to create several types of Windows CE-specific projects.

FIGURE 1.1

Creating a new Windows CE applica-tion project.

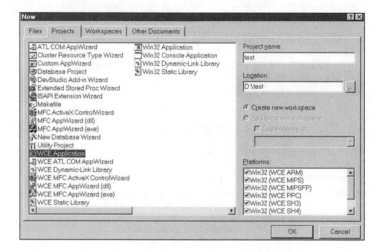

To create your Hello World! application, select WCE Application from the projects list, enter a project name in the Project Name field, and click the OK button.

You will now be prompted for the type of Windows application you would like to create. Select A Typical "Hello World!" Application, as shown in Figure 1.2, and click Finish.

FIGURE 1.2

Selecting the type of application project you would like to create.

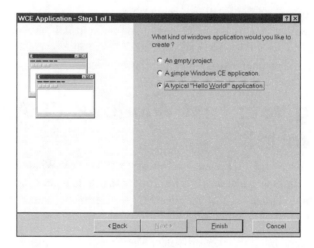

The wizard will create a Windows CE application project for you, in addition to several source files (as well as an RC file) to implement the default Hello World! application. You are now ready to build your first Windows CE application.

Building Your First Windows CE Application

In preparation for building your first Windows CE application, you must perform two preliminary steps:

1. Select the proper platform to target.
2. Select the correct CPU to target.

After you have specified both, you can build, run, and debug your program.

Selecting the Target Platform

The *target platform* is the type of Windows CE device that you want to build your program to run on. The current options are H/PC Ver. 2.00, Palm-size PC 2.01, or H/PC Pro 2.11.

Figure 1.3 shows you how to select the target Windows CE platform from within the Visual C++ IDE.

FIGURE 1.3

Selecting the target platform for which to build.

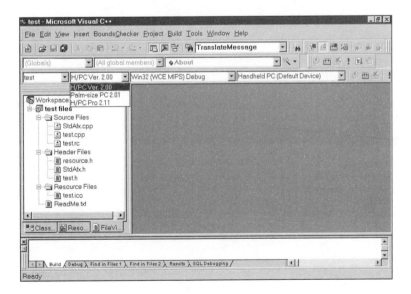

Nothing too serious will go wrong if you accidentally select the wrong target platform. The worst-case scenario is that the target platform you are attempting to run on does not have platform-specific components that your application requires in order to run.

An example of this would be an application that was built for the PsPC and was linked with the PsPC platform's AYGSHELL.LIB (which contains the APIs for interacting with the soft input panel that is available only on the PsPC platform). If you attempted to run this application on an H/PC or an H/PC Professional Edition, you would be warned that there is a mismatch when you tried to download the file.

Selecting the Target CPU

The *target CPU* is the processor that is used in the Windows CE device for which you are building your application.

If you do not know which CPU is used in your Windows CE device, you can find it listed within the System Control Panel applet. On a Hewlett Packard Jornada (an H/PC Professional Edition device), you can find it on the Device tab under the listing Processor Type. On a CASIO E-11 (a PsPC device), you can find it on the General tab under the listing Processor.

When you know which CPU your Windows CE device uses, you can select it from within the Visual C++ IDE, as shown in Figure 1.4.

FIGURE 1.4

Selecting the target CPU for which to build.

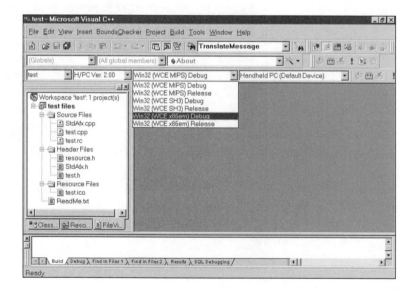

If you select the wrong CPU, you will see the error message displayed in Figure 1.5 when you attempt to download the application to the device from within the Visual C++ IDE.

FIGURE 1.5

This error dialog is displayed when you attempt to download a program built for a MIPS CPU to a device using a StrongARM CPU.

Running Your Application Under the Desktop Emulation Environment

Building for the desktop Windows CE emulator is as simple as selecting WCE x86em as the target CPU you want to build for and then rebuilding. When your build completes, your EXEs and DLLs will automatically be copied to the emulator's object store. If the emulator is not running, it will automatically be started. If a different emulator is running than the shell you have built for (that is, you built for the H/PC emulator, but the PsPC emulator is already running), a warning dialog will inform you of the mismatch. You resolve this issue by simply shutting down the currently running emulator and allowing the correct emulator to start the next time you rebuild or select Update Remote Output File from the Build menu within the Visual C++ IDE.

Go ahead and build your Hello World! application for the H/PC emulator now. After the executable is copied to the emulator's object store, you are free to execute and/or debug your application. This is as simple as selecting CTRL-F5 (Execute) from within the Visual C++ IDE to execute your application, or simply F5 (Go) to debug it. Figure 1.6 shows a debug session for Hello World!

FIGURE 1.6

Debugging Hello World! under the H/PC emulator.

In the preceding paragraphs, I mention the emulator's object store. This is where the files, databases, and Registry accessible to a Windows CE program running within the emulator are stored. An emulator's entire object store is contained within a single OBS file on your desktop computer. Separate OBS files exist for each emulator you have installed on your system. Table 1.2 lists the names of each OBS file and the default installation location on your computer.

TABLE 1.2   The Default Location of Object Store Files on Your Desktop Computer

File	Location
hpc.obs	\Windows CE Tools\WCE200\MS HPC\Emulation
palm_size_pc.obs	\Windows CE Tools\WCE201\MS Palm Size PC\Emulation\Palm
hpcpro.obs	\Windows CE Tools\WCE211\MS HPC Pro\Emulation\HpcPro

If you want to reset your emulator's object store and restart from scratch, you can. This is achieved by shutting down the emulator (if it is currently running) and then copying the default OBS file on the Windows CE Toolkit for Visual C++ 6.0 installation CD-ROM over the corresponding OBS file on your hard drive.

Migrating Existing Win32 Projects to Windows CE

You must perform three main steps to create a Windows CE project for existing Win32 source code:

1. Create a new project that explicitly targets Windows CE.
2. Add the existing source files to the project.
3. Modify the source code so that it will build and run on Windows CE.

You can create a new project the same way you did for your Hello World! application earlier in this hour. Rather than select A Typical "Hello World!" Application as the type of application you would like to create (on the last page of the WCE Application wizard), select An Empty Project instead. This will cause a project file to be created for you, with no additional source files.

You add your source files to your new project by selecting the Project menu, then the Add to Project menu item, and then the Files menu item. This will display an Insert Files into Project dialog that allows you to add multiple source files to your current project.

The last step is to modify your source code so that it builds and executes properly for Windows CE. This is where most of your time will be spent. The major difference that most programmers encounter when they transition to programming for Windows CE is the use of Unicode strings. All the Windows CE APIs using Unicode strings instead of single byte or multi-byte strings. Typically, Windows code such as

```
MessageBox( hWnd, "File not found", "Error", MB_OK );
```

needs to be written in its Unicode equivalent, such as

```
MessageBox( hWnd, L"File not found", L"Error", MB_OK );
```

If you would like to maintain compatibility between Unicode and non-Unicode builds, use the TEXT or _T macros, such as

```
MessageBox( hWnd, TEXT( "File not found" ), TEXT( "Error" ), MB_OK );
```

Here are some hints to help you modify your source code to build for Windows CE:

1. You should first determine whether this code will always be used on Windows CE or you would like to maintain portability between other versions of the Windows operating-system family. If you want to maintain portability, all Windows CE-specific source code and all Unicode-specific source code should be #ifdef'd for _WIN32_WCE and UNICODE, respectively (this is illustrated in Listing 1.2).

2. If you want to maintain portability, convert your strings to TCHAR. If portability is not important, your strings can be changed to WCHAR if you do not want to use TCHAR. Some examples of strings that you would want to leave as CHAR (or char) are strings that are read from or written to ASCII text files or hardware devices (such as modems).

   What are TCHAR strings? It depends. If you are building a Unicode version of your application (for example, –DUNICODE is defined at compile time), the TCHAR will expand to WCHAR. If you are building a non-Unicode version of your application, TCHAR will expand to CHAR. Some commonly used TCHAR string functions include _tcscpy, _tcsstr, _tcscat, and _tcslen. If you are using WCHAR variables, you should use the Unicode equivalent of these string functions explicitly (for example, wcscpy, wcsstr, wcscat, and wcslen). If you have to support ASCII strings, use the mbstowcs and wcstombs functions to convert the strings to and from Unicode (for example, when you have to display text in the user interface or retrieve text input from the user).

3. STDIO functions are not supported on Windows CE. Source code that uses them should be rewritten to use the corresponding Win32 APIs. An example would be to replace calls to fopen, fprintf, and fclose with calls to CreateFile, WriteFile, and CloseHandle.

4. Rewrite any X86 assembly code in C or C++ to make your application easier to port to additional processors. The alternative is porting X86 assembly to SH3, SH4, R3900, R4100, StrongARM, and Power PC assembly. This might sound like fun to some people, but I'm sure you have better things to do. The optimizing compilers included with the Windows CE toolkits do a great job of producing small and fast machine code from your high-level C/C++ code.

The following example shows you how to handle the point raised in hint 1: converting strings between ASCII and Unicode. The source code in Listing 1.1 shows a "before" snapshot of source code that is used to load ASCII text into an edit control.

LISTING 1.1 Loading ASCII Text into an Edit Window on Windows 95 or Windows 98

```
 1: /*********************************************************
 2:  * This function loads the contents of the file specified
 3:  * by 'tcFileName' into the edit control specified by
 4:  * 'hEditWindow'.
 5:  *********************************************************/
 6: VOID LoadFile( TCHAR *tcFileName, HWND hEditWindow )
 7: {
 8:     HANDLE     hFile;
 9:     DWORD      dwSize, dwBytesRead, dwBytes;
10:     CHAR       *szBuffer;
11:
12:     // attempt to open the specified file
13:     hFile = CreateFile( tcFileName, GENERIC_READ, 0, NULL,
14:                         OPEN_EXISTING, 0, NULL );
15:
16:     if ( hFile == INVALID_HANDLE_VALUE ) {
17:
18:         MessageBox( NULL, TEXT( "Could not open specified file!" ),
19:                     TEXT( "Error!" ), MB_OK | MB_ICONEXCLAMATION );
20:
21:     } else {
22:
23:         // create a buffer to hold the contents of the file
24:         dwSize = GetFileSize( hFile, NULL );
25:         szBuffer = (CHAR*) malloc( dwSize + 1 );
26:
27:         if ( szBuffer != NULL ) {
28:
29:             // loop until the entire contents of the file have
30:             // been read into the buffer
31:             dwBytesRead = 0;
32:             while ( dwBytesRead < dwSize ) {
33:
34:                 ReadFile( hFile, szBuffer+dwBytesRead,
```

```
35:                               dwSize-dwBytesRead, &dwBytes, NULL );
36:
37:                  dwBytesRead += dwBytes;
38:
39:              }
40:
41:              szBuffer[dwSize] = 0;
42:
43:              // transfer the buffer contents to the edit control
44:              SetWindowText( hEditWindow, szBuffer );
45:
46:              // free the temporary buffers
47:              free( szBuffer );
48:
49:          }
50:
51:          // close the open file handle
52:          CloseHandle( hFile );
53:
54:      }
55:
56: }
```

The source code in Listing 1.2 shows you how to modify the code in Listing 1.1 so that it will work on Windows CE.

LISTING 1.2   Loading Text into an Edit Window on Windows CE

```
 1: /**********************************************************
 2:  * This function loads the contents of the file specified
 3:  * by 'tcFileName' into the edit control specified by
 4:  * 'hEditWindow'.
 5:  **********************************************************/
 6: VOID LoadFile( TCHAR *tcFileName, HWND hEditWindow )
 7: {
 8:     HANDLE    hFile;
 9:     DWORD     dwSize, dwBytesRead, dwBytes;
10:     CHAR      *szBuffer;
11:
12: #ifdef UNICODE
13:     WCHAR     *wcBuffer;
14: #endif
15:
16:     // attempt to open the specified file
17:     hFile = CreateFile( tcFileName, GENERIC_READ, 0, NULL,
18:                         OPEN_EXISTING, 0, NULL );
19:
20:     if ( hFile == INVALID_HANDLE_VALUE ) {
```

continues

LISTING 1.2　continued

```
21:
22:            MessageBox( NULL, TEXT( "Could not open specified file!" ),
23:                        TEXT( "Error!" ), MB_OK | MB_ICONEXCLAMATION );
24:
25:     } else {
26:
27:         // create a buffer to hold the contents of the file
28:         dwSize = GetFileSize( hFile, NULL );
29:         szBuffer = (CHAR*) malloc( dwSize + 1 );
30:
31: #ifdef UNICODE
32:         wcBuffer = (WCHAR*) malloc( ( dwSize + 1 ) * sizeof( WCHAR ) );
33:         if ( szBuffer && wcBuffer ) {
34: #else
35:         if ( szBuffer != NULL ) {
36: #endif
37:
38:             // loop until the entire contents of the file have
39:             // been read into the buffer
40:             dwBytesRead = 0;
41:             while ( dwBytesRead < dwSize ) {
42:
43:                 ReadFile( hFile, szBuffer+dwBytesRead,
44:                           dwSize-dwBytesRead, &dwBytes, NULL );
45:
46:                 dwBytesRead += dwBytes;
47:
48:             }
49:
50:             szBuffer[dwSize] = 0;
51:
52:             // if this is a Unicode build, convert the buffer
53:             // contents to Unicode
54: #ifdef UNICODE
55:             mbstowcs( wcBuffer, szBuffer, dwSize+1 );
56: #endif
57:
58:             // transfer the buffer contents to the edit control
59: #ifdef UNICODE
60:             SetWindowText( hEditWindow, wcBuffer );
61: #else
62:             SetWindowText( hEditWindow, szBuffer );
63: #endif
64:
65:
66:             // free the temporary buffers
67:             free( szBuffer );
68: #ifdef UNICODE
69:             free( wcBuffer );
```

```
70: #endif
71:
72:          }
73:
74:          // close the open file handle
75:          CloseHandle( hFile );
76:
77:      }
78:
79: }
```

Now, take a brief tour of the remote tools available for Windows CE application developers.

Using Visual C++ Remote Tools for Windows CE

When you installed the Windows CE toolkits, the Windows CE remote tools were also installed. These remote tools include

- Remote File Viewer
- Remote Heap Walker
- Remote Process Viewer
- Remote Registry Editor
- Remote Spy
- Remote Zoomin

The remote tools can be used with the Windows CE applications running under the desktop emulators or on actual Windows CE devices.

How do you run them? The remote tools can be launched from within the Visual C++ IDE or directly from the Start menu. Within the Visual C++ IDE, they can be launched individually by selecting the Windows CE Remote Tools pop-up menu from the Tools menu. The remote tools can also be launched from outside the Visual C++ IDE by selecting Start, Programs, Microsoft Visual C++ 6.0, Windows CE Tools.

The following sections discuss three of the remote tools you are most likely to use often.

How to Make Screenshots: Remote Zoomin

Remote Zoomin enables you to make screen captures from Windows CE emulators or devices. Figure 1.7 shows a screen capture in progress.

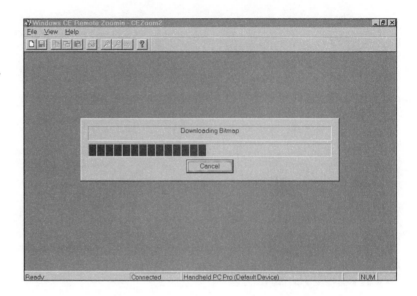

FIGURE 1.7

Using the Remote Zoomin Tool to perform a screen capture.

After the screen capture is completed, you have the following options:

1. Save it to a bitmap file.
2. Copy it to the Clipboard (for pasting into other graphics programs).
3. Print it.

If you would like to perform a screen capture without using a desktop tool, Hour 8, "Working with Graphic Devices", includes source code for a Windows CE–based screen capture utility.

How to Modify the Registry: The Remote Registry Editor

The Remote Registry Editor enables you to view and modify the Registry on Windows CE emulators and devices. It behaves very similarly to Registry editors included with desktop Windows.

Figure 1.8 shows the Remote Registry Editor in action.

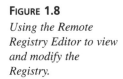

FIGURE **1.8**

Using the Remote Registry Editor to view and modify the Registry.

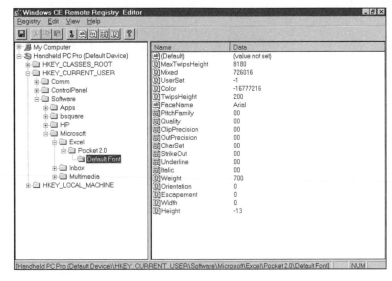

How to Spy: Remote Spy

Remote Spy allows you to spy on messages being sent to various windows running on a Windows CE system. In addition to helping you debug issues within your applications, this can also help you understand how other applications work. Figure 1.9 shows you how to use Remote Spy to spy on Contacts, Calendar, and Pocket Mail applications.

FIGURE **1.9**

Using Remote Spy to spy on some of the standard ROM applications.

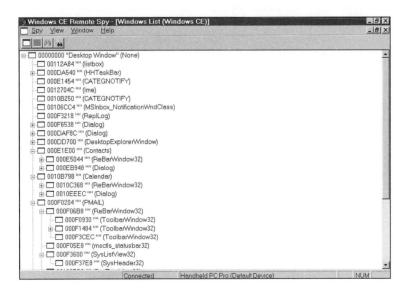

Summary

In this hour, you learned how to install the Visual C++ 6.0 add-on for Windows CE and how to correct any installation errors by performing a complete reinstall. You learned how to create new Windows CE applications and build and run them under the desktop Windows CE emulator and on actual Windows CE devices. You also learned how to use the Visual C++ integrated development environment to retarget your application to build for other Windows CE platforms, such as the H/PC, H/PC Professional Edition, and PsPC. You also learned how to port existing Win32 applications to Windows CE. Finally, you were introduced to the remote tools included with the Visual C++ 6.0 for Windows CE add-on.

Q&A

Q My code uses `sprintf` to format a text string that contains a floating point number. When I ported it to Windows CE, I replaced it with the `wsprintf` function, but it is not properly converting the floating point number to a string. What am I doing wrong?

A The `wsprintf` function does not support floating point numbers on Windows CE. A quick workaround is to use the `_fcvt` function to convert the number to an ASCII string. You can then use the `mbstowcs` function to convert it to a Unicode string.

Q Are there any differences between the `mbstowcs` and `MultiByteToWideChar` functions that I should be aware of?

A The `mbstowcs` function returns the number of characters that have been converted without including the null termination character. The `MultiByteToWideChar` function does include the null termination character in its return value.

Workshop

The Workshop is designed to help you anticipate possible questions, review what you've learned, and begin thinking ahead about putting your knowledge into practice. The answers to the quiz are in Appendix A, "Answers."

Quiz

1. How do you create a screen capture of your application running on a Windows CE device?

2. How do you manually edit the Registry on a Windows CE device?

3. How do you reset the emulation environment to its initial state?

4. How do you determine which type of CPU your Windows CE device uses?

5. What function will convert Unicode text to multibyte text?

6. How do you perform a clean reinstallation of the Visual C++ for Windows CE add-on?

Exercises

1. Create a simple text viewer that loads a text file into an edit control window for viewing. (*Hint*: Edit controls under Windows CE require Unicode text strings.)

2. Add the capability to edit and save text files to the text viewer you created in exercise 1.

Hour **2**

What's Different About Windows CE?

Although a cursory glance might leave you believing that Windows CE is almost identical to its desktop counterparts, when you start digging into it, you will find many big and small differences. This hour, I will break down those differences into four areas:

- The Win32 API
- Additional APIs and SDKs
- The C Runtime Libraries and Language Features
- The C++ Runtime Libraries and Language Features

The driving force behind many of these differences is that Windows CE is designed from the ground up to be as small as possible. Although both desktop operating systems and Windows CE are feature driven, Windows CE takes measures to ensure that features can be selectively included or left out, depending on the specific needs of the device, such as an H/PC or P/PC. Also, where overlap exists between the Win32 APIs and the language runtime libraries (for example, lstrlen/strlen, time/GetSystemTime), only one of the two is provided.

Another major organizational change in Windows CE is the way that system libraries are provided. There are not separate import libraries for GDI, Kernel, and User, as there are on the desktop. Instead, all these modules have been bundled into one file, COREDLL.LIB. Linking against this file provides all the Win32 API functionality, as well as many undocumented internal functions.

The Win32 API

Approximately 3,600 Win32 APIs are supported in Windows NT and Windows 95/98. Windows 2000 will no doubt bump this number up even higher. Version 1.0 of Windows CE supports only about 500 of these APIs. Version 2.0, as configured for the H/PC and the P/PC, triples that to about 1,500 APIs.

> Unfortunately, the C runtime libraries and the Win32 APIs disagree on the necessary define for compiling as UNICODE. To cover all bases, make sure that both UNICODE and _UNICODE_ are defined for all source files. This is done automatically for new Windows CE projects created with Visual C++, but you might have to add it if you're creating a project manually.

Windows CE follows the desktop model of providing function declarations for both ANSI and Unicode versions of every API and choosing between them at compile time, based on the UNICODE macro. However, only the Unicode versions are implemented, so any code that is built for Windows CE must have the UNICODE macro defined. The easiest way to deal with this is to write everything in TCHAR style, rather than directly use char or wchar_t. For example, rather than write

```
char *GetTextFromWindow(HWND hwnd)
{
    char *psz;
    int size = GetWindowTextLength(hwnd);
    psz  = malloc(size + 1);
    GetWindowText(hwnd, psz, size);
    return psz;
}
```

you would write

```
LPTSTR GetTextFromWindow(HWND hwnd)
{
    LPTSTR psz;
    int size = GetWindowTextLength(hwnd);
    psz = malloc((size + 1)*sizeof(TCHAR));
```

```
    GetWindowText(hwnd, psz, size);
    return psz;
}
```

NEW TERM *ANSI* is a standard method of encoding characters in 8 bits (1 byte).

NEW TERM *Unicode* is a standard method of encoding characters in 16 bits (2 bytes).

2

Win32 console programs are not supported under Windows CE; every application is required to use WinMain as its entry point, instead of main. WinMain looks just as it does on the desktop, with one exception: The lpCmdLine parameter is a Unicode string instead of ANSI. This does not mean that your application must have a message loop. Dialog-based applications and "faceless" programs that have no user interface will work just fine without them.

Windows in Windows CE can be in one of two states: minimized or maximized. No support exists for resizable windows. Therefore, messages such as WM_SIZING and WM_WINDOWPOSCHANGING are unnecessary, allowing the Restore item in the system menu to be eliminated as well.

System configuration in Windows CE has been significantly simplified. There are no environment variables or INI files. Everything uses a Registry, which is almost identical to the desktop. The Windows CE Registry is covered in more detail in Hour 9, "The Object Store: Files and the Registry."

For one reason or another, major portions of the standard Win32 API are not available at all in Windows CE. These include

- Hooks
- Generic, flat, and universal thunks
- Services and the event log
- Profiling (GetThreadTime and GetProcessTime)
- Security (SACLs, DACLs, and so on)

Notably absent from this list are the cryptography APIs. Although they are not available on Windows CE v2.0, they have been added to v2.1 and are available on devices such as the H/PC Professional Edition.

One of the big areas of support added in Windows CE v2.0 is COM. Although DCOM and COM+ have not yet come online, the support for basic COM in-process servers is available. COM support in Windows CE is covered extensively in the last hour.

Windows CE support for API sets and SDKs that are not considered part of the Win32 base is the topic of the next section.

Additional APIs and SDKs

Over the years, Win32 has accumulated a huge number of peripheral SDKs and API toolkits, some of which border on the obscure (when was the last time you had to use the OpenType Embedding SDK?).

Rather than support all these features out of the box, Windows CE chose to implement only a select few that are crucially important and then incrementally add new ones. This is identical to the base API approach, as evidenced by the new stdio console and cryptography support in Windows CE v2.1.

Instead of trying to exhaustively list what's not supported in Windows CE, I'll highlight what is available, as a direct port from the desktop and indirectly with new functionality in Windows CE.

Multimedia

The majority of the multimedia functions, such as timeSetEvent, are not available in Windows CE, but v2.0 adds support for a handful of functions for playing and recording sound. sndPlaySound and the entire family of wave functions (waveInStart, waveOutClose, and so on) are available for creating and using WAV files.

Additionally, the P/PC has extra APIs for voice recording and playback. These APIs are discussed in detail in Hour 23, "Debugging Windows CE Applications with Visual C++."

WinSock

A subset of WinSock 1.1 is supported on Windows CE, as well as the Secure Sockets Layer (SSL) feature of WinSock 2.0. A few of the database functions (for example, getservbyname) and all the asynchronous functions (such as WSAAsyncSelect) are not provided. The Windows CE version of WinSock is discussed in more detail in Hour 13, "WinSock and Serial Communications."

WinInet

The bulk of the WinInet API is supported in Windows CE, with the exception of the Gopher protocol. (Does anyone use this anymore?) I'll come back to WinInet in Hour 13.

Remote Access Services (RAS)

A subset of RAS is supported in Windows CE. Only client support is available, and you cannot have more than one simultaneous point-to-point connection.

The Telephony API (TAPI)

A subset of TAPI is provided by Windows CE 2.0 and implements support for outbound calls only. The APIs can be used with built-in or PCMCIA modems. Support for multiple dialog locations and installable service providers is included.

Windows Networking (WNet)

The Windows Networking API is implemented in Windows CE v2.0. This includes support for only the WNet functions (for example, WNetOpenEnum), as opposed to the Net functions (for example, NetFileEnum), which work only with Microsoft networks.

The Mail API (MAPI)

The MAPI that developers love to hate is not provided under Windows CE. Instead, a Windows CE–specific mail API provides functions that create and send mail and manipulate the address book. The Windows CE mail API is covered in Hour 17, "Working with the Contacts Database API."

Active Data Objects (ADO)

ADO is a fairly recent addition to the Windows CE tools arsenal and has full support for Recordset and Field objects. The ADO for the Windows CE SDK is a free download from the Microsoft Web site at
http://www.microsoft.com/windowsce/downloads/pccompanions/adosdk.asp.

ToolHelp

The ToolHelp functions have been supported in Windows CE since inception—no partial coverage or subsets here. TOOLHELP.DLL used to be distributed only in the add-on toolkits for Visual C++, but is now burned into ROM for most devices. If you plan to use ToolHelp in your application, be sure to have your setup verify that it is installed on the device, and copy it down if it's not already there.

Setup

Installing programs on a Windows CE device is fundamentally different than on the desktop because it must be done remotely over some communication medium. For this reason, Windows CE doesn't implement the desktop setup APIs, but instead provides new functionality of its own. Using the Windows CE setup APIs is the focus of Hour 15, "Targeting the Palm-Size PC."

Overall, Windows CE provides a major portion of the functionality that Win32 developers have come to expect, with additional features being added with each new release. Next,

2

you will look at the Windows CE support for C and C++ language features and runtime libraries.

The C Runtime Libraries and Language Features

The ANSI C runtime library (RTL) consists of a couple hundred functions spread out over 15 header files. Table 2.1 lists these headers and whether they are supported under Windows CE v2.0.

TABLE 2.1   ANSI C Header Files Supported by Windows CE v2.0

Header File	Supported Under Windows CE
<assert.h>	No
<ctype.h>	Yes
<errno.h>	No
<float.h>	Yes
<limits.h>	Yes
<locale.h>	No
<math.h>	Yes
<setjmp.h>	Yes
<signal.h>	No
<stdarg.h>	Yes
<stddef.h>	No
<stdio.h>	No
<stdlib.h>	Yes
<string.h>	Yes
<time.h>	No

The biggest omission here are the stdio functions. All friends such as printf and gets have vanished. If you think about it for a moment, though, the reasoning behind this is clear. Because no console support exists, the user has no way to interact with the program via a command line. The Windows CE alternative for these command-line features, such as printf, is to communicate with a user via dialog boxes.

Additionally, all the stdio file functions such as fopen and fwrite have been expunged. As I mentioned previously, where overlap occurs between the Win32 API and the runtime libraries, only one method is provided. In this case, the APIs such as `CreateFile` and `WriteFile` won the battle and dodged the cut.

A couple `stdio` functions are available by including stdlib.h. Unicode versions of `sprintf` and `vsprintf` functions were left in because they are superior to their API equivalent, `wsprintf`, in their support of floating point variables. Also, `sscanf` is implemented.

If your application is dependent on many of these `stdio` functions and you're using v2.0, you might want to consider using the Windows CE `stdio` package written by Ben Goetter (included on the CD-ROM as cestdio.zip). Although the library does provide implementations of `printf`, `fopen`, and the like, the console implementation is left as a hook for users to extend for their applications' specific needs (such as an edit control in a dialog box or what have you).

Luckily, light is on the horizon for Windows CE's console support. Version 2.1, which is running on the new H/PC Professional Edition devices and P/PC devices, includes support for all the `stdio` functions excluded by previous versions. A limited version of a console is available as well, although not a full Win32 console implementation á la `AllocConsole` and `WriteConsole`. It provides enough to work with all the `stdio` functions, but features such as color attributes and standard handle redirection are still missing.

Even though the `stdlib` header is supported, several functions associated with it are not. They are

- `atof`
- `abort`
- `bsearch`
- `calloc`
- `exit`
- `getenv`
- `system`

The functionality of `atof` can be implemented with `sscanf`. The `abort` and `exit` functions map directly to the `TerminateProcess` API, and the absence of `getenv` and `system` results in the lack of console and environment variable support.

The `calloc` function was also eliminated because it duplicates what can easily be accomplished with `malloc` and `memset`, like so:

```
void *calloc(size_t num, size_t size)
{
    void *pv = malloc(num * size);
```

```
    if ( pv )
        memset(pv, 0, num * size);
    return pv;
}
```

That leaves bsearch as a mysterious missing function. My guess is that it was rarely used and easy to implement by hand; therefore, it was dropped.

> If you need a function, such as bsearch, that's missing from the Windows
> CE RTL, you might be able to just steal the desktop implementation and port
> it. The desktop Visual C++ 6 RTL source code is available on the Visual C++ 6
> CD-ROM in the directory \VC98\CRT\SRC. It is also an option to install this
> source on your hard disk as part of the Visual C++ 6 setup process.

To simplify porting of code to and from the desktop, tchar.h supplies the same Unicode/ANSI wrappers (for example, _tcslen, and so on). Whereas all the Unicode functions are implemented, most of the ANSI ones are not. As usual, when you're building applications for Windows CE, be sure to compile everything Unicode.

The Windows CE runtime library supports the ANSI stdlib functions mbstowcs and wcstombs for converting between multibyte and Unicode character strings. These functions, which each take three parameters, are much easier to use than their API counterparts WideCharToMultiByte and MultiByteToWideChar, which take eight and six parameters, respectively. The Windows CE versions of the library functions, though, can pose a porting problem if you use their return value.

NEW TERM   A *multibyte character string* is a method of encoding characters in a variable number of bytes. Under Windows CE, multibyte strings can be considered equivalent to ANSI strings.

The wcstombs function is documented as returning the size needed to store the converted string, minus the null character. The Windows CE version, however, includes the null in the return value count. Thus, the call

```
wcstombs(NULL, L"t", 1);
```

will return 1 on the desktop and 2 under Windows CE. Conversely, mbstowcs has a similar problem deciding to include the null character and expresses the value as the number of bytes instead of the number of wide characters needed. Thus, the call

```
mbstowcs(NULL, "t", 1);
```

will return 1 on the desktop and 4 under Windows CE.

The C++ Standard Library and Language Features

Compared to the C RTL and language support, the C++ version is severely lacking on Windows CE. Although most language features you expect (templates, member function pointers, and so on) are provided, exception handling and runtime-type information (RTTI) are not. As a result of this, the entire Standard Template Library (STL) that relies on exceptions has been omitted. Rumor has it that exception handling and STL will be supported in a future version of Windows CE, but what to do until then? Luckily, you have a few alternatives. In the rest of this section, I will discuss the ins and outs of the limited structured exception handling that Windows CE does support and how you can improve on that. I will also provide some pointers on how you can port the Visual C++ 5.0 STL to Windows CE.

Using C++ under desktop Win32 actually provides you with two distinct types of exception handling. Structured exception handling (SEH) is a Win32 feature and is not inherently tied to C or C++. C++ exception handling is, obviously, tied to the language and is generally more flexible than SEH.

> Even though SEH is discussed here under the C++ heading, it is also available from C. For an excellent discussion of SEH and a comparison to C++ exception handling, see Chapter 16 of *Advanced Windows*, Third Edition, by Jeffrey Richter.

Other than providing easier error handling, the big benefit of C++ exception handling is that all local objects will be destroyed when an exception causes a function to exit. As a side benefit, desktop Win32 also provides this functionality when an SEH exception is thrown. Windows CE does support SEH, but not C++ exception handling, as previously mentioned. Unfortunately, local object destruction is directly tied to the C++ support and thus is not present in the Windows CE version of SEH. To ensure that cleanup of locals is properly handled with SEH under Windows CE, you have to jump through some hoops. Essentially, you have to write code such as this:

```
void foo()
{
    Bar bar;

    __try
    {
        // code that might throw an exception here
```

```
    }
    __finally
    {
        if ( AbnormalTermination() )
        {
            bar.~Bar();
        }
    }
}
```

AbnormalTermination is a Win32 API that returns true if the function is exiting because of an unhandled exception or false if it is exiting under normal circumstances. Assuming that Bar is a C++ object defined elsewhere, this code ensures that the local object is cleaned up regardless of the function's exit status. On desktop Win32, the destructor will automatically be called, so you don't want to do this. Bar's destructor would fire twice, and bad things are guaranteed to happen. This is an issue if you're compiling the same source file on both Windows CE and NT or 95.

Another SEH quirk under Windows CE is the handling of __finally blocks. Desktop Win32 allows return statements inside a __finally block that basically override the normal return value. For example, the code

```
int foo()
{
    __try
    {
        // ....
    }
    __finally
    {
        return 20;
    }
    return 10;
}
```

will always return 20 on desktop Win32. On Windows CE, however, returns are not allowed inside __finally blocks and will cause a compilation error if they are used. To produce the same effect, you can modify a local variable inside the __finally block rather than use an explicit return, like this:

```
int foo()
{
    int ret = 10;

    __try
    {
        // ....
    }
```

```
    __finally
    {
        ret = 20;
    }
    return ret;
}
```

It is possible to emulate C++ exception handling on Windows CE. Vladimir Belkin published an article on how this can be done in the April 1995 issue of the Russian edition of *PC Magazine*, and Fedor Sherstyuk has ported it to Windows CE. Fedor also provides an implementation of RTTI, as outlined in John Lakos's book *Large Scale C++ Software Design*. Both the code and a translation of the article are available on the CD-ROM for this book in the file exclemu.zip.

Getting exception handling to work is great, but what if you just need STL containers? Luckily, I found yet another person to help. David April went through the Visual C++ 5.0 STL implementation and modified it to compile and run under Windows CE. This does not mean that exception handling works correctly—it doesn't—but at least it allows you to access all the containers and algorithms that STL provides. His notes on how to modify STL for Windows CE are available at `http://www.halcyon.com/ast/swdev.htm`.

As you've seen, C++ programming under Windows CE isn't quite as straightforward as C. However, as usual, workarounds are a lot better than no options at all.

Summary

This lesson introduces you to the major differences between Windows CE and desktop Win32. You learned how the philosophies regarding Win32 API versus language runtime functions differ and about the limitations and workarounds for some critical missing pieces.

Q&A

Q How can I support `printf` in my Windows CE program?

A If you are running on v2.1 or better, support is built in and it will automatically work. If you are using v2.0, Ben Goetter's `CeStdio` package is probably the easiest route.

Q My application can't find the function `CreateWindowA` at link time. How come?

A Windows CE provides only the Unicode version of all supported Win32 APIs. Make sure that your application is built with `UNICODE` and `_UNICODE` defined.

Workshop

The Workshop is designed to help you anticipate possible questions, review what you've learned, and begin thinking ahead about putting your knowledge into practice. The answers to the quiz are in Appendix A, "Answers."

Quiz

1. Do `mbstowcs` return the same value on Windows 95 and Windows CE?
2. Does Windows CE support MAPI?
3. What ANSI standard C function can be used to emulate the behavior of the missing `atof` function?
4. Are INI files supported on Windows CE?
5. What is COREDLL.LIB?
6. What is the difference between ANSI, Unicode, and multibyte strings?
7. What WinInet protocols are supported on Windows CE?
8. How do you implement resizable windows on Windows CE?
9. How does structured exception handling (SEH) differ on Windows 95 and Windows CE?
10. What Win32 API function can you use to play WAV files on both Windows 95 and Windows CE?

Exercises

1. Try porting the Visual C++ 6 GENERIC sample to Windows CE.
2. Translate the following code to `TCHAR` style rather than directly use `char`:

```
char *strdup(const char *pcsz)
{
    char *psz = malloc(strlen(pcsz)+1);
    strcpy(psz, pcsz);
    return psz;
}
```

PART II

User Interfaces

Hour

HOUR 3

Building User Interfaces—Command Bars and Bands

When you first see a Windows CE device (particularly H/PCs and P/PCs), you immediately ask yourself, "How can I possibly fit my application on such a small screen?" The answer: Several new controls have been developed specifically to address the limitations in screen size and to maximize user input. Why waste space on a toolbar and a menu when they can be combined into a single control?

In this hour, you will learn

- What command bars are
- How to create and insert objects into a command bar
- How to create command bands
- How to have command bands remember where they are located

What Is a Command Bar?

NEW TERM A *Command Bar* is a single control that combines both a menu and a toolbar. Most of the menu and toolbar messages you are accustomed to using are compatible with the Command Bar control.

NEW TERM A *separator* is a blank space used to divide items in a command bar.

To maximize space on the small-screen Windows CE devices, command bars were created (see Figure 3.1). They can contain menus, combo boxes, buttons, and separators. In addition, several "adornments," such as the OK, Cancel, and Help buttons, can be added for easy user navigation in an application.

FIGURE 3.1

A command bar.

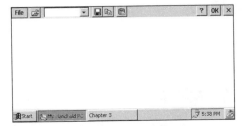

Creating a Command Bar

Several steps are required in building a command bar. To use a command bar, you must first make sure that the Common Controls library is loaded by using the `InitCommonControls()` function. You must also register the command bar class by initializing the extended Common Controls library with the `ICC_BAR_CLASSES` flag, as shown in Listing 3.1.

LISTING 3.1 Initializing the Command Bar Control

```
1: InitCommonControls();
2: INITCOMMONCONTROLSEX iCCS;
3: iCCS.dwSize = sizeof(INITCOMMONCONTROLSEX);
4: iCCS.dwICC = ICC_BAR_CLASSES;
5: InitCommonControlsEx(&iCCS);
```

After you initialize everything, you can create a command bar by using a call to the `CommandBar_Create()` function (see Listing 3.2). `CommandBar_Create()` has three parameters: The first parameter is the program's instance handle; the second is the handle of the parent window; and the third is a user-defined ID value for the control. The function will return a handle to the newly created command bar if it is successful.

LISTING 3.2   Creating the Command Bar

```
1: HWND hCmdBr = CommandBar_Create(ghInstance, ghWnd, ID_COMMANDBAR);
```

> Command bars are automatically set to the size of the parent window's client area and are positioned along the top of the window. The command bar is considered part of the client area of the parent window. To determine the client area of your window, you should use the `CommandBar_GetHeight()` function and subtract it from the height of the window's client rectangle (which you can obtain by using the `GetClientRect()` function).

Inserting Objects into a Command Bar

Now that the basic command bar is created, you're ready to start putting objects into it.

Menus

There are two ways to insert a menu into the Command Bar control. First, you can use the `CommandBar_InsertMenubar()` function, shown in Listing 3.3.

LISTING 3.3   Inserting a Menu with `CommandBar_InsertMenubar()`

```
1: BOOL fOK = CommandBar_InsertMenubar(hCmdBr, ghInstance, IDR_MENU, 0);
```

The `CommandBar_InsertMenubar()` function takes four parameters:

- The handle to the command bar to which you want to add this menu.
- The program's instance handle.
- The resource ID of the menu you want to add.
- The zero-based index of where to put the menu. Typically, for menus, this value is 0.

Second, as of version 2.0 of Windows CE, you can also now use the `CommandBar_InsertMenubarEx()` function to insert a menu. The only difference is the third parameter, which can be either the name of the menu resource you want to add or the handle to a menu created dynamically. If you insert a menu to the command bar by specifying its menu handle, the application's instance parameter must be set to NULL.

After you create a menu in your command bar, you can get its handle by calling the CommandBar_GetMenu() function:

    HMENU hMenu = CommandBar_GetMenu(ghCommandBar, 0);

Two parameters are passed to the function: the command bar handle and the zero-based index to the position of the menu on the command bar.

Toolbar Buttons

Before you can add buttons to your command bar, you must first associate an image with the command bar's internal image list. Images can be added one at a time or as several images in a single bitmap (see Figure 3.2).

FIGURE 3.2

A sample bitmap lay-out of command bar button images.

The easiest way to create command bar button images is to use the resource editor and insert a Toolbar resource into your project. There, you can build multiple images into a single bitmap.

To associate an image into the command bar, you must call the CommandBar_AddBitmap() function:

```
int iImage = CommandBar_AddBitmap(hCmdBar, ghInstance,
➥ IDR_TOOLBAR, 4, 0, 0);
```

The CommandBar_AddBitmap() function has six parameters:

- The handle to the command bar with which you want to associate this image.
- The application's instance handle.
- The resource ID of the bitmap you want to add.
- The number of images in the bitmap.
- Reserved. This parameter is reserved and should be set to 0.
- Reserved. This parameter is also reserved and should be set to 0.

After you have added your command bar images, you can begin to create buttons to go on the control.

The TBBUTTON structure is used to represent a toolbar button. You use this structure when adding or modifying the state of a button. The data members for the TBBUTTON structure are

- iBitmap—Used to indicate the zero-based index of the button image.
- idCommand—The WM_COMMAND to be sent to the parent window when the button is pressed.
- fsState—Used to initialize the button to a state. Possible values are given later in this section.
- fsStyle—Used to specify the style of button. Possible values are given later in this section.
- dwData—An application-defined value that is associated with the button.
- iString—The zero-based index of the button label string.

The TBBUTTON structure's fsState member is used to indicate the button's initial state. It can be one or more of the following values:

- TBSTATE_CHECKED indicates that the button has the TBSTYLE_CHECK style and is clicked.
- TBSTATE_ENABLED indicates that the button is enabled to accept user input. A button that does not have this style is grayed out.
- TBSTATE_HIDDEN indicates that the button is not visible.
- TBSTATE_INDETERMINATE indicates that the button is grayed.
- TBSTATE_PRESSED indicates that the button is being clicked.

The TBBUTTON structure's fsStyle member is used to specify the style of the button. It can be one or more of the following values; its code appears in Listing 3.4:

- TBSTYLE_BUTTON creates a standard button.
- TBSTYLE_CHECK creates a button that toggles between the pressed and nonpressed states each time the user clicks it.
- TBSTYLE_CHECKGROUP creates a check button that stays pressed until another button in the group is pressed.
- TBSTYLE_DROPDOWN creates a drop-down list button. Drop-down buttons send the TBN_DROPDOWN notification message when pressed.
- TBSTYLE_GROUP creates a button that stays pressed until another button in the group is pressed.

- `TBSTYLE_TRANSPARENT` creates a button that allows the background to show through.
- `TBSTYLE_SEP` creates a separator, providing a small gap between button groups.

LISTING 3.4　Creating a `TBBUTTON` Structure

```
 1: static TBBUTTON tbButton[] = {
 2:     { 0, 0, TBSTATE_ENABLED,TBSTYLE_SEP, 0, 0, 0, -1 },
 3:     { 0, ID_FILE_NEW, TBSTATE_ENABLED, TBSTYLE_BUTTON, 0, 0},
 4:     { 0, 0, TBSTATE_ENABLED,TBSTYLE_SEP, 0, 0, 0, -1 },
 5:     { 0, 0, TBSTATE_ENABLED,TBSTYLE_SEP, 0, 0, 0, -1 },
 6:     { 1, ID_FILE_OPEN, TBSTATE_ENABLED, TBSTYLE_BUTTON, 0, 0},
 7:     { 2, ID_FILE_SAVE, TBSTATE_ENABLED, TBSTYLE_DROPDOWN, 0, 0},
 8:     { 0, 0, TBSTATE_ENABLED,TBSTYLE_SEP, 0, 0, 0, -1 },
 9:     { 3, ID_FILE_PRINT, TBSTATE_ENABLED, TBSTYLE_BUTTON, 0, 0},
10: };
```

After you initialize your `TBBUTTON` structure with your button information, two functions are available to add buttons to your command bar.

First, you can call the `CommandBar_InsertButton()` function, shown in Listing 3.5. This will take your `TBBUTTON` array and insert the buttons at the end of the command bar. It takes three parameters: first, the handle to the command bar into which you want to insert the buttons; second, the number of buttons; and finally, a pointer to an array of `TBBUTTON` structures.

LISTING 3.5　Inserting Buttons

```
 1: DWORD dwBtnSize = sizeof(tbButton)/sizeof(TBBUTTON);
 2: CommandBar_AddButtons(ghCommandBar, dwBtnSize, tbButton);
```

The other function you can use to add buttons is the `CommandBar_InsertButton()` function. It is used to insert single buttons into the middle of a command bar. The `CommandBar_InsertButton()` call takes three parameters: first, the handle to the command bar into which you want to insert the button; second, the button position where you want to insert the button; and finally, a pointer to the `TBBUTTON` structure you are inserting.

After your buttons are created, you will receive a standard `WM_COMMAND` notification when a button is pushed.

When you use the TBSTYLE_DROPDOWN style, it creates a button that has an additional down arrow next to the image. Typically, when one of these buttons is pressed, it will drop down a menu underneath it. You should be aware that you will have to manually create the menu, because you receive a notification only that the button has been pressed.

You receive a WM_NOTIFY message with a notification of TBN_DROPDOWN when a button with this style is activated.

Combo Boxes

Another type of control that you can insert into a command bar is a Combo Box. Combo boxes are extremely useful when a user needs to select quickly from a list of items.

To insert a Combo Box into a command bar, you use the CommandBar_InsertComboBox() function:

```
CommandBar_InsertComboBox(hCmdBar, ghInstance, 100, 0, ID_COMBO, 4);
```

The CommandBar_InsertComboBox() function has six parameters:

- The handle to the command bar into which you want to insert the Combo Box control.
- The handle of the application's instance.
- The width of the Combo Box.
- Any additional Combo Box styles you want to add. WS_CHILD and WS_VISIBLE are automatically added when creating the control.
- An identifier for the Combo Box that is used when WM_COMMAND messages are sent.
- The position in the command bar to insert the Combo Box.

After the Combo Box is created, it functions exactly the same as a regular Combo Box control. Handling messages and events is the same as when you created the Combo Box control as a child of the application window.

Adornments

There are three additional objects you can add to a command bar:

1. An OK button
2. A Close button
3. A Help button

To create any of these, you can call the CommandBar_AddAdornments() function:

```
CommandBar_AddAdornments(ghCommandBar, CMDBAR_HELP ¦ CMDBAR_OK, 0);
```

The CommandBar_AddAdornments() function takes three parameters:

- The handle to the command bar you want to add the adornments to.
- Optional flags to indicate what you want to add to the command bar. CMDBAR_HELP adds a question mark button (which sends your main application a WM_HELP message), and CMDBAR_OK adds an OK button (which sends your application an IDOK message through WM_COMMAND).
- A reserved flag. Set this to 0.

According to the Windows CE logo guidelines, applications designed to be run on the P/PC platform are not supposed to have a Close (or Exit) menu option or a close (×) button on the command bar.

ToolTips

To add ToolTips to your command bar, you can use the CommandBar_AddToolTips() function, shown in Listing 3.6.

LISTING 3.6 Inserting ToolTips

```
 1: static LPTSTR lpToolTips[] = {
 2:     { TEXT("File New") },
 3:     { TEXT("") },
 4:     { TEXT("") },
 5:     { TEXT("File Open") },
 6:     { TEXT("File Save") },
 7:     { TEXT("") },
 8:     { TEXT("File Print") },
 9: };
10: CommandBar_AddToolTips(ghCommandBar, 7, lpToolTips);
```

When adding ToolTips, you must add a "blank" tip (that is, – TEXT("")) to handle separator buttons.

The `CommandBar_AddToolTips()` function has the following parameters:

- The handle to the command bar to which you want to add the ToolTips
- The number of ToolTips you are adding
- A pointer to the array of ToolTip strings

Additional Command Bar Information

Although command bars are destroyed when their parent window is destroyed, it is good programming practice to manually destroy the controls yourself.

You can destroy a command bar by calling the function `CommandBar_Destroy()`:

```
CommandBar_Destroy(hCmdbr);
```

The `CommandBar_Destroy()` function takes only one parameter, which is the handle to the command bar you want to destroy.

3

What Is a Command Band?

Starting with version 2.0 of Windows CE, command bands have replaced command bars as the preferred container for menus and toolbars. Command bands are a type of "rebar" control that can contain multiple "bands" of controls (see Figure 3.3).

FIGURE 3.3
A fully loaded command band.

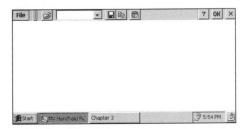

Typically, command bars are placed inside the bands, but any other type of child window may be used. The gripper of each band allows the user to resize and move the bands around, allowing more toolbar items that can be expanded or collapsed.

NEW TERM   A *rebar* control, which has one or more bands, is a container for child windows. Each band can contain one child window, which can be a command bar or any other control.

Creating the Command Band Control

As with the Command Bar control, creating a Command Band is a multistep process. However, you already did most of the initialization necessary when you created your

Command Bar control. All that remains to create a Command Band is that the extended Common Controls library must be initialized with the ICC_COOL_CLASSES flag, shown in Listing 3.7.

LISTING 3.7 Initializing the Command Band Control

```
1: InitCommonControls();
2: INITCOMMONCONTROLSEX iCCS;
3: iCCS.dwSize = sizeof(INITCOMMONCONTROLSEX);
4: iCCS.dwICC = ICC_BAR_CLASSES | ICC_COOL_CLASSES;
5: InitCommonControlsEx(&iCCS);
```

After you initialize everything, you can create your Command Band with the CommandBands_Create() function:

```
HWND hCmdBand = CommandBands_Create(ghInstance, hWnd,
➥ ID_COMMANDBANDS, RBS_BANDBORDERS, NULL);
```

The CommandBands_Create() function has five parameters:

- The program's instance handle
- The handle to the parent window
- A user-defined ID value for the control
- Style bits for the command band (see the next list for more information on the various styles)
- A handle to the command band image list

When creating the Command Band control, you have a choice of several styles to control the look and feel of the command band. The style bit parameter can be one or more of the following values:

- CCS_VERT indicates that the command band should appear vertically down the left side of the parent window.
- RBS_AUTOSIZE indicates that the bands are automatically reformatted when the size or position changes. The control receives an RBN_AUTOSIZE notification when the layout changes.
- RBS_BANDBORDERS indicates that a border is to be drawn between each band.
- RBS_FIXEDORDER indicates that bands can be moved around to different rows, but the order of the bands cannot be changed.
- RBS_SMARTLABELS indicates that the band text label is shown when in a restored state or maximized; otherwise, only the band icon will display when minimized.

- `RBS_VARHEIGHT` indicates that a band should be displayed at the minimum required height for each individual band. If this flag is not set, all bands are equal in height to the tallest band.

- `RBS_VERTICALGRIPPER` indicates that the band should have a vertical gripper. This is used with the `CCS_VERT` style.

Adding Bands

After you create your Command Band control, it is time to start adding bands. Typically, you will have at least two bands: one for your menu and another for your toolbar. To add bands, you have to call the function `CommandBands_AddBands()`, passing it an array of `REBARBANDINFO` structures.

The `REBARBANDINFO` structure, shown in Listing 3.8, is large, but it provides you with a high level of control over what each band looks like and how it behaves.

LISTING 3.8   The `REBARBANDINFO` Structure

```
 1: REBARBANDINFO rbbs;
 2: memset(&rbbs, 0, sizeof(REBARBANDINFO));
 3: rbbs.cbSize;         // Size of the structure
 4: rbbs.fMask;          // Masks for what flags are used
 5: rbbs.fStyle;         // Styles. See the following list
 6: rbbs.clrFore;        // Foreground color
 7: rbbs.clrBack;        // Background color
 8: rbbs.lpText;         // Text label
 9: rbbs.cch;            // Size of text label buffer
10: rbbs.iImage;         // Band image
11: rbbs.hwndChild;      // Handle to the child window in the band
12: rbbs.cxMinChild;     // Minimum width of the child
13: rbbs.cyMinChild;     // Minimum height of the child
14: rbbs.cx;             // Length of the band in pixels
15: rbbs.hbmBack;        // Handle to the background bitmap
16: rbbs.wID;            // User-defined ID for the band
17: rbbs.cyChild;        // Initial height of the band
18: rbbs.cyMaxChild;     // Maximum height of the band
19: rbbs.cyIntegral;     // Step value for the band's growth in pixels
20: rbbs.cxIdeal;        // Ideal width for the band
21: rbbs.lParam;         // User-defined 32-bit value
```

The `fStyle` member can be set to one or more of the following band styles:

- `RBBS_BREAK` indicates that the band is on a new line.

- `RBBS_CHILDEDGE` indicates that the band has an edge at the top and the bottom of the band.

- `RBBS_FIXEDBMP` indicates that the background bitmap does not move when the band is resized.

- `RBBS_FIXEDSIZE` indicates that the band can't be sized. When this flag is on, the gripper is not displayed on the band. This is typically used on bands that contain menus.

- `RBBS_GRIPPERALWAYS` indicates that the band always has a gripper control, even if it is the only band.

- `RBBS_HIDDEN` indicates that the band is not visible.

- `RBBS_NOGRIPPER` indicates that the band will never have a gripper.

- `RBBS_NOVERT` indicates that the band is invisible when used with the `CCS_VERT` style.

- `RBBS_VARIABLEHEIGHT` indicates that the band can be resized by the Command Band control.

Now that you have created the `REBARBANDINFO` structures for your bands, you can add them to the command band by calling the `CommandBands_AddBands()` function, shown in Listing 3.9. This function takes four parameters: first, the handle to the Command Band control; second, the application's instance handle; third, the number of bands to be added; and finally, a pointer to the array of band structures.

LISTING 3.9   Adding Bands to the Command Band

```
 1: REBARBANDINFO rbbs[2];
 2: memset(&rbbs, 0, sizeof(REBARBANDINFO) * 2);
 3:
 4: // Initialize the menu band
 5: rbbs[0].cbSize = sizeof(REBARBANDINFO);
 6: rbbs[0].fMask = RBBIM_ID | RBBIM_SIZE | RBBIM_STYLE;
 7: rbbs[0].fStyle = RBBS_NOGRIPPER;
 8: rbbs[0].wID = ID_MENUBAND;
 9: rbbs[0].cx = 100;
10:
11: // Initialize the toolbar area of the band
12: rbbs[1].cbSize = sizeof(REBARBANDINFO);
13: rbbs[1].fMask = RBBIM_ID | RBBIM_SIZE;
14: rbbs[1].wID = ID_TOOLSBAND;
15: rbbs[1].cx = 100;
16:
17: CommandBands_AddBands(ghCommandBands, ghInstance,
18: ➥sizeof(rbbs)/sizeof(REBARBANDINFO), rbbs);
```

Inserting Items into the Bands

Finally, you are ready to start inserting menus, toolbars, and so on, into the newly created command band. To do so, you must first get a handle to the command bar that is inside each band. To do this, you call the CommandBands_GetCommandBar() function:

HWND hMenuBar = CommandBands_GetCommandBar(hCmdBands, 0);

This call takes two parameters: the handle to the command band, and the zero-based index of the bar for which you want the handle.

Next, to add the menu, you call the CommandBar_InsertMenuBar() function discussed earlier in this lesson, passing the handle you just received:

CommandBar_InsertMenubar(hMenuBar, ghInstance, IDR_MENU, 0);

Finally, you add the buttons to the second band in the same manner you added buttons to the command bar initially. You get the handle to the second band:

HWND hToolBar = CommandBands_GetCommandBar(hCmdBands, 1);

Then, you add the bitmaps and the TBBUTTON structure. Notice that you are still able to add the combo box to the command band in the same manner you did earlier:

```
1: DWORD dwBtnSize = sizeof(tbButton)/sizeof(TBBUTTON);
2: CommandBar_AddBitmap(hToolBar, ghInstance, IDR_TOOLBAR, 4, 0,0);
3: CommandBar_AddButtons(hToolBar, dwBtnSize, tbButton);
4: CommandBar_InsertComboBox(hToolBar, ghInstance, 100, 0, 100, 3);
```

All that's left is to add the adornments (the OK, Close, and Help buttons):

```
CommandBands_AddAdornments(hCmdBands,
➥ghInstance, CMDBAR_HELP | CMDBAR_OK, NULL);
```

And that's it! You've created command bands!

Command Band Notification Messages

Several notification messages are sent to the parent of the Command Band control. These are sent through the WM_NOTIFY message, usually when a user changes the position of a command band.

The two most important notification messages are

- RBN_HEIGHTCHANGE—Sent when the height of the control has changed
- RBN_LAYOUTCHANGE—Sent when the layout of the control has changed

Typically, you will want to repaint your main window when these notifications are sent, so it can adjust for any changes made to the bands.

3

How Do I Restore Command Bands?

Finally, you might be asking yourself, "Self, if the user makes all these changes to my command bands during runtime, how can I save them?" Well, there is an extremely useful function to help out in getting command band state information: CommandBands_GetRestoreInformation(). This function takes three parameters: the handle to the Command Band control, the zero-based index of the band you want to get restore information for, and a pointer to a COMMANDBANDRESTOREINFO structure. This structure, shown in Listing 3.10, contains information necessary to create the command bands with the user's current settings.

LISTING 3.10 Getting Command Band Restore Information

```
COMMANDBANDSRESTOREINFO cbri;
memset(&cbri, 0, sizeof(COMMANDBANDSRESTOREINFO));
cbri.cbSize = sizeof(COMMANDBANDSRESTOREINFO);
CommandBands_GetRestoreInformation(hCmdBands, 0, &cbri);
```

You will typically want to store the contents of the COMMANDBANDSRESTOREINFO structure in the Registry and then, when you create your command bands, read the information back in from the Registry and set up your command bands based on the settings from this structure.

The COMMANDBANDSRESTOREINFO structure is

- cbSize indicates the size of the structure.
- wID indicates the identifier of the band.
- fStyle indicates the current band style flags.
- cxRestored indicates the restored width of the band.
- fMaximized indicates whether the band is maximized.

Summary

In this hour, you were introduced to command bars and command bands. Several examples show how to use these controls in developing a more space-efficient user interface.

Q&A

Q **What is the difference between a Command Bar control and a Command Band control?**

A A Command Bar is a single control that contains a menu and a toolbar. A Command Band control can contain several bands that can be resized and moved.

Q **What types of things can I add to a Command Band control?**

A Any type of child control can be added. Typically, you will add menus and toolbar buttons.

Q **Where is the best place to perform restore logic on a Command Band control?**

A When you are closing your application, it is best to get the Command Band restore information and save it to the Registry. When the application reopens, before you create the bands, you should get the data from the Registry and use it, instead of your default parameters, to create your bands.

Workshop

The Workshop is designed to help you anticipate possible questions, review what you've learned, and begin thinking ahead about putting your knowledge into practice. The answers to the quiz are in Appendix A, "Answers."

Quiz

1. What is the purpose of a command bar?
2. How do I add items to a command bar?
3. How do I handle command bar menu notifications for drop-down buttons?
4. Why is it beneficial to use a command band instead of a command bar?
5. How do I handle a command band resize notification?
6. How do I restore a command band to a preset state?
7. What is the image flag used for in REBARBANDINFO?
8. How do I add ToolTips to command bar buttons?
9. How do you enable and disable command bar buttons?
10. How do I insert a separator into a command bar?

Exercises

1. Modify the example of inserting command bands to add a bitmap to the band background.

2. Add ToolTips to the command band rather than to the Command Bar example.

HOUR **4**

Using the HTML Viewer

Built in to Windows CE is a new type of view control, the HTML Viewer, which automatically handles the parsing and displaying of HTML pages. It can be used as an online Web browser or as an easy way to view reports or other formatted documents, using a standardized markup language.

In this hour, you will learn

- How to create an HTML View control
- How to display an HTML document
- How to respond to notification messages sent from the HTML View control
- Messages you can send to the HTML View control
- How to build a basic Web browser

What Is the HTML Viewer?

The HTML View control is a standard control on Windows CE devices that allows you, the programmer, to create a viewer that uses HTML as its source for formatted documents.

Both Pocket Internet Explorer (H/PCs and H/PC Professional Edition) and Microsoft Mobile Channels (P/PCs, H/PCs, and H/PC Professional Edition) use it to display text and graphics. HTML is also the basis for the Windows CE help system, so the Windows Help Viewer uses it to display on device help files.

You can use the HTML View control (see Figure 4.1) to display any type of HTML text and have it properly formatted. This is extremely useful for not only creating Internet applications but also for displaying reports, status logs, or any other type of formatted document, all using HTML as the source for your display.

NEW TERM   The *Hypertext Markup Language (HTML)* is the backbone of the World Wide Web. It is used to create formatted documents, typically Web pages, and can contain images, sounds, and a variety of other items. Please see RFC 1866 for futher information on HTML.

FIGURE 4.1

The HTML Viewer control.

It should be noted, the HTML View control supports only BMP files internally to display graphics. If you want to display an image that is in another format, you need to have your application convert it to a BMP before displaying it.

Creating an HTML Control

Before you can create an HTML View control, you must first load htmlview.dll into memory and initialize the control library. To use the HTML View control, you must also include the htmlctrl.h header in your application.

To initialize the HTML View control, you first call the LoadLibrary() function, passing in "htmlview.dll" as the module to load (see Listing 4.1). After it is loaded, you then initialize the control with the InitHTMLControl() call, passing in the instance handle to your application.

LISTING 4.1   Initializing the HTML View Control

```
1: // Initialize the HTML view Control
2: HINSTANCE ghHTML = LoadLibrary(TEXT("htmlview.dll"));
```

```
3: if(!InitHTMLControl(ghInstance))
4:     return FALSE;
```

If the InitHTMLControl() call succeeds, it will return TRUE.

Also, you must remember that when your application terminates, you will have to free the handle to the htmlview.dll library by calling the FreeLibrary() function.

Now that the control has been initialized, you can proceed to create the actual HTML View control. This is done by using the standard Windows call to CreateWindow(), using DISPLAYCLASS as the window classname (see Listing 4.2). You will typically want to create your HTML View control in the entire client area of your application, but it is perfectly acceptable to create it as a small view window if your application requires it.

LISTING 4.2   Creating the HTML View Control

```
1: if(ghHTML) {
2: RECT rc;
3: GetClientRect(hWnd, &rc);
4: HWND ghHTMLView = CreateWindow(DISPLAYCLASS, NULL,
    ➥WS_CHILD ¦ WS_VISIBLE ¦ WS_CLIPSIBLINGS, rc.left, rc.top,
    ➥rc.right - rc.left, rc.bottom - rc.top, hParentWnd,
    ➥(HMENU)ID_HTMLVIEW, ghInstance, NULL);
5: }
```

Displaying an HTML Page

Now that you have created an HTML Viewer, it is a straightforward task to display an HTML document.

Sending Text to the Control

To send a text document to the HTML View control, follow these steps:

1. Clear the previous document out of the control. To do this, send the control a WM_SETTEXT message with an empty string as the lParam value (that is, (LPARAM)(LPCTSTR)TEXT("")).

2. Send the document to the control. This is done by sending a series of DTM_ADDTEXT (for ASCII) or DTM_ADDTEXTW (for Unicode) messages that contain the chunks of the document you want to display.

3. After all the document has been sent to the control, you must send the DTM_ENDOFSOURCE message to the HTML View so that it can render the document.

After the document is completely sent to the control, you will receive additional notifications based on the HTML View, depending on the content of your document. These notifications are covered later in this lesson.

As previously mentioned, when sending text to the control, you will want to use the DTM_ADDTEXT (or DTM_ADDTEXTW) message. When you send this message, the wParam value should be TRUE if you're sending straight text or FALSE if you're sending HTML to the control.

```
SendMessage(ghHTMLView, DTM_ADDTEXTW, TRUE,
➡(LPARAM)(LPCTSTR)TEXT("Welcome to HTML"));
```

Listing 4.3 is an example of how to send a small HTML document to the HTML View control.

LISTING 4.3   Sending Text to the HTML View Control

```
1: // Clear the contents of the control
2: SendMessage(ghHTMLView, WM_SETTEXT, 0L, (LPARAM)(LPCTSTR)TEXT(""));
3:
4: // Send a basic document to the control
5: SendMessage(ghHTMLView, DTM_ADDTEXTW, FALSE,
   ➡(LPARAM)(LPCTSTR)TEXT("<HTML><TITLE>HTML Viewer</TITLE><BODY>
   ➡HTML is cool</BODY></HTML>"));
6: SendMessage(ghHTMLView, DTM_ENDOFSOURCE, 0L, 0L);
```

Although this example displays the basic idea of sending text to the control, more than likely you will be loading the HTML document that you want to display from a file located on the device. To do this, you send multiple DTM_ADDTEXT messages as the file loads into memory (see Listing 4.4). When you have completed sending text to the control, you will have to send the DTM_ENDOFSOURCE message to let the control know that no more HTML source will be sent.

LISTING 4.4   Sending Text to the HTML View Control from a File

```
1: BOOL LoadHTMLPage(TCHAR *tchFileName)
2: {
3: DWORD dwRead = 0;
4: char cBuffer[4096] = "\0";
5: // Get a handle to the file to load
6: if(!tchFileName)
7: return FALSE;
8:
9: // Clear the contents of the control
10: SendMessage(ghHTMLView, WM_SETTEXT, 0L, (LPARAM)(LPCTSTR)TEXT(""));
11:
```

```
12: HANDLE hFile = CreateFile(tchFileName, GENERIC_READ, 0, NULL,
    ➥OPEN_EXISTING, FILE_ATTRIBUTE_NORMAL, NULL);
14: if(!hFile)
15: return FALSE;
16: // Load in the file in 4K chunks, and send it to the view control
17: while(ReadFile(hFile, &cBuffer, 4096, &dwRead, NULL)) {
18: SendMessage(ghHTMLView, DTM_ADDTEXT, FALSE, (LPARAM)cBuffer);
19: if(dwRead == 0)
20: break;
21: memset(&cBuffer, 0, 4096);
22: }
23: // Tell the control that we're done sending source to it
24: SendMessage(ghHTMLView, DTM_ENDOFSOURCE, 0L, 0L);
25: CloseHandle(hFile);
26: return TRUE;
27: }
```

As you can see, it is easy to load the control with complex documents formatted in HTML.

HTML Control Notifications

After the HTML View control is sent a document and the DTM_ENDOFSOURCE message is processed, the control sends several notifications to you. These help the control process images, sounds, and meta tags, as well as provide information about the current document that's loaded (that is, the documents title, and so on).

These notifications are sent through WM_NOTIFY, and it is the responsibility of the application to process those messages if you want to use the control to the fullest extent.

When you receive this notification, you will be sent a NM_HTMLVIEW structure as the lParam of WM_NOTIFY. The structure contains the following:

- A NMHDR structure that identifies the window sending the notification.
- LPSTR szTarget. The data contained here is determined by what notification message is being sent:
    - If NM_HOTSPOT is sent, this string contains the contents of the HREF parameter of the HTML <A> tag.
    - If NM_INLINE_IMAGE is sent, this string contains the contents of the SRC parameter of the HTML <IMG> tag.
    - If NM_INLINE_SOUND is sent, this string contains the contents of the SRC parameter of the HTML <BGSOUND> tag.

- If NM_META is sent, this string contains the contents of the HTTP-EQUIV parameter of the HTML <META> tag.
- If NM_TITLE is sent, this string contains the title of the HTML document.
- LPSTR szData. The data contained here is determined by what notification message is being sent:
  - If NM_HOTSPOT is sent, this string contains the query data from a form submitted via the POST command.
  - If NM_META is sent, this string contains the contents of the CONTENT parameter of the HTML <META> tag.
  - If NM_INLINE_IMAGE, NM_INLINE_SOUND, or NM_TITLE is sent, this string is not used.
- DWORD dwCookie. This is a unique value specific to the type of notification message:
  - If NM_INLINE_IMAGE is sent, this value must be sent to the control, within the DTM_SETIMAGE or DTM_IMAGEFAIL message. See the section on handling image requests for further information.
  - If NM_INLINE_SOUND is sent, this value is the loop count from the LOOP parameter in the HTML <BGSOUND> tag. If this is 0, the LOOP parameter is set to INFINITE.
  - If NM_HOTSPOT, NM_META, or NM_TITLE is sent, this value is not used.

Listing 4.5 is an example of how to handle the WM_NOTIFY notification message from within your application's main message loop.

LISTING 4.5   Handling the WM_NOTIFY Message

```
 1: case WM_NOTIFY: {
 2:     if(((NMHDR *)lParam)->idFrom == ID_HTMLVIEW) {
 3:         NM_HTMLVIEW *pHTML = (NM_HTMLVIEW *)lParam;
 4:         if(!pHTML)
 5:             return FALSE;
 6:         switch (pHTML->hdr.code) {
 7:             case NM_INLINE_IMAGE: HandleHTMLImage(pHTML); break;
 8:             case NM_INLINE_SOUND: HandleHTMLSound(pHTML); break;
 9:             case NM_META: HandleHTMLMeta(pHTML); break;
10:             case NM_HOTSPOT: HandleHTMLHotSpot(pHTML); break;
11:             case NM_BASE: HandleHTMLBase(pHTML); break;
12:             case NM_CONTEXTMENU: HandleHTMLContext(pHTML);break;
13:             case NM_TITLE: HandleHTMLTitle(pHTML); break;
14:         }
15:         break;
16:     }
17: }
18: break;
```

Handling Images (`NM_INLINE_IMAGE`)

Most HTML documents contain at least one HTML `<IMG>` tag to specify an embedded image. Although most Web sites use GIF and JPG graphics, the HTML View control only internally supports BMPs. It is the responsibility of the application to convert any images to a bitmap format for the control to process it.

The HTML View control will send your application a `WM_NOTIFY` message with the notification `NM_INLINE_IMAGE` when it encounters an `<IMG>` tag for processing.

After you receive this notification, it is the application's responsibility to send either `DTM_IMAGEFAIL` or `DTM_SETIMAGE` to the control. Both require that the `dwCookie` that was sent as part of the notification be sent back to the control.

`DTM_IMAGEFAIL` is sent when the application cannot load the image. An image that represents a broken image will be displayed in its place. When you're sending this message, the `wParam` should be 0, and the `lParam` should be the cookie value.

If the application is successful in loading the image, it should send the control a `DTM_SETIMAGE` message. This will associate a bitmap with the HTML document image. When sending this message, the `wParam` should be 0, and the `lParam` should be an `INLINEIMAGEINFO` structure, resulting in Figure 4.2.

FIGURE 4.2

Displaying an image in the HTML View control.

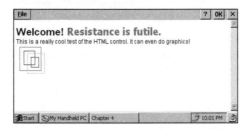

The `INLINEIMAGEINFO` structure contains the following members:

- `DWORD dwCookie`—This is the value that was sent to the application from the control in the original `NM_HTMLVIEW` notification.
- `int iOrigHeight`—This is the original height of the image.
- `int iOrigWidth`—This is the original width of the image.
- `HBITMAP hbm`—This is a handle to the bitmap to be displayed.
- `BOOL bOwnBitmap`—If set to `TRUE`, the HTML control becomes responsible for destroying the bitmap when the page is destroyed. If set to `FALSE`, the application must destroy it.

Listing 4.6 shows how to process a NM_INLINE_IMAGE notification message. After NM_NOTIFY has been processed (from Listing 4.5), it sends the notification to the HandleHTMLImage() function.

LISTING 4.6   Displaying a Bitmap in the HTML View

```
1.  BOOL HandleHTMLImage(NM_HTMLVIEW *nmHTML)
2.  {
3.  HBITMAP hBitmap = NULL;
4.  UINT uiResource = 0;
5.
6.  if(!nmHTML)
7.  return FALSE;
8.
9.  // For the sake of this sample, the image is located inside the
10. // resource of our application and is called IDB_TEST.
11. // Typically, you will need to load the image from the file system
12. // and, if it's not in a BMP format, to convert it over to a
13. // HBITMAP so that the control can show it.
14. if(strcmp(nmHTML->szTarget, "test.bmp") == 0)
15. uiResource = IDB_TEST;
16. else
17. return FALSE;
18.
19. hBitmap = (HBITMAP)LoadImage(ghInstance, MAKEINTRESOURCE(uiResource),
    ➥IMAGE_BITMAP, 0, 0, LR_DEFAULTCOLOR);
20. if(!hBitmap) {
21. // Oops! Couldnt load it, lets fail out
22. SendMessage(ghHTMLView, DTM_IMAGEFAIL, (WPARAM)0L, (LPARAM)nmHTML->
    ➥dwCookie);
23. return FALSE;
24. }
25.
26. // Okay, we got the image and set up the structure, and
27. // now we send it to the control
28. INLINEIMAGEINFO iiInfo;
29. BITMAP bmp;
30.
31. memset(&iiInfo, 0, sizeof(INLINEIMAGEINFO));
32. GetObject(hBitmap, sizeof(BITMAP), &bmp);
33.
34. iiInfo.dwCookie = nmHTML->dwCookie;
35. iiInfo.iOrigHeight = bmp.bmHeight;
36. iiInfo.iOrigWidth = bmp.bmWidth;
37. iiInfo.hbm = hBitmap;
38. iiInfo.bOwnBitmap = TRUE;
39.
40. SendMessage(ghHTMLView, DTM_SETIMAGE, (WPARAM)0L, (LPARAM)&iiInfo);
41. return TRUE;
42. }
```

Embedding Sound into Your HTML Document (NM_INLINE_SOUND)

If the HTML document you have sent to the control contains a <BGSOUND> tag, you will receive a notification of NM_INLINE_SOUND. This indicates that the HTML document has a sound file associated with it.

When you receive this notification, it is the application's responsibility to load and play the sound. Information about what sound to play and its duration is passed in the NM_HTMLVIEW structure, as mentioned previously.

Listing 4.7 shows how to process the NM_INLINE_SOUND notification.

LISTING 4.7 Handling a Sound Request

```
1: BOOL HandleHTMLSound(NM_HTMLVIEW *pHTML)
2: {
3:     if(!pHTML)
4:         return FALSE;
5:
6:     // For the sake of this sample, we will look in  \Windows for
7:     // the sound file. We are passing in a default wave file
8:     // (default.wav) that is known to be on the device.
9:     TCHAR tchSndFile[MAX_PATH+1] = TEXT("\0");
10:
11:     // Convert the path to a unicode string
12:     mbstowcs(tchSndFile, pHTML->szTarget, MAX_PATH);
13:
14:     // Play the sound.
15:     if(pHTML->dwCookie == 0)
16:         PlaySound(tchSndFile, NULL, SND_LOOP | SND_ASYNC);
17:     else {
18:         // Play the sound file for a specific number of times.
19:         for(UINT uiLoop = 0; uiLoop<pHTML->dwCookie; uiLoop++)
20:             PlaySound(tchSndFile, NULL, SND_FILENAME);
21:     }
22:     return TRUE;
23: }
```

You will notice that when pHTML->dwCookie is set to 0, you call the PlaySound() API call with the SND_LOOP | SND_ASYNC flag. This will continuously loop the sound sample.

Handling Hyperlinks (NM_HOTSPOT)

One of the most important tags in an HTML document is the <A> Anchor tag. This enables an HTML document to load another document when a hyperlink is selected.

When an anchor is selected on a document that is loaded into the HTML View control, the application will receive a NM_HOTSPOT notification. This alerts the program that a new document has to be loaded.

As previously mentioned, information about what document to load, as well as any form data, is sent to the application in the NM_HTMLVIEW notification structure.

For HTML forms, the form data can be sent to the application in two ways:

- For a GET form, the HREF string will include the form data.
- For a POST form, the HREF string will include only the base link, and the form data will be sent as the szData member of the NM_HTMLVIEW notification.

Listing 4.8 shows how to handle the NM_HOTSPOT notification. After the user selects a link, it calls in to your function, which will call the HandleHTMLHotSpot function (as shown in Listing 4.4).

LISTING 4.8   Handling a Hyperlink

```
 1: BOOL HandleHTMLHotSpot(NM_HTMLVIEW *pHTML)
 2: {
 3:     if(!nmHTML)
 4:         return FALSE;
 5:
 6:     // The nmHTML->szTarget will contain the new page to load
 7:     if(nmHTML->szTarget) {
 8:         TCHAR tchFileName[MAX_PATH+1] = TEXT("\0");
 9:         mbstowcs(tchFileName, pHTML->szTarget, MAX_PATH);
10:         if(LoadHTMLPage(tchFileName))
11:             return TRUE;
12:     }
13:
14: return FALSE;
15: }
```

You might also want to check the pHTML->szTarget string for an HTML bookmark. A bookmark is denoted at the end of the anchor tag:

```
<A HREF = "mypage.html#bookmark">Click Here</a>
```

This tells the document to jump to another part of the current document rather than load a new page. The best way to handle this is to search the pHTML->szTarget string for the bookmark character . If it is present, you can just send the control a DTM_ANCHOR message instead of loading the new page. The DTM_ANCHOR message is described later in this lesson.

Other Notification Messages

The HTML View control will send your application several other notification messages:

- The NM_BASE notification is sent when the <BASE> HTML tag is in your HTML document. This is used to set the internal "base URL" for all documents. If it was set to <BASE HREF="http://www.myhost.com/">, for example, myhost.com would be the base for all relative URL paths on the page.

- The NM_META notification is sent when the <META> HTML tag is in your HTML document. This is used to embed information inside your HTML document that is not defined by HTML tags. For example, most Web site rating systems use the meta tag to provide information about adult Web content.

- The NM_TITLE notification is sent when the <TITLE> HTML tag is defined in your HTML document. This is used to set the title of the current document.

- The NM_CONTEXTMENU notification is sent when the user presses Alt+Tab on the HTML View window. When this is sent, the notification points to an NM_HTMLCONTEXT structure instead of the NM_HTMLVIEW structure.

> The NM_CONTEXTMENU notification is sent so that a developer can modify the pop-up menu that is created, to fit more within the scope of his or her application.

4

HTML View Control Messages

You can send several messages to the HTML View control:

- DTM_ADDTEXT and DTM_ADDTEXTW—Use this message to send text or the HTML document to the control. The wParam value is set to TRUE if you are sending straight text; otherwise, it's FALSE. The lParam value is a pointer to the data buffer. The only difference with the DTM_ADDTEXTW version of the message is that it is expecting a UNICODE string instead of an ANSI string.

- DTM_ANCHOR and DTM_ANCHORW—Use this message to tell the control to jump to an anchor on the page. The wParam value should be set to 0, and the lParam is a pointer to a string that contains the anchor name. The DTM_ANCHORW message expects a UNICODE string instead of an ANSI string.

- DTM_ENABLESHRINK—Use this message to tell the control to scale images so that the page will fit into the window. The wParam value should be set to 0, and the lParam should be set to TRUE to enable shrink mode and FALSE to disable it.

- `DTM_SETIMAGE`—Use this message to set an image in the HTML View after receiving the `NM_INLINE_IMAGE` notification. The `wParam` value should be set to 0, and the `lParam` is a pointer to the `INLINEIMAGEINFO` structure defining the bitmap.

- `DTM_IMAGEFAIL`—Use this message to fail an image load request after receiving the `NM_INLINE_IMAGE` notification. The `wParam` value should be set to 0, and the `lParam` should be set to the cookie that was passed to you in the `NM_INLINE_IMAGE` notification.

- `DTM_SELECTALL`—Use this message to select all the text in the HTML View control. Both `wParam` and `lParam` should be set to 0.

- `DTM_ENDOFSOURCE`—Use this message to tell the HTML View control that you have completed loading text using the `DTM_ADDTEXT` (or `DTM_ADDTEXTW`) message. Both `wParam` and `lParam` should be set to 0.

Putting It All Together: Building a Basic Web Browser

Now that you have seen how to put together a basic HTML View application, you might be asking yourself how to tie this in to make it a more complete Web browser. Although it is not the purpose of this book to go into details about Web protocols, Microsoft has wrapped much of the functionality required to do this within the WinInet libraries. See Hour 13, "WinSock and Serial Communications," for more detailed information on using Winsock and the WinInet libraries.

What is presented here is a basic description of how to get pages from a remote Web site and display them on your device.

Listing 4.9 shows how to use the WinInet function to load a Web page from the Internet. To use this, you must include the wininet.h header file in your application and link to the wininet.lib import library.

The example shows how to create an Internet session, connect to a Web server, and make a request for a page (in this case, it's asking for /, the root page of a Web site.)

After the request is processed, the page is streamed over the Internet to your read function, which reads data in 4Kb chunks and passes it directly to the control.

After the page is completed, you send the control a `DTM_ENDOFSOURCE` message. The control then sends your application notification messages based on the HTML content you sent the control, including requests for images. To make this a more complete browser, you would have to process the `NM_INLINE_IMAGE` notification, get the image over the

Internet (in the same fashion you requested a page over the Internet), convert the image to a bitmap, and send it to the control through the DTM_SETIMAGE message.

LISTING 4.9 Loading a Web Page over the Internet

```
 1: BOOL GetWebPage(TCHAR *tchWebSite)
 2: {
 3: if(!tchWebSite)
 4: return FALSE;
 5:
 6: // Open up an Internet session
 7: HINTERNET hInternet = NULL, hNetConnect = NULL, hWebRequest = NULL;
 8: hInternet = InternetOpen(TEXT("My App"), INTERNET_OPEN_TYPE_DIRECT,
    ➥NULL, NULL, 0);
 9: if(!hInternet)
10: return FALSE;
11:
12: // Connect to the server
13: hNetConnect = InternetConnect(hInternet, tchWebSite, INTERNET_
    ➥DEFAULT_HTTP_PORT, TEXT("anonymous"), TEXT("anonymous"), INTERNET_
    ➥SERVICE_HTTP, 0, 0);
14: if(!hNetConnect) {
15: InternetCloseHandle(hInternet);
16: return FALSE;
17: }
18:
19: // Make the request
20: hWebRequest = HttpOpenRequest(hNetConnect, NULL, TEXT("/"), NULL,
    ➥NULL, NULL, 0, 0);
21: if(!hWebRequest) {
22: InternetCloseHandle(hNetConnect);
23: InternetCloseHandle(hInternet);
24: return FALSE;
25: }
26:
27: if(!HttpSendRequest(hWebRequest, NULL, NULL, 0, 0)) {
28: InternetCloseHandle(hNetConnect);
29: InternetCloseHandle(hInternet);
30: return FALSE;
31: }
32:
33: // Request was successful. Now let's get the page and display it
34: char cWebBuffer[4096] = "\0";
35: DWORD dwRead = 0;
36:
37: // Clear the page
38: SendMessage(ghHTMLView, WM_SETTEXT, (WPARAM)0L, (LPARAM)TEXT(""));
39:
40: // Loop through the read data and send it in pieces to the control
```

continues

4

LISTING 4.9   continued

```
41: while(InternetReadFile(hWebRequest, &cWebBuffer, 4096, &dwRead)) {
42: if(dwRead == 0)
43: break;
44: SendMessage(ghHTMLView, DTM_ADDTEXT, FALSE,
       ➥(LPARAM)(LPCTSTR)&cWebBuffer);
45: memset(&cWebBuffer, 0, sizeof(cWebBuffer));
46: }
47:
48: // Now that it's complete, send the end of page
49: SendMessage(ghHTMLView, DTM_ENDOFSOURCE, 0L, 0L);
50: InternetCloseHandle(hWebRequest);
51: InternetCloseHandle(hNetConnect);
52: InternetCloseHandle(hInternet);
53: return TRUE;
54: }
```

HTML Control Command Compatibility

Table 4.1 is a list of commands and their level of compatibility with the HTML View control.

TABLE 4.1   HTML Command Compatibility

HTML Tag	Version 1.0	Version 1.1	Version 2.0
A	Yes	Yes	Yes
ADDRESS	Yes	Yes	Yes
APPLET	No	No	Yes
AREA	Yes	Yes	Yes
B	Yes	Yes	Yes
BASE	No	Yes	Yes
BASEFONT	Yes	Yes	Yes
BGSOUND	Yes	Yes	Yes
BIG	Yes	Yes	Yes
BLINK	No	No	No
BLOCKQUOTE	Yes	Yes	Yes
BODY	Yes	Yes	Yes
BR	Yes	Yes	Yes
CAPTION	Yes	Yes	Yes
CENTER	Yes	Yes	Yes
CITE	Yes	Yes	Yes

HTML Tag	Version 1.0	Version 1.1	Version 2.0
CODE	Yes	Yes	Yes
DD	Yes	Yes	Yes
DFN	Yes	Yes	Yes
DIR	Yes	Yes	Yes
DIV	Yes	Yes	Yes
DL	Yes	Yes	Yes
DT	Yes	Yes	Yes
EM	Yes	Yes	Yes
FONT	Yes	Yes	Yes
FORM	Yes	Yes	Yes
FRAME	No	No	Yes
FRAMESET	No	No	Yes
Hn	Yes	Yes	Yes
HEAD	Yes	Yes	Yes
HR	Yes	Yes	Yes
HTML	Yes	Yes	Yes
I	Yes	Yes	Yes
IMG	Yes	Yes	Yes
INPUT	Yes	Yes	Yes
ISINDEX	No	No	No
KBD	Yes	Yes	Yes
LI	Yes	Yes	Yes
LINK	No	No	No
MARQUEE	No	No	No
MENU	Yes	Yes	Yes
MAP	Yes	Yes	Yes
META	Yes	Yes	Yes
NEXTID	Yes	Yes	Yes
NOBR	Yes	Yes	Yes
OBJECT	No	No	No
OL	Yes	Yes	Yes
OPTION	Yes	Yes	Yes
P	Yes	Yes	Yes

4

continues

TABLE 4.1   continued

HTML Tag	Version 1.0	Version 1.1	Version 2.0
PARAM	No	No	Yes
PLAINTEXT	Yes	Yes	Yes
PRE	Yes	Yes	Yes
S	Yes	Yes	Yes
SAMP	Yes	Yes	Yes
SELECT	Yes	Yes	Yes
SMALL	Yes	Yes	Yes
STRIKE	Yes	Yes	Yes
STRONG	Yes	Yes	Yes
SUB	Yes	Yes	Yes
SUP	Yes	Yes	Yes
TABLE	Yes	Yes	Yes
TD	Yes	Yes	Yes
TEXTAREA	Yes	Yes	Yes
TH	Yes	Yes	Yes
TITLE	Yes	Yes	Yes
TR	Yes	Yes	Yes
TT	Yes	Yes	Yes
U	Yes	Yes	Yes
UL	Yes	Yes	Yes
VAR	Yes	Yes	Yes
WBR	Yes	Yes	Yes
XMP	Yes	Yes	Yes

Summary

In this hour, you were shown how to use the HTML View control to view HTML documents inside your applications. This can be used not only for Internet-based applications, but also for developing fancy formatted document displays while using a standard markup language. You were also shown how to build a basic Web browser using the WinInet functions.

Q&A

Q What is the best way to load a document into the HTML View control?

A The best way to load a document is in small pieces. The HTML View will render as much as it can with the data you have loaded. If you wait to load a 64Kb file in at once, rather than keep calling DTM_ADDTEXT in smaller (4Kb) chunks, the user will notice a long wait period.

Q How do I convert other image types (such as JPG and GIF) to something compatible with the HTML Viewer?

A Unfortunately, there is no easy answer for this. You will have to write your own image decompression libraries to handle this. It should also be noted that UNISYS has strict licensing requirements that are necessary to display GIF files. This is one of the reasons newer graphic formats, such as JPG, are becoming increasingly popular.

Workshop

The Workshop is designed to help you anticipate possible questions, review what you've learned, and begin thinking ahead about putting your knowledge into practice. The answers to the quiz are in Appendix A, "Answers."

Quiz

1. What is the class type for the HTML View control?
2. What is the difference between DTM_ADDTEXT and DTM_ADDTEXTW?
3. How do I clear the HTML View control?
4. What notification will I receive when the user clicks on a hyperlink?
5. What is an anchor?
6. What are some uses for the <META> tag?
7. How can I make sure that images will be shrunk to fit the window?
8. How do I get the title for an HTML document?
9. How do I loop a sound file that is specified as INFINITE?
10. How do I fail an image load request?

Exercises

1. Modify the sample to search for bookmarks.
2. Try experimenting with the DTM_ENABLESHRINK message to see how it changes the images.

Hour 5

Working with Standard Controls

Now that we have discussed the basics of Windows CE application programming, it is time to move on to interacting with users. This is done through *controls*, which allow the user to enter data, select items, and navigate through your application.

In this hour, you will learn

- How to use edit controls to edit and enter text
- How to display information in list controls
- How to use combo boxes to select and enter data
- How to use the various types of button controls provided by Windows CE
- How to use static controls to display text, display images, and draw frames or lines
- How to use the scroll control to allow users to navigate up, down, left, and right

Windows Controls

Windows CE provides several controls to build an interface for your application so that users may interact with data. The basic control set, known as the *Standard Controls*, has been around since the original versions of Windows. Windows CE supports these basic controls to provide not only a method for user interaction, but also compatibility with earlier Windows programs.

The Standard Controls are basically predefined window classes that can be created using the CreateWindow() or CreateWindowEx() function call or that can be placed on a dialog box.

Standard Control windows are typically created as children of the parent main window and interact with other windows through the use of WM_COMMAND messages (the Common Controls, which use WM_NOTIFY, are covered in the next hour).

Because each control basically works the same as its Windows 98/NT counterpart, I will give only a brief overview of each control and how it differs on the Windows CE platform.

FIGURE 5.1

The Windows Standard Controls.

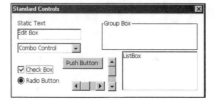

Edit Controls

One of the most basic, but most useful, Standard Controls is the edit control. The edit control, as the name implies, allows users to enter and edit text. The text can then be retrieved by the application in order to do something with it.

It is common user-interface design practice to place a label for the edit control by putting a static control above or next to the edit control with its appropriate label. Because Windows CE has a limited amount of screen real estate, it is also acceptable to place the label as text inside the edit control between angle brackets, like this:

```
<Sample Control Label>
```

An edit control's default processing supports typed text, cursor movement, and text selection using the stylus or keyboard, as well as cut, copy, paste, and undo logic.

To set the text inside an edit control, you must use the WM_SETTEXT message, which takes only a single parameter in the lParam value—that of the null-terminated string to place in the edit control. For example:

```
SendMessage(hWndEdit, WM_SETTEXT, (WPARAM)0L,
➡(LPARAM)(LPCTSTR)TEXT("Sample Text"));
```

To get text from an edit control, you will want to use the WM_GETTEXT message. The message uses both parameters: The wParam should be set to the maximum number of characters to copy, and the lParam should be the buffer in which the text appears. For example:

```
TCHAR tchBuffer[256] = TEXT("\0");
SendMessage(hWndEdit, WM_GETTEXT, (WPARAM) 255, (LPARAM)tchBuffer);
```

Edit controls on Windows CE support only a subset of the available styles on Windows. Table 5.1 describes these styles.

TABLE 5.1 Available Edit Control Styles on Windows CE

Style	Description
ES_AUTOVSCROLL	Scrolls text up a page when the Enter key is pressed.
ES_AUTOHSCROLL	Scrolls text to the right when the end of the edit control has been reached.
ES_CENTER	Centers text in a multiline edit control.
ES_COMBOBOX	The edit control is part of a combo box.
ES_LEFT	Left-aligns text.
ES_LOWERCASE	All characters are converted to lowercase.
ES_MULTILINE	A multiline edit control.
ES_NOHIDESEL	The selected text in an edit control is shown even when the control loses focus.
ES_NUMBER	Allows only numbers to be typed into the edit control.
ES_OEMCONVERT	Converts characters from Windows characters to the OEM character set.
ES_PASSWORD	Masks text input with an asterisk for typed characters. Use the EM_SETPASSWORDCHAR message to change the mask.
ES_READONLY	Makes the edit control read-only so that users cannot change the text in the control.
ES_RIGHT	Right-aligns text.
ES_UPPERCASE	All characters are converted to uppercase.
ES_WANTRETURN	Used with a multiline edit control when you want the carriage return to be inserted into the text, rather than have the default push button pressed.
WS_TABSTOP	Allows the user to navigate to the control with the Tab key.

5

Windows CE does support both single-line edit controls and multiline edit controls. However, Windows CE does not support the Rich Text edit control.

Increasing the Memory of an Edit Control

Edit controls are created with a text buffer that increases as necessary. Single-line edit controls have an internal limit of 32KB, and multiline controls can go to 64KB. You can use the EM_SETLIMITTEXT message to set a hard limit on the number of characters in an edit control.

However, it is important to note that even though the Windows CE API documentation says that the EM_SETHANDLE and EM_GETHANDLE messages are supported (and that they even compile), they are not (and do not).

Unfortunately, if you require an edit control that is greater than 64KB, you will have to design a new edit control class that breaks this barrier.

List Boxes

List boxes contain lists of items that are available for selection. Depending on the style of the control, selection can be made on a single item or multiple items.

Windows CE list boxes support most of the standard Windows API styles, described in Table 5.2.

TABLE 5.2   List Box Control Styles on Windows CE

Style	Description
LBS_DISABLENOSCROLL	Shows the disabled scroll bar for the list box when the list does not have enough items to scroll.
LBS_EXTENDEDSEL	Allows multiple selection of items using the Shift key.
LBS_HASSTRINGS	Specifies that the list box contains strings. This is a default flag on all list boxes in Windows CE.
LBS_MULTICOLUMN	Creates a multicolumn list box.
LBS_MULTIPLESEL	Allows multiple selection of list box items.
LBS_NODATA	For compatibility with earlier versions of windows. Otherwise, owner draw list boxes are not supported.
LBS_NOINTEGRALHEIGHT	Allows list boxes to display partial items.
LBS_NOREDRAW	Prevents the automatic update to list boxes when items are changed.
LBS_NOSEL	Prevents selection of any items.
LBS_NOTIFY	Sends a notification message to the parent when a user clicks or double-clicks on a list box item.

Style	Description
LBS_SORT	Sorts the items in a list box alphabetically.
LBS_STANDARD	Basic format for a list box. It consists of LBS_NOTIFY, LBS_SORT, WS_VSCROLL, and WS_BORDER flags.
LBS_USETABSTOPS	Specifies that the list box should recognize tab characters and expand them.
LBS_WANTKEYBOARDINPUT	Specifies that the WM_VKEYTOITEM message is sent whenever a key is pressed in the list box.
WS_TABSTOP	Allows the user to navigate to the control with the Tab key.
LBS_EX_CONSTSTRINGDATA	Windows CE only. Strings are not stored; the pointer to the string is instead. The application is responsible for managing the memory associated with these strings, because a separate copy of the strings is not stored in the list box.

To add string items to a list box, you can use the LB_ADDSTRING message, which takes a single parameter in the lParam of the message, a null-terminated string. For example:

```
SendMessage(hWndListBox, LB_ADDSTRING, (WPARAM)0L,
➥(LPARAM)(LPCTSTR)TEXT("List Box Entry"));
```

To get the string of the currently selected item, you must first find the current selection by using the LB_GETCURSEL message, followed by a call to the LB_GETTEXT message to retrieve the actual string. Listing 5.1 gives an example of how you get text from a list box.

LISTING 5.1 Getting Text from a List Box

```
1: int nSelection = -1;
2: nSelection = SendMessage(hWndListBox, LB_GETCURSEL, 0L, 0L);
3: if(nSelection != LB_ERR) {
4:     TCHAR tchBuffer[256] = TEXT("\0");
5:     SendMessage(hWndListBox, LB_GETTEXT, nSelection, (LPARAM)tchBuffer);
6: }
```

Windows CE does not support owner draw list boxes.

Combo Controls

Windows CE supports only two of the combo controls found in Windows 98/NT: dropdown and dropdown-list. A *combo control* is a combination of an edit control and a list box. This is an excellent control to use when you are trying to minimize the amount of space used by controls.

5

A *dropdown* combo is a combination control that has an edit control with a button on the right side. When the button is pressed, a list box appears below the edit control. A user can either type in the name of the selection or select one from the list.

A *dropdown-list* combo control is essentially the same as a dropdown combo, except that a static text field replaces the edit control, so the user must select from the list rather than type.

Combo controls on Windows CE support the styles described in Table 5.3.

TABLE 5.3   Combo Box Control Styles on Windows CE

Style	Description
CBS_AUTOHSCROLL	Scrolls text to the right when the end of the edit control has been reached.
CBS_DISABLENOSCROLL	Shows the disabled scroll bar for the list box when the list does not have enough items to scroll.
CBS_DROPDOWN	Default. Displays an edit control so that the user may type a selection.
CBS_DROPDOWNLIST	Displays a static text field for the current selection, instead of an edit control.
CBS_LOWERCASE	All characters are converted to lowercase in the edit control.
CBS_HASSTRINGS	Specifies that the list box contains strings. This is a default flag on all combo boxes in Windows CE.
CBS_NOINTERGRALHEIGHT	Allows the list box to display partial items.
CBS_OEMCONVERT	Converts characters in the edit control from Windows characters to the OEM character set.
CBS_SORT	Sorts the items in the list box alphabetically.
CBS_UPPERCASE	All characters are converted to uppercase in the edit control.
WS_TABSTOP	Allows the user to navigate to the control with the Tab key.
CBS_EX_CONSTSTRINGDATA	Windows CE only. Strings added to the control are not stored; the pointer to the string is instead. The application is responsible for managing the memory associated with these strings, because a separate copy of the strings is not stored in the combo box.

To add a string to a combo box, you can use the CB_ADDSTRING message. It works exactly the same as the list box LB_ADDSTRING message, taking the null-terminated string as the lParam of the message. For example:

```
SendMessage(hWndComboBox, CB_ADDSTRING, (WPARAM)0L,
➥(LPARAM)(LPCTSTR)TEXT("ComboBox Entry"));
```

To get the text from the edit control of a combo box, you can use the standard Windows
WM_GETTEXT message.

Windows CE does not support owner draw combo boxes.

Buttons

Buttons are probably the most widely used and varied Standard Control. They provide
visual communication between the user and the application.

Push Buttons

A push button is what you commonly picture when you think of a button. It is a small,
rectangular, raised button that performs an action when pressed. For example, if the user
presses a Cancel button, whatever action he or she was performing is cancelled.

When a push button is pressed, it sends a WM_COMMAND message to its parent window,
specifying the BN_CLICKED notification in the HIWORD of the wParam and the control ID in
the LOWORD.

Table 5.4 describes the styles of push button controls that Windows CE supports.

TABLE 5.4 Push Button Control Styles on Windows CE

Style	Description
BS_BOTTOM	Aligns the text on the bottom of the button rectangle.
BS_CENTER	Aligns the text in the center of the button rectangle.
BS_DEFPUSHBUTTON	Makes the button the default push button on a dialog. If the user presses the Enter key, this button is selected. It also places a heavy border around the button.
BS_LEFT	Aligns the text to the left side of the button.
BS_NOTIFY	Sends additional notification messages to the parent. The additional notifications are BN_DBLCLK, BN_KILLFOCUS, and BN_SETFOCUS.
BS_OWNERDRAW	Creates an owner draw button. See the next section for more information.
BS_PUSHBUTTON	Creates a push button type of button.
BS_RIGHT	Aligns the text to the right side of the button.
BS_TOP	Aligns the text to the top side of the button.
BS_VCENTER	Aligns the text vertically in the center of the button.
WS_TABSTOP	Allows the user to navigate to the control with the Tab key.

5

Windows CE does not support the BS_BITMAP, BS_FLAT, BS_ICON, BS_PUSHBOX, BS_TEXT, or BS_USERBUTTON styles. To put images on buttons, you have to use an owner draw button.

Owner Draw Push Buttons

Owner draw buttons have been part of the Windows Standard Controls since Windows 3.1 and provide a straightforward method of drawing images on button controls.

To create an owner draw button, create a button with the BS_OWNERDRAW style set. When Windows CE has to draw the button, you will be sent a WM_DRAWITEM, which provides you with information about the control that has to be drawn, including its device context (DC) and control ID.

The code in Listing 5.2, for example, handles the WM_DRAWITEM message and draws a rectangle that looks like a push button.

LISTING 5.2   Handling WM_DRAWITEM

```
 1: case WM_DRAWITEM: {
 2:      LPDRAWITEMSTRUCT lpdis = (LPDRAWITEMSTRUCT)lParam;
 3:      if(lpdis->CtlType == ODT_BUTTON) {
 4:              RECT rct;
 5:              SetRectEmpty(&rct);
 6:              GetClientRect(GetDlgItem(hDlg, (UINT)wParam), &rct);
 7:              if(lpdis->itemState & ODS_SELECTED)
 8:                      DrawFrameControl(lpdis->hDC, &rct, DFC_BUTTON,
 9: ➡DFCS_BUTTONPUSH ¦ DFCS_PUSHED);
10:              else
11:                      DrawFrameControl(lpdis->hDC, &rct, DFC_BUTTON,
12: ➡ DFCS_BUTTONPUSH);
13:      }
14: }
```

Radio Buttons

A *radio button* is a label with a small round button next to it that allows for selection. Typically, you would group radio buttons together to allow the user to choose one from a number of options.

Radio button controls on Windows CE support the styles described in Table 5.5.

TABLE 5.5   Radio Button Control Styles on Windows CE

Style	Description
BS_AUTORADIOBUTTON	Clears all other buttons in the group of selection status when selected.
BS_RADIOBUTTON	Creates a radio button.

Style	Description
BS_LEFT	Aligns the text in the button label to the left side.
BS_LEFTTEXT	Normally, the radio button appears before the text. Setting this style puts the text before the button.
BS_RIGHT	Aligns the text in the button label to the right side.
BS_RIGHTBUTTON	The same as BS_LEFTTEXT.
WS_TABSTOP	Allows the user to navigate to the control with the Tab key.

When the BS_AUTORADIOBUTTON style is set and a user selects that button, Windows CE will automatically set the state of all other radio buttons in the group to unchecked.

Check Boxes

A *check box* is a label with a square box that allows a user to check off an item for selection. You would typically use a check box when you want users to select from a group of independent but related options.

When a check box is selected, it sends a WM_COMMAND message to its parent window, specifying the BN_CLICKED notification in the HIWORD of the wParam and the control ID in the LOWORD.

Table 5.6 shows the check box styles supported by Windows CE.

TABLE 5.6 Check Button Control Styles on Windows CE

Style	Description
BS_3STATE	Creates a three-state check box. The three available states are checked, unavailable, and unchecked.
BS_AUTO3STATE	Creates a three-state check box. The difference between BS_3STATE is that this style will cycle through the check states.
BS_AUTOCHECKBOX	Creates a check box button where the check state toggles automatically when the box is checked and unchecked.
BS_CHECKBOX	Creates a check box button.
BS_LEFT	Align the text in the button label to the left side.
BS_LEFTTEXT	Normally, the checkbox appears before the text. Setting this style will put the text before the check box.
BS_RIGHT	Aligns the text in the button label to the right side.
BS_RIGHTBUTTON	The same as BS_LEFTTEXT.
WS_TABSTOP	Allows the user to navigate to the control with the Tab key.

5

To get the current check state of a check box, you must send the control a BM_GETCHECK message, with no additional parameters in the lParam or wParam of the message. This will return one of the following:

- BST_CHECKED specifies that the button is checked.
- BST_INDETERMINATE specifies that the button is grayed and has the BS_3STATE or BS_AUTO3STATE.
- BST_UNCHECKED specifies that the button is not checked.

Group Boxes

A *group box* is a rectangular area with a label that allows you to group together controls that are related. A group box is used only to organize controls and has only one style, BS_GROUPBOX.

However, it is important to note that because group boxes are opaque on Windows CE, you must add them last in the tab order (which would make the group box control at the end of the Z-order). Otherwise, any other controls will be hidden underneath the group box.

Static Controls

Static controls are used to display text, draw images, or display information that does not require user input. However, if the SS_NOTIFY style (discussed next) is set, you can receive notifications when the static control is tapped on with the stylus.

Static controls on Windows CE support the styles described in Table 5.7.

TABLE 5.7   Static Control Styles on Windows CE

Style	Description
SS_BITMAP	The static control contains a bitmap.
SS_CENTER	Centers text in a static control.
SS_CENTERIMAGE	Centers an image in a static control that displays either a bitmap or an icon. See the following note for more information.
SS_ICON	The static control contains an icon.
SS_LEFT	Left-aligns text in a static control and wraps text if the text is longer than the width of the control.
SS_LEFTNOWORDWRAP	Left-aligns text in a static control and does not wrap text.
SS_NOPREFIX	Prevents conversion of an ampersand to a key accelerator.

Style	Description
SS_NOTIFY	Notifies the parent of the static control by sending an STN_CLICKED notification message when the control is tapped on with the stylus.
SS_RIGHT	Right-aligns text in a static control.

> You can use the SS_CENTERIMAGE style only when you are using the SS_BITMAP style. Icons will not display if this style is set to a static control. If you do not specify either SS_ICON or SS_BITMAP, the static control will act as if SS_BITMAP was set when this style is applied.

To set the image in a static control, you use the STM_SETIMAGE message. STM_SETIMAGE takes both a wParam and an lParam. The wParam should be set to either IMAGE_BITMAP or IMAGE_ICON, depending on the type of image you want to display, and the lParam should be set to the handle of the image. For example:

```
SendMessage(hWndImage, STM_SETIMAGE, IMAGE_ICON,
➥(LPARAM)(HICON)LoadIcon(ghInstance, MAKEINTRESOURCE(IDI_ICON)));
```

Windows CE does have a few limitations when it comes to static controls. Windows CE does not support

- Owner draw static controls.
- Simple static controls (the SS_SIMPLE style). However, these can be emulated using the SS_LEFT or SS_LEFTNOWORDWRAP style.
- Most frame and rectangle styles. SS_BLACKFRAME, SS_BLACKRECT, SS_GRAYFRAME, SS_GRAYRECT, SS_WHITEFRAME, and SS_WHITERECT are all not supported. However, you can use the WM_PAINT message to emulate these styles.

Scroll Bars

Scroll bar controls are used when the contents of a window are larger than the displayed window borders and the user has to scroll to see the information. Table 5.8 describes the scroll bar control styles you can use on Windows CE.

5

TABLE 5.8 Scroll Bar Control Styles on Windows CE

Style	Description
SBS_BOTTOMALIGN	Aligns the bottom of the scroll bar with the bottom of the window. Use with SBS_HORZ.
SBS_HORZ	Specifies that the scroll bar is horizontal in orientation.
SBS_LEFTALIGN	Aligns the left side of the scroll bar with the left of the window. Use with SBS_VERT.
SBS_RIGHTALIGN	Aligns the right side of the scroll bar with the right of the window. Use with SBS_VERT.
SBS_SIZEBOX	Designates a size box.
SBS_SIZEBOXBOTTOMRIGHTALIGN	Aligns the bottom-right corner of the size box with the bottom-right corner of the window. Use with SBS_SIZEBOX.
SBS_SIZEBOXTOPLEFTALIGN	Aligns the upper-left corner of the size box with the upper-left corner of the window. Use with SBS_SIZEBOX.
SBS_TOPALIGN	Aligns the top of the scroll bar with the top of the window. Use with SBS_HORZ.
SBS_VERT	Specifies that the scroll bar is vertical in orientation.

The only difference between Windows CE and Windows 98/NT scroll controls is in the use of the SetScrollInfo() and GetScrollInfo() function calls.

For these functions to work properly, the fnBar parameter *must* be set to SB_CTL, and the hWnd parameter must be set to the handle of the scroll control.

It is also important to note that if you pass in a NULL to the lpsi parameter, SetScrollInfo() will return 0, instead of the current scroll position.

Summary

In this hour, you were shown how to use the Windows CE Standard Controls, and you looked at how they compare to the Windows 95/98/NT standard controls. We also examined what features are not supported on Windows CE, such as images on buttons, and looked at ways to use other functions to achieve the same functionality on Windows CE.

Q&A

Q What is the best way to put images on buttons?

A Because the image styles are not supported on buttons, you yourself have to owner draw the button.

Q Help! I have a dialog, and none of my controls show up in my group box. What did I do wrong?

A Because group boxes are not transparent on Windows CE, you have to put the group box on the bottom of the Z-order (or put it last in the tab order for the window).

Workshop

The Workshop is designed to help you anticipate possible questions, review what you've learned, and begin thinking ahead about putting your knowledge into practice. The answers to the quiz are in Appendix A, "Answers."

Quiz

1. What makes a control a Standard Control?

2. What are the various types of button controls?

3. How do I get my current selection from a list box?

4. How do I set text in an edit control?

5. Does Windows CE support any memory enhancements for combo boxes?

6. Can static controls send me notifications when they are clicked?

7. What does the BS_AUTORADIOBUTTON style do?

Exercise

1. Modify the sample given for owner draw push buttons to draw an icon in the button.

5

HOUR **6**

Incorporating Common Controls

In the preceding lesson, you began to look at the Windows Standard Controls, which have been around since the original version of Windows. Now, we are going to investigate the Windows Common Controls, introduced in Windows 95 and 98.

In this hour, you will learn

- What Common Controls are and how they differ from Standard Controls
- What the major differences are between each Common Control and its Windows 98/NT counterpart
- Which extended Common Controls are supported
- How to use the custom draw services with Common Controls
- Which Common Controls are unsupported on Windows CE

An Introduction to the Common Controls

The Windows Common Controls, as previously mentioned, were first released with Windows 95. Besides providing new types of user input mechanisms, the Common Controls have one distinct difference from the Standard Controls: Windows Standard Controls send WM_COMMAND messages to respond to user interaction, whereas the Common Controls send WM_NOTIFY messages.

As with the Standard Controls, Common Controls are predefined window classes that can be created using the CreateWindow() or CreateWindowEx() function call or can be placed on a dialog box. Figure 6.1 shows some of the Windows common controls.

FIGURE 6.1

Common Controls.

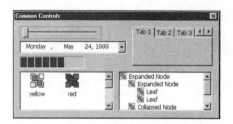

Because each control basically works the same as its Windows 98/NT counterpart, I will give only a brief overview of each control and how it differs on the Windows CE platform. You will also learn what is not supported on Windows CE, as well as some interesting additions for the Windows CE platform.

Initializing the Common Control Library

Before you can use any of the Common Controls, you must make sure that the Common Controls DLL is loaded into memory. You can use the InitCommonControls() function call to load the library and register the controls.

```
void InitCommonControls();
```

If you have to use any of the newer extended Common Controls, such as the month calendar and the date/time picker, you must also call the InitCommonControlsEx() function. This function takes one parameter, a pointer to an INITCOMMONCONTROLSEX structure, shown in Listing 6.1.

LISTING 6.1 Using `InitCommonControlsEx()`

```
1: INITCOMMONCONTROLSEX iccs;
2: memset(&iccs, 0, sizeof(INITCOMMONCONTROLSEX));
3: iccs.dwSize = sizeof(INITCOMMONCONTROLSEX);
4: iccs.dwICC = ICC_DATE_CLASSES | ICC_BAR_CLASSES | ICC_LISTVIEW_CLASSES;
5: InitCommonControlsEx(&iccs);
```

The `INITCOMMONCONTROLSEX` structure is made up of two members. The first is *dwSize*, which specifies the size of the structure. The second, *dwICC*, indicates which controls you want to initialize. Table 6.1 explains each of the initialization flags.

TABLE 6.1 INITCOMMONCONTROLSEX Control Flags

Flag	Description
ICC_LISTVIEW_CLASSES	List view and header controls
ICC_TREEVIEW_CLASSES	Tree view control
ICC_BAR_CLASSES	Toolbar, status bar, slider, and command bar controls
ICC_TAB_CLASSES	Tab control
ICC_UPDOWN_CLASS	Up/down control
ICC_PROGRESS_CLASS	Progress control
ICC_DATE_CLASSES	Month picker, date picker, and time picker controls
ICC_COOL_CLASSES	Rebar (command band) control

List View Controls

As the name implies, a *list view control* displays items in a graphical list with icons that are associated with each item. The control also has the capability to display the items in a multicolumn format and allows in-place editing of items. Figure 6.2 shows a standard list view control.

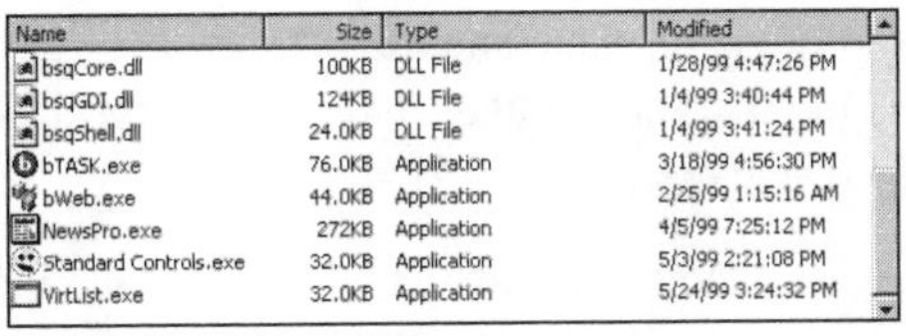

FIGURE 6.2
The list view control.

Under Windows CE, list view controls do not support hot tracking, hover selection, background images, or list view ToolTips.

List view controls support custom draw services under Windows CE. (See the section on how to use custom draw later in this hour.)

List View Extended Styles

Windows CE does support a few of the new extended list view styles. To use these, you call the `ListView_SetExtendedListViewStyle()` function:

```
void ListView_SetExtendedListViewStyle(HWND hWndListView, DWORD dwExStyle);
```

This function takes two parameters: the handle to the list view and a set of flags for the extended style you want to support.

The flag can be one or more of the styles described in Table 6.2.

TABLE 6.2 List View Extended Style Flags

Flag	Description
LVS_EX_GRIDLINES	Draws a grid around each item.
LVS_EX_SUBITEMIMAGES	Subitems can display an image.
LVS_EX_CHECKBOXES	Places a check box next to each item.
LVS_EX_HEADERDRAGDROP	Headers can be rearranged by using drag and drop.
LVS_EX_FULLROWSELECT	When a list view item is selected, highlights the entire row.

To retrieve the extended styles from a list view control, you can use the `ListView_GetExtendedListViewStyle()` function call:

```
DWORD dwExStyles = ListView_GetExtendedListViewStyle(HWND hwndLV);
```

This function takes only one parameter, which is the handle to the list view control for which you want to retrieve the style information.

Advanced: Virtual List Views

One of the long-standing problems with list view controls is that when you start inserting lots of data, the control slows down to a crawl. Fortunately, Microsoft saw this problem and created a new type of style on the standard list view control that allows you just to set the number of items in a list view, rather than insert information for each item. This is known as a *virtual list view control*.

Virtual list views are create exactly the same as a standard list view control, with the addition of the `LVS_OWNERDATA` style. Rather than call `ListView_InsertItem` to add items to the control, you only have to call the function `ListView_SetItemCountEx()` with the number of items you want to insert into the list.

When using a virtual list view, you are sent three notifications to process list view items: LVN_GETDISPINFO, LVN_ODCACHEHINT, and LVN_ODFINDITEM.

LVN_GETDISPINFO is sent to the parent window when the control needs data to display or sort the item.

LVN_ODCACHEHINT is sent to the parent window when the control display has changed. Typically, this occurs when the user scrolls and the control has to update the display. You will receive a NMLVCACHEHINT structure that contains the list-view item index of the start and end items currently visible. This is extremely useful because it enables you to create a cache of items in memory rather than continuously access storage for item information.

Finally, LVN_ODFINDITEM is sent when the control has to find a certain list item. You are sent a NMLVFINDITEM structure that contains information about the item for which the control is looking, including the standard LVFINDINFO structure.

What does this all mean? Well, as an example, the code in Listing 6.2 creates a list view control that has 20,000 items in it, while Listing 6.3 shows how you respond to the notification to draw a list view item.

LISTING 6.2   Creating a Virtual List View Control

```
 1: ghWndList = CreateWindowEx(0L, TEXT("SysListView32"), TEXT(""),
 2:➡ WS_VISIBLE ¦ WS_CHILD ¦ LVS_REPORT ¦ LVS_SHOWSELALWAYS ¦ LVS_OWNERDATA,
 3:➡ 0, nCmdBarHeight, rctClient.right - rctClient.left,
 4:➡rctClient.bottom - rctClient.top - nCmdBarHeight,
 5:➡hWnd, (HMENU)ID_LISTVIEW, ghInstance, NULL);
 6: // Set up the columns
 7: LV_COLUMN lvCol;
 8: memset(&lvCol, 0, sizeof(LV_COLUMN));
 9:
10: // Create the column
11: lvCol.mask = LVCF_FMT ¦ LVCF_TEXT ¦ LVCF_WIDTH;
12: lvCol.fmt = LVCFMT_LEFT;
13: lvCol.cx = 150;
14: lvCol.pszText = TEXT("List Item");
15: ListView_InsertColumn(ghWndList, 0, &lvCol);
16:
17: // Add Items
18: ListView_SetItemCountEx(ghWndList, 20000, LVSICF_NOSCROLL);
```

6

LISTING 6.3   Handling the Virtual List View Notification

```
 1: case WM_NOTIFY: {
 2:     switch(((LPNMHDR)lParam)->code) {
 3:     case LVN_GETDISPINFO: {
 4:             NMLVDISPINFO *pnmv = (NMLVDISPINFO *)lParam;
 5:             TCHAR tchString[25] = TEXT("\0");
 6:             if(pnmv->item.mask & LVIF_TEXT) {
 7:                     wsprintf(tchString, TEXT("Item #%d"),
 8:➡pnmv->item.iItem);
 9:                     _tcsncpy(pnmv->item.pszText, tchString,
10:➡ pnmv->item.cchTextMax);
11:             }
12:     }
13:     break;
14:     }
15: }
16: break;
```

Tree View Controls

When developing applications, you typically will find that data has some sort of parent/child relationship with other data. The most natural way to view this relationship is in a tree or hierarchical list. The tree view control is basically an expandable or collapsible tree that has graphics and text associated with each item. Figure 6.3 shows a standard tree view control.

FIGURE 6.3

The tree view control.

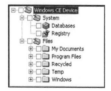

Windows CE fully supports tree view controls, except for the window style `TVS_TRACKSELECT`.

Tree view controls support custom draw services under Windows CE.

Image Lists

Although an image list is not a typical visible control, it is still an important part of the Common Controls library. An *image list* is a *collection* of images that are the same size. An image list can be composed of bitmaps or icons and can contain either masked or nonmasked images. Image lists do not directly display images; rather, they are used to manipulate and track multiple images.

Header, list view, tree view, and tab controls allow you to associate an image list with the control for drawing images.

It is important to note that Windows CE image lists do not support cursors.

Date/Time Picker Controls

The *date/time picker control*, as the name implies, is a control that allows the user to edit the date and/or time. The control displays the information for a specific date and/or time and provides the user with control of individual elements, such as the day, month, and so on. To modify a value, the user can then select a field and type in a new value from the keyboard.

Windows CE supports the styles for the date/time picker control, described in Table 6.3, to determine what is displayed.

TABLE 6.3 Date/Time Picker Control Styles

Style	Description
DTS_LONGDATEFORMAT	Displays the date in long date format. The output is determined by the regional settings. An example would be Sunday, May 23, 1999.
DTS_SHORTDATEFORMAT	Displays the date in short date format. The output is determined by the regional settings. Examples would be 5/23/99 or 5.23.99.
DTS_TIMEFORMAT	Displays the time instead of the date. The output is determined by the regional settings.

Windows CE also supports the DTS_SHOWNONE, DTS_UPDOWN, and DTS_APPCANPARSE styles.

If you would rather use a custom format for displaying your data in the control, you can use the DTM_SETFORMAT message to format the string, sending the new format as the lParam parameter of the message. Date/time format strings can use the characters described in Table 6.4.

6

TABLE 6.4 Date/Time Format Strings

String	Description
d	The one-digit or two-digit day.
dd	The two-digit day. Single digit days have a 0 in front.
ddd	The three-character weekday abbreviation.
dddd	The full weekday name.
gg	The period or era string. Windows CE will ignore this if the date does not have an associated CAL_SERASTRING value.
h	The one-digit or two-digit hour in 12-hour format.
hh	The two-digit hour in 12-hour format. Single-digit hours have a 0 in front.
H	The one-digit or two-digit hour in 24-hour format.
HH	The two-digit hour in 24-hour format. Single-digit hours have a 0 in front.
m	The one-digit or two-digit minute.
mm	The two-digit minute. Single-digit minutes have a 0 in front.
M	The one-digit or two-digit month number.
MM	The two-digit month number. Single-digit months have a 0 in front.
MMM	The three-character month abbreviation.
MMMM	The full month name.
t	The one-letter a.m. or p.m. abbreviation.
tt	The two-letter a.m. or p.m. abbreviation.
X	The callback field. The control queries the application to fill in all X character strings.
y	The single-digit year. For example, 1999 would be 9.
yy	The last two digits of the year.
yyy	The full year.

It is important to note that when you use the X character for formatting strings, the date/time control will send your application the DTN_FORMAT and DTN_FORMATQUERY messages, to which you must respond in order to correctly display your date or time string.

Month Calendar Controls

The *month calendar control* displays a calendar with one or more months in it. Users can use the control to select a particular day, week, month, and so on. Figure 6.4 shows a sample of the month calendar control.

FIGURE 6.4

The month calendar control.

When users tap the month name, they can select from a menu that displays all the months in the year. If they select the year, they can use the up and down arrows to navigate through the years.

On Windows CE, the month calendar control supports the following styles:

- MCS_DAYSTATE—Sends a MCN_GETDAYSTATE notification message to request information about days that should be displayed in bold

- MCS_MULTISELECT—Allows the user to select a range of dates within the control

- MCS_WEEKNUMBERS—Displays week numbers (1–52) to the left of each week

- MCS_NOTODAYCIRCLE—Does not circle the Today date

- MCS_NOTODAY—Does not display the Today date at the bottom of the window

To set the current day, or the current range of selected days, you can use the following messages:

- MCM_SETCURSEL—Passes in a SYSTEMTIME structure to set the current selection

- MCM_SETRANGE—Passes in the address of a two-element SYSTEMTIME array, specifying the minimum and maximum date range

- MCM_SETSELRANGE—Passes in the address of a two-element SYSTEMTIME array, specifying the minimum and maximum selection range

- MCM_SETTODAY—Passes in a SYSTEMTIME structure to specify the Today date

Header Controls

Header controls are typically used in conjunction with list view controls (report mode of a list view uses a header control internally to show column information). A *header* is divided into multiple sections that represent an individual column of information. If the header control is used separately from a list view control, it is up to the application to display the data within the individual columns.

Windows CE enables you to attach an image list to the header so that it can display graphics as well as text.

Header controls support custom draw services under Windows CE.

Tab Controls

Tab controls give the appearance of a set of tab dividers in a file cabinet; when selected, these change the contents of the window. For example, property sheet dialogs use a tab control to allow the user to select each "sheet" in the dialog.

Windows CE supports the TCS_EX_FLATSEPARATORS extended tab style. This style draws a separator between items that have the TCS_BUTTONS or TCS_FLATBUTTONS style.

It important to note that the TCS_HOTTRACK and TCS_EX_REGISTERDROP styles are not supported under Windows CE. Also, Windows CE does not support vertical text. If you create tabs with a vertical orientation, you will have to create a text bitmap, rotate it, and associate it with the tab.

Up/Down (Spin) Controls

Under Windows CE, the only type of up/down control that is supported is one that is attached to another control, which is known as a spin control (or "buddy" window). A spin control is an edit box that has both up and down arrows that are used to increment or decrement the edit control value.

Progress Bar Controls

A progress bar is typically used when a long operation in an application has to occur and progress is incrementally shown. A *progress control* displays a colored bar inside a horizontal rectangle. The length of the bar usually indicates the percentage of the operation that has been completed.

Windows CE supports the new control styles PBS_SMOOTH (for displaying smooth bars instead of segmented) and PBS_VERTICAL (for displaying vertical orientation). Windows CE also supports the new PBM_SETRANGE32 message for setting 32-bit values for the progress bar range.

Slider Controls

A *slider control*, also known as a *trackbar*, allows you to select a value within a range by sliding a thumb to a location on a line. When the user drags the thumb (or slider) or clicks on the line, the slider moves in that direction.

Windows CE supports up to two trackbar buddy windows. These windows are placed by the control to appear at the ends of the trackbar. You can use the TBM_SETBUDDY to set the handle of the buddy controls and the TBM_GETBUDDY message to get the buddy window handle. This can be extremely useful if you must display text or images on either (or both) ends of the trackbar control.

Slider controls support custom draw services under Windows CE.

Status Bar Controls

A *status bar control* is a window that typically resides at the bottom of a parent window and displays information about the status of the application.

Windows CE does not support the SBS_SIZEGRIP style for status bar controls. This is because windows cannot be resized under Windows CE.

Windows CE supports the notification SBN_SIMPLEMODECHANGE, which is sent from the status bar when the simple mode changes from receiving a SB_SIMPLE message.

Custom Draw

Although custom draw is not actually a control, it is an extremely important part of the Common Controls libraries. Basically, *custom draw* makes it simple to customize certain aspects of a common control's appearance, such as its color or font. You can even completely redraw the control if you like.

Why is this important? Before custom draw, if you wanted to change the color of a single list-view item, you had to owner-draw the entire list view control. This entails handling all aspects of the painting of the control. Now, with custom draw, you can specify that you want to override one particular step in the drawing process (in this case, change the color of a single item).

Under Windows CE, command band, header, list view, trackbar, and tree view controls all support custom draw.

When any of these controls begins its drawing process, it will send a notification message, NM_CUSTOMDRAW, to the parent window at specific times during the drawing cycle. Depending on what type of control sends the message, the lParam of the notification is a reference to various types of the NMCUSTOMDRAW structure.

As previously mentioned, NM_CUSTOMDRAW will notify the parent window during the various paint cycles (in the *dwDrawStage* member of the NM_CUSTOMDRAW structure). The custom draw paint cycles are described in Table 6.5.

6

TABLE 6.5 Custom Draw Paint Cycles

Drawing Stage	Description
CDDS_PREPAINT	Before the paint cycle starts
CDDS_POSTPAINT	After the paint cycle completes
CDDS_PREERASE	Before the erase cycle starts
CDDS_POSTERASE	After the erase cycle completes
CDDS_ITEMPREPAINT	Before an item is drawn
CDDS_ITEMPOSTPAINT	After an item is drawn
CDDS_ITEMPREERASE	Before an item is erased
CDDS_ITEMPOSTERASE	After an item is erased

To continue the drawing process, you must return one of the following values after processing the individual drawing stage:

- CDRF_DODEFAULT—Specifies that the control should continue to draw itself and send no further NM_CUSTOMDRAW notification messages for this paint cycle
- CDRF_NOTIFYITEMDRAW—Specifies that the control should notify the parent of any item-specific drawing cycles (CDDS_ITEM notifications)
- CDRF_NOTIFYPOSTPAINT—Specifies that the control should notify the parent of any after-item drawing cycles
- CDRF_SKIPDEFAULT—Specifies that you will handle the drawing for this cycle and prevents the system from continuing to draw
- CDRF_NEWFONT—Specifies that you have changed the current font because the new font might have different system metrics than the old one

What does all this mean? Well, for example, if you wanted to change the color of all list items to blue, you could use the code in Listing 6.4.

LISTING 6.4 Handling Custom Draw

```
 1: case NM_CUSTOMDRAW: {
 2:     NMLVCUSTOMDRAW *lpNMCustomDraw = (NMLVCUSTOMDRAW *)lParam;
 3:     if(lpNMCustomDraw->nmcd.dwDrawStage == CDDS_PREPAINT)
 4:             return CDRF_NOTIFYITEMDRAW;
 5:     if(lpNMCustomDraw->nmcd.dwDrawStage == CDDS_ITEMPREPAINT) {
 6:             lpNMCustomDraw->clrText = RGB(0, 0, 255);
 7:             return CDRF_DODEFAULT;
 8:     }
 9:     return CDRF_DODEFAULT;
10: }
```

If you wanted to change the second item's font, you would use the code in Listing 6.5.

LISTING 6.5 Handling Custom Draw (Custom Font)

```
 1: case NM_CUSTOMDRAW: {
 2:     NMLVCUSTOMDRAW *lpNMCustomDraw = (NMLVCUSTOMDRAW *)lParam;
 3:     if(lpNMCustomDraw->nmcd.dwDrawStage == CDDS_PREPAINT)
 4:             return CDRF_NOTIFYITEMDRAW;
 5:     if(lpNMCustomDraw->nmcd.dwDrawStage == CDDS_ITEMPREPAINT) {
 6:             if(lpNMCustomDraw->nmcd.dwItemSpec == 1) {
 7:                     SelectObject(lpNMCustomDraw->nmcd.hdc, hLargeFont);
 8:                     return CDRF_NEWFONT;
 9:             }
10:     }
11:     return CDRF_DODEFAULT;
12: }
```

As you can see, manipulating individual items for custom drawing is simple with the custom draw service.

> Windows CE does not support the animation control, ComboBoxEx control, drag lists, hot keys, IP address edit control, flat scroll bars, or Rich Edit control.

Summary

In this hour, you were shown how to use the Windows CE Common Controls and how they differ from the Windows 95/98/NT common controls. We also looked at the extended common controls available on Windows CE. Two very important topics covered in this hour are virtual list views and the custom draw support that most common controls support.

Q&A

Q Why would I want to use virtual list view controls?

A Virtual list view controls are great because they do not store any information about the list items. You can create extremely large lists that respond quickly.

Q What is the difference between custom draw and owner draw?

A Owner drawn controls are responsible for drawing every aspect of the control. Items that use the custom draw service can respond to (and override) any individual stage of the drawing process. For example, say that you want to make a single item in a list view a different color. Using owner draw, you would have to manually draw the entire control, whereas using custom draw, you could intercept the draw message for an individual item and set its color.

Workshop

The Workshop is designed to help you anticipate possible questions, review what you've learned, and begin thinking ahead about putting your knowledge into practice. The answers to the quiz are in Appendix A, "Answers."

Quiz

1. What is the major difference between Standard and Common Controls?
2. How do I set full row selection in a list view?
3. For what are tree view controls used?
4. What is a buddy control?
5. What controls support the custom draw service?
6. How can I display a progress bar vertically?
7. How do I set a list view to be virtual?

Exercise

1. Modify the example for the virtual list view control to use the custom draw service. Make every other list view item display in red instead of black.

Hour **7**

Activating the Common Dialogs

To keep a consistent user interface between applications and provide users with familiar screens for commonly used functions, Windows has a set of common dialogs that are built in to Windows CE. These dialogs help a user avoid having to learn similar techniques for performing actions across applications.

In this hour, you will learn

- What common dialogs are available on Windows CE
- How to use the File Open and File Save dialogs
- How to use the Color dialog and customize it
- How to use the Print support dialogs and customize them (on both H/PC and H/PC Professional Edition)
- What dialogs are supported on the P/PC

What Are Common Dialogs?

As previously mentioned, common dialogs are extremely helpful when you are designing an application's user interface. They are a series of dialogs provided by Windows CE to help put a common user interface on tasks that are routinely performed in applications, such as loading a file or saving a file (shown in Figure 7.1).

FIGURE 7.1

The File Save common dialog.

Certain common dialogs (in particular, the Print and Color common dialogs) on Windows CE also support the capability to use a developer-defined dialog while using the common dialog's default processing. This enables the developer to disable or even hide certain user interface elements that are not applicable to his or her application. If a dialog requires even further customization, a *dialog hook* can be used to enable the application to respond to messages from the dialog.

 A *common dialog template* is used to enable the developer to add more controls (or remove unnecessary ones) from a common dialog.

 A *common dialog hook* is used to enable the developer to add special processing to a common dialog by sending messages to and receiving messages from the dialog (refer to Figure 7.1).

It should be noted that even though certain dialogs allow developers to modify their applications' look and functionality, the purpose of a common dialog is to provide users with a consistent look and feel across applications. If you absolutely have to modify a common dialog, take special care to leave as many of the default controls as possible in their original location to avoid user confusion.

 As of Windows CE 2.11 (H/PC Professional Edition), Windows CE supports only four common dialogs: File Open, File Save, Print, and Color. The P/PC supports only File Open and File Save and has some specific flags to support the Palm-size file system (that is, managing projects versus files). You should also be aware that the Print common dialogs have changed between versions 2.0 and 2.1 from using `PrintDlg` to `PageSetupDlg`.

Preparing Your Application to Use Common Dialogs

Windows CE works a bit differently than Windows 95 or NT. The File Open and File Save dialogs are part of coredll.dll, instead of the common dialogs DLL, commdlg.dll.

To use the other dialogs, such as the Color or Print dialogs, you will have to include commdlg.h in your project. To use the common dialog functions, you can either dynamically or statically link to them inside commdlg.dll.

Handling Errors in the Common Dialogs

If a user cancels out of a common dialog, or any type of error occurs when using one of the common dialogs, you will receive a 0 for your return value. You can then call the CommDlgExtendedError() function to obtain more information about why your call to the common dialog failed.

```
DWORD dwError = CommDlgExtendedError();
```

If the user cancelled out of the dialog box, you will get a 0 for the error code; otherwise, you will be returned one of the codes in Table 7.1.

TABLE 7.1 Common Dialog Error Codes

Error Code	Definition
CDERR_DIALOGFAILURE	The dialog box could not be created.
CDERR_STRUCTSIZE	The size of the structure in the initialization of the dialog is incorrect.
CDERR_INITIALIZATION	The creation of the dialog failed during initialization. This usually occurs when there is insufficient memory to create the dialog.
CDERR_NOTEMPLATE	You specified the flag to use a template, but you did not provide one.
CDERR_NOHINSTANCE	You specified the flag to use a template, but you did not include the instance of your application.
CDERR_LOADSTRFAILURE	The dialog failed to load a specific string.
CDERR_FINDRESFAILURE	The dialog failed to find a specific resource.
CDERR_LOADRESFAILURE	The dialog failed to load a specific resource.
CDERR_LOCKRESFAILURE	The dialog failed to lock a specific resource.
CDERR_MEMALLOCFAILURE	The dialog was unable to allocate enough memory.
CDERR_NOHOOK	You specified the flags to use a dialog hook, but you did not include the hook procedure.

continues

7

TABLE 7.1 continued

Error Code	Definition
CDERR_REGISTRYFAILURE	The common dialog could not read from the Registry.
PDERR_SETUPFAILURE	The dialog failed to load the required resources.
PDERR_PARSEFAILURE	The dialog could not get printer information.
PDERR_RETDEFFAILURE	The PD_RETURNDEFAULT flag was set, but the hDevMode or hDevNames flag was not NULL.
PDERR_LOADDRVFAILURE	The dialog could not load the specific printer driver.
PDERR_GETDEVMODEFAIL	The driver could not initialize one of the DEVMODE structures.
PDERR_INITFAILURE	The dialog failed during initialization.
PDERR_NODEVICES	No printer drivers were found.
PDERR_NODEFAULTPRN	No default printer was found.
PDERR_DNDMMISMATCH	The two structures, DEVMODE and DEVNAMES, are not for the same printer.
PDERR_PRINTERNOTFOUND	The dialog could not find the specified printer.
PDERR_NOPORTS	No printer ports are registered on the device.
PDERR_NOPRINTERS	No printers are registered on the device.
PDERR_CREATEDCFAILURE	The dialog could not create a DC compatible with the printer.
FNERR_BUFFERTOOSMALL	The buffer size is too small for the selected filename.
FNERR_INVALIDFILENAME	The filename is invalid.

The FNERR return codes are available only on Windows CE 2.1. On Windows CE 2.0, you still have to call GetLastError() to find out error information for the File Open and File Save common dialogs.

The File Open and File Save Common Dialogs

The File Open and File Save common dialogs are probably the most used because they are present in most applications. As their names imply, the File Open common dialog (see Figure 7.2) is used to select a file to open (on Windows CE 2.1, this can even be from the network). The File Save common dialog is used to open a dialog that allows the user to select a file to save. They both use the OPENFILENAME structure, which is defined next.

FIGURE 7.2

The File Open common dialog.

The OPENFILENAME Structure

The OPENFILENAME structure is used with both the File Open and File Save common dialogs. Depending on what flags are set, the operation of the dialog can vary.

As previously mentioned, you should be aware that both of these dialogs are located inside coredll.dll, instead of commdlg.dll, and do not allow you to use templates or to hook the dialog procedure.

The OPENFILENAME structure is defined in Table 7.2. Member variables that are not present are not supported on Windows CE.

TABLE 7.2   The Member Variables of the OPENFILENAME Structure

Member	Specifies
lStructSize	The size of the structure.
hwndOwner	The handle to the window that owns the dialog.
lpstrFilter	The pointer to a buffer that specifies the filter strings.
nFilterIndex	The index of which filter to use from lpstrFilter.
lpstrFile	The pointer to a buffer that is used to initialize the File Name edit control. It will receive the name of the selected file when the user clicks OK.
nMaxFile	The size of the buffer used in lpstrFile.
lpstrInitialDir	The pointer to a buffer that specifies the directory in which to open the dialog.
lpstrTitle	The pointer to a buffer that specifies the title of the dialog box.
Flags	The flags used to initialize and control the dialog. (See the following list for more details.)
lpstrDefExt	The pointer to a buffer that specifies the default extension that is appended to a filename if the user doesn't type an extension.

The dwFlags parameter can be set to one or more of the following:

- OFN_CREATEPROMPT specifies that the dialog should prompt the user to create the file if it doesn't exist.

7

- OFN_EXTENSIONDIFFERENT is used as a return value to specify whether the user typed an extension that is different from lpstrDefExt.

- OFN_FILEMUSTEXIST specifies that the user can only enter the name of an existing file. If the file does not exist, the dialog will display a warning message.

- OFN_NODEFERENCELINKS specifies that the dialog box should return the select short-cut (.lnk) file path instead of the actual path and filename referenced by the short-cut.

- OFN_OVERWRITEPROMPT specifies that the File Save common dialog box should display a warning message if the selected file already exists.

- OFN_PATHMUSTEXIST specifies that the dialog will only accept valid paths and filenames.

Creating a File Open Dialog

To create a File Open dialog, you must first initialize and fill in the OPENFILENAME structure as in Listing 7.1. After you have done this, all you have to do is call the GetOpenFileName() function and pass in a pointer to the OPENFILENAME structure.

LISTING 7.1   Creating a File Open Dialog

```
 1: TCHAR tchFileName[MAX_PATH+1] = TEXT("\0");
 2: OPENFILENAME ofn;
 3:
 4: memset(&ofn, 0, sizeof(ofn));
 5: ofn.lStructSize = sizeof(OPENFILENAME);
 6: ofn.hwndOwner = hParent;
 7: ofn.lpstrFilter = TEXT("Sounds\0*.wav\
    ➥0All Files (*.*)\0*.*\0");
 8: ofn.nFilterIndex = 0;
 9: ofn.lpstrFile = tchFileName;
10: ofn.nMaxFile = MAX_PATH;
11: ofn.lpstrInitialDir = TEXT("\\Windows");
12: ofn.lpstrTitle = TEXT("File Open Dialog");
13: ofn.Flags = OFN_FILEMUSTEXIST ¦ OFN_PATHMUSTEXIST;
14: ofn.lpstrDefExt = TEXT("wav");
15:
16: GetOpenFileName(&ofn);
```

Creating a File Save Dialog

Creating a File Save dialog is essentially the same as the File Open dialog, except that you change some of the flags to handle file creation. Listing 7.2 shows you the necessary code.

LISTING 7.2   Creating a Save Dialog

```
 1: TCHAR tchFileName[MAX_PATH+1] = TEXT("\0");
 2: OPENFILENAME ofn;
 3:
 4: memset(&ofn, 0, sizeof(ofn));
 5: ofn.lStructSize = sizeof(OPENFILENAME);
 6: ofn.hwndOwner = hParent;
 7: ofn.lpstrFilter = TEXT("Sounds\0*.wav\
    ➥0All Files (*.*)\0*.*\0");
 8: ofn.nFilterIndex = 0;
 9: ofn.lpstrFile = tchFileName;
10: ofn.nMaxFile = MAX_PATH;
11: ofn.lpstrInitialDir = TEXT("\\Windows");
12: ofn.lpstrTitle = TEXT("File Save Dialog");
13: ofn.Flags = OFN_CREATEPROMPT | OFN_OVERWRITEPROMPT;
14: ofn.lpstrDefExt = TEXT("wav");
15:
16: GetSaveFileName(&ofn);
```

> If the return value is 0, an error has occurred. On Windows CE 2.0 and P/PCs, you can call the GetLastError() message, which will return either the ERROR_INVALID_PARAMETER or ERROR_OUTOFMEMORY error. On Windows CE 2.1 and above, you can use the CommDlgExtendedError() function to get error information.

The Color Dialog

The Color dialog, shown in Figure 7.3, is used to select a color from the system colors and the available dithered colors.

FIGURE 7.3

The Color common dialog.

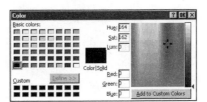

The Color common dialog also allows the user to select from a choice of "custom" colors. It is the developer's responsibility to maintain the array of custom colors.

The CHOOSECOLOR Structure

Before creating the Color dialog, you must first initialize a CHOOSECOLOR structure, which tells the dialog how to operate.

7

The CHOOSECOLOR structure is defined in Table 7.3. Member variables that are not present are not supported on Windows CE.

TABLE 7.3   The Member Variables of the CHOOSECOLOR Structure

Member	Specifies
lStructSize	The size of the structure.
hwndOwner	The handle to the window that owns the dialog.
hInstance	The instance of the application that contains the template for the dialog box if the CC_ENABLETEMPLATE or CC_ENABLETEMPLATEHANDLE flag is set.
rgbResult	If the CC_RGBINIT flag is set, this contains the RGB value of the color to initialize the dialog with; otherwise, the initial color is black. When the dialog returns, this will contain the RGB value of the color the user selected.
lpCustColors	The pointer to an array of 16 COLORREF colors, used to initialize the custom colors portion of the dialog. When the dialog returns, this array will contain any updates the user made to the custom colors. It is the application's responsibility to store this information.
Flags	The flags used to initialize and control the dialog. See the following list for more details.
lCustData	Application-specific data that is sent to the dialog through the hook procedure specified in lpfvHook. This data is sent through the WM_INITDIALOG message in the lParam value to the hook function.
lpfnHook	The pointer to a CCHookProc dialog hook procedure. Active only if the CC_ENABLEHOOK flag is set. See the following list for more details.
lpTemplateName	The pointer to a null-terminated string that is the name of the resource of the dialog template. This template is used instead of the standard template. Active only if the CC_ENABLETEMPLATE flag is set.

The Flags parameter can be set to one or more of the following:

- CC_ANYCOLOR specifies that the dialog should display all available colors.
- CC_ENABLEHOOK specifies that the dialog should use the hook procedure that is pointed to by the lpfnHook member of the structure.
- CC_ENABLETEMPLATE specifies that the dialog should use the template specified by lpTemplateName instead of the standard dialog. hInstance also has to be initialized to use this.
- CC_ENABLETEMPLATEHANDLE specifies that the dialog should use the hInstance parameter as a handle to a memory block that contains a dialog template.

- CC_FULLOPEN specifies that the dialog should automatically open with the Custom Colors area exposed.
- CC_PREVENTFULLOPEN specifies that the dialog should gray out the Define Custom Colors button.
- CC_RGBINIT specifies that the rgbResult member contains a color with which to initialize the dialog box.
- CC_SOLIDCOLOR specifies that the dialog should display only solid (not dithered) colors.

Creating the Color Dialog

To create a Color dialog (see Listing 7.3), you must first initialize and fill in the CHOOSECOLOR structure. After you have done this, all you have to do is call the ChooseColor() function and pass in a pointer to the CHOOSECOLOR structure.

LISTING 7.3 Creating the Color Dialog

```
 1: COLORREF crCustomColors[16];
 2: COLORREF crNewColor = NULL;
 3: CHOOSECOLOR cc;
 4:
 5: memset(&cc, 0, sizeof(CHOOSECOLOR));
 6: memset(&crCustomColors, 0, sizeof(COLORREF) * 16);
 7: cc.lStructSize = sizeof(CHOOSECOLOR);
 8: cc.hwndOwner = hParent;
 9: cc.rgbResult = crNewColor;
10: cc.lpCustColors = (COLORREF *)crCustomColors;
11: cc.Flags = CC_RGBINIT | CC_FULLOPEN | CC_SOLIDCOLOR;
12: ChooseColor(&cc);
```

When the dialog returns, the value of rgbResult will contain the RGB value of the color that the user selected.

The Printer Common Dialogs

Windows CE supports two Print common dialogs. Your choice is dependent on which version of the operating system you are using. If you are using an H/PC (version 2.0), you must use the PrintDlg common dialog, whereas if you are using an H/PC Professional Edition (version 2.1 and beyond), you must use the PageSetupDlg common dialog.

This lesson covers the use of the common dialogs. For further information about printing, see Hour 14, "Printing."

7

Version 2.0: Using `PrintDlg`

On Windows CE version 2.0, you will have to use the `PrintDlg` dialog (see Figure 7.4) to get information from the user about the pending print job.

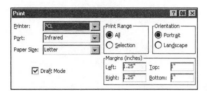

Before creating the `PrintDlg` dialog, you must first initialize a `PRINTDLG` structure. This structure contains information about the page margins, printer configurations, page orientation, and print mode.

The `PRINTDLG` structure is defined in Table 7.4. Member variables that are not present are not supported on Windows CE.

TABLE 7.4 The Member Variables of the `PRINTDLG` Structure

Member	Specifies
cbStruct	The size of the structure.
hwndOwner	The handle to the window that owns the dialog box.
hdc	When the dialog returns, this will contain a handle to the printer's device context.
dwFlags	The flags used to initialize and control the dialog. See the following list for more details.
rcMinMargin	Contains the minimum widths of the left, right, top, and bottom margins if the `PD_MINMARGINS` flag is set.
rcMargin	Contains the widths of the left, right, top, and bottom margins if the `PD_MARGINS` flag is set.
hinst	The handle to the instance that contains the dialog template if the `PD_ENABLEPRINTTEMPLATE` flag is set.
lCustData	Application-specific data that is sent to the dialog through the hook procedure specified in `lpfvHook`. This data is sent through the `WM_INITDIALOG` message in the `lParam` value to the hook function.
pfnPrintHook	The pointer to a PrintHookProc dialog hook procedure. Active only if the `PD_ENABLEPRINTHOOK` flag is set. See the following list for more details.

Member	Specifies
pszPrintTemplateName	The pointer to a null-terminated string that is the name of the resource of the dialog template. This template is used instead of the standard template. Active only if the PD_ENABLEPRINTTEMPLATE flag is set.
hglbPrintTemplateResource	The handle to a memory object that contains a dialog box template if the PD_ENABLEPRINTTEMPLATEHANDLE flag is set.

The dwFlags parameter can be set to one or more of the following:

- PD_SELECTALLPAGES specifies that the All button should be selected when the dialog is initialized. After the dialog closes, this specifies that the user has clicked it.

- PD_SELECTSELECTION specifies that the Selection button should be selected when the dialog is initialized. After the dialog closes, this specifies that the user has clicked it.

- PD_SELECTDRAFTMODE specifies that the user has selected Draft Mode.

- PD_SELECTA4 specifies that the user has selected the A4 paper size.

- PD_SELECTLETTER specifies that the user has selected the letter paper size.

- PD_SELECTINFRARED specifies that the user has selected the infrared printer port.

- PD_SELECTSERIAL specifies that the user has selected the serial printer port.

- PD_DISABLEPAPERSIZE specifies that the paper size selection should be disabled.

- PD_DISABLEPRINTRANGE specifies that the print range selection should be disabled.

- PD_DISABLEMARGINS specifies that the margin selection should be disabled.

- PD_DISABLEORIENTATION specifies that the page orientation (portrait or landscape) should be disabled.

- PD_RETURNDEFAULTDC specifies that the dialog should not show and should just return the printer's device context.

- PD_ENABLEPRINTHOOK specifies that the dialog should use the hook procedure that is pointed to by the pfnPrintHook member of the structure.

- PD_ENABLEPRINTTEMPLATE specifies that the dialog should use the template specified by pszPrintTemplateName instead of the standard dialog. hinst also has to be initialized to use this.

- PD_ENABLEPRINTTEMPLATEHANDLE specifies that the dialog should use the hglbPrintTemplateResource parameter as a handle to a memory block that contains a dialog template.

7

- PD_SELECTPORTRAIT specifies that portrait mode is selected by default. After the dialog closes, this specifies that the user has selected portrait mode.

- PD_SELECTLANDSCAPE specifies that landscape mode is selected by default. After the dialog closes, this specifies that the user has selected landscape mode.

- PD_MARGINS specifies that the rcMargin value contains the initial margin values.

- PD_INTHOUSANDTHSOFINCHES specifies the unit of measurement for the margins.

- PD_INHUNDREDTHSOFMILLIMETERS specifies the unit of measurement for the margins.

- PD_MINMARGINS specifies that the rcMinMargin value contains the minimum margin values.

After you have created the PRINTDLG structure and filled it with the values you need, you can then call the PrintDlg() function (see Listing 7.4). You have to pass this function a pointer to your PRINTDLG structure.

LISTING 7.4 Creating the Print Dialog Using PrintDlg

```
1: PRINTDLG prntDlg;
2:
3: memset(&prntDlg, 0, sizeof(PRINTDLG));
4: prntDlg.cbStruct = sizeof(PRINTDLG);
5: prntDlg.hwndOwner = hParent;
6: prntDlg.dwFlags = PD_SELECTALLPAGES ¦ PD_SELECTPORTRAIT;
7: PrintDlg(&prntDlg);
```

Version 2.1: Using `PageSetupDlg`

On Windows CE 2.1 devices, you should be using the PageSetupDlg function call instead of PrintDlg to create the Print dialog shown in Figure 7.5.

FIGURE 7.5

The Print common dialog in version 2.1.

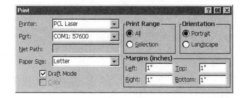

As far as the end user sees, the PageSetupDlg dialog basically provides the same functionality as PrintDlg did, with the noted exception of color printing, networking, and so on. To accommodate any extra controls you add to the dialog, the structure used to set up the dialog is very different.

Before being able to use the `PageSetupDlg` dialog, you must first create a `PAGESETUPDLG` structure. This structure contains information about the page margins, network printer support, printer configurations, page orientation, and so on.

The `PAGESETUPDLG` structure is defined in Table 7.5. Member variables that are not present are not supported on Windows CE.

TABLE 7.5   The Member Variables of the `PAGESETUPDLG` Structure

Member	Specifies
lStructSize	The size of the structure.
hwndOwner	The handle to the window that owns the dialog box.
hDevMode	The handle to a `DEVMODE` structure. See the following list for more details.
hDevNames	The handle to a `DEVNAMES` structure. See the following list for more details.
Flags	The flags used to initialize and control the dialog. See the following list for more details.
ptPaperSize	Specifies the dimensions of the paper specified by the user.
rtMinMargin	Contains the minimum widths of the left, right, top, and bottom margins if the `PSD_MINMARGINS` flag is set.
rtMargin	Contains the widths of the left, right, top, and bottom margins if the `PSD_MARGINS` flag is set.
hInstance	The handle to the instance that contains the dialog template if the `PSD_ENABLEPRINTTEMPLATE` flag is set.
lCustData	Application-specific data that is sent to the dialog through the hook procedure specified in `lpfnPageSetupHook`. This data is sent through the `WM_INITDIALOG` message in the `lParam` value to the hook function.
lpfnPageSetupHook	The pointer to a `PageSetupHook` dialog hook procedure. Active only if the `PSD_ENABLEPAGESETUPHOOK` flag is set. See the following list for more details.
lpPageSetupTemplateName	The pointer to a null-terminated string that is the name of the resource of the dialog template. This template is used instead of the standard template. Active only if the `PSD_ENABLEPAGESETUP` flag is set.
hPageSetupTemplate	The handle to a memory object that contains a dialog box template if the `PSD_ENABLEPAGESETUPTEMPLATEHANDLE` flag is set.

7

The DEVMODE structure is used to initialize controls on the dialog. When the dialog returns, it contains the user's selections.

The parameters of the DEVMODE structure that are not present are not supported on Windows CE. The structure is composed of the following:

- dmSpecVersion specifies the version of the initialization structure. This must be set to SPEC_VERSION.
- dmSize specifies in bytes the size of the DEVMODE structure.
- dmOrientation specifies the page orientation. Use DMORIENT_PORTRAIT for portrait mode or DMORIENT_LANDSCAPE for landscape mode.
- dmPaperSize specifies the paper size. Use DMPAPER_LETTER for 8 1/2 by 11 paper, or DMPAPER_A4 for 210 by 297 millimeters.
- dmPrintQuality specifies the quality of the print job. Use DMRES_DRAFT for draft mode or DMRES_HIGH for high quality mode.
- dmColor specifies whether the printout should be in color or monochrome. Use DMCOLOR_COLOR for color and DMCOLOR_MONOCHROME for black and white print jobs.

The DEVNAMES structure is used to get strings that are associated with the printer, such as driver, device, and port names.

The following are the parameters of the DEVNAMES structure:

- wDriverOffset specifies the offset in bytes from the beginning of this structure to the driver name.
- wDeviceOffset specifies the offset in bytes from the beginning of this structure to the device name.
- wOutputOffset specifies the offset in bytes from the beginning of this structure to the name of the output port.
- wDefault specifies whether the names contained in this structure are for the default printer.

The Flags member can be one or more of the following:

- PSD_DISABLEMARGINS specifies that the margin selection should be disabled.
- PSD_DISABLEORIENTATION specifies that the page orientation (portrait or landscape) should be disabled.
- PSD_DISABLEPAPER specifies that the paper size selection should be disabled.
- PSD_DISABLEPRINTRANGE specifies that the print range selection should be disabled.

- **PSD_DISABLEPRINTER** specifies that the Printer button should be disabled, preventing the user from additional printer setup information.

- **PSD_ENABLEPAGESETUPHOOK** specifies that the dialog should use the hook procedure that is pointed to by the lpfnPageSetupHook member of the structure.

- **PSD_ENABLEPAGESETUPTEMPLATE** specifies that the dialog should use the template specified by pszPageSetupTemplateName instead of the standard dialog. hInstance also has to be initialized to use this.

- **PSD_ENABLEPAGESETUPTEMPLATEHANDLE** specifies that the dialog should use the hPageSetupTemplate parameter as a handle to a memory block that contains a dialog template.

- **PSD_INHUNDRESTHSOFMILLIMETERS** specifies the unit of measurement that the margins are in.

- **PSD_INTHOUSANDTHSOFINCHES** specifies the unit of measurement that the margins are in.

- **PSD_MARGINS** specifies that the rtMargin value contains the initial margin values.

- **PSD_MINMARGINS** specifies that the rtMinMargin value contains the minimum margin values.

- **PSD_RANGESELECTION** specifies the Selection button on the dialog as the default range, instead of All.

- **PSD_RETURNDEFAULT** specifies that the dialog should not display, but instead return immediately with the hDevNames and hDevMode handles for the system default printer.

To successfully call the PageSetupDlg() function call, you must first set up the PAGESETUPDLG structure as in Listing 7.5. When this is done, you only have to call PageSetupDlg() and pass a pointer to your structure.

LISTING 7.5 Creating the PageSetupDlg Dialog

```
1: PAGESETUPDLG pgSetupDialog;
2: memset(&pgSetupDialog, 0, sizeof(PAGESETUPDLG));
3:
4: pgSetupDialog.lStructSize = sizeof(PAGESETUPDLG);
5: pgSetupDialog.hwndOwner = hParent;
6: PageSetupDlg(&pgSetupDialog);
```

7

Customizing a Common Dialog

Even though the common dialogs were designed to meet the needs of most applications, at times custom functionality must be added to the dialog to better fit your application. To accomplish this, you can either use a custom template or a dialog hook to add extra functionality and control over the dialogs.

This functionality is currently supported only on the Color and the Print common dialogs.

Using a Custom Template

If you have to make visual changes to the dialog, you will want to use a custom dialog template. This is most commonly used if you want to remove controls or add unique controls that are specific to your application.

For this example, you can make some small visual changes to the PrintDlg dialog. To do this, you modify the dialog template (print.dlg, which is located in your include directory) and also include the header printdlg.h in your project.

Next, you modify the dialog template to fit your needs. For example, add a button (to use the button, you will have to hook the dialog procedure, as shown in Figure 7.6), a text field, and, just for fun, change some of the text in one of the controls. You should be careful not to change the resource IDs of the controls because without a custom hook procedure to handle them, they will not function properly.

FIGURE 7.6

Your own modified PrintDlg *common dialog.*

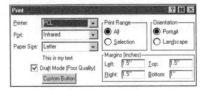

Now that the dialog has been modified, you make some small modifications to the PRINTDLG structure to tell it to use the template dialog instead of the default (see Listing 7.6).

LISTING 7.6   Using a Custom Dialog Template

```
1: PRINTDLG prtDlg;
2: memset(&prtDlg, 0, sizeof(PRINTDLG));
3:
4: prtDlg.cbStruct = sizeof(PRINTDLG);
5: prtDlg.hwndOwner = hParent;
```

```
6: prtDlg.dwFlags = PD_SELECTALLPAGES | PD_SELECTPORTRAIT |
   ➡PD_ENABLEPRINTTEMPLATE;
7: prtDlg.hinst = ghInstance;
8: prtDlg.pszPrintTemplateName = MAKEINTRESOURCE(ID_MYPRINTDLG);
9: PrintDlg(&prtDlg);
```

Although custom templates are useful for modifying the visual aspect of the dialog, you now have to hook the dialog procedure to get the functionality you need.

Using Your Own Dialog Hook Procedure

If the common dialog you are using requires you to override some of its processing, you will have to hook the dialog procedure. This basically allows you to stub in your own DialogProc to take over the default dialog's functionality.

To hook the dialog procedure, you create a *hook function*. This is basically a DialogProc that you will create to handle custom messages to the dialog. You will have to tell the dialog in its initialization structure that you are using a hook function, by providing a pointer to the function and a flag turning on the hook.

For this example, in Listing 7.7, you will add additional functionality to the sample template in the last section, which modified the PrintDlg.

LISTING 7.7 *Using a Custom Dialog Hook Function*

```
 1: BOOL PrintMe(HWND hParent)
 2: {
 3:     PRINTDLG prtDlg;
 4:     memset(&prtDlg, 0, sizeof(PRINTDLG));
 5:
 6:     prtDlg.cbStruct = sizeof(PRINTDLG);
 7:     prtDlg.hwndOwner = hParent;
 8:     prtDlg.dwFlags = PD_SELECTALLPAGES | PD_SELECTPORTRAIT |
 9:     ➡PD_ENABLEPRINTTEMPLATE | PD_ENABLEPRINTHOOK;
10:     prtDlg.hinst = ghInstance;
11:     prtDlg.pszPrintTemplateName = MAKEINTRESOURCE(ID_MYPRINTDLG);
12:     prtDlg.pfnPrintHook = PrintHookProc;
13:     PrintDlg(&prtDlg);
14:     return TRUE;
15: }
16:
17: UINT CALLBACK PrintHookProc(HWND hDlg, UINT uiMessage,
    ➡WPARAM wParam,LPARAM lParam)
18: {
19:     switch(uiMessage)
20:     {
21:         case WM_COMMAND: {
22:         switch(LOWORD(wParam)) {
```

7

continues

LISTING 7.7   continued

```
23:                    case IDC_MY_BUTTON:
24:                        MessageBox(hDlg, TEXT("My Custom Button"),
                           ➥TEXT("Print Dialog Sample"), MB_OK);
25:                    break;
26:                }
27:            break;
28:            }
29:      }30:31:      return FALSE;
32: }
```

P/PC Specifics

The P/PC devices also support some of the common dialogs, with minor variations.
These include the following:

- Opening and saving files
- Folders
- File properties
- What's not supported on P/PCs

Opening and Saving Files

Calling in to the File Open and File Save common dialogs is exactly the same as the
H/PC: You create an OPENFILENAME structure and pass it to the GetOpenFileName or
GetSaveFileName function call. There are only a few minor differences to be aware of in
the OPENFILENAME structure:

- Flags can be set to the OFN_PROJECT flag, which opens the folder dialog instead of
  the File Open dialog, or to the OFN_PROPERTY flag to show a file property sheet.
- lpstrFile returns the full path of the selected file.
- lpstrFileTitle returns the project folder name.
- lpstrInitialDir points to a string that receives the folder name, but not the full
  path.

Folders

On the P/PC, you can use the GetOpenFileName function to manage folders on the
device. This variation of the dialog will allow you to create, delete, or rename folders. To
use this, you have to set the Flags field of the OPENFILENAME structure to OFN_PROJECT.

File Properties

If your application requires more information about a particular file, such as modified times, and so on, you will want to view it as a File Property dialog. This is a variation of the GetSaveFileName dialog. To view file properties, set the Flags field of the OPENFILENAME structure to OFN_PROPERTY.

What's Not Supported on P/PCs

The Color and Print common dialogs are not supported on P/PCs, nor is the capability to use dialog hooks or dialog templates.

Summary

In this hour, you learned how to use common dialogs to help users employ a standard interface for common tasks. You were shown how to create them, extract data from them, and in some instances, customize them. You were also shown differences between H/PC and P/PC versions of the dialogs.

Q&A

Q Why use common dialogs?

A To provide a familiar look and feel for the most commonly used functionality on the device.

Q Why would you want to hook the Print or Color common dialogs?

A If you wanted to disable certain functionality or provide new functionality on the dialogs.

Workshop

The Workshop is designed to help you anticipate possible questions, review what you've learned, and begin thinking ahead about putting your knowledge into practice. The answers to the quiz are in Appendix A, "Answers."

Quiz

1. Can I hook or template the File Open or File Save dialogs?
2. Are the Print and Color dialogs supported on the P/PC platform?
3. On the H/PC Professional Edition, should I use PrintDlg to print?

7

4. On the File Open or File Save common dialog, how can I change the dialog title?

5. How do I get error information for my common dialogs?

6. How do I get the color that the user selected in the Color dialog?

7. What does the CC_SOLIDCOLOR flag do in the CHOOSECOLOR structure?

Exercises

1. Modify the sample code so that the File Save dialog will not prompt for overwrite errors.

2. Create a PrintDlg common dialog that has default margins of 1 1/2 inches and a minimum margin of 1/2 inch.

PART III

Tap in to the System

Hour

Hour 8

Working with Graphics Devices

Now it is time to introduce you to the Windows CE graphics device interface (GDI) subsystem.

In this hour, you will learn

- How to work with device contexts, pens, brushes, lines, and shapes
- How to determine which fonts are available on a Windows CE system and how to use them
- How to work with bitmaps

An Introduction to the Windows CE GDI Subsystem

Like desktop Windows, the Windows CE graphics device interface (GDI) subsystem is based on performing output operations on a device context (DC). Applications can draw text and graphics to the DC using the GDI functions.

Objects (such as pens, brushes, fonts, bitmaps, regions, or palettes) are selected into a DC by using the SelectObject function. Objects are deleted from a DC using the DeleteObject function.

Windows CE supports three types of DCs: display, memory, and printing. Display DCs are used for drawing on the screen. Memory DCs are used for drawing on device-independent bitmaps. Print DCs are used for outputting to printers (this is supported only in Windows CE 2.0 and above).

Pens and Brushes

Pens are created and used in the same manner as in desktop versions of Windows. Pens are created by the use of the CreatePen or the CreatePenIndirect functions. They are selected into a DC using the SelectObject function, and they are deleted from the DC after they are no longer needed by using the DeleteObject function.

Pen styles supported on Windows CE include solid pens (PS_SOLID), dashed pens (PS_DASHED), and null pens (PS_NULL). The following pen styles are not supported: PS_DOT, PS_DASHDOT, PS_DASHDOTDOT, and PS_INSIDEFRAME.

Brushes are used to fill in the interior regions of shapes. Solid brushes can be created with the CreateSolidBrush function, and a *pattern brush* (a brush that paints with a bitmap image) can be created with the CreatePatternBrush function. You can create a brush based on a device-independent bitmap with the CreateDIBPatternBrushPt function.

Like other GDI objects, brushes are selected into a DC by the use of the SelectObject function, and they are deleted by the use of the DeleteObject function.

Dithered brushes are not supported on Windows CE.

Drawing Shapes on Windows CE

Table 8.1 lists the shape-drawing APIs supported on Windows CE.

TABLE 8.1 Windows CE Shape-Drawing Functions

Function	Purpose
Ellipse()	To draw and fill an ellipse
Polygon()	To draw and fill a polygon
Polyline()	To draw a series of connected lines
Rectangle()	To draw and fill a rectangle
RoundRect()	To draw and fill a rectangle with rounded corners

Windows CE does not support arcs, Bezier curves, chords, and pie graphs, as well as the PolyPolygon, PolyPolyLine, LineTo(), and MoveTo() functions.

The biggest effect on porting drawing code from desktop Windows to Windows CE is produced by the desktop LineTo() and MoveTo() functions. These are not supported on Windows CE. In their place, you should use the PolyLine() function. Listing 8.1 demonstrates how to do this, with code that will draw a triangle on desktop Windows.

LISTING 8.1 Drawing a Triangle on Traditional Desktop Windows

```
1: case WM_PAINT:
2:         {
3:                 PAINTSTRUCT     ps;
4:                 HDC             hdc;
5:
6:                 hdc = BeginPaint( hWnd, &ps );
7:                 MoveToEx( hdc, 100, 100, NULL );
8:                 LineTo( hdc, 150, 50 );
9:                 LineTo( hdc, 150, 150 );
10:                 LineTo( hdc, 100, 100 );
11:                 EndPaint( hWnd, &ps );
12:         }
13:         break;
```

Listing 8.1 will not compile for Windows CE because of the use of LineTo() and MoveToEx(). To build and execute properly on Windows CE, you must rewrite the code to use PolyLine() as shown in Listing 8.2.

LISTING 8.2 Drawing a Triangle on Windows CE

```
1:     case WM_PAINT:
2:         {
3:                 PAINTSTRUCT ps;
4:                 HDC             hdc;
5:                 POINT           points[] = { { 100, 100 }, { 150, 50 },
                                    ➥{ 150, 150 }, { 100, 100 } };
6:
7:                 hdc = BeginPaint( hWnd, &ps );
8:                 Polyline( hdc, (const POINT*)&points,
                            ➥sizeof(points)/sizeof(POINT));
9:                 EndPaint( hWnd, &ps );
10:         }
11:         break;
```

Drawing Text on Windows CE

Text is drawn to a DC on Windows CE using the ExtTextOut API. The TextOut and PolyTextOut APIs supported on desktop Windows are not supported on Windows CE.

The GetTextAlign function retrieves the current text alignment settings for the specified DC. Your application can set the text alignment value by utilizing the SetTextAlign function.

Your application can determine the width and height of a string before outputting by using the GetTextExtentPoint function. This function is identical to the GetTextExtentPoint32 function. Both of these functions use the font selected for the current DC to determine the size, which is returned by the pointer to a SIZE structure parameter.

The GetTextExtentExPoint function is used to determine the number of characters in a specified string that can be displayed within a specified width.

Fonts on Windows CE

Windows CE supports both TrueType and raster fonts, but only one or the other can be used on a particular platform. Which type of fonts that are used on a platform is determined when the operating system is built for that platform. Typically, Windows CE PC Companion devices running Windows CE 1.0 or 1.1 use raster fonts, and devices running Windows CE 2.0 or later use TrueType fonts.

> The default system font for Windows CE 2.0 and above is Tahoma, and the size is 9 pt. This is the font you should use within the Developer Studio resource editor when creating your dialog boxes.

Creating and Querying Fonts

Your application can apply a font to a DC by creating the font using the CreateFontIndirect function and then selecting it into the DC using SelectObject. If CreateFontIndirect fails to find an exact match for the logical font specified by the LOGFONT parameter, it will create a font that is the closest match.

If your application has to examine the characteristics of a font currently selected in a DC, you can use the GetTextMetrics function to retrieve its TEXTMETRIC values. GetTextFace can be used to retrieve the name of the currently selected font.

Adding and Removing Fonts from the System Font Table

8

Applications can add and remove fonts from the system font table by using the AddFontResource and RemoveFontResource functions. If your application does this, it should notify the other applications on the system of the change, using the following code:

```
SendMessage( HWND_BROADCAST, WM_FONTCHANGE, 0, 0 );
```

Determining Which Fonts Are Available on a System

As in other versions of Windows, the EnumFontFamilies function can be used to enumerate through the fonts available on the system. The third function parameter specifies an application-defined callback function (of type EnumFontFamProc) that processes each font enumerated. Font enumeration continues until all fonts are enumerated, or the EnumFontFamProc callback function returns 0.

In the next section, you will learn how to use this to implement the Select Font common dialog that is missing from Windows CE.

Adding a Font Selection Dialog to Your Editor

Current versions of Windows CE do not include the font selection common dialog. Figure 8.1 shows you how to implement your own font selection dialog and uses the selected font to display Hello within the application's main window.

FIGURE 8.1

Implementing your own Select Font dialog.

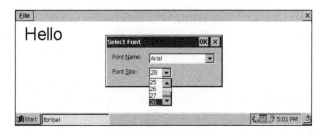

To implement this, there are four main pieces to the code: the function to enumerate the fonts on the system, the DLGPROC function to allow the user to select the font he or she wants, the function to create the font, and the code that uses the font.

Listing 8.3 uses a function that enumerates the fonts available on the system. It is a callback function invoked when you call the EnumFontFamilies function.

LISTING 8.3   Implementing the Callback Function Invoked by `EnumFontFamilies`

```
 1: #define MAX_FONTS 20
 2:
 3: TCHAR        g_tcFontNames[MAX_FONTS][40];
 4: DWORD        g_dwFontCount = 0;
 5:
 6: int CALLBACK FamFontEnumProc(const LOGFONT *pLogFont,
                 ➥const TEXTMETRIC *pTextMet, DWORD wParam,
                 ➥LPARAM lParam)
 7: {
 8:     DWORD    dwRet = 0;
 9:
10:      UNREFERENCED_PARAMETER( pTextMet );
11:
12:     // if we have more than MAX_FONTS, we are done
13:     if ( g_dwFontCount >= MAX_FONTS ) return 0;
14:
15:     // save the name of the font
16:     _tcsncpy( g_tcFontNames[g_dwFontCount], pLogFont->lfFaceName, 40 );
17:
18:     // increment the current index to the array
19:     g_dwFontCount++;
20:     return 1;
21: }
```

> The third parameter to the EnumFontFamilies function is a pointer to a
> FONTENUMPROC callback function. FONTENUMPROC is not defined in the help
> system, but can be found in the WINGDI.H header file. It is
>
> typedef int (CALLBACK* FONTENUMPROC)(CONST LOGFONT *,
>   ➥CONST TEXTMETRIC *, DWORD, LPARAM);

Listing 8.4 shows the dialog proc displaying the font information to the user and
capturing his or her selection. The fonts available on the system are displayed in the first
list box, and the font sizes available for the currently selected font are displayed in the
second list box.

LISTING 8.4   Creating a Font Selection Dialog in the RC File

```
 1: IDD_SELECTFONT DIALOG DISCARDABLE 0, 0, 140, 46
 2: STYLE DS_MODALFRAME ¦ DS_CENTER ¦ WS_POPUP ¦ WS_CAPTION ¦ WS_SYSMENU
 3: EXSTYLE WS_EX_CAPTIONOKBTN
 4: CAPTION "Select Font"
 5: FONT 9, "Tahoma"
```

```
 6: BEGIN
 7:     LTEXT           "Font &Name:",IDC_STATIC,7,7,38,10
 8:     COMBOBOX        IDC_NAME_COMBO,52,7,81,64,CBS_DROPDOWNLIST ¦
 9:                     CBS_SORT ¦ WS_VSCROLL ¦ WS_TABSTOP
10:     LTEXT           "Font &Size:",IDC_STATIC,7,25,37,10
11:     COMBOBOX        IDC_SIZE_COMBO,52,24,28,52,CBS_DROPDOWNLIST ¦
12:                     CBS_SORT ¦ WS_VSCROLL ¦ WS_TABSTOP
13: END
```

Listing 8.5 demonstrates how the dialog proc is implemented.

LISTING 8.5   Implementing a Font Selection Dialog

```
 1: LOGFONT         g_lf;
 2:
 3: TCHAR    *g_tcFontSizes[] = {
 4:             TEXT(" 8"), TEXT(" 9"), TEXT("10"), TEXT("11"),
 5:             TEXT("12"), TEXT("13"), TEXT("14"), TEXT("15"),
 6:             TEXT("16"), TEXT("17"), TEXT("18"), TEXT("19"),
 7:             TEXT("20"), TEXT("21"), TEXT("22"), TEXT("23"),
 8:             TEXT("24"), TEXT("25"), TEXT("26"), TEXT("27"),
            ➥TEXT("28"), NULL };
 9:
10: LRESULT CALLBACK SelectFontDlgProc(HWND hDlg, UINT message,
                  ➥WPARAM wParam, LPARAM lParam)
11: {
12:     HWND    hControl;
13:     HDC     hDC;
14:     INT     i;
15:     static INT iNameIndex = 0, iSizeIndex = 0;
16:
17:     switch (message) {
18:
19:         case WM_INITDIALOG:
20:
21:             memset( &g_tcFontNames, 0x00, sizeof( g_tcFontNames ) );
22:             hDC = GetDC( hDlg );
23:             g_dwFontCount = 0;
24:
25:             EnumFontFamilies( hDC, NULL, FamFontEnumProc, (LPARAM)hDC );
26:
27:             // load the font names to use
28:             hControl = GetDlgItem( hDlg, IDC_NAME_COMBO );
29:             i = 0;
30:             while( ( _tcslen( g_tcFontNames[i] ) > 0 ) &&
                  ➥( i < MAX_FONTS ) ) {
31:                 ComboBox_AddString( hControl, g_tcFontNames[i] );
32:                 i++;
33:             }
34:             ComboBox_SetCurSel( hControl, iNameIndex );
```

continues

LISTING 8.5   continued

```
35:
36:                     // load the font sizes to use
37:                     hControl = GetDlgItem( hDlg, IDC_SIZE_COMBO );
38:                     i = 0;
39:                     while( g_tcFontSizes[i] != NULL ) {
40:                         ComboBox_AddString( hControl, g_tcFontSizes[i] );
41:                         i++;
42:                     }
43:                     ComboBox_SetCurSel( hControl, iSizeIndex );
44:
45:                     return TRUE;
46:                     break;
47:
48:             case WM_COMMAND:
49:
50:                 switch( LOWORD( wParam ) ) {
51:
52:                     case IDOK:
53:                         TCHAR     tcFontName[40];
54:                         INT       iFontSize;
55:
56:                         hControl = GetDlgItem( hDlg, IDC_NAME_COMBO );
57:                         ComboBox_GetText( hControl, tcFontName, 40 );
58:
59:                         iNameIndex = ComboBox_GetCurSel( hControl );
60:                         hControl = GetDlgItem( hDlg, IDC_SIZE_COMBO );
61:
62:                         iSizeIndex = ComboBox_GetCurSel( hControl );
63:                         iFontSize = iSizeIndex + 8;
64:
65:                         SetGlobalFont( GetDC( hDlg ), tcFontName,
                                           ➥iFontSize );
66:                         EndDialog( hDlg, TRUE );
67:                         break;
68:
69:                     case IDCANCEL:
70:                         EndDialog( hDlg, FALSE );
71:                         break;
72:
73:                 }
74:                 break;
75:
76:     }
77:
78:     return FALSE;
79:
80: }
```

The code in Listing 8.5 uses a `SetGlobalFont` function to create the font, based on the font name and size selected by the user. Listing 8.6 shows how this function is implemented.

LISTING 8.6 Creating a Font of a Specified Name and Size

```
 1: VOID SetGlobalFont( HDC hDC, TCHAR *tcFontName, INT iSize )
 2: {
 3:     POINT       pt;
 4:     FLOAT       cyDpi;
 5:
 6:     cyDpi = (FLOAT) GetDeviceCaps( hDC, LOGPIXELSY );
 7:     pt.y = (int) ( ( iSize * cyDpi * 10 ) / 72 );
 8:
 9:     memset( &g_lf, 0, sizeof( LOGFONT ) );
10:     g_lf.lfHeight       = - (int) ( fabs( pt.y ) / 10.0 + 0.5 );
11:     g_lf.lfCharSet      = DEFAULT_CHARSET;
12:     _tcscpy( g_lf.lfFaceName, tcFontName );
13:     g_hFont = CreateFontIndirect( &g_lf );
14: }
```

In this particular case, you are using your font selection dialog to specify which font to use when writing `Hello` in the application's main window. This is accomplished by handling the paint message as shown in Listing 8.7.

LISTING 8.7 Using the Font the User Selected

```
 1: case WM_PAINT:
 2:     PAINTSTRUCT     ps;
 3:     RECT        r;
 4:     HDC         hDC;
 5:     HFONT       hOrigFont;
 6:
 7:     hDC = BeginPaint( hWnd, &ps );
 8:     GetClientRect( hWnd, &r );
 9:     hOrigFont = (HFONT)SelectObject( hDC, g_hFont );
10:     ExtTextOut( hDC, 20, 30, 0, NULL, TEXT( "Hello" ), _
                  ➥tcslen( TEXT( "Hello" ) ), NULL );
11:     SelectObject( hDC, hOrigFont );
12:     EndPaint( hWnd, &ps );
13:     break;
```

Bitmaps on Windows CE

Versions of Windows CE before version 2.0 support two levels of bit depths in bitmaps: a bit depth of 1 (that is, a black-and-white bitmap) and a bit depth of 2 (a 2bp bitmap).

NEW TERM The term *2bp* means two bits per pixel. A color representation of two bits per pixel yields a total possibility of four colors (such as white, black, light gray, and dark gray). Only on Windows CE are 2bp bitmaps supported.

Windows CE 2.0 introduces support for color bitmaps. This includes support for pixel depths of 1, 2, 4, 8, 16, 24, and 32 bits per pixel.

Windows CE does not contain native support for compressed bitmaps or dithering.

Table 8.2 lists the bitmap functions implemented on Windows CE.

TABLE 8.2 Windows CE Bitmap Functions

Function	Purpose
CreateBitmap	Creates a bitmap of the specified size and bit depth
CreateCompatibleBitmap	Creates a bitmap compatible with the specified DC
CreateDIBSection	Creates a device-independent bitmap

The following section shows you how to use these functions to write your own screen-shot application.

A Screenshot Example

The development tools for Windows CE include a screenshot utility that allows you to do Windows CE device screen captures from your desktop machine. The drawback is that you must be connected to your desktop machine, preventing you from doing screenshots of dial-up networking sessions.

> If you have an ethernet connection to your Windows CE device, you can use the Remote Zoomin tool included with Visual C++ to do a screenshot of a dial-up networking session. This assumes that you can use a modem at the same time as an ethernet card, implying that your Windows CE device has a built-in modem or that you are using an external modem (the PCMCIA slot will be in use with the ethernet card).

Craig Peacock maintains a useful Windows CE information FAQ Web site at http://www.craigtech.co.uk. He needed the ability to do color screen captures of dial-up networking sessions, so I wrote a Windows CE–based screenshot utility program for him, based on the code in Listing 8.8.

LISTING 8.8 Implementing a Screen Shot Utility

```
 1: #include <windows.h>
 2: #include <tchar.h>
 3:
 4: #pragma pack( 1 )
 5:
 6: INT WINAPI WinMain(    HINSTANCE hInstance,
 7:                HINSTANCE hPrevInstance,
 8:                LPTSTR lpCmdLine,
 9:                INT nShowCmd )
10: {
11:
12:     static struct {
13:         BITMAPINFOHEADER bmih;
14:         RGBQUAD rgq[16];
15:     } bmi;
16:
17:     BITMAPFILEHEADER    bmfh;
18:
19:     INT     rectH, rectW;
20:     HDC     hDC, hDC_Screen;
21:     HBITMAP hBitmap, hOldBitmap;
22:     BYTE    *pBitmapBits;
23:     TCHAR   tcFileName[80], tcString[256];
24:     HANDLE  hFile;
25:     DWORD   dwBytes, dwSize, dwTotalWritten;
26:
27:     // wait for the start-up wait cursor to go away
28:     Sleep( 500L );
29:
30:     // get the screen dimensions
31:     rectH = GetSystemMetrics( SM_CYSCREEN );
32:     rectW = GetSystemMetrics( SM_CXSCREEN );
33:
34:     // initialize the bitmap info struct
35:     memset( &bmi.bmih, 0x00, sizeof( BITMAPINFOHEADER ) );
36:     bmi.bmih.biWidth = rectW;
37:     bmi.bmih.biHeight = rectH;
38:     bmi.bmih.biSize = sizeof(bmi.bmih);
39:     bmi.bmih.biPlanes = 1;
40:     bmi.bmih.biBitCount = 4;
41:     bmi.bmih.biCompression = BI_RGB;
42:
43:     // set the 16 color values
44:     memset( &bmi.rgq[0], 0x00, sizeof( RGBQUAD ) * 16 );
45:     bmi.rgq[1].rgbRed    = 128;
46:     bmi.rgq[2].rgbGreen  = 128;
47:     bmi.rgq[3].rgbRed    = bmi.rgq[3].rgbGreen = 128;
48:     bmi.rgq[4].rgbBlue   = 128;
```

continues

LISTING 8.8 continued

```
49:    bmi.rgq[5].rgbRed    = bmi.rgq[5].rgbBlue   = 128;
50:    bmi.rgq[6].rgbGreen  = bmi.rgq[6].rgbBlue   = 128;
51:    bmi.rgq[7].rgbRed = bmi.rgq[7].rgbGreen =
                        ➥bmi.rgq[7].rgbBlue = 192;
52:    bmi.rgq[8].rgbRed = bmi.rgq[8].rgbGreen =
                        ➥bmi.rgq[8].rgbBlue = 128;
53:    bmi.rgq[9].rgbRed = 255;
54:    bmi.rgq[10].rgbGreen  = 255;
55:    bmi.rgq[11].rgbRed    = bmi.rgq[11].rgbGreen = 255;
56:    bmi.rgq[12].rgbBlue   = 255;
57:    bmi.rgq[13].rgbRed    = bmi.rgq[13].rgbBlue   = 255;
58:    bmi.rgq[14].rgbGreen  = bmi.rgq[14].rgbBlue   = 255;
59:    bmi.rgq[15].rgbRed    = bmi.rgq[15].rgbGreen  =
                        ➥bmi.rgq[15].rgbBlue = 255;
60:
61:    // the screen's DC
62:    hDC_Screen = GetDC( NULL );
63:
64:    // create the bitmap
65:    hBitmap = CreateDIBSection(    hDC_Screen, (PBITMAPINFO)&bmi.bmih,
66:                    DIB_RGB_COLORS, &pBitmapBits, NULL, 0 );
67:
68:    // dwSize = LocalSize( pBitmapBits );
69:    dwSize = abs( bmi.bmih.biWidth * bmi.bmih.biHeight )
70:                * ( bmi.bmih.biPlanes + 1 ) * ( bmi.bmih.biBitCount );
71:
72:    dwSize /= 16;
73:
74:    // inintialize the bitmap file header struct
75:    memset( &bmfh, 0x00, sizeof( bmfh ) );
76:    bmfh.bfType = 0x4D42;
77:    bmfh.bfSize = sizeof( bmfh ) + sizeof( bmi ) + dwSize;
78:    bmfh.bfOffBits = sizeof( bmfh ) + sizeof( bmi );
79:
80:    // create a compatible DC, select the bitmap into it, and then
            ➥copy from the screen
81:    hDC = CreateCompatibleDC( hDC_Screen );
82:    hOldBitmap = SelectObject( hDC, hBitmap );
83:    BitBlt( hDC, 0, 0, rectW, rectH, hDC_Screen, 0, 0, SRCCOPY );
84:
85:    // determine a unique filename
86:    wsprintf( tcFileName, (TCHAR*) TEXT( "\\%d.bmp" ), GetTickCount() );
87:
88:    // open the file for writing
89:    hFile = CreateFile(    tcFileName, GENERIC_WRITE,
90:                0, NULL, CREATE_ALWAYS, 0, NULL );
91:
92:    // write the bitmap file header to file
93:    WriteFile( hFile, &bmfh, sizeof( bmfh ), &dwBytes, NULL );
```

```
 94:
 95:     // write the bitmap info header to file
 96:     WriteFile( hFile, &bmi, sizeof( bmi ), &dwBytes, NULL );
 97:
 98:     // write the bitmap bits to file
 99:     dwTotalWritten = 0;
100:     while( dwTotalWritten < dwSize ) {
101:         WriteFile(    hFile, pBitmapBits+dwTotalWritten,
102:                   dwSize-dwTotalWritten, &dwBytes, NULL );
103:         dwTotalWritten += dwBytes;
104:     }
105:
106:     // close the file
107:     CloseHandle( hFile );
108:
109:     // ask the user whether he or she would like to view the image
110:     wsprintf( tcString,
         ➥(TCHAR*)TEXT("The screen image was saved to file \"%s\".")
111:      TEXT( "Do you want to view it?" ), tcFileName );
112:     dwSize = MessageBox( GetFocus(), tcString,
                            ➥(TCHAR*)TEXT( "ScreenShot" ), MB_YESNO );
113:
114:     if ( dwSize == IDYES ) {
115:
116:         SHELLEXECUTEINFO    si;
117:
118:         memset( &si, 0, sizeof(SHELLEXECUTEINFO) );
119:         si.cbSize = sizeof( si );
120:         si.lpFile = tcFileName;
121:         ShellExecuteEx( &si );
122:
123:     }
124:
125:     return 0;
126:
127: }
```

Bit Block Transfers

Listing 8.8 makes use of the BitBlt function to copy an image from one DC to another.
Table 8.3 lists the bit manipulation functions implemented on Windows CE.

TABLE 8.3 Windows CE Bit Block Transfer Functions

Function	Purpose
BitBlt	Transfers an image, altering the image based on selected raster operation codes
MaskBit	Combines color data for source and destination images
PatBlt	Paints a rectangle based on combining surface pixels and the current brush's pixel
StretchBlt	Transfers an image, stretching or compressing as necessary
TransparentImage	Transfers an image, excluding portions drawn in a specified color

The TransparentImage function is currently implemented only on Windows CE. It enables you to transfer a bitmap from one DC to another, but specifically excludes all portions of the image that contain a color of your choosing.

Not all these operations are supported on all devices. Your application should use the GetDeviceCaps function to retrieve the capabilities of a particular device.

The main difference between Windows CE and other versions of Windows is that the foreground application has ownership of the system palette. Applications that use more than the standard Windows colors (the first and last 10 colors in the stock palette) might not display properly after they lose foreground focus.

Summary

In this hour, you learned about the functionality implemented in the Windows CE GDI subsystem. You learned how to work with DCs, pens, brushes, lines, shapes, fonts, and bitmaps. You also saw hands-on examples for creating a screen capture program that saves to the bitmap file format, as well as a simple font selection dialog. You also learned about differences between the palette on Windows CE and desktop Windows.

Q&A

Q I am interested in directly accessing the bits that compose a bitmap. When I use the CreateDIBSection function, I expect to have the fourth parameter set to point to the bitmap's bits. Sometimes my program crashes when attempting to access these bits. What is going wrong?

A In low memory conditions, the CreateDIBSection function may succeed on Windows CE, even though the pointer to the bitmap's bits is not successfully set. In addition to checking the return value of the CreateDIBSection function, your program should also verify the following before proceeding with any operations on the bits:

1. Check to make sure that the pointer to the bitmap's bits is not set to NULL.

2. Check to make sure that the buffer to which this pointer is pointing is the expected size. The GetLocalSize function can be used to perform this check.

Q When I call DeleteObject on Windows CE to delete my bitmap, it fails by returning FALSE. When I run the code on desktop Win32, it succeeds. What might the problem be?

A You must make sure that you deselect your GDI object (which can be returned by the SelectObject function) before deleting the object. This is proper Win32 programming, but desktop Win32 is more forgiving than Windows CE in this scenario, which may lead to problems when porting code from the desktop to Windows CE.

Workshop

The Workshop is designed to help you anticipate possible questions, review what you've learned, and begin thinking ahead about putting your knowledge into practice. The answers to the quiz are in Appendix A, "Answers."

Quiz

1. What does the term *2bp* mean?

2. Your program eventually fails to create a GDI object because of lack of memory. Shutting down the program and restarting it does not help. The only way you and your users can get it to start working again is to reset the Windows CE device. What is the likely culprit?

3. My desktop Win32 code will not compile for Windows CE because MoveTo and LineTo are unrecognized. How do I fix this?

4. Which bit block transfer function is only available on Windows CE?

5. What function do you use to create a compressed bitmap on Windows CE?

6. My desktop Win32 code uses TextOut, but doesn't compile for Windows CE. How do I fix this?

7. When EnumFontFamilies invokes your callback function, how do you determine if you have received a pointer to a raster font or a TrueType font?

Exercises

1. Create a simple text editor that allows the user to select the font used in the edit window, using the font selection dialog sample code covered in this chapter.

2. Modify the screen capture utility in this chapter to create black-and-white screen captures.

HOUR 9

The Object Store: Files and the Registry

As you are already aware, most Windows CE devices do not have an internal storage device such as a hard disk to store information. Instead, Windows CE creates an area of RAM known as the *object store*, where files, databases, and Registry settings are stored.

In this hour, you will learn

- What the Windows CE object store is
- How to work with files in Windows CE
- How to work with the Windows CE Registry
- How to modify the sort order and retrieve information from the Contacts database

The Windows CE File System: The Object Store

Because of limited battery life and device size, Windows CE devices do not use a normal storage medium such as a hard drive or floppy disk for storage. Instead, Windows CE implements a persistent storage mechanism known as the object store. The object store is a user-defined chunk of RAM used for the storage of files, Registry entries, and databases, and the remaining RAM is used for program memory. A user can adjust these settings by going to the Control Panel and selecting the System applet.

End users typically do not know of the object store because Microsoft has provided the Windows CE Explorer to view the contents of it (on H/PC and H/PC Professional Edition handhelds). Users should feel comfortable with Explorer because it closely mimics its desktop counterpart, as shown in Figure 9.1.

FIGURE 9.1
The Windows CE Explorer.

To make life easier for developers, building applications that have to access items in the object store was designed to be extremely similar to Win32 programming. This lesson discusses designing applications that use the Windows CE file system and Registry services. For more information about the Windows CE Database API, please see Hour 10, "Advanced Object Store: The Database API."

 An *object store* is a user-defined amount of RAM that is used for the storage of files, databases, and Registry settings.

Files on Windows CE

The Windows CE file system is a robust set of APIs that enable a developer to access files that are both ROM and RAM based. Think of the object store as the hard drive of a Windows CE device. APIs are available to allow you to create, open, delete, read, write, and so on.

The first major difference you will notice about the Windows CE object store is the lack of drive letters. Windows CE uses directory entries under the root for installed user devices. For example, if the user inserts a flash card, a directory /Storage Card 1 is created. For each additional flash card inserted, the number is incremented (so /Storage Card 2 would be the second card, and so on).

File paths are limited to the standard length of MAX_PATH, which is set to 260 bytes, the same as Windows. However, because there is no internal concept of current directories, files should be accessed using their full paths. As with Windows 95 and NT, files, paths, and extensions cannot contain the characters \ / : * ? " <> ¦.

Also, it is important to note that on Windows CE 2.0, files can grow only to a maximum of 4MB.

Finally, because files can be internally stored in either RAM and ROM, Windows CE also supports additional file attributes. See the section titled "Additional File Information" for more information about these attributes.

Creating and Opening Files

As with Windows 95 and NT, you can use the CreateFile() function call to either create a new file or open an existing one:

```
HANDLE CreateFile(LPCTSTR lpFileName, DWORD dwAccess,
➥DWORD dwShareMode, LPSECURITY_ATTRIBUTES lpSecurity,
➥DWORD dwCreationDistribution, DWORD dwFlags, HANDLE hTemplate);
```

If the call succeeds, it will return a handle to the specified file. The CreateFile() function takes the following parameters:

- lpFileName specifies the name of the file (including the full path) that you want to create or open.

- dwAccess specifies the access mode for the file. It can be set to one or more of the following: 0 for query access if you just want the attributes of a file, GENERIC_READ for read access, and GENERIC_WRITE for write access to the file.

- dwShareMode specifies how a file can be shared. If set to 0, the file cannot be shared with other processes. If set to FILE_SHARE_READ, other processes will have read access. If set to FILE_SHARE_WRITE, other processes will have write access.

- lpSecurity is ignored and should be set to NULL.

- dwCreationDistribution specifies how to open or create the file. It can be set to CREATE_NEW, which will create a new file; and CREATE_ALWAYS, which will create a new file regardless of whether it already exists. OPEN_EXISTING opens a file if it already exists. OPEN_ALWAYS opens a file if it exists; otherwise, it creates it. TRUNCATE_EXISTING opens a file and truncates it to 0 bytes in length.

- dwFlags specifies flags and attributes for the file. See the following list for more information on the supported flags.

- hTemplate is ignored and should be set to NULL.

The following are the file flags and attributes supported on Windows CE:

- FILE_ATTRIBUTE_NORMAL specifies the default file attributes.

- FILE_ATTRIBUTE_READONLY sets the file to read-only. Any attempts to write to this file will fail.

- FILE_ATTRIBUTE_ARCHIVE sets the archive bit for the file.

- FILE_ATTRIBUTE_SYSTEM sets the system bit for the file. This is typically used for files in the operating system.

- FILE_ATTRIBUTE_HIDDEN sets the hidden bit. This prevents the file from being shown in a normal directory listing.

- FILE_FLAG_WRITE_THROUGH flags that the file shouldn't be cached in memory.

- FILE_FLAG_RANDOM_ACCESS flags that the file will be randomly accessed. This helps optimize caching.

For example, to create a new file:

```
HANDLE hFile = CreateFile(tchFileName, GENERIC_WRITE, 0, NULL,
➥CREATE_NEW, FILE_ATTRIBUTE_NORMAL, NULL);
```

Reading from Files

Reading and writing from files is exactly the same as it is on Windows 95 and NT. Windows CE uses the ReadFile() and WriteFile() functions to perform file I/O, as well as the concept of a current file pointer to indicate position within the file. Further information on the file pointer can be found later in this chapter.

To read data from an open file, you can use the ReadFile() function call, which is defined as

```
BOOL ReadFile(HANDLE hFile, LPVOID lpBuffer, DWORD dwNumBytestoRead,
➥ LPDWORD lpNumberOfBytesRead, LPOVERLAPPED lpOverlapped);
```

The ReadFile() API takes five parameters: a handle to the file you want to read data from; a pointer to a buffer that will receive the data; a DWORD value specifying the number of bytes you want to read from the file; a pointer, which receives the number of bytes actually read from the file; and finally, lpOverlapped, which must be set to NULL because Windows CE does not support overlapped file operations.

The file pointer is internally incremented for the number of bytes that are read from the file. If you attempt to call ReadFile() past the end of the file, no error will occur, but no bytes are read. That is why it is important to check the return value of the `lpNumberOfBytesRead` variable to make sure that it is not 0.

Listing 9.1 is an example of this.

LISTING 9.1 Reading from a File

```
 1: TCHAR tchBuffer[1024] = TEXT("\0");
 2: DWORD dwRead = 0;
 3: memset(tchBuffer, 0, 1024);
 4: while(ReadFile(hFile, tchBuffer, 1024, &dwRead, NULL) != 0) {
 5:     if(dwRead == 0)
 6:         break;
 7:     // Do something with tchBuffer here,
 8:     // such as send it to an edit control
 9:     SendMessage(hEdit, WM_SETTEXT, 0, (LPARAM)(LPCTSTR)tchBuffer);
10:     memset(tchBuffer, 0, 1024);
11:     dwRead = 0;
12: }
```

Writing to Files

To write data to a file, use the `WriteFile()` function call, which is defined as

```
BOOL WriteFile(HANDLE hFile, LPCVOID lpBuffer, DWORD dwNumBytesToWrite,
➥LPDWORD lpNumOfBytesWritten, LPOVERLAPPED lpOverlapped);
```

The `WriteFile()` function takes five parameters: the handle to the file to which you are going to write data, a pointer to a buffer of data to be written, an integer specifying how many bytes you are going to write, a pointer to an integer that receives how many bytes were written, and `lpOverlapped`, which must be set to `NULL` because Windows CE does not support overlapped file operations.

Data is written to the file at the point specified by the current file pointer, which is also incremented by the number of bytes written to the file.

Listing 9.2 is an example of `WriteFile()`.

LISTING 9.2 Writing a Buffer to a File

```
1: DWORD dwNumBytes = sizeof(tchBuffer);
2: DWORD dwWritten = 0;
3: while(dwNumBytes > 0) {
4: if(!WriteFile(hFile, tchBuffer, 1024, &dwWritten, NULL))
5:     break;
6: dwNumBytes-=dwWritten;
7:     dwWritten = 0;
8: }
```

The File Pointer

Every open file has a file pointer, which points to the next byte of data to be read or written to. When a file is initially opened, it contains 0. The current file pointer can be set using the SetFilePointer() function call.

```
DWORD SetFilePointer(HANDLE hFile, LONG lDistance,
➥PLONG lpDistanceToMoveHigh, DWORD dwMoveMethod);
```

The SetFilePointer() function takes four parameters: the handle to an open file, an offset to move the file pointer, a 32-bit offset to move the offset, and dwMoveMethod, which determines how to move the pointer. If dwMoveMethod is set to FILE_BEGIN, it is from the beginning of the file. If it is set to FILE_END, the offset is at the end of the file. If it is set to FILE_CURRENT, the current position is used for the offset.

For example, to move a pointer lBytes from the beginning of the file:

```
dwFilePointer = SetFilePointer(hFile, lBytes, NULL, FILE_BEGIN);
```

To get the current file position, you can call the SetFilePointer function with an offset of 0, specifying the FILE_CURRENT move method.

Closing a File

To close an open file handle, simply call the CloseHandle() function call:

```
BOOL CloseHandle(HANDLE hFile);
```

The function takes one parameter: the handle to an open file. It will return TRUE if the function succeeded, and FALSE if it fails. Failure typically indicates that the handle that was passed to CloseHandle() was incorrect.

Additional File Information

To get additional information about a file, you can use the GetFileAttributes() function call on a file or directory:

```
DWORD dwAttributes = GetFileAttributes(LPCTSTR lpFileName);
```

This function only takes one parameter: the full path to the file (or directory) for which you want to get the attribute. The attributes returned can be one or more of the following:

- FILE_ATTRIBUTE_NORMAL specifies the default file attributes.
- FILE_ATTRIBUTE_READONLY specifies that the file is read-only.
- FILE_ATTRIBUTE_ARCHIVE specifies that the archive bit is set.
- FILE_ATTRIBUTE_SYSTEM specifies that this is a system file used in the operating system.

- `FILE_ATTRIBUTE_HIDDEN` specifies that the file is hidden.
- `FILE_ATTRIBUTE_INROM` specifies that the file is stored in ROM.
- `FILE_ATTRIBUTE_ROMMODULE` specifies that the file is stored in ROM and is designed to execute in place.
- `FILE_ATTRIBUTE_DIRECTORY` specifies that the file is a directory.
- `FILE_ATTRIBUTE_TEMPORARY` specifies that the file is located on a user-installed device, such as a PC card.

9

To set the attributes for a file that already exists, you can use the `SetFileAttributes()` function call:

```
BOOL SetFileAttributes(LPCTSTR lpFileName, DWORD dwAttributes);
```

The `SetFileAttributes()` function takes two parameters: the full path to the file or directory and the attributes you want to set on the file.

To get the size of a file, you can call the `GetFileSize()` function:

```
DWORD dwFileSize = GetFileSize(HANDLE hFile, LPDWORD lpFileSizeHigh);
```

The function takes two parameters: the full path to the file and an optional pointer to receive the upper 32 bits of the file size (if the file is more than 4GB).

To get full file or directory information in a single function call, you can use the `GetFileInformationByHandle()` function:

```
BOOL GetFileInformationByHandle(HANDLE hFile,
➥LPBY_HANDLE_INFORMATION lpFileInfo);
```

This function takes two parameters: the full path to the file or directory and a pointer to a `BY_HANDLE_INFORMATION` structure. The `BY_HANDLE_INFORMATION` structure is defined in Table 9.1.

TABLE 9.1 The Member Variables of the `BY_HANDLE_INFORMATION` Structure

Member	Specifies
dwFileAttributes	File attributes (as previously described) for the file or directory
ftCreationTime	The FILETIME that the file was created
ftLastAccessTime	The FILETIME that the file was last accessed
ftLastWriteTime	The FILETIME to which the file was last written
dwVolumeSerialNumber	0 if the file is located in the object store
nFileSizeHigh	The high-order DWORD of the file size
nFileSizeLow	The low-order DWORD of the file size

continues

TABLE 9.1 continud

Member	Specifies
nNumberOfLinks	(Not used in Windows CE)
nFileIndexHigh	The high-order DWORD of a unique index identifier
nFileIndexLow	The low-order DWORD of a unique index identifier
dwOID	The object ID of the file (See the section titled "File Object Identifiers" for more information.)

File System Management

Several Win32-compatible functions are provided for managing the file system.

To copy files, use the CopyFile() function call:

```
BOOL CopyFile(LPCTSTR lpExistingFileName, LPCTSTR lpNewFileName,
➥BOOL bFailIfExists);
```

The CopyFile() function takes three parameters: the source filename (with path), the destination path and filename, and a flag that indicates whether the function should fail if the destination file already exists. You should also make sure that the destination directory already exists, because the operation will not create it for you.

To move files, use the MoveFile() function call:

```
BOOL MoveFile(LPCTSTR lpExistingFileName, LPCTSTR lpNewFileName);
```

The MoveFile() function takes two parameters: the source path and filename and the destination path and filename. As with CopyFile, you must make sure that the destination directory already exists.

To delete a file, use the DeleteFile() function call:

```
BOOL DeleteFile(LPCTSTR lpFileName);
```

This takes only a single parameter: the path and filename of the file to delete.

To create a directory, use the CreateDirectory() function:

```
BOOL CreateDirectory(LPCTSTR lpPath, LPSECURITY_ATTRIBUTES lpSecurity);
```

CreateDirectory() takes two paramaters: the path to the directory to create and a NULL because Windows CE does not support security. One thing to note: The path to the new directory must already exist to succeed. For example, you cannot call

```
CreateDirectory(TEXT("\\My Path\\My Folder");
```

If the path \My Path does not already exist, the CreateDirectory call will fail.

To delete a directory, use the RemoveDirectory() function:

```
BOOL RemoveDirectory(LPCTSTR lpPathName);
```

It takes only a single parameter: the path to the directory to remove. You must also make sure that the directory is empty before trying to remove it.

Finally, Windows CE adds an additional call, GetStoreInformation(), which returns basic information about the size and free space of the current *object store*:

```
BOOL GetStoreInformation(LPSTORE_INFORMATION lpSi);
```

This function takes a pointer to an LPSTORE_INFORMATION structure, which is defined in Table 9.2 and appears in Listing 9.3.

TABLE 9.2 The Member Variables of the STORE_INFORMATION Structure

Member	Specifies
dwStoreSize	The size of the object store
dwFreeSize	The amount of free space in the object store

LISTING 9.3 Using the GetStoreInformation() Function

```
1: STORE_INFORMATION si;
2: memset(&si, 0, sizeof(STORE_INFORMATION));
3: GetStoreInformation(&si);
```

Finding Files

To search for files, you can use the Win32-compatible FindFirstFile() function and then call FindNextFile() to enumerate through the files that match your search criteria:

```
HANDLE hSearchHandle = FindFirstFile(LPCTSTR lpFileName,
➥LPWIN32_FIND_DATA lpFindFileData);
```

FindFirstFile() takes two parameters: the filename or pattern to be searched and a pointer to a WIN32_FIND_DATA structure that receives information about the found file.

Table 9.3 defines the WIN32_FIND_DATA structure.

TABLE 9.3   The Member Variables of the WIN32_FIND_DATA Structure

Member	Specifies
dwFileAttributes	The attributes of the file (See the preceding section for more information.)
ftCreationTime	The FILETIME value of when the file was created
ftLastAccessTime	The FILETIME value of when the file was last accessed
ftLastWriteTime	The FILETIME value of when the file was last written to
nFileSizeHigh	The high-order DWORD of the file size
nFileSizeLow	The low-order DWORD of the file size
dwOID	The file object identifier (See the section "File Object Identifiers" for more information.)
cFileName	The null-terminated name of the file

After calling FindFirstFile(), if you want to enumerate through the files, you can call the FindNextFile() function, passing in the handle you received from the previous call to FindFirstFile, as well as a pointer to the WIN32_FIND_DATA structure to get the file information. If no more files are found, FindNextFile() will return 0. At this point, a call to GetLastError will return an ERROR_NO_MORE_FILES error message.

After your search is completed, you have to call the FindClose() function, passing in the handle that was opened from your initial call to FindFirstFile():

```
BOOL FindClose(HANDLE hFindHandle);
```

Therefore, to search through the \Windows directory for all .WAV files, you would use the code in Listing 9.4.

LISTING 9.4   Searching, Using FindFirstFile()

```
 1: BOOL FindAllWavFiles(HWND hParent)
 2: {
 3:     HANDLE hFind = NULL;
 4:     WIN32_FIND_DATA wFindData;
 5:     BOOL fFinished = FALSE;
 6:
 7:     memset(&wFindData, 0, sizeof(WIN32_FIND_DATA));
 8:
 9:     hFind = FindFirstFile(TEXT("\\Windows\\*.wav"), &wFindData);
10:     if(hFind == INVALID_HANDLE_VALUE)
11:         return FALSE;
12:
13:     while(!fFinished) {
14:         // Show a message with the Wav File Name
```

```
15:            MessageBox(hParent, wFindData.cFileName, TEXT("Wav File"),
               ➥ MB_OK);
16:
17:            // Get the next file
18:            memset(&wFindData, 0, sizeof(WIN32_FIND_DATA));
19:            if(!FindNextFile(hFind, &wFindData)) {
20:                if (GetLastError() == ERROR_NO_MORE_FILES)
21:                    fFinished = TRUE;
22:            }
23:        }
24:
25:    return TRUE;
26: }
```

File Object Identifiers

Object identifiers (OIDs) are unique values that identify each individual object in the object store. For example, every file, database, database record, and directory has its own unique identifier.

For more information on a particular OID, you can use the CeOidGetInfo() function:

```
BOOL CeOidGetInfo(CEOID oid, CEOIDINFO *poidInfo);
```

This call takes two parameters: the OID you want to get more information on and a pointer to a CEOIDINFO structure to receive information about the object. Table 9.4 defines the CEOIDINFO structure.

TABLE 9.4 The Member Variables of the CEOIDINFO Structure

Member	Specifies
wObjType	The type of object. This can be OBJTYPE_INVALID, OBJTYPE_FILE, OBJTYPE_DIRECTORY, OBJTYPE_DATABASE, and OBJTYPE_RECORD.
wpad	The alignment for a double-byte entry.
infFile	The CEFILEINFO structure that contains information about a file if the wObjType is OBJTYPE_FILE.
infDirectory	The CEDIRINFO structure that contains information about a directory if the wObjType is OBJTYPE_DIRECTORY.
infDatabase	The CEDBASEINFO structure that contains information about a file if the wObjType is OBJTYPE_DATABASE.
infRecord	The CERECORDINFO structure that contains information about a file if the wObjType is OBJTYPE_RECORD.

Because this lesson deals with the file system, take a look at structures that work with files (CEFILEINFO and CEDIRINFO). The other structures are covered in the next lesson, which discusses *object store* database information.

The CEFILEINFO structure is defined in Table 9.5.

TABLE 9.5   The Member Variables of the CEFILEINFO Structure

Member	Specified
dwAttributes	The attributes of the file
oidParent	The OID of the parent directory
szFileName	The null-terminated name of the file
ftLastChanged	The FILETIME indicating when the file was last modified
dwLength	The length, in bytes, of the file

The CEDIRINFO structure is defined in Table 9.6.

TABLE 9.6   The Member Variables of the CEDIRINFO Structure

Member	Specified
dwAttributes	The attributes of the directory
oidParent	The OID of the parent directory
szFileName	The null-terminated name of the path and directory name

The Registry

The Registry is an internal database that Windows CE uses to store information about the operating system, program configuration, user profiles, applications, hardware, and so on. Although Windows CE uses similar functions to create, read, and write to the Registry as Windows 95 and NT, the internal layout of the Registry keys and values, shown in Figure 9.2, is different.

Windows CE stores data in the Registry the same as Windows 95 and NT, in a hierarchical tree, and is made up of keys and values. Each entry in the tree is called a *key*, which can contain both subkeys and data known as *values*.

Each key and value name can consist of printable ANSI characters, and cannot include spaces, backslashes, or wildcard characters (* or ?). Key names are not supposed to be localized, although values can be in Unicode.

FIGURE 9.2

The Windows CE Registry.

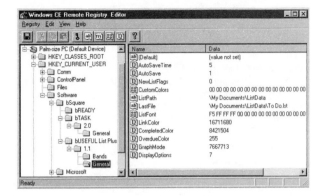

Windows CE has three defined "root" keys:

- HKEY_LOCAL_MACHINE, which stores hardware and software information
- HKEY_CURRENT_USER, which stores preferences of the current user
- HKEY_CLASSES_ROOT, which defines data types of documents and OLE objects

It is also important to note that the Windows CE Registry does not support security.

Opening and Creating Keys

To create a Registry key, you must call the RegCreateKeyEx() function. When the function is called, it will return the handle to the new Registry key. If the Registry key you attempt to create already exists, this will return the key handle to the original key, but does not overwrite it.

The RegCreateKeyEx() function looks like this:

```
LONG lResult = RegCreateKeyEx(HKEY hKey, LPCTSTR lpSubKey,
➥DWORD dwReserved, LPTSTR lpClass, DWORD dwOptions,
➥REGSAM samDesired, LPSECURITY_ATTRIBUTES lpSecurity,
➥PHKEY phkResult, LPDWORD lpdwDisposition);
```

RegCreateKeyEx() has nine parameters, including the handle to the parent key (or one of the predefined keys), a null-terminated string for the new subkey, a reserved value that must be 0, and a null-terminated classname (which can be NULL). The dwOptions, samDesired, and lpSecurity attributes are ignored and can be set to 0. Next is a pointer to an HKEY that receives the new key handle, and finally, lpdwDisposition is a pointer that tells you whether it opened an old key or a new one was created.

Listing 9.5 is an example of creating a new Registry key.

LISTING 9.5 Creating a Registry key

```
1: HKEY hKey = NULL;
2: DWORD dwWord = 0;
3: if (RegCreateKeyEx(HKEY_CURRENT_USER,
4: ➥TEXT("Software\\bSquare\\bTASK\\1.0\\General"), 0, TEXT(""), 0, 0,
5: ➥ NULL, &hKey, &dwWord) == ERROR_SUCCESS) {
6:   // Continue with program
7: }
```

If you just need to open the Registry key, rather than create it, you can use the RegOpenKeyEx() function:

```
LONG lResult = RegOpenKeyEx(HKEY hKey, LPCTSTR lpSubKey, DWORD ulOptions,
➥REGSAM samDesired, PHKEY phkResult);
```

The parameters for RegOpenKeyEx() are the same as RegCreateKeyEx(), as previously defined.

After you either create or open a Registry key, you can read and write values from it.

Reading from the Registry

To read a value from the Registry, you can call the RegQueryValueEx() function:

```
LONG lResult = RegQueryValueEx(HKEY hKey, LPCWSTR lpszValueName,
➥LPDWORD lpReserved, LPDWORD lpType, LPBYTE lpData, LPDWORD lpcbData);
```

The RegQueryValueEx() function takes six parameters:

- The handle to the opened key
- A null-terminated name of the value
- A reserved parameter, which should be set to NULL
- A pointer to a variable that received the type associated with the value (see Table 9.7 for type definitions)
- A pointer to a buffer that receives the data
- A pointer to a DWORD that specifies the size of the buffer lpData

When you are reading (and writing) data to the Registry, all data values have a *data type*, which describes the type of data stored.

TABLE 9.7 Registry Data Types

Data Type	Definition
REG_BINARY	Binary data in any form.
REG_DWORD	A 32-bit number.

Data Type	Definition
REG_DWORD_LITTLE_ENDIAN	Equivalent to REG_DWORD.
REG_DWORD_BIG_ENDIAN	A 32-bit number in big endian format.
REG_EXPAND_SZ	A null-terminated string that contains environment variables.
REG_LINK	A Unicode symbolic link.
REG_MULTI_SZ	An array of null-terminated strings. This has to be terminated by two null characters.
REG_NONE	No defined data type.
REG_RESOURCE_LIST	A device driver resource list.
REG_SZ	A null-terminated string.

Writing to the Registry

To write a value to a Registry, you must call the `RegSetValueEx()` function:

```
LONG RegSetValueEx(HKEY hKey, LPCWSTR lpszValueName, DWORD Reserved
➥DWORD dwType, const BYTE *lpData, DWORD cbData);
```

The `RegSetValueEx()` function takes six parameters:

- The handle to the parent key (or one of the predefined handles)
- A null-terminated string specifying the value name
- A reserved parameter, for which you can pass in NULL
- One of the data types described in Table 9.7
- A pointer to the buffer of data to be put in the Registry
- A DWORD specifying the size of the data buffer lpData

Deleting Keys and Values

To delete a Registry key, you call the `RegDeleteKey()` function:

```
LONG lResult = RegDeleteKey(HKEY hKey, LPCWSTR lpszSubKey);
```

The two parameters are the handle to the parent key and a null-terminated string specifying the subkey you want to delete.

To delete a Registry value, you call the `RegDeleteValue()` function:

```
LONG lResult = RegDeleteValue(HKEY hKey, LPCWSTR lpszValueName);
```

The two parameters are the handle to the parent key and a null-terminated string specifying the value name you want to delete.

Enumerating Items in the Registry

When querying the Registry, you might want to get a list of all the keys under a particular parent. To do so, you can use the RegEnumKeyEx() function call:

```
LONG lResult = RegEnumKeyEx(HKEY hKey, DWORD dwIndex, LPTSTR lpName,
➥LPDWORD lpcbName, LPDWORD lpReserved, LPTSTR lpClass,
➥LPDWORD lpcbClass, PFILETIME lpftLastWriteTime);
```

The RegEnumKeyEx() function takes eight parameters:

- The handle to the parent key (or one of the predefined keys).
- The index of the subkey to enumerate, which should initially be set to 0.
- A pointer to a buffer to receive the key name.
- A pointer to the size of the buffer lpName.
- A reserved parameter, which should be set to NULL.
- A pointer to a buffer to receive the classname.
- A pointer to the size of the buffer lpClass.
- Because Windows CE does not support FILETIME write information to the Registry, the last parameter should be NULL.

Listing 9.6 shows how to walk through all the top-level Registry keys.

LISTING 9.6   Top-level Registry keys

```
 1: BOOL EnumTopKeys(HWND hWnd)
 2: {
 3:     DWORD dwKeyIndex = 0, dwKeySize = 0;
 4:     TCHAR tchSubKey[MAX_PATH+1] = TEXT("\0");
 5:
 6:     dwKeySize = MAX_PATH;
 7:     while(RegEnumKeyEx(HKEY_LOCAL_MACHINE, dwKeyIndex,
 8:     ➥tchSubKey, &dwKeySize, NULL, NULL, NULL, NULL) != ERROR_NO_MORE_ITEMS)
{
 9:         // MessageBox each Key out
10:         MessageBox(hWnd, tchSubKey, TEXT("Registry Key"), MB_OK);
11:
12:         memset(tchSubKey, 0, MAX_PATH);
13:         dwKeySize = MAX_PATH;
14:     }
15:     return TRUE;
16: }
```

You can also enumerate through all the values of a specific Registry key using the RegEnumValue() function:

```
LONG lResult = RegEnumValue(HKEY hKey, DWORD dwIndex,
➥LPWSTR lpszValueName, LPDWORD lpcchValueName,
➥LPDWORD lpReserved, LPDWORD lpType, LPBYTE lpData,
➥ LPDWORD lpcbData);
```

The RegEnumValue() function takes eight parameters:

- The handle to the parent key or to one of the predefined keys
- The index of the value to retrieve, which should initially be set to 0
- A pointer to a buffer that receives the value name
- A pointer to a pointer to the size of the buffer lpszValueName
- A reserved parameter, which should be set to NULL
- A pointer to receive the type of value, as specified in Table 9.7
- A pointer to a buffer that receives the value data
- A pointer to the size of the buffer lpData

Finally, to get some basic information about a Registry key and its values, you can use the RegQueryInfoKey() function. Basically, this function gets information about the largest value sizes, classnames, and so on, that are useful when querying information from the Registry.

```
LONG lResult = RegQueryInfoKey(HKEY hKey, LPWSTR lpClass,
➥LPDWORD lpcbClass, LPDWORD lpReserved, LPDWORD lpcSubKeys,
➥ LPDWORD lpcbMaxSubKeyLen, LPDWORD lpcbMaxClassLen,
➥ LPDWORD lpcValues, LPDWORD lpcbMaxValueNameLen,
➥LPDWORD lpcbMaxValueLen, LPDWORD lpcbSecurityDescriptor,
➥ PFILETIME lpftLastWriteTime);
```

As with all the Registry functions, the RegQueryInfoKey() function takes the handle to the opened Registry key (or a predefined one) to process the function. Table 9.8 describes the other parameters, all of which receive information from the Registry.

TABLE 9.8 RegQueryInfoKey() Parameters

Parameter	Definition
lpClass	The buffer that receives the classname
lpcbClass	The pointer to the size of the lpClass buffer
lpReserved	The reserved value, set to NULL
lpcSubKeys	The pointer to a variable that gets the number of subkeys
lpcbMaxSubKeyLen	The pointer to a variable that gets the largest length of a subkey name
lpcbMaxClassLen	The pointer to a variable that gets the largest length of a subkey class
lpcValues	The pointer to a variable that gets the number of values for the key

continues

TABLE 9.8 continued

Parameter	Definition
lpcbMaxValueNameLen	The pointer to a variable that gets the largest length of a value name
lpcbMaxValueLen	The pointer to a variable that gets the largest length of value data
lpcbSecurityDescriptor	Not used, set to NULL
lpftLastWriteTime	Not used, set to NULL

As an example, if you wanted to enumerate through all the values in the HKEY_LOCAL_MACHINE\Explorer\Databases Registry key, you would use the code in Listing 9.7.

LISTING 9.7 Enumerating Registry Values

```
 1: BOOL EnumValuesKeys(HWND hWnd)
 2: {
 3:     DWORD dwMaxValName = 0, dwMaxValData = 0, dwIndex = 0,
 4:     ➥ dwCurValNameLen = 0, dwCurDataLen = 0, dwValType = 0;
 5:     LPTSTR lpValueName = NULL;
 6:     LPBYTE lpValueData = NULL;
 7:     HKEY hSubKey = NULL;
 8:
 9:     // Open up the key to look at
10:     if(RegOpenKeyEx(HKEY_LOCAL_MACHINE, TEXT("Explorer\\Database"),
11:     ➥ 0, NULL, &hSubKey) != ERROR_SUCCESS)
12:       return FALSE;
13:
14:     // Query for the largest key
15:     RegQueryInfoKey(hSubKey, NULL, NULL, NULL, NULL, NULL, NULL,
16:     ➥NULL, &dwMaxValName, &dwMaxValData, NULL, NULL);
17:     if(dwMaxValName) {
18:         if((lpValueName = (LPTSTR)LocalAlloc(LPTR,
19:         ➥++dwMaxValName*sizeof(TCHAR))) == NULL)
20:           return FALSE;
21:
22:         if((lpValueData = (LPBYTE)LocalAlloc(LPTR, ++dwMaxValData))
23:         ➥ == NULL) {
24:           LocalFree(lpValueName);
25:           return FALSE;
26:         }
27:     } else
28:         return FALSE;
29:
30:     // Enumerate the values
31:     dwCurValNameLen = dwMaxValName;
32:     dwCurDataLen = dwMaxValData;
```

```
33:
34:     while(RegEnumValue(hSubKey, dwIndex, lpValueName,
35:       ➥&dwCurValNameLen, NULL, &dwValType, lpValueData, &dwCurDataLen) !=
36:       ➥ERROR_NO_MORE_ITEMS){
37:       // MessageBox the results
38:       TCHAR tchOutputBuffer[255] = TEXT("\0");
39:       wsprintf(tchOutputBuffer, TEXT("RegKey: %s, Value: %s"),
40:         ➥ lpValueName, lpValueData);
41:       MessageBox(hWnd, tchOutputBuffer, TEXT("Registry Values"),
42:         ➥ MB_OK);
43:
44:       // Increment and loop through the eval
45:       dwIndex++;
46:       dwCurValNameLen = dwMaxValName;
47:       dwCurDataLen = dwMaxValData;
48:       memset(lpValueName, 0, dwMaxValName);
49:       memset(lpValueData, 0, dwMaxValData);
50:     }
51:
52:     // Free memory
53:     if(lpValueName)
54:         LocalFree(lpValueName);
55:     if(lpValueData)
56:         LocalFree(lpValueData);
57:
58:     // Close the key
59:     RegCloseKey(hSubKey);
60:     return TRUE;
61: }
```

Closing the Registry

Any time you open a handle to a key in the Registry, you have to call the RegCloseKey()
function to close the handle, as you would with any file.

```
LONG lResult = RegCloseKey(HKEY hKey);
```

The function takes only a single parameter, the handle of the key you want to close.

Summary

In this hour, you were shown the differences between the object store and a normal
file system. You learned that the object store is a persistent storage area of memory that
contains files, the Registry, and databases. You were also shown how to use the object
store for manipulating individual files and items stored in the Registry.

Q&A

Q Can I copy or write to a ROM file?

A Even though you can use `GetFileAttributes` on a ROM file, you cannot use the `MoveFile`, `CopyFile`, or `DeleteFile` functions on a ROM-based file.

Q Can I create my own root-level Registry entries?

A No, you have to use the Windows default root entries.

Workshop

The Workshop is designed to help you anticipate possible questions, review what you've learned, and begin thinking ahead about putting your knowledge into practice. The answers to the quiz are in Appendix A, "Answers."

Quiz

1. What is the object store?
2. What flags do you use to create a new file?
3. If there were four mounted devices on your Windows CE device, what would their device names be?
4. How do you set the file pointer?
5. How do you delete a directory?
6. What is an OID?
7. What are the types of Registry values?
8. What is the largest file you can have on a Windows CE device?

Exercises

1. Modify Listing 9.4 to automatically create the Registry key if it does not already exist.

HOUR 10

Advanced Object Store: The Database API

This lesson builds on what you learned in the last hour about the object store and looks at the Windows CE Database API and how to use it.

In this hour, you will learn

- What the Windows CE Database API is
- How to create new databases
- How to store and retrieve data from databases
- How to sort data in the databases
- How to understand the Windows system databases

The Object Store and Databases

As with any database, the Windows CE Database API provides a simplistic way of organizing and storing data. Most of the internal applications (Contacts, Tasks, and so on) use the Database API to store information.

Figure 10.1 shows you a basic database folder.

FIGURE 10.1

The Databases folder.

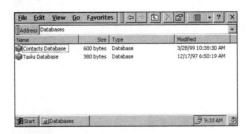

Each database consists of a collection of records that contain one or more properties of information and their values.

Databases created from the Database API do have some basic limitations:

- A maximum of four sort indices.
- A maximum property size of 64KB.
- A maximum record size of 128KB.
- Windows CE databases have one hierarchy.
- Database locking is not supported (but notification of changes is).
- Records cannot contain other records or be shared between databases.

As you can see, the Windows CE Database API is limited. Complex relational databases are not possible with the current implementation. Instead, the Database API should be used for storing simple related data, such as a shopping list or contact information.

NEW TERM   A database contains one or more *records*. Each record has properties that contain data, and records cannot contain other records. Each record also has an associated CEOID (defined in Hour 9, "The Object Store: Files and the Registry").

NEW TERM   Details about an individual record are stored as *properties*. Each property has a property identifier, a data type, and the actual data.

Databases on Windows CE

Each database property is defined as a specific data type. Table 10.1 presents the data types available to Windows CE databases.

TABLE 10.1   Available Database API Data Types

Property	Description
CEVT_BLOB	A block of memory, stored as a CEBLOB structure
CEVT_FILETIME	A FILETIME structure
CEVT_I2	A 16-bit signed integer
CEVT_I4	A 32-bit signed integer
CEVT_LPWSTR	A null-terminated string
CEVT_UI2	A 16-bit unsigned integer
CEVT_UI4	A 32-bit unsigned integer
CEVT_BOOL	A Boolean value (Windows CE 2.1 and later)
CEVT_R8	A 64-bit signed double (Windows CE 2.1 and later)

10

It is also important to note that as of Windows CE version 2.1 and later, databases can reside on mountable volumes.

> Databases that begin with a \ are system databases. A system database is hidden from the Windows CE Explorer, but can be used as a normal database.

Mounting Database Volumes

Starting with Windows CE 2.1, you are now able to store databases on externally mounted devices, such as flash cards. To use an external device for database storage, you must first mount the database.

To mount a database volume, you call the CeMountDBVol() function call:

```
BOOL fMounted = CeMountDBVol(PCEGUID pCeGUID, LPWSTR lpszVol,
➥DWORD dwFlags);
```

The CeMountDBVol() function takes three parameters: a pointer to a CEGUID that is used by the Database API Ex functions, a null-terminated string that contains the name of a file that will contain one or more databases (that is, \\Storage Card\\Databases.cdb), and a dwFlags field that can specify volume creation flags.

The dwFlags parameter can be any of the following values:

- CREATE_NEW specifies that a new database volume should be created. If it already exists, the function will fail.

- `CREATE_ALWAYS` specifies that a new database volume should always be created. If it already exists, it will overwrite the old one.
- `OPEN_EXISTING` specifies that it should open a database volume. If it doesn't exist, the function will fail.
- `OPEN_ALWAYS` specifies that it should always open the volume. If it doesn't exist, the function will create a new one.
- `TRUNCATE_EXISTING` specifies that it should open an existing database volume and truncate it to 0 bytes.

In order to use a mounted database volume, make sure that you use the Ex version of the Database API calls.

After you have finished using a database volume, you must unmount it. To do so, call the `CeUnmountDBVol()` function:

```
BOOL fUnmounted = CeUnmountDBVol(PCEGUID pCeGUID);
```

The function takes a single parameter: a pointer to a CEGUID of a mounted database volume.

> If you want to use the Ex Database API with the internal object store databases, you can get the object store's CEGUID by calling `CREATE_SYS-TEMGUID(PCEGUID pCeGUID)`. It will fill in the pointer value with a pointer to the system CEGUID.

Finally, if you want to flush all pending data to the mounted volume, you can call the `CeFlushDBVol()` function:

```
BOOL fFlushed = CeFlushDBVol(PCEGUID pCeGUID);
```

The function takes only one parameter: the pointer to the mounted database volume.

Enumerating Databases

To determine a group of databases, the Database API provides functionality to enumerate databases that are in the object store, are of a certain type, or are mounted on a particular volume.

To walk through the database list, you can use the function `CeFindFirstDatabase()`, followed by a series of calls to `CeFindNextDatabase()` to continue the enumeration. This technique is similar to the `FindFirstFile()` and `FindNextFile()` APIs discussed in Hour 9.

To begin the enumeration, we first call CeFindFirstDatabase():

```
HANDLE hDB = CeFindFirstDatabase(DWORD dwType);
```

CeFindFirstDatabase() takes only one parameter: a type identifier for the database. If you want to enumerate all the databases, just use 0. The function will return a handle to the enumeration context that should be used in calls to CeFindNextDatabase():

```
CEOID ceOID = CeFindNextDatabase(HANDLE hDB);
```

CeFindNextDatabase() will return a CEOID (as described in Hour 9 and later in this hour) that you can use to access the database. Listing 10.1 is an example.

LISTING 10.1   Enumerating Databases

```
 1: BOOL fEnumerate = TRUE;
 2: HANDLE hDB = CeFindFirstDatabase;
 3: if(!hDB)
 4:     return FALSE;
 5: while(fEnumerate) {
 6:     CEOID dbOID = CeFindNextDatabase(hDB);
 7:     if(!dbOID) {
 8:         if(GetLastError() == ERROR_NO_MORE_ITEMS) {
 9:             fEnumerate = FALSE;
10:             continue;
11:         }
12:     }
13:
14:     // Get the information for the database
15:     CEOIDINFO ceOIDInfo;
16:     memset(&ceOIDInfo, 0, sizeof(CEOIDINFO));
17:     if (!CeOidGetInfo(dbOID, &ceOIDInfo)) {
18:         // An error has occurred, so let's quit the loop
19:         fEnumerate = FALSE;
20:         continue;
21:     }
22: }
```

If you are using Windows CE 2.1 or later, you can also use CeFindFirstDatabaseEx() and CeFindNextDatabaseEx() instead:

```
HANDLE hDB = CeFindFirstDatabaseEx(PCEGUID pCeGUID, DWORD dwType);
```

The only difference is that the first parameter is a pointer to a CEGUID that identifies the database volume. (Refer to the section "Mounting Database Volumes" for more information.)

```
CEOID ceOID = CeFindNextDatabaseEx(HANDLE hDB, PCEGUID pCeGUID);
```

10

Again, with `CeFindNextDatabaseEx`, the only new parameter is the pointer to the database volume.

Creating Databases

Depending on which version of Windows CE you are using, you can create databases in one of two ways. If you are using Windows CE 2.0 and earlier, you can use the `CeCreateDatabase()` function call. If you are using Windows CE 2.1 and later, you may also use the `CeCreateDatabaseEx()` to create a database on an external volume outside the object store.

First, take a look at `CeCreateDatabase()`:

```
CEOID ceOIDDB = CeCreateDatabase(LPWSTR lpszName, DWORD dwType,
➥WORD wNumSortOrder, SORTORDERSPEC *rgSortSpecs);
```

`CeCreateDatabase` takes four parameters:

- The name of the new database (which is limited to 32 characters)
- A user-defined identifier for the database (it is *not* a unique identifier, but used just for enumeration)
- The number of sort orders in your database
- A pointer to an array of `SORTORDERSPEC` structures that define your sort order

The `SORTORDERSPEC` structure has two members: `propid`, which is the identifier of the property to sort on, and `dwFlags`, which specifies the actual sort. Table 10.2 lists the `Sort` flags and their definitions.

TABLE 10.2 The `SORTORDERSPEC` Sorting Flags

Sort Flag	Definition
CEDB_SORT_DESCENDING	Descending order sort.
CEDB_SORT_CASEINSENSITIVE	Case-insensitive sort.
CEDB_SORT_UNKNOWNFIRST	Records that do not have this property are placed before all other records.
CEDB_SORT_GENERICORDER	Ascending case-sensitive sort. This is the default.

For example, Listing 10.2 shows you how to use them.

LISTING 10.2 Creating a Database

```
 1: CEOID ceOIDDB = NULL;
 2: SORTORDERSPEC sos[5];
 3: HANDLE hDB = NULL;
 4:
 5: // Set up the columns
 6: memset(sos, 0, sizeof(sos));
 7: sos[0].propid = MAKELONG(CEVT_LPWSTR, 1);
 8: sos[1].propid = MAKELONG(CEVT_UI4, 2);
 9: sos[2].propid = MAKELONG(CEVT_FILETIME, 3);
10: sos[3].propid = MAKELONG(CEVT_UI4, 4);
11:
12: // Create the database
13: ceOIDDB = CeCreateDatabase(TEXT("Shopping"), 123, 4,
14:     ➡(SORTORDERSPEC *)sos);
15: if(!ceOIDDB) {
16:     MessageBox(ghWnd, TEXT("Failed to Create Database"),
17:         ➡TEXT("DB Manager"), MB_OK);
18:     return FALSE;
19: }
```

10

Under Windows CE 2.1 or later, you can use the `CeCreateDatabaseEx()` function:

```
CEOID ceOIDDB = CeCreateDatabaseEx(PCEGUID pCeGUID,
➡CEDATABASEINFO *pInfo);
```

The `CeCreateDatabaseEx()` function takes two parameters: a pointer to a CEGUID database volume and a pointer to a CEDATABASEINFO structure. The CEDATABASEINFO structure is defined in Table 10.3.

TABLE 10.3 The Member Variables of the CEDATABASEINFO Structure

Member	Specifies
dwFlags	The dwFlags member is divided into two parts, an upper and a lower word. The LOWORD flags for what the valid members of this structure are. It can be one or more of CEDB_VALIDMODTIME, CEDB_VALIDNAME, CEDB_VALIDTYPE, CEDB_VALIDSORTSPEC, and CE_VALIDDBFLAGS. The HIWORD can only be set to CEDB_NOCOMPRESS, which means that the database is not compressed. To set this flag, use the MAKELONG (low word, high word) macro.
szDbaseName	A null-terminated string that contains the name of the database.
dwType	Specifies the user-defined type identifier.
wNumRecords	Returns the number of records in the database.
wNumSortOrder	The number of active sort orders.
dwSize	Returns the size of the database in bytes.
ftLastModified	Returns the FILETIME of the last database modification.
rgSortSpecs	A pointer to an array of sort order descriptions.

Opening Databases

Depending on whether your database is located on a mounted volume on Windows CE 2.1 and later, you can use either the CeOpenDatabase() or CeOpenDatabaseEx() function call to open a database.

Under Windows CE 2.0 and earlier, you call

```
HANDLE hDB = CeOpenDatabase(PCEOID pCeOID, LPWSTR lpszName,
➡CEPROPID propid, DWORD dwFlags, HWND hWndNotify);
```

When opening a database, you can use either the database name or the database's OID. The CeOpenDatabase function takes five parameters:

- The OID of the database to open (0 if opening by name)
- The null-terminated name of the database to open (NULL if opening by OID)
- The sort order to sort the database when opened
- The increment flag, which can be set to 0 or CE_DBAUTOINCREMENT (the database pointer will automatically advance after a record is read)
- A handle of a window to receive notification messages if the database is modified while open (this can be NULL)

Table 10.4 lists the database notifications you can receive.

TABLE 10.4 Database Notifications

Notification	Definition
DB_CEOID_CHANGED	The database has been modified by another thread. The message sends the database OID.
DB_CEOID_CREATED	A new object has been created in the object store. The message sends the CEOID.
DB_CEOID_RECORD_DELETED	A record has been deleted by another thread. The message sends the record's OID.

For example, if you want to open a database, Listing 10.3 will help.

LISTING 10.3 Opening a Database

```
1: // Open the database
2: if(!(hDB = CeOpenDatabase(0, TEXT("\\Cookies"), 0,
3: ➡CEDB_AUTOINCREMENT, NULL)))
4:     return FALSE;
5: CloseHandle(hDB);
```

If you are using Windows CE 2.1 or later and want to open a database on a mounted volume, you can use the function

```
HANDLE hDB = CeOpenDatabaseEx(PCEGUID pCeGUID, PCEOID pOid,
➥LPWSTR lpszName, CEPROPID propid, DWORD dwFlags,
➥CENOTIFYREQUEST *pRequest);
```

The CeOpenDatabaseEx() function takes six parameters. Most are the same as the CeOpenDatabase() function call, except that pCeGUID is a pointer to the CEGUID of the mounted database volume, pOid is a pointer to the OID of the database (NULL if opening by Name), and the last parameter is a pointer to a CENOTIFYREQUEST structure.

The CENOTIFYREQUEST structure is defined in Table 10.5.

TABLE 10.5   The Member Variables of the CENOTIFYREQUEST Structure

Member	Specifies
dwSize	The size of the CENOTIFYREQUEST structure.
hWnd	The window handle of the window to receive notifications.
dwFlags	Flags on how notifications are handled. If set to 0, it is the same as previously mentioned. If set to CEDB_EXNOTIFICATION, your application will receive a CENOTIFICATION structure that defines the notification. If you are using a mounted database, you must set the CEDB_EXNOTIFICATION flag.
hHeap	The handle to a memory heap. If set to NULL, the system will allocate memory.
dwParam	A user-defined parameter that is sent in the CENOTIFICATION structure.

If you set the dwFlags member to 0, you will receive the same notifications that you would as if you used the CeOpenDatabase function call. However, if you used CEDB_EXNOTIFICATION, you will receive a WM_DBNOTIFICATION message, with the lParam pointing to a CENOTIFICATION structure. It should be noted that you are responsible for freeing the memory that contains the CENOTIFICATION structure by calling

```
BOOL CeFreeNotification(PCENOTIFYREQUEST pRequest,
➥PCENOTIFICATION pNotify);
```

The function takes two parameters: a pointer to the original CENOTIFYREQUEST structure and a pointer to the CENOTIFICATION structure that was sent in WM_DBNOTIFICATION.

Finally, to close a database, you can call the Windows standard CloseHandle() function, passing in the handle to the open database.

Sort Order

When creating a database, you specified up to four sort orders for it. When you opened that database, you chose to open it with either the default sort order or a particular one. However, it might be necessary to redefine the sort order for a particular database.

Under Windows CE 2.0 and earlier, you can call CeSetDatabaseInfo():

```
BOOL CeSetDatabaseInfo(CEOID oidDB, CEDBASEINFO *pNewInfo);
```

It takes two parameters: the OID of the database to change and a pointer to a CEDBASE-INFO structure (refer to the section "Creating Databases").

Under Windows CE 2.1 and later, you can use the CeSetDatabaseInfoEx() functions:

```
BOOL CeSetDatabaseInfoEx(PCEGUID pCeGUID, CEOID oidDB,
➥CEDBASEINFO *pNewInfo);
```

The only difference is the first parameter, which is a pointer to a CEGUID of the mounted database volume.

It should be noted that re-sorting a database is time-intensive and can be annoying to users if done frequently.

Searching for Records

After the database has been opened, you can find a particular database record by using the CeSeekDatabase() function call. This will move the database pointer to a record that matches the criteria you specified in your search:

```
CEOID ceOID = CeSeekDatabase(HANDLE hDB, DWORD dwSeekType, DWORD dwValue,
➥LPDWORD lpdwIndex);
```

The function takes four parameters:

- The handle to an open database
- A dwSeekType parameter (described in Table 10.6) that tells the function how to search
- A dwValue that specifies the value for the seek (and depends on the dwSeekType)
- A pointer to a variable that receives the index from the start of the database to the record that was found

Table 10.6 defines the dwSeekType parameters.

TABLE 10.6   Database Search Parameters

Parameter	Definition
CEDB_SEEK_CEOID	Find a particular record by OID. The dwValue parameter is the object identifier of the record to search for.
CEDB_SEEK_VALUESSMALLER	Find a record from the current location that has a property smaller than the specified value. The dwValue parameter is a pointer to a CEPROPVAL structure.
CEDB_SEEK_VALUEFIRSTEQUAL	Find a record from the current location that contains a property equal to the specified value. The dwValue parameter is a pointer to a CEPROPVAL structure.
CEDB_SEEK_VALUE_NEXTEQUAL	Find a record from the next position that contains a property equal to the specified value. The dwValue parameter is a pointer to a CEPROPVAL structure.
CEDB_SEEK_VALUEGREATER	Find a record from the current location that has a property greater than the specified value. The dwValue parameter is a pointer to a CEPROPVAL structure.
CEDB_SEEK_BEGINNING	Find a record at a specified position from the beginning of the database. The dwValue parameter specifies the index of the record.
CEDB_SEEK_CURRENT	Find a record at a specified position starting at the current database record. The dwValue parameter specifies a positive value to seek forward or a negative number to seek backward.
CEDB_SEEK_END	Find a record at a specified position from the end of the database. The dwValue parameter specifies the number of records to go backward.

Reading from Databases

After you have moved the database pointer to a particular record you are interested in (or if you are reading all the records, you can start at 0), you can use the CeReadRecordProps() function to read the record's property information.

```
CEOID ceOIDRecord = CeReadRecordProps(HANDLE hDB, DWORD dwFlags,
➥LPDWORD lpcPropID, CEPROPID *rgPropID, LPBYTE *lplpBuffer,
➥LPDWORD lpcbBuffer);
```

The function takes six parameters:

- A handle to an open database

- A flags field that can have the CEDB_ALLOWREALLOC flag if you want the function to automatically enlarge the buffer for data (you will have to free the buffer after the function returns)

- A pointer to the number of CEPROPID structures in rgPropID
- A pointer to an array of CEPROPID structures that specifies what record properties you want to receive
- A pointer to a buffer to receive the data
- A pointer that receives the size of the data stored in lplpBuffer

If you want to receive all the properties for a record, you can make rgPropID NULL, and lpcPropID will return the number of properties retrieved.

Under Windows CE 2.1 and later, you can use the CeReadRecordPropsEx() function:

```
CEOID ceOIDRecord = CeReadRecordPropsEx(HANDLE hDB, DWORD dwFlags,
➥LPDWORD lpcPropID, CEPROPID *rePropID, LPBYTE *lplpBuffer,
➥LPDWORD lpcbBuffer, HANDLE hHeap);
```

The only difference is the hHeap parameter, which is a handle to a user-created heap. It will use this heap's memory instead of the local heap when allocating the buffer. If you want to use the local heap, just pass in a 0 for this parameter.

For example, if you wanted to retrieve all the properties for all records and export them to a file, you could use the code in Listing 10.4.

LISTING 10.4 Reading from a Database

```
 1: BOOL ExportToFile(CEOID ceOIDDB, TCHAR *tchFileName)
 2: {
 3:     HANDLE hDB = NULL, hExport = NULL;
 4:     LPBYTE pBuf = NULL;
 5:     CEOID ceOIDRecord = NULL;
 6:     WORD wNumProps = 0;
 7:     DWORD dwBufSize = 0, dwWritten = 0;
 8:
 9:     if(!tchFileName ¦¦ !ceOIDDB)
10:         return FALSE;
11:
12:     // Open the database
13:     if(!(hDB = CeOpenDatabase(&ceOIDDB, NULL, 0, CEDB_AUTOINCREMENT,
        ➥ NULL)))
14:         return FALSE;
15:
16:     // Create the file
17:     if((hExport = CreateFile(tchFileName, GENERIC_WRITE, 0, NULL,
        ➥ CREATE_ALWAYS, FILE_ATTRIBUTE_NORMAL, NULL)) ==
        ➥INVALID_HANDLE_VALUE) {
18:         CloseHandle(hDB);
19:         return FALSE;
20:     }
```

```
21:
22:         // Loop through each item in the database
23:         while((ceOIDRecord = CeReadRecordProps(hDB, CEDB_ALLOWREALLOC,
           ➥&wNumProps, NULL, &pBuf, &dwBufSize))) {
24:             // We got a record (all the properties); let's write it out
25:             WriteFile(hExport, pBuf, dwBufSize, &dwWritten, NULL);
26:
27:             // Add a NULL separator
28:             WriteFile(hExport, TEXT("\0"), sizeof(TCHAR), &dwWritten,
               ➥ NULL);
29:
30:             // Clean up
31:             if(pBuf)
32:                 LocalFree(pBuf);
33:             wNumProps = 0;
34:             dwBufSize = 0;
35:             pBuf = NULL;
36:             dwWritten = 0;
37:         }
38:
39:         // Close
40:         CloseHandle(hDB);
41:         CloseHandle(hExport);
42:
43:         return TRUE;
44: }
```

Writing to Databases

To write a record to a database, you can use the CeWriteRecordProps() function:

```
CEOID ceOIDRecord = CeWriteRecordProps(HANDLE hDB, CEOID oidRecord,
➥WORD cPropID, CEPROPVAL *rgPropVal);
```

The function takes four parameters:

- A handle to an open database
- The OID of the record to write to (if you are modifying a record; otherwise, set to 0 for a new record)
- The number of properties specified in rgPropVal
- A pointer to an array of CEPROPVAL structures containing the record to write

LISTING 10.5   Writing to a Database

```
 1: for(int x = 0; x<100; x++) {
 2:     CEPROPVAL cePropVal[5];
 3:     SYSTEMTIME sysTime;
 4:     FILETIME ftTime;
 5:
 6:     memset(&cePropVal, 0, sizeof(cePropVal));
 7:     cePropVal[0].propid = MAKELONG(CEVT_LPWSTR, 1);
 8:     cePropVal[0].val.lpwstr = TEXT("Item");
 9:     cePropVal[1].propid = MAKELONG(CEVT_UI4, 2);
10:     cePropVal[1].val.ulVal = (DWORD)x;
11:     GetLocalTime(&sysTime);
12:     SystemTimeToFileTime(&sysTime, &ftTime);
13:     cePropVal[2].propid = MAKELONG(CEVT_FILETIME, 3);
14:     cePropVal[2].val.filetime = ftTime;
15:     cePropVal[3].propid = MAKELONG(CEVT_UI4, 4);
16:     cePropVal[3].val.ulVal = x;
17:     if(!CeWriteRecordProps(hDB, 0, 4, (CEPROPVAL *)cePropVal))
18:         break;
19: }
```

Deleting Records

To delete a record in a database, call the `CeDeleteRecord()` function:

```
BOOL fDeleted = CeDeleteRecord(HANDLE hDB, CEOID oidRecord);
```

The function takes two parameters: a handle to an opened database and an OID of the record to delete. If successful, the function will return TRUE.

Deleting Databases

You can delete a database by using either `CeDeleteDatabase()` or `CeDeleteDatabaseEx()`.

If you are using Windows CE 2.0 and earlier versions, call the CeDeleteDatabase() function:

```
BOOL fDeleted = CeDeleteDatabase(CEOID oidDB);
```

The `CeDeleteDatabase()` function takes only one parameter: the OID of the database to delete. If successful, it will return TRUE.

If you have to delete a database on a mounted volume in Windows CE 2.1 or later, call the `CeDeleteDatabaseEx()` function:

```
BOOL fDeleted = CeDeleteDatabaseEx(PCEGUID pCeGUID, PCEOID oidDB);
```

This function takes two parameters: a pointer to the mounted database volume CEGUID and a pointer to the OID of the database to delete. If successful, it will return TRUE after the database is deleted.

Object Identifiers and Databases

As mentioned in Hour 9, all databases and database records have an OID (object identifier) that is uniquely associated with them. The OID can also be used to query, read, or delete data from the database.

Under Windows CE 2.0 and earlier, you can use the CeOidGetInfo() function:

```
BOOL fInfo = CeOidGetInfo(CEOID ceOID, CEOIDINFO *pOidInfo);
```

The function takes two parameters: an OID and a pointer to a CEOIDINFO structure.

Under Windows CE 2.1 and later, you can use the CeOidGetInfoEx() function:

```
BOOL fInfo = CeOidGetInfo(PCEGUID pCeGUID, CEOID oid,
➥CEOIDINFO *oidInfo);
```

As with all other Ex functions, the only difference in this function is the first parameter, a pointer to a CEGUID mounted database volume.

See Hour 9 for more information about the CEOIDINFO structure with regards to the file system. CEOIDINFO also contains information pertaining to databases and the CEDATABASEINFO (refer to Table 10.3) and CERECORDINFO structures.

The CERECORDINFO structure is defined by its member variable, oidParent. The oidParent member is an OID of the parent database.

Summary

In this hour, you were shown how to use the Windows CE Database APIs and how they relate to other items in the object store. You also explored the differences between normal and mounted databases, as well as various techniques for manipulating database records. Finally, you looked at the limitations of Windows CE databases.

Q&A

Q Under Windows CE 2.1, should I use the Ex database functions?

A You only have to use the extended database API functions if you are working with mounted database volumes.

10

Q Can I sort off a property type `CEVT_BLOB`?

A No, you cannot sort off binary data.

Workshop

The Workshop is designed to help you anticipate possible questions, review what you've learned, and begin thinking ahead about putting your knowledge into practice. The answers to the quiz are in Appendix A, "Answers."

Quiz

1. Can you lock a database?

2. What is the maximum number of sort indices?

3. What are database properties?

4. What are the new property types under Windows CE 2.1?

5. How can I seek a database for a particular index?

6. What is the major difference between databases on Windows CE 2.0 and on Windows CE 2.1?

7. How do I delete a database record?

Exercises

1. Write a function to delete a database, based on its OID. Make sure that the function prompts the user to continue, providing the database name.

Hour 11

Threads and Processes

Similar to its desktop counterparts, Windows CE is a fully multitasking and preemptive multithreaded operating system. To this end, most of the APIs you use to create and manage threads and processes are the same. Of course, those that don't fall under the "most of the APIs" blanket are the ones you need to know about, and they are the focus of this hour's discussion.

In this hour, you will learn

- The size and feature restrictions of the Windows CE thread and process model
- Thread synchronization
- Thread local storage (TLS) support
- Measurement and profiling features

Limitations

On desktop Win32 operating systems, no restrictions are placed on the number of processes that can be running at the same time, and each process has its own 4GB virtual address space. Windows CE changes this architecture significantly, allowing only 32 concurrently running processes. Each of these processes, commonly referred to as *slots*, supports a 32MB virtual address space, giving a total addressable memory space of 1GB. Modules that provide operating system functionality, such as device drivers and the graphical windowing and event subsystem (GWES), take the first few slots when the device is booted up. Typically, a running device with a shell and communications services has about 24 slots available for user applications.

On the other hand, Windows CE places no restrictions on the number of threads a process can create—you can have as many as you like. Each thread has full access to the entire 32MB address space of the process.

Unlike Windows NT or 95, the stack space for a thread does not grow dynamically and is the same fixed size for all threads in a process. Versions previous to 2.1 have a hard-coded thread stack size of 58KB that is not modifiable by the user. Starting with version 2.1, the default stack size is set by the linker /stack switch. If the switch is not present, the old value of 58KB is used.

It is important to note that the stack size of a secondary thread cannot be changed at runtime by specifying a value in the dwStackSize parameter of the CreateThread API or beginthreadex C runtime library routine. This parameter is simply ignored, and the default value set by the linker switch or the operating system is always used.

The thread priority scheme is also different on Windows CE. Unlike Windows NT, there is no priority class, and threads are not scheduled differently based on the process to which they belong. Instead, all processes are treated equally, and scheduling is based solely on thread priority. The "priority boosting" strategy of Windows NT is also not implemented. Windows CE supports eight levels of thread priorities:

- THREAD_PRIORITY_TIME_CRITICAL indicates three points above normal priority. See the next paragraph for special scheduling behavior.
- THREAD_PRIORITY_HIGHEST indicates two points above normal priority.
- THREAD_PRIORITY_ABOVE_NORMAL indicates one point above normal priority.
- THREAD_PRIORITY_NORMAL indicates normal priority. This is the default priority for all threads.
- THREAD_PRIORITY_BELOW_NORMAL indicates one point below normal priority.
- THREAD_PRIORITY_LOWEST indicates two points below normal priority.
- THREAD_PRIORITY_ABOVE_IDLE indicates three points below normal priority.
- THREAD_PRIORITY_IDLE indicates four points below normal priority.

Scheduling is done in a round robin fashion based on priority, which means that all higher priority threads are run before those with a lower priority.

There are two exceptions to the round robin rules of thread scheduling on Windows CE. Any thread with `THREAD_PRIORITY_TIME_CRITICAL` will never be preempted, even by another `THREAD_PRIORITY_TIME_CRITICAL` thread; it will remain in control until it finishes or blocks. Threads with this priority are usually reserved for servicing interrupts in device drivers and operating system components and should not generally be used by an application.

The second exception occurs when a lower priority thread owns a resource that a higher priority thread must continue running. In this case, known *as priority inversion*, the lower priority thread is temporarily given the priority of the thread that is waiting for it so that the resource will be released and the higher priority thread can continue running. After the resource is released, the thread's priority is set back to its original value.

It is good practice to never depend on the actual numeric value of a thread's priority, but rather to just compare it to the defined constants. However, when the priority value is actually directly referenced, a common mistake is to assume that a higher number represents a higher priority. On Windows NT and Windows 95, this is true, but it is the exact opposite on Windows CE. The value of `THREAD_PRIORITY_TIME_CRITICAL` is zero, and as the priority decreases, the numeric value increases to a maximum of seven for the lowest priority, `THREAD_PRIORITY_IDLE`. This means that code such as

```
// Does thread1 have a higher priority than thread2?
if ( GetThreadPriority(hThread1) > GetThreadPriority(hThread2) )
    // thread1 has higher priority
else
    // thread2 has equal or higher priority
}
```

is wrong (except for equal priorities) and

```
// lower the priority of thread1
SetThreadPriority(hThread1, GetThreadPriority(hThread1)-1);
```

will actually raise the priority of `thread1`. As mentioned before, the best approach is to avoid relying on the relationship of these numeric values. However, if you must, be sure to change your logic to accommodate the difference on Windows CE. This code compares thread priorities correctly on Windows NT, Windows 95, and Windows CE:

```
/*
Return TRUE if thread1 is higher priority than thread2, otherwise return FALSE
*/
BOOL IsThreadPriorityHigher(HANDLE hThread1, HANDLE hThread2)
{
```

11

```
   DWORD dwPri1 = GetThreadPriority(hThread1);
   DWORD dwPri2 = GetThreadPriority(hThread2);

#ifdef WIN32_WCE
   if (dwPri1 < dwPri2 )
#else
   if (dwPri1 > dwPri2 )
#endif
        return TRUE
   else
        return FALSE;
}
```

On Windows NT, each thread has a data structure called a thread information block
(TIB) associated with it. The TIB contains information such as the GetLastError value,
thread local storage (TLS) values, and the structured exception handling (SEH) chain. A
similar structure known as the *thread environment block* (TEB) is available on Windows
95/98. Unfortunately, Windows CE does not support a feature similar to the TIB/TEB.
The kernel does have a data structure that stores this information, but it is not available to
applications.

The last Windows CE limitation I'll discuss is how ending a process is different. On
Windows NT, calling the C runtime library exit function or the ExitProcess API closes
the process immediately. On Windows CE, neither exit nor ExitProcess is available.
Instead, the main thread must terminate or return for the process to exit. For some
applications, this is fine, but in many situations, exiting a process from outside the main
thread is very convenient (especially when porting code from desktop Win32). Luckily,
you can simulate ExitProcess like this:

```
void WINAPI ExitProcess(UINT uExitCode)
{
    TerminateProcess(GetCurrentProcess(), uExitCode);
}
```

Although it is usually a good rule of thumb to avoid using TerminateProcess, this is the
cleanest way to exit a process outside the main thread under Windows CE. This snippet
also benefits from the fact that, unlike its desktop counterparts, TerminateProcess on
Windows CE fires DllMain's DLL_PROCESS_DETACH event for any loaded DLLs. This
gives the process more chance to clean up properly, but the typical TerminateProcess
drawbacks of not having file buffers flushed or compromising the state of shared memory blocks still apply.

Thread Synchronization

Having multiple threads in a process can be both a blessing and a curse at the same time. If you've ever had to chase down a really nasty race condition or deadlock scenario, you know exactly what I mean. If you haven't had this opportunity, you almost certainly have some interesting, but extremely frustrating, debugging sessions in your near future.

Proper thread synchronization is no less important on Windows CE than on any other platform, and the Win32 API provides several tools that enable you to handle basic scenarios and build more sophisticated solutions for the complicated ones. There are three basic categories for these synchronization features:

- Critical sections
- Interlocked APIs
- Kernel objects

Critical sections are used to ensure that no more than one thread at a time is executing a block of code. Typically, this code modifies a shared data structure or inspects some state variable, but anything is fair game. There are four operations for manipulating a critical section (`initialize`, `delete`, `enter`, and `leave`), and their behavior is identical to that of Windows NT and Windows 95.

A simple example of using a critical section appears in Listing 11.1. The example increments an integer variable from 0 to 31, cooperatively sharing the work between two threads via a critical section. Notice that you initialize the critical section before it is used and delete it when you are finished and that the calls to `EnterCriticalSection` and `LeaveCriticalSection` are always balanced. If you're paying close attention, you will wonder why `WinMain` uses sequential calls to `WaitForSingleObject` instead of `WaitForMultipleObjects`. I'll discuss the reasons a little later on.

LISTING 11.1 A Sample Use of a Critical Section

```
 1: /*
 2:     Sample code for using a critical section.
 3:     Works identically under Windows NT/95/CE.
 4: */
 5:
 6: #include <windows.h>
 7: #include <tchar.h>
 8:
 9: #define MAX_THREADS    2
10: #define MAX_VALUE      32
11:
12: CRITICAL_SECTION g_CritSec;
```

continues

LISTING 11.1 continued

```
13: TCHAR            g_chBuf[64];
14:
15:
16: DWORD WINAPI IncVarThreadFunc(PVOID pv)
17: {
18:
19:     int     *pint = (int*)pv;
20:     BOOL    bDone = FALSE;
21:
22:     while ( bDone == FALSE )
23:     {
24:         EnterCriticalSection(&g_CritSec);
25:
26:         if ( *pint < MAX_VALUE )
27:         {
28:             wsprintf(g_chBuf,
29:                     _T("thread id = %08X, value = %d\n"),
30:                     GetCurrentThreadId(),
31:                     *pint);
32:             OutputDebugString(g_chBuf);
33:
34:             (*pint)++;
35:         }
36:         else
37:             bDone = TRUE;
38:
39:         LeaveCriticalSection(&g_CritSec);
40:     }
41:
42:     return 0;
43: }
44:
45:
46: int WINAPI WinMain(    HINSTANCE hInstance,
47:                        HINSTANCE hPrevInstance,
48:                        LPTSTR    lpCmdLine,
49:                        int       nCmdShow)
50: {
51:
52:     DWORD   dwTID;
53:     HANDLE  hThreads[MAX_THREADS];
54:     int     iValue = 0;
55:
56:     InitializeCriticalSection(&g_CritSec);
57:
58:     for ( int i = 0; i < MAX_THREADS; i++ )
59:         hThreads[i] = CreateThread(NULL, 0, IncVarThreadFunc,
60:                                    &iValue, 0, &dwTID);
61:
```

```
62:
63:     for ( i = 0; i < MAX_THREADS; i++ )
64:         WaitForSingleObject(hThreads[i], INFINITE);
65:
66:     DeleteCriticalSection(&g_CritSec);
67:
68:     return 0;
69: }
70:
```

Actually, there is one other critical section–related API: TryEnterCriticalSection. This is supported only in Windows NT v4.0 and isn't available on Windows CE. If you need this functionality, you're probably better off switching to a mutex, which I'll discuss shortly.

The interlocked functions are provided as a way of performing a simple atomic operation without having to use a critical section or a mutex to provide thread safety. The APIs are

- InterlockedCompareExchange
- InterlockedTestExchange
- InterlockedIncrement
- InterlockedDecrement
- InterlockedExchange
- InterlockedExchangeAdd

InterlockedTestExchange is the only one in this list that is unique to Windows CE. Essentially, it is nothing more than InterlockedCompareExchange, with the last two parameters reversed and changed to the LONG data type instead of PVOID. Any call such as this

```
InterlockedCompareExchange((PVOID*)&lDestValue,
                           (PVOID)lNewValue,
                           (PVOID)lOldValue);
```

is identical to this:

```
InterlockedTestExchange(&lDestValue, lOldValue, lNewValue);
```

In fact, if you look in the Windows CE header file winbase.h, you will see that for some CPU architectures InterlockedTestExchange is actually a macro that just calls InterlockedCompareExchange with a properly rearranged and typecast argument list.

Given that the interlocked functions provide simple thread-safe integer comparison and increment functions, you should be able to rewrite the thread function from Listing 11.1 without using critical sections, right? Actually, the answer is no. The problem is that there is no way to conditionally increment *pint based on the less than comparison to

MAX_VALUE. InterlockedTestExchange provides only an equality comparison. If you split it into more than one statement, a thread could be interrupted between statements, and you are back to the necessity for a critical section to guarantee an atomic operation.

The interlocked functions can be very useful for situations such as implementing reference counting in a multithreaded application (via InterlockedIncrement and InterlockedDecrement), but for more complicated problems, you're probably better off with a critical section or a mutex.

That leaves you with the last synchronization item: kernel objects. This is a much bigger topic than the other two combined and encompasses several types of flexible synchronization facilities under a common umbrella.

NEW TERM   A *kernel object* is an operating system resource that can be referenced, via a handle, from any process. Examples of a kernel object include a mutex, thread, and process.

Win32 provides four synchronization kernel objects:

- A *mutex* provides similar functionality to a critical section.
- An *event* allows you to notify other threads when some condition has been met.
- A *semaphore* gives you the ability to restrict resource access to a limited number of users.
- A *waitable timer* allows you to notify other threads on regular time intervals.

I'll cover each of these items in detail this hour, but first will discuss some Windows CE–specific issues that affect kernel objects as a whole.

When you create a kernel object, you have the option of giving it a name. Unnamed objects can be accessed only from the process in which they are created, whereas named objects can be opened and used by another process. Names are *case-sensitive*, which means that goo, Goo, and GOO refer to different objects. In Windows CE 2.0, there was a problem with giving objects names greater than 760 characters long. It would crash the system—not exactly the desired behavior. In Windows CE 2.1, this problem has been corrected and matches the Windows NT behavior of limiting names to 260 characters.

In Windows NT, kernel object names are all drawn from a common pool, regardless of the type of object. For example, you cannot have a mutex and a semaphore named BSQUARE. Windows CE, however, would allow this because it has a separate name pool for each object type. This can cause havoc if you're trying to keep code portable, so it is probably best to avoid using this "feature."

Another portability issue that crops up on Windows CE is that kernel object handles are not specific to a given process, but instead are common across all processes. This enables you to create an event in one process, pass that handle to another process, and have things work correctly. Windows NT and Windows 95 don't allow this, choosing to restrict handles to the process in which they were created.

Apart from the obvious portability issues, Windows CE's handle-sharing scheme has bigger problems. If you create an object and pass the handle to another process, the reference count is not incremented. This means that if the other process closes the handle, the object will be destroyed even though the originating process hasn't closed the handle. This can lead to nasty race conditions and scenarios that are very difficult to reproduce, so it's better to stick with portable constructs and use a named object to provide access from multiple processes.

Typical scenarios that share kernel objects across processes use the Create API (such as CreateMutex) for the first process and the Open API (such as OpenMutex) for subsequent ones. Unfortunately, Windows CE does not implement the Open APIs, relying on the Create API to provide both create and open features (which it does on NT as well). To distinguish which operation occurred, you test the GetLastError value like this:

```
HANDLE hMutex = CreateMutex(NULL, FALSE, "KWYJIBO");
If ( hMutex && (GetLastError() == ERROR_ALREADY_EXISTS) )
{
    // the mutex was opened, not created
}
else if ( hMutex )
{
    // the mutex was created
}
else
{
    // the sky is falling - must be a Y2K issue…
}
```

When you are porting code to Windows CE, sometimes it's nice to provide an implementation of an open function to minimize changes. (For an example of how it can be done, see this lesson's exercise section.)

To obtain ownership on a kernel object, you have to use one of the Win32 wait functions. Windows CE provides implementations of WaitForSingleObject, WaitForMultipleObjects, and MsgWaitForMultipleObjectsEx. The caveat here is that WaitForMultipleObjects and MsgWaitForMultipleObjectsEx support waiting only for any one handle to become signaled and not all of them. If you request that all handles be waited on, the function will immediately return with the error code ERROR_INVALID_PARAMETER. If the timing constraints on your application are not too strict, you can simply call WaitForSingleObject on each handle in a loop. It's not exactly the same thing, but works for most situations.

Now, let's mull over the details of each synchronization kernel object primitive.

As mentioned previously, a mutex provides similar functionality to a critical section, limiting access to a block of code to a single thread at a time. To acquire the mutex, you use WaitForSingleObject, and ownership is ended with ReleaseMutex. The biggest benefit of a mutex over a critical section is that, because a mutex is a kernel object, it can be used with multiple processes instead of only the process in which it is created. If you don't have to synchronize across multiple processes, you are much better off using a critical section for performance reasons.

Figure 11.1 compares the speed of repeatedly acquiring and releasing a critical section with that of acquiring and releasing a mutex on a Handheld PC Pro with a StrongARM processor. As you can see, for more than nearly 2,000 iterations, using a critical section is much more efficient.

FIGURE 11.1

Mutex versus critical section performance comparison.

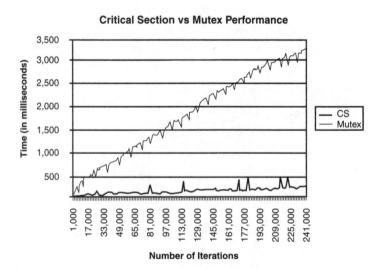

Events are a much more flexible feature than mutexes and provide you with a way to notify other threads when an arbitrary condition is met. Other than the previously mentioned naming problem in v2.0, events under Windows CE work the same as their Windows NT and Windows 95 counterparts. Table 11.1 (courtesy of Johnson Hart, author of *Win32 System Programming*) shows the four behaviors, based on whether an event is manual or auto reset and whether SetEvent or PulseEvent is used to signal it.

TABLE 11.1 Event Behaviors

Event	Auto Reset	Manual Reset
SetEvent	Exactly one thread is released. If none are currently waiting on the event, the first thread to wait on it in the future will be released immediately.	All currently waiting threads are released. The event remains signaled until reset by some thread.
PulseEvent	Exactly one thread is released, but only if a thread is currently waiting on the event.	All currently waiting threads are released, and the event is then reset.

Unlike mutexes and events, semaphores and waitable timers are not supported on Windows CE. Luckily, semaphores aren't difficult to simulate using mutexes and events (I'll present an implementation this hour). Waitable timers, on the other hand, are more difficult to simulate. You can, however, use the Windows CE Notification APIs (covered in depth in Hour 19, "Managing Power and System Resources") to get some of the functionality.

Semaphores are a way of restricting access to a resource to a limited number of users. Although Windows CE doesn't natively support them, it is possible to simulate the same functionality using mutexes and events. Johnson Hart, author of *Win32 System Programming*, wrote just such a system; it closely mimics the native Win32 interfaces and is freely available. The full source code is available on the CD-ROM, and Listing 11.2 presents an example.

LISTING 11.2 A Sample Use of Johnson Hart's Semaphore Implementation for Windows CE

```
1: /*
2:    Test Windows CE semaphore emulation
3: */
4:
5: #define STRICT
6: #include <windows.h>
7: #include <tchar.h>
8: #include <stdlib.h>
9: #include "wcesem.h"
10:
11: SYNCHHANDLE g_hSem = NULL;
12:
13: #define MAX_THREADS 64
14: #define QUEUE_SIZE  5
15:
```

continues

LISTING **11.2**   continued

```
16: long g_iCurSize = 0;
17:
18:
19:
20:
21: void DebugOut(LPTSTR psz, ...)
22: {
23:     TCHAR    szbuf[256];
24:     va_list arglist;
25:
26:     va_start(arglist, psz);
27:
28:     wvsprintf(szbuf, psz, arglist);
29:     OutputDebugString(szbuf);
30:
31:     va_end(arglist);
32:
33: }
34:
35:
36: UINT WINAPI PrintJob(PVOID pv)
37: {
38:     long lPrev;
39:
40:     WaitForSemaphoreCE(g_hSem, INFINITE);
41:
42:     InterlockedIncrement(&g_iCurSize);
43:
44:     DebugOut(_T("%08lX - entered queue: size = %d\n"),
45:             GetCurrentThreadId(), g_iCurSize );
46:
47:     Sleep(500);  // print job....
48:
49:     InterlockedDecrement(&g_iCurSize);
50:
51:     DebugOut(_T("%08lX - exited queue: size = %d\n"),
52:             GetCurrentThreadId(), g_iCurSize );
53:
54:     ReleaseSemaphoreCE(g_hSem, 1, &lPrev);
55:
56:     return 0;
57: }
58:
59: int WINAPI WinMain( HINSTANCE hInstance, HINSTANCE hPrevInstance,
60:                     LPTSTR lpCmdLine, int nCmdShow )
61: {
62:     HANDLE hThreads[MAX_THREADS];
63:     UINT dwTID;
64:     int  i;
```

```
65:
66:       g_hSem = CreateSemaphoreCE(NULL, QUEUE_SIZE,
67:                                  QUEUE_SIZE, NULL );
68:
69:       for ( i = 0; i < MAX_THREADS; i++ )
70:           hThreads[i] =  CreateThread(NULL, 0, PrintJob,
71:                                     NULL, 0, &dwTID);
72:
73:       // CE does not support the all handles version of
74:       // WaitForMultipleObjects, so we do each handle in
75:       // sequence instead
76:       for ( i = 0; i < MAX_THREADS; i++ )
77:           WaitForSingleObject(hThreads[i], INFINITE);
78:
79:       CloseSynchHandle(g_hSem);
80:
81:       return 0;
82: }
```

The code simulates a simple print queue, limiting the number of concurrently submitted jobs to QUEUE_SIZE. Although the names of the semaphore functions are different, their signatures are identical to the Win32 API functions, which makes it much easier to port code. Notice that you have to use WaitForSemaphoreCE instead of WaitForSingleObject because the handle returned by CreateSemaphoreCE is a proprietary structure and not a kernel object handle.

Although it is rarely used for thread synchronization, the SuspendThread API can be useful for many other situations. Unfortunately, Windows CE does not support suspending a thread if it is currently executing a system call. By *system call*, I mean any exported Win32 API or internal operating system function. This means that threads that sit in a tight loop calling OutputDebugString or that are synchronizing with a call to WaitForSingleObject are almost impossible to suspend.

A couple remedies exist for some, but not all, situations. If a thread is sitting in a tight loop around a system call, there is still an opportunity to suspend it between calls. Attempting the suspension multiple times, like this, will increase your chances:

```
BOOL AttemptToSuspendThread(HANDLE hThread)
{
    BOOL bSuccess = FALSE;
    const int MAX_TRIES = 5;

    for ( int i = 0; i < MAX_TRIES && !bSuccess; i++ )
    {
        bSuccess = (SuspendThread(hThread) != -1);
        if ( !bSuccess )
            Sleep;     // give up current thread's time slice
    }
```

11

```
    return bSuccess;
}
```

Granted, this is not recommended multithreading practice and still has a probability of failure, but it is better than the more naive single-attempt approach.

Also, if you have the opportunity to redesign the code, you should consider having the thread that you are suspending check a Win32 manual reset event at the top of its control loop. This would enable you to pause the thread's execution by setting the event state to nonsignaled when you want it to stop execution.

Thread Local Storage Support

Thread local storage (TLS) is a very useful feature of Win32 and enables you to associate state information with a thread without having to manage a thread-safe list yourself.

There are two kinds of TLS: static and dynamic. Dynamic TLS is managed with `TlsAlloc`, `TlsFree`, `TlsGetValue`, and `TlsSetValue`. It is fully supported by Windows CE and has the same behavior as its Windows NT counterpart. The capacity is the same in both implementations as well, supporting up to 64 slots per process.

Static TLS, specified with the `__declspec(thread)` attribute in variable declarations, is not supported on Windows CE. Although v2.0 compilers for some processors (for example, SH3 and 80x86) accepted the syntax without error, the attribute was just ignored, and the data was not actually kept on a per-thread basis. This—and some misinformation in widely read magazine articles about Windows CE development—has led to some confusion about Windows CE's static TLS support, but the bottom line is that it is not currently supported and you should use dynamic TLS instead.

Measurement and Profiling

When your application's performance or memory consumption isn't meeting its goals, how can you find out where the problem spots are? Unfortunately, there aren't as many tools for Windows CE as there are for Windows NT and Windows 95, but Windows CE provides a few nuggets that enable you to track application behavior.

Although a simple profiling system could be built on the `GetThreadTimes` and `GetProcessTimes` APIs, they are, unfortunately, not supported on Windows CE. However, if you have Platform Builder and are willing to create a specialized kernel, you can choose from three types of profiling: Monte Carlo, Instrumented Kernel, and Hardware-Assisted. Detailed information on how to utilize these profiling features is beyond the scope this book, but is available in Jean Gareau's article "Profiling Support in Windows CE" in the Spring 1999 issue of the *Windows CE Tech Journal*. You can read it online at http://www.cetj.com/archives/9903/f3.shtml.

Tracking a process's memory consumption is much easier and can be done without having to resort to building a special version of the OS. ToolHelp provides the ability to walk the list of memory heaps and track the blocks that belong to a specific process. You can then simply add up the size of each block to find the amount of memory taken up by the heaps. Listing 11.3 shows sample code for an application that does exactly this.

LISTING 11.3   Using the `ToolHelp` Functions to Display a Process's Memory Footprint

```
 1: /*
 2:     Display the size of the memory heaps for all running processes
 3: */
 4:
 5: #include <windows.h>
 6: #include <tlhelp32.h>
 7:
 8: void DebugOut(LPTSTR psz, ...)
 9: {
10:     TCHAR    szbuf[256];
11:     va_list arglist;
12:
13:     va_start(arglist, psz);
14:
15:     wvsprintf(szbuf, psz, arglist);
16:     OutputDebugString(szbuf);
17:
18:     va_end(arglist);
19:
20: }
21:
22: void DumpProcessHeapSizes(HANDLE hSnapShot, LPPROCESSENTRY32 ppeinfo)
23: {
24:     HEAPLIST32 hl = { sizeof(HEAPLIST32) };
25:
26:     // print the EXE name and process id
27:     DebugOut(_T("%s (%08X):\n"),
28:             ppeinfo->szExeFile,
29:             ppeinfo->th32ProcessID);
30:
31:     HANDLE hHeapSnapShot;
32:     hHeapSnapShot = CreateToolhelp32Snapshot(TH32CS_SNAPHEAPLIST,
33:                                     ppeinfo->th32ProcessID);
34:
35:     if ( Heap32ListFirst(hHeapSnapShot, &hl) )
```

continues

LISTING 11.3 continued

```
36:     {
37:         do
38:         {
39:             HEAPENTRY32 he = { sizeof(HEAPENTRY32) };
40:             DWORD       dwHeapSize  = 0;
41:
42:             if ( Heap32First(hHeapSnapShot, &he,
43:                             ppeinfo->th32ProcessID,
44:                             hl.th32HeapID) )
45:             {
46:                 do
47:                 {
48:                     dwHeapSize += he.dwBlockSize;
49:                 } while ( Heap32Next(hHeapSnapShot, &he) );
50:
51:                 DebugOut(_T("\tHeap %d: %d bytes"),
52:                         hl.th32HeapID,
53:                         dwHeapSize);
54:
55:                 // indicate the default heap
56:                 if ( (hl.dwFlags & HF32_DEFAULT) == HF32_DEFAULT )
57:                     DebugOut(_T(" (default)\n"));
58:                 else
59:                     DebugOut(_T("\n"));
60:             }
61:             else
62:                 DebugOut(_T("\tError getting size of heap %d\n"),
63:                         hl.th32HeapID);
64:
65:         } while ( Heap32ListNext(hHeapSnapShot, &hl) );
66:     }
67:     else
68:         DebugOut(_T("\tNo heaps available\n"));
69:
70:     CloseHandle(hHeapSnapShot);
71: }
72:
73:
74: int WINAPI WinMain(    HINSTANCE hInstance,
75:                        HINSTANCE hPrevInstance,
76:                        LPTSTR    lpCmdLine,
77:                        int       nCmdShow)
78: {
79:     HANDLE hSnapShot = CreateToolhelp32Snapshot(TH32CS_SNAPPROCESS,
80:                                                 0);
81:
82:     if ( hSnapShot )
83:     {
84:         PROCESSENTRY32 peinfo = { sizeof(PROCESSENTRY32) };
```

```
 85:
 86:          if ( Process32First(hSnapShot, &peinfo) )
 87:          {
 88:              do
 89:              {
 90:                  // skip the current process...
 91:                  if ( peinfo.th32ProcessID != GetCurrentProcessId() )
 92:                      DumpProcessHeapSizes(hSnapShot, &peinfo);
 93:
 94:              } while ( Process32Next(hSnapShot, &peinfo) );
 95:          }
 96:          else
 97:              DebugOut(_T("Error retrieving process list\n"));
 98:
 99:          CloseHandle(hSnapShot);
100:      }
101:      else
102:          DebugOut(_T("Error creating ToolHelp snapshot\n"));
103:
104:
105:
106:      return 0;
107: }
```

The information is displayed with OutputDebugString for maximum portability between Windows CE devices and operating system versions. To see the text, run the program under the Visual C++ debugger or use the DBWinCE utility from Hour 23, "Debugging CE Applications with Visual C++."

11

Summary

Whew! We've covered a lot of ground this hour. I started off discussing some general differences in the behavior of threads and processes between Windows CE and Windows NT and 95. I then discussed how thread synchronization differs and how to work around some missing features in Windows CE (such as semaphores). Finally, I cleared up some confusion on Windows CE's TLS support and discussed some options for profiling and measuring a process's memory consumption.

Q&A

Q How can I increase the stack space available to my process?

A On Windows CE 2.0, all threads have a fixed size stack of 58KB each. For v2.1 or greater, use the /stack switch when you link your executable or DLL.

Q How can I use semaphores in Windows CE?

A Semaphores are not in the Win32 API for Windows CE, but Johnson Hart has a freely available replacement that works on Windows CE. See Listing 11.2 for an example and the CD-ROM for the implementation.

Workshop

The Workshop is designed to help you anticipate possible questions, review what you've learned, and begin thinking ahead about putting your knowledge into practice. The answers to the quiz are in Appendix A, "Answers."

Quiz

1. How many thread priorities are available on Windows CE?

2. How many concurrent processes can run on Windows CE?

3. Why do you need thread safety to do a simple integer increment (such as `InterlockedIncrement`)?

4. What is the difference between dynamic and static TLS? Which one should you use on Windows CE?

5. What is the difference between a mutex and a critical section?

6. Are kernel object names case-sensitive?

7. How much virtual memory space does each process have on Windows CE?

8. Can `WaitForMultipleObjects` be used to wait for more than one handle to be signaled?

9. How is the scope of kernel object handles different on Windows CE than on Windows NT or 95? Should you make use of it in your applications?

10. What's the best way to implement thread suspension on Windows CE?

Exercises

1. Implement a completely thread-safe `OpenEvent` function using the `CreateEvent` API.

2. Describe what priority inversion is and how Windows CE solves it.

HOUR 12

Controlling Interprocess Communication

Sharing data between processes is a fundamental problem that almost any nontrivial application will eventually have to conquer. In the old days, when the operating system was one big address space, life was easy. You could freely pass pointers and directly read or write data anywhere. Win32's introduction of a separate virtual address space for each process complicates matters, but also provides methods that can be utilized to achieve the same goal.

In this hour, you will learn

- How interprocess communication (IPC) works in Win32 and how it is different on Windows CE
- The benefits and drawbacks of all the available methods
- Windows CE–specific issues

Windows CE Support for Win32 IPC Features

Win32 provides the following 10 IPC methods:

- The Clipboard
- WinSock
- ReadProcessMemory and WriteProcessMemory
- Memory-mapped files (MMF)
- Shared data segments
- WM_COPYDATA
- Dynamic data exchange (DDE)
- Remote Procedure Calls (RPC)
- Named and anonymous pipes
- Mailslots

The last four methods in the list (DDE, RPC, pipes, and mailslots) are not supported on Windows CE, but it's still a good idea to know something about them. If you ever have to port an application that utilizes them, it will be much easier to pick an alternative solution if you understand what they do. After I cover the other six items, I'll return to these four and discuss how you can simulate them.

The *Clipboard* is managed by a set of Win32 APIs and is shared by all processes in the operating system. Windows CE doesn't support the Clipboard viewer functions and provides only a subset of the built-in Clipboard formats. All the other features, including custom formats, are supported. Although the Clipboard is one of the most obvious and easiest methods of IPC, it is rarely used in practice for anything other than the most trivial applications. This is because there is no way to control access to the data, and a simple user cut-and-paste action can easily cause things to go haywire. You will revisit the Clipboard APIs in the section titled "Clipboard Issues" in this lesson.

WinSock is the Windows implementation of the UNIX sockets interface for network communications. Although sockets are usually used to communicate with other nodes on a network, they can also be used to communicate between processes on the same machine. The capability to use a single method that is scalable from interprocess communication to network communication is extremely useful for applications such as database front ends. I'll cover WinSock in depth in Hour 13, "WinSock and Serial Communications."

ReadProcessMemory and WriteProcessMemory are low-level Win32 APIs that allow you to manipulate memory in another process's address space. They are typically used by debuggers and other system utilities and are not well suited as a general IPC mechanism. Both are fully supported on Windows CE and work identically to their desktop counterparts, with the exception that you can't write to ROM addresses.

Memory-mapped files (MMF) are probably the most commonly used Win32 mechanism for IPC. The idea behind them is that a "file" can be treated as a pointer to a memory buffer, and changes are automatically reflected on disk. This provides a very convenient method for doing file I/O, as well as IPC, and beats the pants off the old `ReadFile` and `WriteFile` methods. Memory-mapped files can also be used as generic memory buffers by utilizing the operating system paging file instead of a specific user file. I'll discuss Windows CE's MMF implementation and give some sample code in the section "Memory-Mapped File Issues" in this lesson.

Every executable file on Win32—whether it be an EXE, DLL, or some custom extension—is made up of sections. There are standard sections for code and data, but users can add their own custom sections as well. When Win32 loads the same file into memory multiple times (for example, multiple EXEs using the same DLL), the default behavior is to share code sections across all processes and give each process its own copy of the data sections. For example, this is why global variables are unique in multiple instances of the same program. However, when custom sections are included, the user has full control over their behavior. A *shared data segment* is created by specifying a custom data section that is common to all processes. I'll give some sample code for doing this and discuss some Windows CE quirks in the section "Shared Data Segment Issues."

If your application is based on a message loop, like the majority of Windows CE applications, it is sometimes easiest to do IPC by sending a window message. Win32 provides the `WM_COPYDATA` message for exactly this purpose and allows you to send an arbitrarily large block of data across process boundaries. There's a gotcha on Windows CE, though, and I'll discuss it in the section "`WM_COPYDATA` Issues."

12

Win32 IPC Features Not Supported on Windows CE

Now that I've touched on all the supported IPC mechanisms, I'll discuss how to work around the four methods that Windows CE doesn't support.

Dynamic data exchange (DDE) started out as an update notification mechanism on old Windows 3.1 systems and graduated to a simple form of IPC with the advent of Win32. It has gradually been replaced by more sophisticated systems such as COM. Simulating the basics of DDE doesn't necessarily require COM, though. An event and an MMF will do nicely. Whenever the data changes, it is written to the file, and the event is signaled. Readers wait on the event and, when it is signaled, read the update from the file.

Remote procedure calls (RPC) are a general mechanism for making a function call in another process or machine on a network. The Windows CE Remote API is a good example of an RPC from a desktop machine to a Windows CE device and is covered in detail in Hour 20, "Communicating with the Desktop." Windows CE doesn't have built-in support for RPC, as Windows NT does, but it gives you all the underlying tools for implementing it yourself. The basic idea is to have a "stub" application on each machine and make a Winsock connection to transfer requests and replies. The same method can be applied between two processes with a separate thread that handles the Winsock transactions.

Pipes (both named and anonymous) and *mailslots* are not as easy to emulate as DDE and RPC. They are both essentially special types of files and require operating system support to work correctly. Depending on how they are being used, you can sometimes get similar functionality with Winsock or normal file I/O.

Clipboard Issues

Edit controls have built-in capability to perform cut, copy, and paste actions by responding to the WM_CUT, WM_COPY, and WM_PASTE messages, respectively, but it's also possible to manually put data on the Clipboard and retrieve it.

Listing 12.1 shows how to transfer a text buffer to the Clipboard.

LISTING 12.1 An Example of Using Clipboard APIs

```
 1: /*
 2:     Put a text buffer on the Clipboard
 3: */
 4: BOOL PutTextOnClipboard(HWND hwnd, LPSTR pszText)
 5: {
 6:     BOOL bSuccess = FALSE;
 7:
 8:     if ( IsWindow(hwnd) && OpenClipboard(hwnd) )
 9:     {
10:         EmptyClipboard();
11:
12:         LPTSTR pszCopy = (LPTSTR)LocalAlloc(LMEM_MOVEABLE,
            ➥ (_tcslen(pszText)+1) * sizeof(TCHAR));
13:
14:         if ( pszCopy )
```

```
15:        {
16:                _tcscpy(pszCopy, pszText);
17:
18:                UINT uiFormat;
19: #ifdef UNICODE
20:                uiFormat = CF_UNICODETEXT;
21: #else
22:                uiFormat = CF_TEXT;
23: #endif
24:                bSuccess = (SetClipboardData(uiFormat, pszCopy) != NULL);
25:
26:            // if the Clipboard doesn't own the data, we need to free it
27:            if ( bSuccess == FALSE )
28:                LocalFree(pszCopy);
29:        }
30:
31:        CloseClipboard();
32:    }
33:
34:    return bSuccess;
35: }
```

There are a few interesting items to note about Listing 12.1. Although the documentation states that the OpenClipboard API allows a NULL parameter, this does not work for Windows CE. The call, and all subsequent Clipboard calls, will still return TRUE, but the data will not end up on the Clipboard. Instead, Windows CE requires a valid window handle for the OpenClipboard call and, additionally, the window must have been created by the process calling OpenClipboard. If the window was created by another process, you can put data on the Clipboard, but any paste operation to remove it will cause a series of access violation exceptions and require a warm boot of the device.

Also, the desktop requires that the data being put on the Clipboard be allocated with GlobalAlloc. Windows CE doesn't support GlobalAlloc, so LocalAlloc with the LMEM_MOVEABLE flag should be used. If PutTextOnClipboard succeeds, the Clipboard now owns the data, and it should not be freed by you—that's why you call LocalFree only if bSuccess is false on line 27.

Memory-Mapped File Issues

On desktop Win32 platforms, any valid file handle can be used with CreateFileMapping and MapViewOfFile to read and write the file through a pointer instead of file I/O routines. Windows CE, on the other hand, can only memory map a file that was opened with the CreateFileForMapping API; any other file handle results in an error return value of ERROR_INVALID_HANDLE. The return type and parameter list of CreateFileForMapping is identical to CreateFile, so porting code is usually a snap.

12

Additionally, support for writeable MMFs was not added to Windows CE until recently with version 2.1. In previous versions, `CreateFileForMapping`, `CreateFileMapping`, and `MapViewOfFile` all return `INVALID_PARAMETER` if write access is requested.

Listing 12.2 shows an example of using MMFs as an IPC mechanism. The full project for the Windows CE Toolkit for Visual C++ 6 is on the CD-ROM.

LISTING 12.2   An Example of Using a Memory-Mapped File

```
 1: /*
 2:     Sample code to demonstrate sharing data between
 3:     processes with memory-mapped files
 4: */
 5:
 6: #include <windows.h>
 7: #include <windowsx.h>
 8: #include "resource.h"
 9:
10:
11: #define MAX_TEXT_DATA_CHARS   256
12: #define MAX_TEXT_DATA_SIZE    (MAX_TEXT_DATA_CHARS*sizeof(TCHAR))
13:
14: static HANDLE g_hMMF = NULL;
15: static LPTSTR g_pszData = NULL;
16:
17: /*
18:     Close the MMF handle and release the data view
19: */
20: BOOL CloseMMF()
21: {
22:     if ( g_pszData )
23:     {
24:         UnmapViewOfFile(g_pszData);
25:         g_pszData = NULL;
26:     }
27:
28:     if ( g_hMMF )
29:     {
30:         CloseHandle(g_hMMF);
31:         g_hMMF = NULL;
32:     }
33:
34:     return TRUE;
35: }
36:
37:
38: /*
39:     Open the MMF and data view. If it is not already opened by
40:     someone, initialize the data to all zeroes
```

```
41: */
42: BOOL OpenMMF()
43: {
44:     BOOL bSuccess = FALSE;
45:
46:     g_hMMF = CreateFileMapping(INVALID_HANDLE_VALUE,
47:                                NULL,
48:                                PAGE_READWRITE,
49:                                0,
50:                                MAX_TEXT_DATA_SIZE,
51:                                _T("TEXT_DATA"));
52:
53:     if ( g_hMMF )
54:     {
55:         BOOL bOpened = (GetLastError() == ERROR_ALREADY_EXISTS);
56:
57:         g_pszData = (LPTSTR)MapViewOfFile(g_hMMF,
58:                                           FILE_MAP_READ | FILE_MAP_WRITE,
59:                                           0,
60:                                           0,
61:                                           MAX_TEXT_DATA_SIZE);
62:
63:         // If we have a pointer and we created the MMF object,
64:         // initialize the data to all zeroes
65:         if ( g_pszData && (bOpened == FALSE))
66:             memset(g_pszData, 0, MAX_TEXT_DATA_SIZE);
67:     }
68:
69:     bSuccess = (g_hMMF && g_pszData);
70:
71:     if ( !bSuccess )
72:         CloseMMF();
73:
74:     return bSuccess;
75: }
76:
77: /*
78:     Put the MMF data into an edit box
79: */
80: BOOL TransferMMFToEditBox(HWND hwndDlg)
81: {
82:     BOOL bSuccess = FALSE;
83:
84:     if ( g_pszData )
85:     {
86:         HWND hwndEdit = GetDlgItem(hwndDlg, IDC_TEXTDATA);
87:         bSuccess = SetWindowText(hwndEdit, (LPCTSTR)g_pszData);
88:     }
89:
90:     return bSuccess;
91: }
```

12

continues

LISTING 12.2 continued

```
 92:
 93: /*
 94:     Put the edit box data into an MMF
 95: */
 96: BOOL TransferEditBoxToMMF(HWND hwndDlg)
 97: {
 98:     BOOL bSuccess = FALSE;
 99:
100:     if ( g_pszData )
101:     {
102:         HWND hwndEdit = GetDlgItem(hwndDlg, IDC_TEXTDATA);
103:         if ( GetWindowTextLength(hwndEdit) )
104:             bSuccess = GetWindowText(hwndEdit, g_pszData, MAX_TEXT_
                ➥DATA_CHARS);
105:         else
106:         {
107:             _tcscpy(g_pszData, _T(""));
108:             bSuccess = TRUE;
109:         }
110:     }
111:
112:     return bSuccess;
113: }
114:
115:
116: // window function for the dialog box
117:
118: BOOL CALLBACK DlgProc(HWND hwndDlg, UINT uMsg,
119:                       WPARAM wParam, LPARAM lParam)
120: {
121:     BOOL bRet = FALSE;
122:
123:     switch( uMsg )
124:     {
125:         case WM_INITDIALOG:
126:             if ( OpenMMF() )
127:             {
128:                 Edit_LimitText(GetDlgItem(hwndDlg, IDC_TEXTDATA),
                    ➥ MAX_TEXT_DATA_SIZE);
129:                 TransferMMFToEditBox(hwndDlg);
130:             }
131:             else
132:             {
133:                 MessageBox(hwndDlg, _T("Could not initialize
                    ➥MMF data"), _T("Error"), MB_OK);
134:                 EndDialog(hwndDlg, IDCANCEL);
135:             }
136:             break;
137:
```

```
138:        case WM_COMMAND:
139:        {
140:            int     nID = LOWORD(wParam);
141:            int     wNotify = HIWORD(wParam);
142:            HWND    hwndCtl = (HWND)lParam;
143:
144:            if ( wNotify == BN_CLICKED )
145:            {
146:              switch( nID )
147:              {
148:                case IDCANCEL:
149:                    CloseMMF();
150:                    EndDialog(hwndDlg, IDCANCEL);
151:                    bRet = TRUE;
152:                    break;
153:
154:                case IDC_READDATA:
155:                    TransferMMFToEditBox(hwndDlg);
156:                    break;
157:
158:                case IDC_WRITEDATA:
159:                    TransferEditBoxToMMF(hwndDlg);
160:                    break;
161:              }
162:            }
163:         }
164:         break;
165:      }
166:
167:      return bRet;
168: }
169:
170:
171: int WINAPI WinMain(    HINSTANCE hInstance,
172:                        HINSTANCE hPrevInstance,
173:                        LPWSTR    lpCmdLine,
174:                        int       nCmdShow)
175: {
176:      DialogBox(hInstance, MAKEINTRESOURCE(IDD_MAINDLG),
177:              NULL, (DLGPROC)DlgProc);
178:      return 0;
179: }
```

12

Listing 12.2 requires Windows CE version 2.1 or greater because it uses writeable MMFs. Previous versions would return NULL from the call to CreateFileMapping and cause OpenMMF to return FALSE.

Shared Data Segment Issues

Listing 12.3 shows code for a DLL with a shared data segment that provides read and write routines that are mutually exclusive across all processes.

LISTING 12.3   An Example of a DLL with a Shared Data Segment

```
 1: #include <windows.h>
 2: #include <tchar.h>
 3:
 4:
 5: #pragma comment(linker, "-section:Shared,rws")
 6: #pragma data_seg("Shared")
 7:
 8: static DWORD g_dwData = 0;
 9:
10: #pragma data_seg()
11:
12:
13: /*
14:     Get the current value of the data in a
15:     shared data segment
16: */
17: DWORD GetSharedValue()
18: {
19:     HANDLE hMutex = CreateMutex(NULL, FALSE, _T("SHARED_DATA_MUTEX"));
20:     DWORD  dwData;
21:
22:     WaitForSingleObject(hMutex, INFINITE);
23:
24:     dwData = g_dwData;
25:
26:     ReleaseMutex(hMutex);
27:     CloseHandle(hMutex);
28:
29:     return dwData;
30: }
31:
32: /*
33:     Set the value of data in a shared data
34:     segment and return the old value.
35: */
36: DWORD SetSharedValue(DWORD dwNewData)
37: {
38:     HANDLE hMutex = CreateMutex(NULL, FALSE, _T("SHARED_DATA_MUTEX"));
39:     DWORD  dwData;
40:
41:     WaitForSingleObject(hMutex, INFINITE);
42:
```

```
43:      dwData = g_dwData;
44:      g_dwData = dwNewData;
45:
46:      ReleaseMutex(hMutex);
47:      CloseHandle(hMutex);
48:
49:      return dwData;
50: }
```

The key to a shared segment is how and where variables are declared. At the top of Listing 12.3, notice that you wrap the declaration g_dwData in three pragma statements. The first one tells the linker that you want to create a custom data segment called Shared and give it permissions of read, write, and shared. This will allow all processes to modify a common copy of the data and will override the default behavior of giving each process its own copy of the data segment. The next two pragma statements tell the linker what data to place into the segment. In this case, you only need g_dwData, but if you wanted more data to be in your shared segment, you would declare as many variables as you need between the data_seg pragma statements.

> A key point to note here is that the linker has a quirk about placing data in custom shared segments and requires them to be set to an initial value. If you omitted the initialization of g_dwData, it would be placed in the normal data segment, and each process would get its own separate copy.
>
> This step is easy to omit and can be the source of bugs that are very hard to find. Be sure that you initialize all variables in a shared segment, or it will come screaming back to haunt you (probably at a most inopportune time).

12

WM_COPYDATA Issues

WM_COPYDATA is a useful feature when you have to pass a block of memory across process boundaries. Windows CE, however, has a bug that requires you to be aware of how you allocate your COPYDATASTRUCT variable. If it is a local stack variable, everything works fine. Changing it to a global or static variable or dynamically allocating it from the heap, however, will cause the data in the COPYDATASTRUCT received by the target process's window procedure to be corrupt. All three members will have garbage values, and you will not be able to retrieve the data from the sender.

The workaround here should be obvious: Always use a local COPYDATASTRUCT stack variable with WM_COPYDATA. Listing 12.4 shows sample code using WM_COPYDATA under Windows CE.

LISTING 12.4   An Example of Using WM_COPYDATA for Windows CE

```
 1: /*
 2:     Send data to a specified HWND via WM_COPYDATA
 3: */
 4: BOOL SendData(HWND hwnd, LPBYTE pb, DWORD cb, DWORD dwUser)
 5: {
 6:     COPYDATASTRUCT cds;
 7:     BOOL bSuccess = FALSE;
 8:
 9:     if ( IsWindow(hwnd) )
10:     {
11:         cds.dwData = dwUser;
12:         cds.cbData = cb;
13:         cds.lpData = pb;
14:
15:         SendMessage(hwnd, WM_COPYDATA, (WPARAM)hwnd, (LPARAM)&cds);
16:         bSuccess = TRUE;
17:     }
18:
19:     return bSuccess;
20: }
```

WM_COPYDATA always requires the use of SendMessage instead of PostMessage. This is because the pointer to the COPYDATASTRUCT is used directly by the operating system and is not buffered during the message transfer. If PostMessage were used, the call would return without waiting for the recipient to process the data. In the example in Listing 12.4, this means that you could return from SendData before the procedure for the hwnd had a chance to process your message. Your COPYDATASTRUCT would then be a dangling pointer, and the hwnd procedure would cause an access violation when it tries to read the data. SendMessage avoids this by guaranteeing that the recipient is finished processing the message and arguments before returning control to the caller.

Summary

In this hour, I covered the variety of IPC methods provided by Win32 and their support on Windows CE. It's important to remember that coordinating communication between processes is no different than between threads and is just as crucial. See Hour 11, "Threads and Processes," for more information on the available synchronization tools.

Q&A

Q **Why is my call to `CreateFileMapping` failing with status code `ERROR_INVALID_HANDLE`?**

A Windows CE requires files for memory mapping to be opened with the `CreateFileForMapping` API instead of the `CreateFile` API.

Q **I declared a variable in a custom shared segment, but each separate process gets its own copy. How come?**

A The linker will place only initialized variables in a shared segment, even when they are declared between `pragma` statements. Make sure that any variables you want in the shared segment are being assigned an initial value.

Workshop

The Workshop is designed to help you anticipate possible questions, review what you've learned, and begin thinking ahead about putting your knowledge into practice. The answers to the quiz are in Appendix A, "Answers."

Quiz

1. How are the Clipboard APIs different on Windows CE?

2. How do I avoid problems with `WM_COPYDATA` on Windows CE?

3. How do I simulate DDE on Windows CE?

4. What is a Remote Procedure Call (RPC)?

Exercise

1. Listing 12.2 is not thread-safe because `OpenMMF`, `TransferMMFToEditBox`, and so on, use shared data without a mutex. Change the code so that it is thread-safe.

12

HOUR **13**

Winsock and Serial Communications

Communication with other computers is necessary on almost any operating system, but it is becoming increasingly important with the skyrocketing use of mobile devices. Because Windows CE is right in the thick of the mobile device market, communication features are a big key to its success.

Communication with other computers can be divided into three general categories: desktop partnerships, serial communication, and network communication. Windows CE's desktop partnership capabilities are discussed in Hour 20, "Communicating with the Desktop," and Hour 21, "Creating `ActiveSync` Modules."

In this hour, you will learn

- The details of serial and network communication on Windows CE
- An overview of WinSock support
- An overview of WinInet support

Serial Communications Support

The capability to communicate with the outside world over a serial port has been around almost as long as the modern computer. Devices of every size and variety—from a deeply embedded system with no user interface to a dedicated graphics desktop machine—usually have at least one serial port into which users can plug.

Windows CE is no different in this regard. Full support is provided for the typical serial port you would expect, as well as a special dedicated infrared (IR) serial port. I'll first cover how to use traditional serial ports and then delve into the features of the IR support.

Windows CE uses the same programming model for the serial port that is used on Windows NT. Each valid port is treated as a file with the name COMx:, in which x is a small integer number (usually between 1 and 4). The port is actually opened with a call to CreateFile, and read/write operations are performed with the ReadFile and WriteFile APIs. There are some key differences to reading and writing serial ports on Windows CE, as you will soon see.

After you have an open handle to a serial port, you can use a number of APIs for configuration and for querying information. Win32 supports exactly 23 communication APIs, and Windows CE currently implements 16 of them. As is the usual case in Windows CE, the APIs that are not supported have overlapping functionality and can easily be implemented with other methods.

Table 13.1 lists the Win32 communication APIs and the ones not supported on Windows CE.

TABLE 13.1 The Breakdown of API Functions

Supported on Windows CE	Not Supported on Windows CE
ClearCommBreak	BuildCommDCB
ClearCommError	BuildCommDCBAndTimeouts
EscapeCommFunction	SetDefaultCommConfig
GetCommMask	SetCommConfig
GetCommModemStatus	GetDefaultCommConfig
GetCommProperties	GetCommConfig
GetCommState	CommConfigDialog
GetCommTimeouts	
PurgeComm	
SetCommBreak	

Supported on Windows CE	Not Supported on Windows CE
SetCommMask	
SetCommState	
SetCommTimeouts	
SetupComm	
TransmitCommChar	
WaitCommEvent	

BuildCommDCB allows you to specify information about the serial port in a string and build up a device control block (DCB) from that information. BuildCommDCBAndTimeouts does the same thing and also specifies the serial port timeout configuration. Internally, these functions just parse the string and fill structure values. The same effect can be achieved by filling in the DCB and/or timeout structures by hand or manually parsing a configuration string.

The config APIs are essentially duplicates of the SetCommState/GetCommState APIs that allow vendors to provide their own custom information and a configuration dialog box. The net effect of these APIs can be achieved by directly using SetCommState/GetCommState instead.

When it comes to reading and writing a serial port, Windows CE requires some changes. To minimize delays encountered with blocking reads and writes, desktop Win32 platforms use a feature called *overlapped I/O*. This enables you to read and write a file simultaneously from multiple threads without having to wait for the operation to complete. Overlapped I/O also takes care of thread synchronization for you, allowing multiple reads and writes from any number of threads without the user having to use a mutex or a critical section.

Windows CE does not support the overlapped I/O features as they are implemented via CreateFile, ReadFile, and WriteFile. However, it does implement overlapped I/O inside the device driver that is used when the file APIs are actually reading and writing a serial port. This means that as long as you are talking to a serial port on Windows CE, you can treat it as an overlapped file and perform reads and writes from multiple threads without having to coordinate them.

Although this use of overlapped I/O in the serial driver solves multithreading issues, it does not address the issue of knowing when an event on the comm port has occurred. The WaitCommEvent API takes care of this. However, waiting for a character to arrive takes an unknown amount of time because you don't really know when it will be sent. Windows CE solves this problem by guaranteeing that a call to SetCommMask with a

13

mask of 0 will cause a blocking WaitCommEvent call to return, thus allowing a read thread to break out of its loop when no more data is available.

Another quirk of serial ports on Windows CE is the timeout settings. Some devices do not work well with nonzero values for the timeout multipliers or constants, and it is best to always set them to zero. In general, the best timeout values for Windows CE devices usually look like this:

```
CommTimeOuts.ReadIntervalTimeout = MAXDWORD;
CommTimeOuts.ReadTotalTimeoutMultiplier = 0;
CommTimeOuts.ReadTotalTimeoutConstant = 0;
CommTimeOuts.WriteTotalTimeoutMultiplier = 0;
CommTimeOuts.WriteTotalTimeoutConstant = 0 ;
```

To demonstrate the comm APIs on Windows CE, I ported the Win32 SDK TTY example. This application, CETTY, allows the user to configure and connect to a serial port, then echoes data read from the port, and sends any keystrokes typed over the port. If you connect another terminal program (for example, the SDK TTY example) to the serial port on the host side, the connection acts like a teletype, displaying typed keystrokes on the other machine. Figure 13.1 shows the port configuration dialog from CETTY.

FIGURE 13.1

The CETTY port configuration dialog.

The application spins off a read thread to monitor data coming in over the serial port. The thread uses the WaitCommEvent method already mentioned by reading the data, shown in Listing 13.1.

LISTING 13.1   Reading Data from the Serial Port

```
1: DWORD FAR PASCAL CommWatchProc( LPSTR lpData )
2: {
3:    DWORD      dwEvtMask ;
4:    NPTTYINFO  npTTYInfo = (NPTTYINFO) lpData ;
5:    int        nLength ;
6:    BYTE       abIn[ MAXBLOCK + 1] ;
```

```
 7:      if (!SetCommMask( COMDEV( npTTYInfo ), EV_RXCHAR ))
 8:      return ( FALSE ) ;
 9:      while ( CONNECTED( npTTYInfo ) )
10:    {
11:      dwEvtMask = 0 ;
12:        WaitCommEvent( COMDEV( npTTYInfo ), &dwEvtMask, NULL );
13:        if ((dwEvtMask & EV_RXCHAR) == EV_RXCHAR)
14:      {
15:        do
16:        {
17:          if (nLength = ReadCommBlock( hTTYWnd,
18:                                       (LPSTR) abIn,
19:                                       MAXBLOCK ))
20:          {
21:            WriteTTYBlock( hTTYWnd, (LPSTR) abIn, nLength ) ;
22:                // force a paint
23:            UpdateWindow( hTTYWnd ) ;
24:          }
25:        }
26:        while ( nLength > 0 ) ;
27:      }
28:    }
29:      // clear information in structure (kind of a "we're done" flag)
30:    THREADID( npTTYInfo ) = 0 ;
31:    HTHREAD( npTTYInfo ) = NULL ;
32:      return( TRUE ) ;
33: }
```

Although you're connected, you wait for data to arrive on the port via the SetCommMask and WaitCommEvent APIs. When WaitCommEvent returns with a mask indicating that data is available, you read the data and loop back around. When the user disconnects from the port or closes the application, you call SetCommMask with a mask of 0 to indicate that the connection is closed and the thread should exit.

Wireless Serial Communications Support

To provide the capability to connect devices over a wireless link, Windows CE supports communication over an IR serial port. The protocols used for this communication are not specific to Windows CE. Rather, the Infrared Data Association (IRDA) specifies and publishes them. Much information and many technical articles on IRDA are available at http://www.irda.org.

Windows CE's IR port can actually be used in three modes: raw, IrComm, and IrSock. I'll cover raw and IrComm in this section and revisit IrSock in the next section on WinSock support.

13

Raw mode is the underlying primitive on which the other two port modes are built. Under raw mode, the communication link is only *half-duplex*, meaning that data can be transmitted in only one direction at a time. It is up to you as the developer to detect read/write collisions and handle the inevitable dropped or corrupted bytes.

The port supporting raw IR mode is specified in the Port value under the Registry key `HKEY_LOCAL_MACHINE\Comm\IrDA`. The value is specified as an integer and should be used as the *x* in the `COMx:` filename for `CreateFile`. After you have an open handle, you use the `EscapeCommFunction` API to set it to raw mode. The `SETIR` function sets the port to raw mode, and the `CLRIR` function sets it back to normal serial mode.

IrComm is a much easier alternative to the primitive raw IR mode. It takes care of collision detection and buffering reads and writes. Raw mode and IrComm don't necessarily share the same port number; the IrComm port is specified in the Index value under the Registry key `HKEY_LOCAL_MACHINE\Drivers\Builtin\IrCOMM`. After the `CreateFile` call successfully returns, no other steps are necessary to configure IrComm. The port can be treated like a normal serial port. If you write data to an IrComm port that is not yet connected, it will buffer the data until a connection is available and then send the data on its way.

Unfortunately, IrComm acts like a typical serial port in that it does not guarantee that bits will not be dropped on their trip across the wire. The best way to accomplish guaranteed delivery is via WinSock, which is the next topic.

An Overview of WinSock Support

WinSock is the Windows adaptation of the UNIX network programming interface known as *sockets*. It has been around since the Windows 3.1 days and is the standard way of communicating with another machine across a network. Regardless of whether the machine is across the room or across the globe, the WinSock programming model is the same.

Over the years, WinSock has picked up many features and has a few backwards compatibility warts as well. Currently, Windows CE supports a subset of version 1.1 of the WinSock API, with one notable addition from the version 2.0 specification. I'll discuss the pluses and minuses of Windows CE's WinSock implementation and present some sample code that gets a socket connection to a desktop machine over Windows CE Services. In Hour 20, I'll cover alternative methods for communicating with the desktop machine.

One of the biggest differences about Windows CE's WinSock implementation is that it does not include support for any of the WSAAsync functions. These functions allow you to avoid blocking while a function is completing or waiting for input. Instead, they return control immediately, operate in the background, and notify you of completion via window messages. This strategy became necessary because Windows 3.1 does not have multiple threads; therefore, the user interface would not be updated properly if any function blocked for a long period of time. With the advent of a full multithreaded operating system such as Windows CE, window message notifications become unnecessary. For blocking reads or writes, you should spin off a separate thread rather than block your main thread and cause your user interface to suffer.

Another Windows CE–supported alternative to the WSAAsync view of the world is to set a socket as nonblocking. Windows CE supports the ioctlsocket API that allows you to change a socket to nonblocking via the FIONBIO command. When a socket operates in this mode, calls to methods that would block (for example, recv) instead return WSAEWOULDBLOCK via the WSAGetLastError API. This allows you to avoid blocking and retry the call later. The ioctlsocket API also allows you to query how much data is available to be read from the socket with the FIONREAD command.

Another feature left out of Windows CE's WinSock implementation is the database functions getservbyname, getservbyport, getprotobyname, and getprotobynumber. These functions allow you to map well-known protocol and service names to their port numbers, and vice versa.

As mentioned at the beginning of this section, Windows CE supports only one WinSock 2.0 method. This method, WSAIoctl, is used for specifying Secure Socket Layer (SSL) options such as digital certificate validation.

Now, take a look at some WinSock code for Windows CE. The example for this section is a client/server application that can be compiled for both the desktop and the device. The desktop side is the "server" in this case, and the device is the "client." The dialog box interfaces to the server and client components appear in Figures 13.2 and 13.3, respectively.

13

FIGURE **13.2**

The server dialog.

FIGURE **13.3**

The client dialog.

Clicking the Connect button on both sides establishes a connection and allows the user to type text in the edit box on the server and send it to the client. Although this example doesn't do anything exciting, the underlying techniques are used in many applications. You will see it again in Hour 20 and Hour 23, "Debugging Windows CE Applications with Visual C++."

The easiest way to accomplish this connection to a desktop machine is to establish a connection with Windows CE Services first. This initializes a Point-to-Point Protocol (PPP) or ethernet link and provides the basis for communicating over WinSock.

One of the first hurdles you must conquer is how to get the IP address of the desktop machine from the device. If the Windows CE Services connection is via PPP over the serial port, you can use the pseudo hostname ppp_peer to accomplish this. Using this string in a call to gethostbyname, like this,

```
PHOSTENT phe = gethostbyname("ppp_peer");
```

returns the address of the associated desktop computer to which you want to connect.

If the Windows CE Services connection is established over ethernet, there is no automatic way to find the desktop machine. The easiest method is to pass the hostname of the machine to the device-side application on the command line and use that in a call to gethostbyname.

Listings 13.2 and 13.3 show the functions that establish the server and client side of the socket connection.

LISTING 13.2   A Server-Side Connection Routine

```
 1: BOOL ServerConnect(SOCKET *psock, HWND hwndDlg)
 2: {
 3:     BOOL                fSuccess = FALSE;
 4:     int                 nRetries = 0;
 5:     struct sockaddr_in  addrT;
 6:     int                 nRet;
 7:
 8:     memset(&addrT, 0, sizeof(addrT));
 9:     addrT.sin_family = AF_INET;
10:     addrT.sin_port = htons(iSockPort);
11:     addrT.sin_addr.s_addr = INADDR_ANY;
12:
13:     nRet = bind(*psock, (PSOCKADDR)&addrT, sizeof(addrT));
14:
15:     if ( nRet != SOCKET_ERROR )
16:     {
17:         if ( listen(*psock, 0) != SOCKET_ERROR )
```

```
18:        {
19:            while ((fSuccess == FALSE) &&
20:                    (++nRetries < MAX_RETRIES))
21:            {
22:                struct fd_set  fds;
23:                struct timeval tv = { DELAY_TIME / 1000,
24:                                      DELAY_TIME % 1000 };
25:
26:                FD_ZERO (&fds);
27:                FD_SET (*psock, &fds);
28:
29:                if (select(0, &fds, NULL, NULL, &tv) == 0)
30:                {
31:                    continue;
32:                }
33:
34:                if (FD_ISSET(*psock, &fds))
35:                {
36:                    // accept the connection and close the
37:                    // socket we were listening to
38:                    SOCKET oldsock = *psock;
39:
40:                    *psock = accept(oldsock, NULL, 0);
41:                    closesocket(oldsock);
42:                    fSuccess = (*psock != INVALID_SOCKET);
43:                }
44:            }
45:        }
46:    }
47:
48:    return fSuccess;
49: }
```

LISTING 13.3   A Client-Side Connection Routine

```
1: BOOL ClientConnect(SOCKET *psock, HWND hwndDlg)
2: {
3:     BOOL               fSuccess = FALSE;
4:     int                nRetries = 0, nRet;
5:     struct sockaddr_in addrT;
6:     PHOSTENT           phe;
7:
8:     // ppp_peer returns the IP address of the host machine
9:     // if Windows CE Services is running or NULL otherwise
10:     if ( !(phe = gethostbyname("ppp_peer")) )
11:     {
12:         MessageBox(hwndDlg, _T("Error"),
13:                     _T("Can't get ppp_peer"), MB_OK);
14:
15:         return FALSE;
```

continues

13

LISTING 13.3 continued

```
16:     }
17:
18:     for (fSuccess = FALSE;
19:          nRetries < MAX_RETRIES && !fSuccess;
20:          nRetries++, Sleep(DELAY_TIME)
21:          )
22:     {
23:         memset(&addrT, 0, sizeof(addrT));
24:         addrT.sin_family = AF_INET;
25:         addrT.sin_port = htons(iSockPort);
26:         addrT.sin_addr.s_addr = *(long *)phe->h_addr;
27:
28:         nRet = connect(*psock, (PSOCKADDR)&addrT, sizeof(addrT));
29:
30:         if ( nRet != SOCKET_ERROR)
31:         {
32:             fSuccess = TRUE;
33:         }
34:     }
35:
36:     return fSuccess;
37: }
```

The code is mostly standard WinSock mechanics, so I won't go over it in detail.

I've only scratched the surface of what WinSock can accomplish. If you'd like to learn more about WinSock development, the book *Window Sockets Network Programming* by Bob Quinn and Dave Shute is a great tutorial and reference. Bob Quinn also maintains a WWW site for information on the Windows CE WinSock implementation at http://www.sockets.com/ws_wince.htm.

Using IrSock

Another common need is the communication between two Windows CE devices rather than between a device and a desktop machine. IrSock is designed to meet this need and provides a way to utilize wireless infrared communication with familiar socket interfaces.

IrSock has a couple drawbacks. It does not support UDP datagrams or SSL encryption. You can visualize the IR port as an underpowered TV remote control—it transmits only a couple feet, and the devices must be pointed toward each other to establish and maintain a connection.

Establishing an IrSock connection differs from a regular socket connection in two fundamental ways: socket creation and addressing.

Socket creation is an easy one to solve—just replace the AF_INET constant with AF_IRDA in all calls to the socket API. This constant is defined in the af_irda.h header file, which you have to include. This tells WinSock that this socket will be treated as an infrared socket instead of the typical "over the wire" type.

Modifying your code to utilize IrSock addressing is a little more difficult. Instead of the typical socket strategy of an IP address and a port number, IrSock uses a numeric device ID and a service name. The service name can be any arbitrary string up to 25 characters long, but it must be the same on both sides of the connection, as you will see in the sample code.

Rather than use ppp_peer or a hostname to determine the address of the other device, IrSock provides a method for dynamically enumerating all devices in proximity and retrieving their addresses. This enumeration is done by calling getsockopt like this:

```
char            szDevice[256];
DWORD           dwSize = sizeof(szDevice);
DEVICELIST      *pDevList = (DEVICELIST*)szDevice;
nRet = getsockopt(sockHandle,

            SOL_IRLMP,

            IRLMP_ENUMDEVICES,

            szDevice, &dwSize);
```

sockHandle had to be created as an AF_IRDA socket, or the call will fail. On success, getsockopt will return 0 and fill the szDevice buffer with as many available IRDA_DEVICE_INFO structures as it can. By casting the buffer to a DEVICELIST pointer, you can enumerate each entry and determine the address to connect to. If no devices are available, pDevList->numDevice will be 0.

After a device has been detected and you have its IRDA_DEVICE_INFO structure, you can use this information to fill in a SOCKADDR_IRDA address. The irdaAddressFamily member should always be set to AF_IRDA, and the device ID is directly copied from the IRDA_DEVICE_INFO entry. The service name is specific to the application and is usually just a constant string in the source code.

To show IrSock code in action, I modified the socket test application from the preceding section to use IrSock. The full irsocktest code and a Windows CE Toolkit for Visual C++ 6.0 workspace are available on the CD-ROM.

Porting the code to IrSock was a very easy task. After changing all the socket API calls to use AF_IRDA, I modified the server and client connection loops as shown in Listings 13.4 and 13.5, respectively.

13

LISTING 13.4   An IrSock Client-Side Connection Routine

```
 1: BOOL ClientConnect(SOCKET *psock, HWND hwndDlg)
 2: {
 3:     BOOL              fSuccess = FALSE;
 4:     int               nRetries = 0, nRet;
 5:     SOCKADDR_IRDA     addrT;
 6:     char              szDevice[256];
 7:     DWORD             dwSize = sizeof(szDevice);
 8:     DEVICELIST        *pDevList = (DEVICELIST*)szDevice;
 9:
10:
11:     for (fSuccess = FALSE;
12:          nRetries < MAX_RETRIES && !fSuccess;
13:          nRetries++, Sleep(DELAY_TIME)
14:          )
15:     {
16:         // find an IrSock server to connect to
17:         nRet = getsockopt(*psock,
                              SOL_IRLMP,
                              IRLMP_ENUMDEVICES,
                              szDevice,
                              &dwSize);
18:         if ( (nRet != 0) || (pDevList->numDevice == 0))
19:             continue;
20:
21:         memset(&addrT, 0, sizeof(addrT));
22:         addrT.irdaAddressFamily = AF_IRDA;
23:         memcpy(addrT.irdaDeviceID, pDevList->Device[0].irdaDeviceID, 4);
24:         strcpy(addrT.irdaServiceName, IR_SOCK_APP);
25:
26:         nRet = connect(*psock, (PSOCKADDR)&addrT, sizeof(addrT));
27:
28:         if ( nRet != SOCKET_ERROR)
29:         {
30:             fSuccess = TRUE;
31:         }
32:     }
33:
34:     return fSuccess;
35: }
```

LISTING 13.5   An IrSock Server-Side Connection Routine

```
 1: BOOL ServerConnect(SOCKET *psock, HWND hwndDlg)
 2: {
 3:     BOOL              fSuccess = FALSE;
 4:     int               nRetries = 0;
 5:     SOCKADDR_IRDA     addrT;
 6:     int               nRet;
```

```
 7:
 8:        memset(&addrT, 0, sizeof(addrT));
 9:        addrT.irdaAddressFamily = AF_IRDA;
10:        memset(&addrT.irdaDeviceID, 0, 4);
11:        strcpy(addrT.irdaServiceName, IR_SOCK_APP);
12:
13:        nRet = bind(*psock, (PSOCKADDR)&addrT, sizeof(addrT));
14:
15:        if ( nRet != SOCKET_ERROR )
16:        {
17:            if ( listen(*psock, 0) != SOCKET_ERROR )
18:            {
19:                while ((fSuccess == FALSE) &&
20:                        (++nRetries < MAX_RETRIES))
21:                {
22:                    struct fd_set  fds;
23:                    struct timeval tv = { DELAY_TIME / 1000,
24:                                          DELAY_TIME % 1000 };
25:
26:                    FD_ZERO (&fds);
27:                    FD_SET (*psock, &fds);
28:
29:                    if (select(0, &fds, NULL, NULL, &tv) == 0)
30:                    {
31:                        continue;
32:                    }
33:
34:                    if (FD_ISSET(*psock, &fds))
35:                    {
36:                        // accept the connection and close the
37:                        // socket we were listening to
38:                        SOCKET oldsock = *psock;
39:
40:                        *psock = accept(oldsock, NULL, 0);
41:                        closesocket(oldsock);
42:                        fSuccess = (*psock != INVALID_SOCKET);
43:                    }
44:                }
45:            }
46:        }
47:
48:        return fSuccess;
49: }
```

Listing 13.4 uses the enumeration technique just discussed to determine any devices in close proximity that are available for a connection. After a device is found, you build up a SOCKADDR_IRDA structure and try to connect to it. The process is repeated MAX_RETRIES times to give the servers a few seconds to become available.

Listing 13.5 shows how to implement a server side of an IrSock connection. The SOCKADDR_IRDA is built the same way, except that you zero out the device ID. This tells IrSock that you want to connect to any available device with the given service name. This technique is similar to the INADDR_ANY strategy I used for regular sockets in Listing 13.2. You then attempt to listen for someone connecting to you MAX_RETRIES times and return a status code indicating whether a connection was established.

IrSock can be a valuable ally if you have to send information between Windows CE devices—especially because you don't have to tote around any cables. Porting is a snap as well because, after a connection is established, it entails pretty much all the same socket calls.

An Overview of WinInet Support

WinInet is a Win32 wrapper around WinSock that implements the common Internet protocols HTTP, Gopher, and FTP. It abstracts the underlying details of how they work and provides a much higher-level API that is easy to work with.

The only difference between Windows CE's WinInet implementation and the desktop's is which protocols are supported. Because the Gopher protocol has gone the way of the dinosaur and is rarely used, it is not implemented.

FTP support is implemented for Windows CE, but many OEMs choose to not include it in their version of the operating system for size reasons. It is not in any Windows CE 2.0 H/PCs, but it is included on most P/PCs. Also, it is available on the new H/PC Professional Edition. If a device you're targeting doesn't have WinInet FTP support and you want to add it, you can use Platform Builder to create a new WinInet DLL with the support you need and distribute it with your application.

Because writing WinInet code for Windows CE is the same as desktop development, I won't dig into the details. For the scoop on all the WinInet tricks and techniques, have a look at Aaron Skonnard's excellent book *Essential WinInet*.

Summary

This hour I've covered the gist of the communication features of Windows CE. I discussed how to utilize the standard and IR serial port and how to get a connection to a desktop machine and talk over WinSock. I also covered using WinSock over the IR port and how Windows CE's WinInet implementation is different from the desktop's.

Q&A

Q Is overlapped I/O supported on Windows CE?

A Generic overlapped I/O via `CreateFile` is not supported on Windows CE, but the serial driver in Windows CE uses overlapped I/O under the hood. This means that it is okay to do parallel reads and writes from multiple threads if you are talking to a serial port on Windows CE.

Q What is different about establishing a connection with IrSock compared to regular sockets?

A There are two main areas of difference: socket creation and addressing. Socket creation has to be done with the `AF_IRDA` constant instead of `AF_INET` in all socket API calls. Addressing is accomplished with a device ID and a service name instead of an IP address and a port number.

Workshop

The Workshop is designed to help you anticipate possible questions, review what you've learned, and begin thinking ahead about putting your knowledge into practice. The answers to the quiz are in Appendix A, "Answers."

Quiz

1. How can I work around Windows CE's lack of the `WSAAsync` WinSock APIs?

2. How can I work around Windows CE's lack of support for the `SetCommConfig` API?

3. How can I force a thread to return from a call to `WaitCommEvent`?

4. How can I set a serial port to raw IR mode?

5. How can I set a socket to be nonblocking?

Exercises

1. Change the socket test example to use nonblocking sockets rather than rely on the blocking properties of `recv` and `send`.

2. Modify CETTY to support the IR serial port via IrComm.

13

HOUR 14

Printing

How to add printing support to your Windows CE application is the topic of this hour. The Windows CE printing APIs are a subset of the desktop Win32 Print APIs, and this lesson helps you explore them.

In this hour, you will learn

- What printing options are available with various versions of Windows CE
- How to use the Win32 Print APIs to produce printer output
- How to add the Print common dialog to your application

What Printing Options Are Available in Versions of Windows CE?

Printing support varies among versions of Windows CE and among Windows CE platforms. The following sections clarify what functionality is available for a given operating system version and platform.

Windows CE Version 1.0 and 1.1

In Windows CE 1.0, the printing subsystem is not included in the operating system. This means that if you want straight-text or WYSIWYG printing, you yourself have to fully implement it or rely on third-party application software to do it for you.

In Windows CE 1.1, the printing subsystem is still not present, but text-only printing is added to Microsoft's Pocket Word application in ROM.

Windows CE Version 2.0: What Is, What Is Not

In Windows CE 2.0, a subset of the Win32 Print APIs have been added to the operating system. The APIs for creating printer output are included, but the APIs for managing the spooling of print jobs are not. Additionally, network printing and the capability to preview print jobs onscreen are not currently supported.

Print preview gives you the ability to preview a representation of the print output onscreen before committing to send it to an actual printer. *Print job spooling* is the capability to queue print jobs until a printer is available. If your users require either of these features, your application can integrate with third-party applications to help achieve this.

> The Print to bFAX print driver included on the CD-ROM allows the user to select bFAX or bPRINT as a target printer. As your application prints, this printer driver compresses the image your user wants to print, stores it in a TIFF file, and adds it to bPRINT's print queue. When a printer is available, the user can then use bPRINT to output the queued print jobs. This is especially useful for developers because it speeds up the print debugging process; you can generate and view output without printing to an actual printer.

The `PrintDlg` common dialog is available for applications to use. This API displays a system dialog where the user can specify how and where he or she wants to print. This is discussed in depth later in this hour.

Windows CE Version 2.1 and Beyond

The underlying printing APIs have not changed between Windows CE 2.0 and 2.1, but the common dialog to configure the print job has. Specifically, the `PrintDlg` function has been replaced with the `PageSetupDlg` function. How to use `PageSetupDlg` is discussed in more detail later in this hour.

Windows CE is a *modular* operating system. This means that including the printing subsystem within a build of the Windows CE operating system is optional. The following list is an overview of printing support on the Windows CE platforms currently available:

- The printing subsystem is included in H/PC and H/PC Professional Edition PC Companion devices that are running Windows CE 2.0 or greater.

- The printing subsystem is *NOT* included in the P/PCs that run Windows 2.0 or 2.1. Very likely, it will be included in the next wave of P/PCs, expected in late 1999.

- The printing subsystem was not included with the first version of the Windows CE Auto PC.

The actual connection to the printer can be established using the Windows CE device's serial or infrared ports. If your printer does not have a serial or infrared port, you will need either a serial-to-parallel adapter or an infrared-to-parallel converter. Depending on the serial-to-parallel converter used, a null-modem cable might also be necessary.

> Greenwich Instruments, Aegis, and Belkin produce serial-to-parallel converters. Canon and Parallax Research produce infrared-to-parallel converters. You can visit the bPRINT homepage at `http://www.bsquare.com/development/products/bprint.htm` for an up-to-date list of manufacturers and model numbers.

Another option would be to invest in a small portable printer. Most models have either a serial or infrared port built in, and some run off batteries. Citizen's PN series, Pentax Technologies' PocketJet series, and Canon's BubbleJet series might be of interest to you. You can visit the online mobile accessory reseller Mobile Planet at `http://www.mplanet.com` for the latest selection and specifications.

Adding Printing Support to Your Application

Printing on Windows CE is very similar to printing using Win32 on the desktop. The basic steps are

1. Get or create a handle to a printer device context (DC).
2. Use GDI APIs to write text and graphics to the printer DC.
3. When the page is completed, have the operating system send it to the printer.

Table 14.1 shows the printing APIs available to help you achieve this. They work very much like their desktop Win32 counterparts.

14

TABLE 14.1   Print APIs Available on Windows CE 2.0 and Above

Function	Use
StartDoc	Start a print job.
StartPage	Start a new page.
EndPage	End the current page.
EndDoc	End a print job.
AbortDoc	Abort the current print job.
SetAbortProc	Register your AbortProc function.

Because these functions work the same on Windows CE as on the desktop, I will not examine them in depth in this book. If you are unfamiliar with them, you should read *The Windows NT Win32 API SuperBible* by Richard Simon (Waite Group Press).

The DOCINFO structure looks exactly as it does on the desktop:

```
typedef struct {
        int       cbSize;
        LPCTSTR   lpszDocName;
        LPCTSTR   lpszOutput;
        LPCTSTR   lpszDatatype;
        DWORD     fwType;
} DOCINFO;
```

DOCINFO is used the same way that it is on the desktop, except that only the first two fields are supported. *cbSize* should be set to "sizeof(DOCINFO)" and *lpszDocName* should be set to a null-terminated Unicode string that specifies the name of the document to be printed. Windows CE does not support printing to files, so *lpszOutput* should be set to NULL. Likewise, *lpszDatatype* and *fwType* are not supported and should be set to zero.

The Windows CE 2.0 Common Dialog for Printing

Printing on Windows CE 2.0 involves using the PRINTDLG structure with the PrintDlg function.

Unlike the DOCINFO structure, the Windows CE version of PRINTDLG varies slightly from its desktop counterpart. Specifically, because the Print Setup dialog is not available on Windows CE, the associated members in PRINTDLG have been removed. Additionally, two members have been added:

- *rcMargin* specifies the width of the top, bottom, left, and right margins.

- *rcMinMargin* specifies the minimum allowable width for the top, bottom, left, and right margins.

One interesting observation is that some of the members of this structure have been named differently than their desktop Win32 siblings, even though they perform the same function. If you are porting existing code to Windows CE that uses the *lStructSize*, *Flags*, or *hDC* members, you will have to rename them to *cbStruct*, *dwFlags*, and *hdc*.

As you can see in Figure 14.1, the PrintDlg function is used the same way as its desktop Win32 namesake. However, you should take note of the following differences:

- The user cannot specify a range of pages to print.

- The user cannot specify the number of copies to print.

- The function always attempts to return the printer DC in the *hdc* member of the PRINTDLG parameter.

FIGURE 14.1

The PrintDlg *common dialog in action on Windows CE 2.0.*

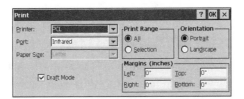

This function will fail and return FALSE if it is unable to return the printer DC in *hdc*. The desktop Win32 version of this function attempts to do this only if *Flags* is set to PD_RETURNDC. This flag is not defined on Windows CE, but can be easily confused with the Windows CE–specific PD_RETURNDEFAULTDC flag. The PD_RETURNDEFAULTDC flag specifies that the PrintDlg function should return the printer DC in the *hdc* member without displaying the Print dialog at all. The PrintDlg function will succeed in retrieving the printer DC in the absence of a connection to an actual printer if you are attempting to print to a third-party spooler/preview application, such as bPRINT.

The Windows CE 2.1 (and Above) Common Dialog for Printing

The Windows CE help system recommends that you use the PAGESETUPDLG structure with the PageSetupDlg function when providing printing support on Windows CE 2.1 and higher.

14

The PageSetupDlg function is *not* available on Windows CE 2.0, but backward compatibility support for the PrintDlg function *is* available on Windows CE 2.1. Therefore, if you want your application to run on both Windows CE 2.0 and 2.1 devices, you should use the PrintDlg function.

The PAGESETUPDLG structure and PageSetupDlg function are implemented much the same on Windows CE as in desktop Win32.

FIGURE 14.2

On Windows CE 2.1, the appearance (to the user) of the PageSetupDlg *common dialog is identical to that of the Windows CE 2.1 version of the* PrintDlg *common dialog.*

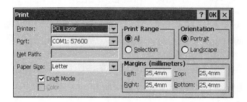

Sending `Hello` to Your Printer

To maintain compatibility with a wider range of Windows CE devices, Listings 14.1 and 14.2 are written to use the PrintDlg function. Listing 14.1 shows you how to generate some output on your printer, and Listing 14.2 shows you how to add a Print Status dialog to your application.

The code in Listing 14.1 demonstrates how to print *Hello* on a page. It uses the PrintDlg function to allow the user to select the printer he or she wants to print to and uses StartDoc, StartPage, EndPage, and EndDoc to produce the printer output.

LISTING 14.1   Sending `Hello` to the Printer

```
 1:     /*************************************************************
 2:     * print "Hello!" on the currently attached printer
 3:     *************************************************************/
 4:
 5:     PRINTDLG pd;
 6:     BOOL      fReturn = FALSE;
 7:
 8:     memset( &pd, 0x00, sizeof( PRINTDLG ) );
 9:     pd.hwndOwner = hWnd;
10:     pd.cbStruct = sizeof( PRINTDLG );
11:     pd.hinst = hInst;
12:
```

```
13:      fReturn = PrintDlg( &pd );
14:
15:      /***********************************************************
16:       * if the user did not select cancel, and we have a
17:       * connection to a printer, proceed to print
18:       ***********************************************************/
19:
20:      if ( fReturn ) {
21:
22:              DOCINFO             DocInfo;
23:              memset( &DocInfo, 0x00, sizeof( DocInfo ) );
24:              DocInfo.cbSize = sizeof( DocInfo );
25:
26:              if ( StartDoc( pd.hdc, &DocInfo ) > 0 ) {
27:
28:                      StartPage( pd.hdc );
29:                      ExtTextOut( pd.hdc, 50, 50, 0, NULL,
                                ➥TEXT( "Hello!" ), 6, NULL );
30:                      EndPage( pd.hdc );
31:                      EndDoc( pd.hdc );
32:
33:              }
34:
35:      }
36:
37:      /***********************************************************
38:       * if a printer DC was successfully allocated, it
39:       * needs to be deleted
40:       ***********************************************************/
41:      if ( pd.hdc != NULL ) DeleteDC( pd.hdc );
```

Now that you have sent a message to the printer, you should provide your users with a
way to cancel the print job in-progress. This is implemented by adding a Print Status
dialog with a Cancel button. When the user clicks Cancel, the AbortDoc function shown
in Listing 14.2 should be invoked.

LISTING 14.2   Invoking the AbortDoc Function

```
1: BOOL CALLBACK PrintDlgProc( HWND hDlg, UINT uiMsg, WPARAM wParam,
                              ➥LPARAM lParam )
2: {
3:     static HDC    hPrintDC;
4:
5:     UNREFERENCED_PARAMETER( lParam );
6:
7:     switch ( uiMsg ) {
8:
9:             case WM_INITDIALOG:
10:                    g_fAbortPrinting = FALSE;
```

continues

14

LISTING 14.2   continued

```
11:                        hPrintDC = (HDC)lParam;
12:                        return TRUE;
13:                        break;
14:
15:            case WM_COMMAND:
16:                    if ( LOWORD( wParam ) == IDCANCEL ) {
17:                            g_fAbortPrinting = TRUE;
18:                            AbortDoc( hPrintDC );
19:                            return TRUE;
20:                    }
21:                    break;
22:
23:        }
24:
25:    return FALSE;
26:
27: }
```

For this to work, you must make several changes to the code in Listing 14.1. The first change involves implementing the AbortProc function:

```
BOOL CALLBACK AbortProc( HDC hPrintDC, INT iCode )
{
    MSG     message;

    UNREFERENCED_PARAMETER( hPrintDC );
    UNREFERENCED_PARAMETER( iCode );

    while( !g_fAbortPrinting &&
          PeekMessage( &message, NULL, 0, 0, PM_REMOVE ) ) {
        if ( !g_hPrintDlg ||
             !IsDialogMessage( g_hPrintDlg, &message ) ) {
           TranslateMessage( &message );
           DispatchMessage( &message );
        }
    }
    return !g_fAbortPrinting;
}
```

The remainder of the changes involves using the SetAbortProc function and adding abort-checking code to the printing code, as shown in listing 14.3.

LISTING 14.3   Adding the Capability to Abort a Print Job

```
1: /************************************************************
2:  * print "Hello!" on the currently attached printer
3:  ************************************************************/
4:
```

```
 5: PRINTDLG  pd;
 6: BOOL      fReturn = FALSE;
 7:
 8: memset( &pd, 0x00, sizeof( PRINTDLG ) );
 9: pd.hwndOwner = hWnd;
10: pd.cbStruct = sizeof( PRINTDLG );
11: pd.hinst = hInst;
12:
13: fReturn = PrintDlg( &pd );
14:
15: /***********************************************************
16:  * if the user did not select cancel, and we have a
17:  * connection to a printer, proceed to print
18:  ***********************************************************/
19:
20: if ( PrintDlg( &pd ) ) {
21:
22:         DOCINFO         DocInfo;
23:         memset( &DocInfo, 0x00, sizeof( DocInfo ) );
24:         DocInfo.cbSize = sizeof( DocInfo );
25:
26:         // use SetAbortProc() to set "AbortProc" to
27:         // be the abort proc for this print job
28:         SetAbortProc( pd.hdc, (ABORTPROC)AbortProc );
29:
30:         if ( StartDoc( pd.hdc, &DocInfo ) > 0 ) {
31:
32:                 StartPage( pd.hdc );
33:
34:                 // print out the entire document here or (in this case)
35:                 // just one word.
36:                 ExtTextOut( pd.hdc, 50, 50, 0, NULL, TEXT( "Hello!" ), 6,
NULL );
37:
38:                 // check to see whether we are supposed to abort
39:                 if ( !g_fAbortPrinting && EndPage( pd.hdc ) ) {
40:                         EndDoc( pd.hdc );
41:                 }
42:
43:         }
44:
45: }
46:
47: /***********************************************************
48:  * if a printer DC was successfully allocated, it
49:  * needs to be deleted
50:  ***********************************************************/
51: if ( pd.hdc != NULL ) DeleteDC( pd.hdc );
```

14

Summary

In this hour, you learned how to update your Windows CE application to print by using the Windows CE printing subsystem. You also learned about the issues affecting printing support on various versions of Windows CE, as well as some strategies for dealing with them.

Q&A

Q How can I add printing support to my P/PC application?

A Windows CE 2.0 for P/PCs does not include the printing APIs. It might be included in a future version of the P/PC. In the meantime, you can either write your own straight-text printing or use a third-party product such as BSQUARE's bPRINT (included on the CD-ROM) to do serial and infrared straight-text and WYSIWYG (What You See Is What You Get) printing from your P/PC.

Q I can print to a Hewlett Packard printer, but I can't successfully print to a Canon BubbleJet or EPSON printer.

A Windows CE PC Companion devices ship with a Hewlett Packard PCL–compatible printer driver in CD-ROM, which is not compatible with ESC/P2-compatible printers. You have to install ESC/P2-compatible printer drivers on your Windows CE device to print to ESC/P2 printers. ESC/P2 is a printer control language developed by EPSON.

Workshop

The Workshop is designed to help you anticipate possible questions, review what you've learned, and begin thinking ahead about putting your knowledge into practice. The answers to the quiz are in Appendix A, "Answers."

Quiz

1. How do you get a valid printer DC?

2. `PrintDlg()` returns `FALSE` no matter what values you specify for the *dwFlags* member of the `PRINTDLG` structure. `CommDlgExtendedError` returns `4100`. What is going wrong?

3. Which members are the same in the `PRINTDLG` structure used on desktop Win32 and the version used on Windows CE?

4. What are the four main functions used for actually printing a document?

5. How do you print on Windows CE 1.0?

6. From the user's perspective, what is different between the desktop Win32 version of the `PrintDlg` function and the Windows CE version?

7. How do you spool a print job on Windows CE?

Exercises

1. Create a simple text editor that prints out the contents of its edit control window.

2. Change the program in exercise 1 to include a working Cancel dialog.

14

Hour 15

Targeting the Palm-Size PC

You will learn how to customize your Windows CE application for the Palm-size PC (P/PC) in this hour. The Windows CE interface for the P/PC has some significant differences from the Handheld PC (H/PC), and this lesson helps you through them.

In this hour, you will learn

- How to modify your user interface to target the Palm-size PC
- How to interact with the pop-up software keyboard
- How to use the Palm-size PC–specific APIs
- Simple strategies for maintaining a Handheld PC version and a Palm-size PC version of your application from the same code base

Standard Palm-Size PC Hardware

Understanding the hardware elements that are common to all Palm-size PCs is useful. It helps to ensure that you design your application so that it works well on all devices on the market. This helps to reduce the time and expense that you need to expend on application<->device compatibility testing, and the number of problems that may turn up during this testing.

- The touch screen and stylus
- Navigation controls
- Audio input and output
- Notifications
- CPUs, memory, and power
- Communication ports, serial and infrared

The Touch Screen and the Stylus

Palm-size PCs include a 240×320–pixel touch screen. Unlike Handheld PCs, Palm-size PCs currently come with only a single screen size, making it easier for you to design and test your applications. The first wave of Palm-size PCs shipped in early 1998 with 2-bit grayscale screens. Devices with color screens started shipping in early 1999.

> Although it does not appear that the Palm-size PC screen size will change in the *foreseeable* future, you should take care to design your applications so that they will work well on multiple screen sizes.

Palm-size PCs do not include keyboards. Text entry is accomplished via the stylus and the soft input panel (SIP). The SIP displays the input method (IM) currently selected by the user for text entry. Palm-size PCs typically ship with at least two IMs: a QWERTY-like software keyboard from Microsoft and a handwriting recognition IM named *Jot* (from Communication Intelligence Corporation, http://www.cic.com). Device manufacturers and end users have the option of installing additional IMs if they like. Which IM is being used by the end user is entirely transparent to your applications. Input from the IM is received by your application as if it was input from a regular physical keyboard.

Navigation Controls

Palm-size PCs come with a standard set of hardware buttons. The following describe what they are and how they behave:

- The Exit button is used as the Esc key on a normal keyboard.
- The Action button is used as the Enter key.
- The Record button activates the voice recorder application.

15

- The Application buttons launch applications (these are preconfigured to launch specific applications, but they can be reconfigured to launch other applications).
- The Up button acts as the up-arrow key.
- The Down button acts as the down-arrow key.

Audio Input and Output

Palm-size PCs include a built-in microphone for audio input and a speaker for audio output. The minimum sample rate for the microphone is 8KHz. Some devices may have jacks for external microphones and headphones, but these should be transparent to software (that is, no special coding is required to receive input from or generate output to these jacks).

Notifications

All Palm-size PCs include audio notification capabilities. Additionally, some devices include a flashing LED and a vibration control (similar to vibrating pagers) to attract the user's attention.

CPUs, Memory, and Power

Currently, a Palm-size PC uses either an SH3 chip or a MIPS chip. The HP Jornada 420 uses the SH3 CPU, and all others use a MIPS CPU. All devices contain at least 6MB of ROM and 2MB of RAM. Palm-size PCs should be able to run at least 15 hours from their main power source (usually, two AAA batteries).

Communication Ports: Serial and Infrared

The serial port can be used to communicate with other hardware devices, including desktop computers. Some devices may require an optional docking cradle (available from the manufacturer) to do this. The serial port is accessible programmatically as COM1:.

The infrared port conforms to IrDA data specifications and can be used to communicate with other Windows CE devices, desktop computers, and printers (if the appropriate third-party software is used). The infrared port is accessible programmatically as COM3:.

Modifying Your User Interface for the Palm-Size PC

In this section, I will review the major recommendations of the Palm-size PC logo recommendations and requirements, as well as some common-sense tips and suggestions for Palm-size PC user-interface design.

Although earning the "Designed for Windows CE" logo for your application might not be a necessity for your current situation, it is wise to follow the requirements in case a customer needs your application to be certified as Windows CE logo compliant. You can find and download the latest copy of the Palm-size PC logo requirements from http://www.microsoft.com/ windowsce or http://www.veritest.com.

The following points give an overview of the logo requirements for Windows CE Palm-size PC applications:

- The object store file system should not be exposed to the user. This means that your application should not make the end user aware of the directory structure present on the device.

- Allow only a single instance of your application to run. No taskbar is available on Palm-size PCs to enable the user to switch between different instances of your application.

- Do not provide a user-visible method of closing your applications. This means that your applications should have neither a close button in the upper-right corner of your command bands nor an Exit or Close option within your menus. When system resources are low, Windows CE will ask your application to close by sending it a WM_CLOSE message.

- When your application receives the WM_CLOSE or WM_DESTROY message, it should shut down "quietly." This includes *not* asking users whether they would like to save their changes. Their changes should automatically be saved (to a temporary file, if necessary) and reloaded automatically when the application is restarted, so that users are never even aware that the application has been shut down.

- The help button should not be present in your application. Your application will receive a WM_HELP message when the user selects the Help menu item from the system's Start menu when your application is in the foreground.

- Do not include keyboard-centric visual cues within your application. Your application's menus and dialogs should not include menu shortcuts (Alt+) or accelerators (Ctrl+).

While you are developing your application, it will be necessary to shut it down so that you can download and test new versions. One way to do this is to include a Close option within your user interface while you are debugging your application and then remove the option when you are ready to ship. Another way is to use a third-party task manager (such as bTASK™ from http://www.bsquare.com/development) to close your application.

15

Figure 15.1 contrasts two applications running on a Palm-size PC. The application on the left does not adhere to the Windows CE Palm-size PC logo guidelines. The application on the right is the same program adapted to specifically target the Palm-size PC form-factor.

FIGURE 15.1

The application on the left violates the Palm-size PC logo guidelines, whereas the application on the right does not.

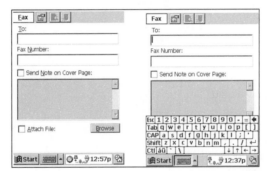

Three main issues were fixed between the two versions of the applications:

- The menu no longer has a shortcut key (the underlined F, indicating that Alt+F can be used to activate the Fax menu).

- The static controls in the main window no longer have shortcut keys (To is replaced with To, Fax Number with Fax Number:).

- When focus is set to an edit control (the To field in this case), the soft input panel (SIP) is automatically activated so that the user can start entering text if he or she wants to.

Be sure to check your ToolTips for accelerators. It is a common mistake to remove the accelerators from your menus but forget to remove them from the ToolTips of your toolbar buttons.

Figures 15.2 and 15.3 show some suggestions for how to optimize your user interface for the Palm-size PC.

FIGURE 15.2

The default Handheld PC screen layout for the BSQUARE HTML Editor.

FIGURE 15.3

The default Palm-size PC screen layout for the BSQUARE HTML Editor.

The following is a checklist to help you optimize your user interface for the Palm-size PC's narrower screen:

- If your main application view uses a tab control to navigate between views, it is better to make the tab control horizontal (across the top or bottom) instead of vertical.

- If your application uses several command bands, you might want to consider stacking them vertically the first time the user starts the program, so that they are not hidden from the user. If the user is not interested in them, he or she is free to move them to the top of the screen.

- If your application has a high number of top-level menus (such as File, Edit, View, Tools, and Options), it might be too wide to view on a Palm-size PC screen. If this is the case, you will want to combine some of your menus. A possibility might be to move the Options menu to be a pop-up submenu on the Edit menu.

- Redesign all your dialogs so that they fit on the narrower screen.

- Make sure that the help and close buttons are not present on your command bands. In addition to taking up space, they also violate the Windows CE logo guidelines.

Introducing the CAPEDIT Control

There are situations where you can be 99% sure that your user will want to capitalize the first character of a string they are entering into an edit control. An example would be an edit control that is used to input the proper name of an individual. Depending on the input method the user has selected within the SIP, capitalizing the first letter entered in the edit control is likely to slow your user down by requiring an extra screen tap (to tap the "shift" key). The CAPEDIT control was created to address this issue. It automatically capitalizes the first character in an edit control for your user, saving them time and effort.

The following steps illustrate how to use the CAPEDIT control:

1. Call SHInitExtraControls before your program attempts to create a CAPEDIT control.

2. Change your EDIT controls to CAPEDIT in your resource file or in your explicit calls to CreateWindow or CreateWindowEx.

The ToolTip Control

ToolTips can be added to buttons and static text on Palm-size PCs, using the following steps:

1. Call SHInitExtraControls before your program attempts to create a ToolTip control.

2. Change your BUTTON controls to TTBUTTON and your STATIC controls to TTSTATIC. This can be done in either your resource file or your explicit calls to CreateWindow or CreateWindowEx.

3. Write your ToolTip control text in the format Control Text~~ToolTip Text. For example, if you have a Browse button that allows the user to browse for a file, you would want to use Browse~~Browse for a File to Open. The button would display Browse, and if the user places the stylus on the button, the ToolTip Browse for a File to Open will be displayed.

If your ToolTip text is too wide to fit on a single line, the control will automatically create additional lines. You can force it to create a line break by using \r within the ToolTip text.

Working with the Pop-Up Software Keyboard

It is your application's responsibility to display and hide the pop-up software keyboard at the appropriate times. The controls that accept text entry should display the SIP when they get focus, and they should hide the SIP when they lose focus. The API you use to do this is SHSipInfo.

Listing 15.1 is a function that will show and hide the SIP on demand. It first checks to see what state the SIP is currently in. If it differs from the desired state, it tells the SIP to toggle its state.

LISTING 15.1   Showing and Hiding the SIP

```
 1: VOID ShowSIP( BOOL fShowSip )
 2: {
 3:     SIPINFO    si;
 4:     BOOL    fSipIsUp;
 5:     if ( SHSipInfo( SPI_GETSIPINFO, 0, &si, 0 ) ) {
 6:         fSipIsUp = ( si.fdwFlags & SIPF_ON );
 7:         if ( fSipIsUp != fShowSip ) {
 8:             if ( fSipIsUp )
 9:                 si.fdwFlags -= SIPF_ON;
10:             else
11:                 si. fdwFlags += SIPF_ON;
12:             SHSipInfo( SPI_SETSIPINFO, 0, &si, 0 );
13:         }
14:     }
15: }
```

It is your application's responsibility to resize itself when the SIP is shown or hidden. If the state of the SIP is changed by a program or by the user, you will receive a WM_SETTINGCHANGE message whose wParam parameter is set to SPI_SETINFO. You should resize your main application window similarly to Listing 15.2.

LISTING 15.2   Resizing the SIP

```
 1: case WM_SETTINGCHANGE:
 2:     switch( wParam ) {
 3:         case SPI_SETSIPINFO:
 4:             SIPINFO    si;
 5:             memset( &si, 0x00, sizeof( si ) );
 6:             si.cbSize = sizeof( si );
 7:             if ( SHSipInfo( SPI_GETSIPINFO, 0, &si, 0 ) ) {
 8:                 MoveWindow(    hWndMain,
```

```
 9:                        si.rcVisibleDesktop.left,
10:                        si.rcVisibleDesktop.top,
11:                        si.rcVisibleDesktop.right -
12:                        si.rcVisibleDesktop.left,
13:                        si.rcVisibleDesktop.bottom -
14:                        si.rcVisibleDesktop.top,
15:                        TRUE );
16:            }
17:        break;
18:    }
19:    break;
```

If the preceding code fails to link when you attempt to build it, make sure that your Visual C++ project is configured to link with the library AYGSHELL.LIB. This library contains the SIP-specific APIs and is therefore available only when building for Palm-size PCs. If you mistakenly link with it when building for other platforms (such as the Handheld PC Pro), Windows CE will tell you that it is unable to run your program because of missing components.

Using the Flash Card APIs

First-generation Palm-size PCs include a single slot for flash cards. Because potential exists for multiple flash cards in the future, there is an API for accessing the flash card that is very similar to the `FindFirstFile`/`FindNextFile` API you are accustomed to with desktop Win32 programming. `FindFirstFlashCard` returns a handle to the first flash card found on the system. If it is successful, you can call `FindNextFlashCard` to find the next flash card. `FindNextFlashCard` returns `FALSE` when there are no more flash cards on the device.

When you find a flash card, you can use the `EnumProjects` and `EnumProjectFiles` APIs to enumerate all folders and files on your flash card. If you are attempting to locate particular files, use the `FindFirstProjectFile` and `FindNextProjectFile` APIs.

Using the Voice Recorder Control

The Voice Recorder control allows you to record and play sounds within your application. You create a Voice Recorder control by using the `VoiceRecorder_Create` API. This function takes one parameter: a pointer to a properly initialized `CM_VOICE_RECORDER` structure. Listing 15.3 shows how to do this using the style flags for `CM_VOICE_RECORDER` in Table 15.1.

LISTING 15.3 Using the `VoiceRecorder_Create` API

```
 1: HWND StartVoiceRecorder( HWND hwndParent, TCHAR *tcWaveFile )
 2: {
 3:     CM_VOICE_RECORDER    VoiceRecorder;
 4:     if ( !IsWindow( hwndParent ) ) return NULL;
 5:     memset( &VoiceRecorder, 0, sizeof(CM_VOICE_RECORDER) );
 6:     VoiceRecorder.cb = sizeof(CM_VOICE_RECORDER);
 7:     VoiceRecorder.dwStyle = VRS_NO_MOVE;
 8:     // center control relative to hwndParent
 9:     VoiceRecorder.xPos = -1;
10:     VoiceRecorder.hwndParent = hwndParent;
11:     VoiceRecorder.lpszRecordFileName = tcWaveFile;
12:     return VoiceRecorder_Create( &VoiceRecorder );
13: }
```

TABLE 15.1 Style Flags Supported by the `CM_VOICE_RECORDER` Structure

Notification Message	Meaning
VRS_NO_OKCANCEL	The OK and Close buttons are hidden.
VRS_NO_NOTIFY	Notification messages are not sent to the parent window.
VRS_MODAL	Control is not returned to your application until the control is dismissed.
VRS_NO_OK	The Cancel button is hidden.
VRS_NO_RECORD	The Record button is hidden.
VRS_PLAY_MODE	The control starts playing the specified WAV file after the control is created.
VRS_NO_MOVE	The grip is not displayed on the control; the user cannot move the control.

The Voice Recorder control communicates with your application's topmost window-processing loop using `WM_NOTIFY` messages. The `lParam` parameter is a pointer to an `NMHDR` structure containing information about the notification message. Table 15.2 describes the notifications that are sent.

TABLE 15.2 Notifications Sent by the Voice Recorder Control

Notification Message	Meaning
VRN_ERROR	An error was encountered.
VRN_RECORD_START	The user started recording.
VRN_RECORD_STOP	The user stopped recording.
VRN_PLAY_START	The user started playback.

Notification Message	Meaning
VRN_PLAY_STOP	The user stopped playback.
VRN_CANCEL	The user clicked Cancel.
VRN_OK	The user clicked OK.

15

Strategies for Maintaining Handheld Versions of Your Application from the Same Code Base

One of the keys to successful Windows CE programming is organizing your projects so that they are easy to port to new versions of the Windows CE shell. The capability to quickly port your Palm-size PC recipe-tracking application to a microwave oven running Windows CE can be the difference that determines whether or not your product even has the opportunity to be pre-loaded on a new Windows CE device. This section provides you with some ideas on how to achieve this through resource file and source code management.

Resource File Management

How do you name your resource files? It's typical for programmers to name them after the product name they are building. This naming strategy does not lend itself well to porting to seven language versions targeting three Windows CE shells. Ideally, your resource filename will contain information about the following:

- The product you are building
- The target language it was created for
- The Windows CE platform it was created for

An example of this would be

Notepad_English_Hpc.rc

Notepad_English_Ppc.rc

Notepad_German_Hpc.rc

Notepad_German_Ppc.rc

It now becomes very obvious which target you are building for when viewing your project from within Developer Studio.

You can easily remove a particular resource file from your Visual C++ project by selecting it within the FileView view of your project and pressing the Delete key. You can easily insert another resource file into your project by right-clicking on your project in the FileView view and selecting Add Files to Project from the pop-up menu.

Source Code Management

In some cases, you will want to include only portions of your source code when building for a Palm-size PC. The best way to handle this is to establish a #define that is used only with Palm-size PC product builds. An example would be PALM_SIZE_PC. Listing 15.4 demonstrates how to show and hide the SIP based on whether your edit controls are getting or losing focus:

LISTING 15.4   Showing and Hiding the SIP Based on Focused Controls

```
1: case WM_COMMAND:
2:     switch( LOWORD( wParam ) ) {
3: #ifdef PALM_SIZE_PC
4:         // building for the Palm-size PC is the only time
5:         // we are interested in showing or hiding the SIP
6:         // when an editing control receives or loses focus.
7: case IDC_AN_EDIT_CONTROL:
8: switch( HIWORD( wParam ) ) {
9: case EN_SETFOCUS:
10:     ShowSIP( TRUE );
11:     break;
12: Case EN_KILLFOCUS:
13:     ShowSIP( FALSE );
14:     break;
15:         }
16:         break;
17: #endif    // PALM_SIZE_PC
18:         // include code common to all types of CE platforms here
19:     }
```

You can #define PALM_SIZE_PC in your builds in three ways:

- Add it as a hard-coded #define in one of your header files. You would set it to

  #define PALM_SIZE_PC   1

  when you want to create a Palm-size PC build of your application and to

  #undef PALM_SIZE_PC

  when you want to create a Handheld PC build of your application.

- Configure it as a #define within the Microsoft Visual C++ IDE. You can do this by

  1. Pressing Alt+F7 (or selecting Settings from the Project menu)
  2. Selecting the C/C++ tab in the property sheet
  3. Setting the Category to General
  4. Appending PALM_SIZE_PC to the Preprocessor Definitions settings

- Specify it in your command-line build procedures by adding -DPALM_SIZE_PC=1 to your compiler flags.

Summary

In this hour, you learned how to modify your Windows CE application to target Palm-size PCs. You learned about the minimum hardware configuration for a Palm-size PC. Not only did you learn how to interact with the SIP, but you also learned how to work with other Palm-size PC-specific controls and APIs. You ended the hour by learning some simple strategies for maintaining a Handheld PC version and a Palm-size PC version of your application from the same code base.

Q&A

Q How can I add printing support to my Palm-size PC application?

A Windows CE 2.0 for Palm-size PCs does not include the printing APIs. It might be included in a future version of the Palm-size PC. In the meantime, you can either write your own "straight text" printing or use a third-party product such as BSQUARE's bPRINT (included on the CD-ROM) to do serial and infrared straight text and WYSIWYG (What You See Is What You Get) printing from your Palm-size PC. Appendix B, "What's on the CD," contains more information on bPRINT's command line and how your application can use it to provide seamless printing support.

Q When my application uses the File Open common dialog, it does not list files on the flash card inserted in my Palm-size PC. What is going on?

A This common dialog will only find files stored in the \My Documents folder on your flash card.

Workshop

The Workshop is designed to help you anticipate possible questions, review what you've learned, and begin thinking ahead about putting your knowledge into practice. The answers to the quiz are in Appendix A, "Answers."

Quiz

1. How many Palm-size PC–specific issues are there with the application in Figure 15.4?

FIGURE 15.4

How many issues are there with this application?

2. How does an application know when to resize itself after the user has hidden the SIP?

3. What are the two types of controls that can have ToolTips?

4. How do you launch the Voice Recorder control to automatically start playing a WAV file?

Exercises

1. Create a program that uses the Voice Recorder control to record and play WAV files.

2. Add a dialog to the program that you created in the preceding step. This dialog should contain a CAPEDIT control for the name of the WAV file, and a TTBUTTON control to browse for WAV files. The Browse button should include ToolTip text.

HOUR 16

Using AppInstall to Redistribute Your Programs

How to install your applications onto Windows CE devices is the focus of this lesson.

In this hour, you will learn

- How to create CAB files
- How to help your users install CAB files
- How to gain greater control over your installs by creating your own SETUP.DLL
- How to handle installs on Windows CE 1.0 devices

Introducing Your CAB File

Install scenarios for Windows CE devices running Windows CE 2.0 and above are based on using a *cabinet* (CAB) file. The CAB file extraction engine resides on the Windows CE device, so a desktop computer is not necessary to properly install applications. The Application Manager program (CeAppMgr.exe, discussed later in this hour) is provided on the desktop computer to help manage the installation, deinstallation, and reinstallation of Windows CE applications.

Installing on Windows CE 1.0 devices is a special case that does not involve using CAB files. Windows CE 1.0 installs are discussed at the end of this hour.

CAB files work pretty much the same on Windows CE as they do with desktop windows. Within a single CAB file, there can be multiple compressed files, as well as directions for where and how to install them. Additionally, on Windows CE, you can include a SETUP.DLL file that will be executed at install time, giving you greater control over the install process. First, you will learn to create a CAB file and then see what goes into your INF file.

How Do I Create a CAB File?

The process of creating a CAB file involves using the CABWIZ.EXE tool to process an INF file as input and create a CAB file as output. CABWIZ.EXE is located in the \Windows CE Tools\Wce201\MS Palm Size PC\Support\AppInst\Bin directory.

The INF file format is discussed in detail in the next section.

These are the command-line options for CABWIZ.EXE:

```
cabwiz.exe <file>.inf [/DEST dir] [/ERR file] [/CPU cpu1 cpu2 … ]
```

The /DEST flag specifies the directory in which to create the CAB files. If it is not specified, the CAB files will be created in the current directory.

The /ERR flag specifies the output file to which you log CAB file compilation errors and warnings. If /ERR is not used, the errors and warnings will be reported to you via pop-up message boxes. The /ERR flag is helpful for implementing command-line build procedures.

The parameters to the /CPU flag specify the CPUs for which you are building.

This is an example of how to use CABWIZ.EXE to build CAB files:

```
cabwiz.exe "c:\test.inf" /err errors.txt /cpu mips sh3
```

This will create a CAB file named test.sh3.cab (for SH3 installs) and a CAB file named test.mips.cab (for MIPS installs).

What Goes in My INF File?

The INF file is a file you create to specify which files you want installed, where you want them installed, what Registry entries you want created, and more.

The [Version] Section of the INF File

Version is an interesting name for this section because it doesn't actually contain version information pertaining to Windows CE (Windows CE version information comes later, in the section on CEDevice). The fields that should be specified in this section are

```
[Version]
Signature = "$Windows NT$"  ; or "$Windows 95$"
Provider = "Your Company"  ; replace with your company name
CESignature = "$Windows CE$"
```

The [CEStrings] Section

This section is used to specify the application's name and default install location:

```
[CEStrings]
AppName = "Dog Bite"    ; name of your application
InstallDir = %CE1%\%AppName%  ; default install path
```

I just sneaked %CE1% into the definition of InstallDir. What is it? It is one of the available variables, listed in Table 16.1, that can be used to specify one of the default Windows CE system folders.

TABLE 16.1   Variables Representing Default System Folders

Value	Meaning
%CE1%	\Program Files
%CE2%	\Windows
%CE3%	\Windows\Desktop
%CE4%	\Windows\Startup
%CE5%	\My Documents
%CE6%	\Program Files\Accessories
%CE7%	\Program Files\Communication
%CE8%	\Program Files\Games
%CE9%	\Program Files\Pocket Outlook
%CE10%	\Program Files\Office
%CE11%	\Windows\Programs
%CE12%	\Windows\Programs\Accessories
%CE13%	\Windows\Programs\Communications

continues

16

TABLE 16.1 continued

Value	Meaning
%CE14%	\Windows\Programs\Games
%CE15%	\Windows\Fonts
%CE16%	\Windows\Recent
%CE17%	\Windows\Favorites

The [CEDevice], [CEDevice.SH3], [CEDevice.MIPS] (and So On) Sections

This section describes the OS requirements and device characteristics required for the installation to complete.

These include supported processors, minimum OS version, maximum OS version, minimum OS build number, and maximum OS build number. You can also explicitly specify any CPUs you don't want to install on.

> The OS build number can be found in the System Control Panel applet. It is reported as *XXXX-YYYY*, in which *XXXX* is the OS build number, and *YYYY* is the build number for the built-in applications.

Any values specified in the [CEDevice] section will apply to all CPUs, unless overridden in a [CEDevice.<CPU>] subsection.

Here is a sample entry in the INF file:

```
[CEDevice]
VersionMin = 2.0    ; install on CE 2.0 and greater
[CEDevice.SH3]
ProcessorType = 10003  ; 10003 == SH3
[CEDevice.MIPS]
ProcessorType = 4000  ; 4000 == MIPS
[CEDevice.STRONGARM]
ProcessorType = 2577  ; 2577 == StrongArm
```

The [DefaultInstall] Section

This section defines what subsequent sections should specify:

- Which files to install
- Which Registry entries to create

- Which shortcuts to create
- Whether there is a SETUP.DLL that should be used during setup
- Whether there are COM objects that should be registered automatically by the setup process

It looks like this:

```
[DefaultInstall]
RegSettings = RegSettings.All
CEShortcuts = Shortcuts.All
CopyFiles = Files.Common
[DefaultInstall.SH3]
CopyFiles = Files.SH3
[DefaultInstall.MIPS]
CopyFiles = Files.MIPS
```

The [SourceDisksNames] and [SourceDisksFiles] Sections

Entries in the [SourceDisksNames] section follow this convention:

ordinal = ,"*<disk label>*",,*<path>*

<path> is absolute for common files and is relative for CPU-specific files.

This is how it looks in practice:

```
[SourceDisksNames]
1 = ,"Common",,C:\MYAPP
[SourceDisksNames.SH3]
2 = ,"SH3 Files",,sh3
[SourceDisksNames.MIPS]
3 = ,"MIPS Files",,mips
[SourceDisksFiles]
MyAppHelp.htc = 1
[SourceDisksFiles.SH3]
NyApp.exe = 2
[SourceDisksFiles.MIPS]
MyApp.exe = 3
```

The [DestinationDirs] Section

This section specifies where particular groups of files are installed. The format of an entry looks like this:

```
<files section> = 0,<location to install>
```

The following is an example of how to use this:

```
[DestinationDirs]
Files.SH3 = 0,%InstallDir%   ; install the SH3 bits
                             ; in the selected install directory
Files.MIPS = 0,%InstallDir%  ; install the MIPS bits
                             ; in the selected install directory
```

```
Files.Common = 0,%CE2%  ; place the help file in the \WINDOWS folder
Shortcuts.All = 0,%CE3%  ; create the shortcuts on the desktop
```

The [CopyFiles] Section

These sections specify which files to copy, what to rename them to, and how to handle particular circumstances that might arise when copying the files. The format is

<destination name>,<original name>,,flags

<destination name> is the desired target filename on the Windows CE device. *<original name>* is the name of the file before it was incorporated into the CAB file. It can be left blank if it is the same as *<destination name>*. The *flags* parameter specifies how to handle special cases. Table 16.2 shows you the flag values.

TABLE 16.2   [CopyFiles] Flag Values

Value	Meaning
0x00000001	Warn if the copying of a file is skipped.
0x00000002	The user is not allowed to skip copying a file.
0x00000010	Never overwrite the target file.
0x00000400	Only copy if the target already exists.
0x20000000	Do not copy if the target is newer.
0x40000000	Copy over the target, ignoring the date.
0x80000000	Reference-count this shared component.

The following is an example of how to use this:

```
[DefaultInstall.SH3]
CopyFiles=Files.Common, Files.SH3
[Files.Common]
; rename 'myapp.htc' to 'My App Help Files.htc'
My App Help Files.htc,myapp.htc,,0
[Files.SH3]
; rename 'myapp.exe' to 'My App.exe'
My App.exe,myapp.exe,,0
```

The [AddReg] Section

This section enables you to create Registry entries on the Windows CE device when your application is installed. The format for an entry looks like this:

<registry root>,<subkey>,<value>,<flags>,<value>(,<value>)

The *<registry root>* string specifies the Registry root location, described in Table 16.3.

TABLE 16.3   Registry Root Strings

String	Registry Root
HKCR	HKEY_CLASSES_ROOT
HKCU	HKEY_CURRENT_USER
HKLM	HKEY_LOCAL_MACHINE

<subkey> specifies the Registry path. *<value>* specifies the name of the Registry value. If it is left blank, the name (default) will be used.

<flags> specifies the type of entry and how it should be created, as shown in Table 16.4.

TABLE 16.4   Registry Entry Creation Flags

Value	Meaning
0x00000000	This is a REG_SZ entry.
0x00000001	This is a REG_BINARY entry.
0x00010000	This is a REG_MULTI_SZ entry.
0x00010001	This is a REG_DWORD entry.
0x00000002	Do not modify the entry if it already exists.

REG_BINARY values are comma-separated and are in hex format (without the 0x prefix). REG_MULTI_SZ values are comma-separated strings.

This is how it is implemented:

```
[RegSection]
; create a multi-sz entry (without clobbering any previous entry)
; of highest scorers
HKLM,Software\DogBite,HighScores,0x00010002,"JN:50","RN:45"
; create a binary entry with 6 values
HKLM,Software\DogBite,Layout,0x000000001,B,A,D,C,A,B
 The [CEShortCuts] Section
```

This section specifies which shortcuts to create when your application is installed. The format for an entry looks like this:

<shortcut name>,<type>,<file/path>,<location>

<shortcut name> is the name to use for the shortcut. If *<type>* is 0 or blank, this specifies that it is a shortcut to a file; otherwise, it is a shortcut to a folder. *<file/path>* specifies the file or path to which the shortcut provides a shortcut. The optional *<location>* parameter specifies where the shortcut is created.

This is how the [CEShortCuts] section could be implemented:

```
[CEShortCuts]
; create a desktop (%C3%) shortcut to a program
; named "dogbite.exe"
"ShortCut to DogBite",0,dogbite.exe,%C3%
```

It is not Working—How Do I Debug My CAB File?

Next, we will examine how to troubleshoot CAB file problems.

Resolving CAB File Problems

If your CAB file is failing to build, you should be able to isolate and resolve the problem using the /ERR flag and examining the error log file that is created.

If your CAB file builds successfully but fails to completely install your application correctly, it becomes a little trickier. Figure 16.1 shows the message that you and your users will see if your application does not successfully install.

FIGURE 16.1

This installation did not complete successfully.

The following two methods help isolate the reason for the failure:

- Experiment with different hardware (does it fail on SH3 but not MIPS, or does it work with Palm-size PCs but not Handheld PCs).

- Experiment with commenting out sections of the INF file to isolate whether they are causing the error. Removing the sections that aren't related to installing files (such as the Registry or shortcut creation sections) is a good starting place.

You can comment out a line in your INF file by prepending a semicolon to it.

Hey! Ho! Let's Go! Getting Your CAB File onto a Windows CE Device

Okay, you've created your CAB file. How do you get it into your users' hands so that they can install your application onto their Windows CE devices? You have two approaches:

1. Create and distribute a desktop-based setup program that oversees the installation of the CAB file. This approach works best when shipping on physical media, such as CD-ROM or diskettes.

2. Distribute the CAB file by itself. This works best for Internet downloads, especially if the user is downloading the setup directly to his or her Windows CE device (that is, a desktop computer is not involved).

Both these scenarios are discussed in the following sections.

Using a Setup Program to Install from a Desktop Machine

One option is to provide a desktop setup program that oversees the product installation and helps the user get started with your product. As with desktop setup programs, you can write your own setup program or use third-party tools. Either way, you will have to work with the Windows CE Application Manager on the desktop.

Working with the Windows CE Application Manager on the Desktop

The Windows CE Application Manager is a desktop program provided by Microsoft that allows users to manage which applications are installed on their Windows CE device. Your setup program interacts with it via its command line:

```
CEAPPMGR.EXE /REPORT <your INI file>.INI
```

If the /REPORT parameter is specified, extra information will be generated for install errors. This parameter is used for debugging and should not be used when generating your final build of setup.

The <your INI File>.INI parameter specifies the full path and filename of your INI file for your application. Your INI file is different from the INF file you created for CABWIZ.EXE and is discussed in the next section. If your application is composed of multiple CAB files, you can specify multiple INI files on the CEAPPMGR.EXE command line.

The File Format for the INI File Used by the Application Manager

The following sample shows how a Windows CE Application Manager INI file could be organized:

```
[CEAppManager]
Version  = 1.0  ; AppMgr version is 1.0
Component = Games  ; subsequent section containing needed info
[Games]
Description  = A non-existent game involving a wayward virtual pet
Uninstall  = DogBite
IconFile = dogbite.ico
IconIndex  = 0
DeviceFile  = dogbite.exe
CabFiles  = SH3\dogbite.cab, MIPS\dogbite.cab
```

Non-Desktop Installs

A desktop-based install scenario is not the only option for installing programs onto a Windows CE device. Your users can also get the CAB file onto their device by

- Copying it directly from the desktop machine (using Windows CE Services)
- Downloading the CAB file from a Web site directly to the device
- Transferring the CAB file to the Windows CE device using the Infrared port

When providing a CAB file on your Web site, be sure to include clear directions on how to download and install it. Keep in mind that Windows CE users are not necessarily power users of Windows 95, Windows 98, or Windows NT. I fielded one of the earliest end-user support calls for bFAX Pro and discovered that the users' problem was that they didn't know how to use Open File common dialog to navigate to other folders.

Where did my CAB file go? The Windows CE program that extracts your files will automatically delete the CAB file from your Windows CE device after the installation is complete. This frees up much needed space on the device, but can be frustrating if you are attempting to run your CAB file multiple times under various test circumstances (that is, with various applications running, under low memory conditions, under low storage space conditions, and so on). In these cases, you will want to make copies of your CAB file on your Windows CE device to save you the time and trouble of copying the same file multiple times from your desktop machine.

SETUP.DLL: More Control, More Control!

What if you need to tweak the Windows CE portion of the installation process to do more than the basics provided by the INF files syntax? No problem, there is a device-side DLL you can include in your CAB file that will be called on installation and when the user attempts to uninstall your program (using Remove Programs within the Control Panel).

This device-side DLL is SETUP.DLL, and you will have to build it for each CPU on which you want it to run. Table 16.5 shows the four functions that you implement in your SETUP.DLL to direct the install process.

TABLE 16.5 Functions to Implement in Your SETUP.DLL

Function	When It Is Invoked During Setup
Install_Init	Before installation begins
Install_Exit	After installation completes
Uninstall_Init	Before uninstall begins
Uninstall_Exit	After uninstall completes

The prototypes for these functions are found in the CE_SETUP.H header file. This header file can be found in the \Windows CE Tools\Wce201\MS Palm Size PC\Support\AppInst\Inc directory. This DLL does not declare these functions as exported functions. You must modify CE_SETUP.H to place __declspec(dllexport) in front of the functions listed in Table 16.5 in order to compile your SETUP.DLL.

One thing to keep in mind about SETUP.DLL is that it won't necessarily be named *SETUP.DLL* while it resides on the Windows CE device. You should not make any assumptions about its name or location when it is installed.

Installing on Windows CE 1.0 Devices

The CAB file approach to setup was not implemented (and made a logo requirement) until Windows CE 2.0 was released. In plain English, a CAB file extraction engine was not included in ROM on Windows CE 1.0 devices. If your users copy a CAB file onto a Windows CE device and launch it, nothing will happen. If it is necessary for your setup program to support installing to Windows CE 1.0 devices, you must learn a few extra APIs that are implemented on the desktop.

Table 16.6 shows the Windows CE 1.0 setup functions and the typical order in which you will likely want to use them. The functions are prototyped in PPCLOAD.H, and you will have to link with PPCLOAD.LIB to use them.

TABLE 16.6 The Windows CE 1.0 Setup Functions

Function	What It Does
Load_Init	Initializes RAPI
Load_AlreadyInstalled	Determines whether the application is already installed
Load_PegCpuType	Determines which CPU is used on the Windows CE device
Load_PegFreeSpace	Determines the amount of Windows CE storage space
Load_PegGetPlatformName	Determines which CPU is used on the Windows CE device
Load	Installs your application
Load_RegisterFileInfo	Associates an icon with your application
Load_Exit	Releases RAPI

Load_PegCpuType tells you whether you are installing on an SH3 or a MIPS device. The Load_PegGetPlatformName function returns more information about the CPU, such as whether it is a MIPS R3910 or MIPS R4100 CPU.

If you have versions of your application for both Windows CE 1.0 and Windows CE 2.0 devices, your setup program will have to determine at runtime which version of Windows CE your user is attempting to install on.

One way to determine which version of Windows CE your user is installing on is to check whether the Windows CE Application Manager is installed on the desktop machine. It is not present on desktop machines that are configured to work only with Windows CE 1.0 devices.

If you determine that it is a Windows CE 1.0 device, use these load functions to install the Windows CE 1.0 version. Otherwise, use the Windows CE Application Manager to install your Windows CE 2.0–compatible CAB files.

Summary

In this hour, you learned how to install your application on different versions of Windows CE devices. You learned how to use CABWIZ.EXE with an INF file to create CAB files and how to use CEAPPMGR.EXE with an INI file to install your CAB files on the Windows CE 2.0 devices. You also learned how to use the load functions on the desktop to install your application onto Windows CE 1.0 devices.

Q&A

Q How do you explicitly determine whether the Windows CE Application Manager is installed on the desktop computer?

A By checking the following location in the Registry on the desktop machine:
`HKLM\Software\Microsoft\Windows\CurrentVersion\App Paths`

Q How do I have my setup program automatically register my self-registering COM DLL?

A Modify your INF file to include the [`CESelfRegister=DLL filename`] key in the [`DefaultInstall`] section. The DLL must export the `DllRegisterServer` and `DllUnregisterServer` COM functions to be a self-registering DLL.

Workshop

The Workshop is designed to help you anticipate possible questions, review what you've learned, and begin thinking ahead about putting your knowledge into practice. The answers to the quiz appear in Appendix A, "Answers."

Quiz

1. Your application is failing to install because it shares a DLL with another product of yours that is already installed and running on the device. For your install to complete successfully, the other application using the DLL must be shut down so that the CAB file extraction engine can successfully examine the DLL and overwrite it with the version within your CAB file, if necessary. How do you do this programmatically from within the setup?

2. You have a file TEST.DLL that you would like to install as MYAPP.DLL in the \WINDOWS folder on the Windows CE device. You do not want to install this file if there is already a newer version of MYAPP.DLL installed. You also want to reference-count this shared component. What line would you add to your INF file's [`CopyFiles`] section to achieve this?

3. How do you install a file to the My Documents directory on the Windows CE device?

4. What is the difference between the `Load_PegCpuType` function and the `Load_PegGetPlatformName` function?

Exercises

1. Create a CAB file that installs your application (or one of the sample programs).
2. Modify the CAB file in exercise 1 to display a pop-up `Hello` message to the user before installing.

PART IV

Advanced Windows CE Programming

Hour

HOUR 17

Working with the Contacts Database API

Because Windows CE devices such as the Handheld PC (H/PC) and Palm-size PC (P/PC) are designed as personal organizers, one of their most basic functions is to store contact information. Although you typically work with the built-in Contacts application, you might have to access contact data inside your own application. To do this, a thorough Contact API was put in place.

In this hour, you will learn

- How to open and create the Contacts database
- How to add new address cards
- How to modify existing address cards
- How to delete address cards
- How to modify the sort order and retrieve information from the Contacts database

What Is the Contacts Database?

The Contacts database is the storage house for all on-device contacts. Typically, a user would use the built-in Contacts application to get and store information about personal contacts. However, you might find it necessary to access this information directly from your application. This is extremely useful because you do not have to replicate contact storage in your own application.

Contacts are stored in a system database and are organized by address cards. *Address cards* store all the contact fields in what are also known as *properties*. There are several properties per address card, such as name, address, telephone, and so on. See Hour 10, "Advanced Object Store: The Database API," for more information on how databases, records, and properties interact.

 An *address card* is the basic storage for a contact entry. Each address card contains several properties that describe the contact.

FIGURE 17.1

The Contacts application.

Providing access to the Contacts database enables you to fully integrate your application with the Windows CE system. For example, your application has to select an email address. It is extremely easy to give users a list of email addresses that are already stored on the device in the Contacts application. This makes life much simpler for both you and your end user.

Address Card Properties

Each address card contains a series of properties that describe the current contact. Your application can use a property tag when retrieving an address card or specifying the sort order.

 Details about an individual address card are stored as *address card properties*. Some property types are Name, Address, Birthday, Anniversary, Email Address, and so on.

A list of the available property tags appears in Table 17.1.

TABLE 17.1   The Contacts Database Property Tags

Property Tag	Description
HHPR_ANNIVERSARY	Anniversary date
HHPR_ASSISTANT_NAME	Assistant's name
HHPR_ASSISTANT_TELEPHONE_NUMBER	Telephone number
HHPR_BIRTHDAY	Birth date
HHPR_BUSINESS_FAX_NUMBER	Business fax number
HHPR_CAR_TELEPHONE_NUMBER	Car phone number
HHPR_CATEGORY	Category used by the Contacts application
HHPR_CHILDREN_NAME	Children's names
HHPR_COMPANY_NAME	Company name
HHPR_DEPARTMENT_NAME	Department name
HHPR_EMAIL1_EMAIL_ADDRESS	Primary email address
HHPR_EMAIL2_EMAIL_ADDRESS	Secondary email address
HHPR_EMAIL3_EMAIL_ADDRESS	Third email address
HHPR_GENERATION	Generation (2nd, 3rd, and so on)
HHPR_GIVEN_NAME	First name
HHPR_HOME2_TELEPHONE_NUMBER	Second phone number
HHPR_HOME_ADDRESS_CITY	Home city
HHPR_HOME_ADDRESS_COUNTRY	Home country
HHPR_HOME_ADDRESS_POSTAL_CODE	Home zip code
HHPR_HOME_ADDRESS_STATE	Home state
HHPR_HOME_ADDRESS_STREET	Home street address
HHPR_HOME_FAX_NUMBER	Home fax number
HHPR_HOME_TELEPHONE_NUMBER	Home phone number
HHPR_MIDDLE_NAME	Middle name
HHPR_MOBILE_TELEPHONE_NUMBER	Mobile phone number
HHPR_NAME_PREFIX	Name prefix
HHPR_NOTES	Any notes
HHPR_OFFICE_ADDRESS_CITY	Office city

17

continues

TABLE 17.1 continued

Property Tag	Description
HHPR_OFFICE_ADDRESS_COUNTRY	Office country
HHPR_OFFICE_ADDRESS_POSTAL_CODE	Office zip code
HHPR_OFFICE_ADDRESS_STATE	Office state
HHPR_OFFICE_ADDRESS_STREET	Office street address
HHPR_OFFICE_LOCATION	Office location
HHPR_OFFICE_TELEPHONE_NUMBER	Office phone number
HHPR_OFFICE2_TELEPHONE_NUMBER	Second office phone number
HHPR_OTHER_ADDRESS_CITY	Other address city
HHPR_OTHER_ADDRESS_COUNTRY	Other country
HHPR_OTHER_ADDRESS_POSTAL_CODE	Other zip code
HHPR_OTHER_ADDRESS_STATE	Other state
HHPR_OTHER_ADDRESS_STREET	Other street
HHPR_PAGER_NUMBER	Pager number
HHPR_SPOUSE_NAME	Spouse's name
HHPR_SURNAME	Last name
HHPR_TITLE	Title
HHPR_WEB_PAGE	Home page
HHPR_FILEAS	File as name (P/PC only)
HHPR_EMAIL_TYPE	Type of email
HHPR_EMAIL_OR_PAGER_TYPE	Email or pager

Opening the Contacts Database

Before writing an application that uses the Contacts database, you must make sure that your project includes the addrstor.h header file and links with addrstor.lib.

When you want to start using the Contacts database, you must first open it using the OpenAddressBook() function call:

```
BOOL fOpened = OpenAddressBook(HWND hwnd, HHPRTAG hhProp);
```

This function takes two parameters: the handle to the parent window to receive notifications and the property tag to specify what property to sort on. The tag can be set to 0 if the sort order is not needed.

To open an address book with a certain sort order requires one of the property tags that was used when the database was created. In the case of the default Contacts database, it must be one of the following: HHPR_SURNAME, HHPR_COMPANY_NAME, HHPR_OFFICE_TELEPHONE_NUMBER, or HHPR_HOME_TELEPHONE_NUMBER.

The window handle that you pass in is used to receive any notification messages if another application modifies the database while you have it open. These notifications are further discussed in Hour 10, but the two you should watch for are DB_PEGOID_CREATED and DB_PEGOID_RECORD_DELETED. The OpenAddressBook function automatically counted the number of contacts when it was opened. If you receive either one of these messages, you should call the RecountCards() function so that the system will internally recount the number of address cards.

If OpenAddressBook returns FALSE, the system could not open the Contacts database. You can use the GetLastError() function to find out why it failed. If it failed with the error ERROR_FILE_NOT_FOUND, the Contacts database does not yet exist, and you can create it using the CreateAddressBook() function:

BOOL fCreated = CreateAddressBook(HHPRTAG *rghhProps,

➥int numProps);

CreateAddressBook also takes two parameters: an array of up to four properties to define sort order (which, if NULL, will use the default order of HHPR_SURNAME, HHPR_COMPANY_NAME, HHPR_OFFICE_TELEPHONE_NUMBER, and HHPR_HOME_TELEPHONE_NUMBER) and the number of properties in the array.

Listing 17.1 is an example of how to open or create the Contacts database.

LISTING 17.1 Opening the Contacts Database

```
1: // Open or create the contacts database (sort by default)
2: BOOL OpenContacts(HWND hWndParent)
3: {
4:     if(!hWndParent)
5:         return FALSE;
6:     // Open or create the contacts database (sort by default)
7:     BOOL fOpened = FALSE;
8:     fOpened = OpenAddressBook(hWndParent, NULL);
9:     if(!fOpened) {
10:         if(GetLastError() == ERROR_FILE_NOT_FOUND) {
11:             // The database did not exist, so let's create it
```

LISTING 17.1   Opening the Contacts Database

```
12:               HHPRTAG prTags[4];
13:               prTags[0] = HHPR_EMAIL1_EMAIL_ADDRESS;
14:               prTags[1] = HHPR_COMPANY_NAME;
15:               prTags[2] = HHPR_OFFICE_TELEPHONE_NUMBER;
16:               prTags[3] = HHPR_HOME_TELEPHONE_NUMBER;
17:
18:               // Create the address book
19:               if(!CreateAddressBook((HHPRTAG *)prTags, 4))
20:                   return FALSE;
21:               // Open up the newly created address book
22:               if(!OpenAddressBook(hWndParent, 0))
23:                   return FALSE;
24:           } else
25:               return FALSE;
26:       }
27:     return TRUE;
28: }
```

When you have finished using the Contacts database, it is important to call the `CloseAddressBook()` function. It takes no parameters and ensures that the Contacts database has closed and all pending changes have been written.

Adding a New Contact

Before you can add an address card to the Contacts database, you must perform a few steps. First, you must create a new `AddressCard` structure and fill in the properties you want to include in this record.

The `AddressCard` structure is a series of strings (and two system times) that define the new contact. It consists of the following:

- `stBirthday` specifies a `SYSTEMTIME` with the contact's birthday.
- `stAnniversary` specifies a `SYSTEMTIME` with the contact's anniversary.
- `pszBusinessFax` specifies the contact's business fax number.
- `pszCompany` specifies the contact's company name.
- `pszDepartment` specifies the contact's department.
- `pszEmail` specifies the contact's email address.
- `pszMobilePhone` specifies the contact's mobile phone number.
- `pszOfficeLocation` specifies the contact's office location.
- `pszPager` specifies the contact's pager number.
- `pszWorkPhone` specifies the contact's work phone number.

- `pszTitle` specifies the contact's title.
- `pszHomePhone` specifies the contact's home phone number.
- `pszEmail2` specifies the contact's secondary email address.
- `pszSpouse` specifies the name of the contact's spouse.
- `pszNotes` specifies any additional notes on this contact.
- `pszEmail3` specifies the contact's third email address.
- `pszHomePhone2` specifies the contact's second home phone.
- `pszHomeFax` specifies the contact's home fax number.
- `pszCarPhone` specifies the contact's car phone number.
- `pszAssistant` specifies the name of the contact's assistant.
- `pszAssistantPhone` specifies the phone number of the contact's assistant.
- `pszChildren` specifies the names of the contact's children.
- `pszCategory` specifies the contact's category used in the Contacts application for sorting.
- `pszWebPage` specifies the contact's home page.
- `pszWorkPhone2` specifies the contact's secondary phone number.
- `pszNamePrefix` specifies the contact's prefix (that is, *Mr.*, *Mrs.*, and so on).
- `pszGivenName` specifies the contact's first name.
- `pszMiddleName` specifies the contact's middle name.
- `pszSurname` specifies the contact's last name.
- `pszGeneration` specifies the contact's generation (III, IV, and so on).
- `pszHomeAddrStreet` specifies the contact's home street address.
- `pszHomeAddrCity` specifies the contact's home city.
- `pszHomeAddrState` specifies the contact's home state.
- `pszHomeAddrPostalCode` specifies the contact's home postal code.
- `pszHomeAddrCountry` specifies the contact's home country.
- `pszOtherAddrStreet` specifies the contact's alternative street address.
- `pszOtherAddrCity` specifies the contact's alternative city.
- `pszOtherAddrState` specifies the contact's alternative state.
- `pszOtherAddrPostalCode` specifies the contact's alternative postal code.
- `pszOtherAddrCountry` specifies the contact's alternative country.
- `pszOfficeAddrStreet` specifies the contact's office street address.

17

- `pszOfficeAddrCity` specifies the contact's office city.
- `pszOfficeAddrState` specifies the contact's office state.
- `pszOfficeAddrPostalCode` specifies the contact's office postal code.
- `pszOfficeAddrCountry` specifies the contact's office country.

After you have filled out what parameters you need, you must make several calls to the `SetMask()` function, one for each property that is defined in your `AddressCard`. It takes two parameters, a pointer to the new `AddressCard`, and the property tag that you want to make active (one of the `HHPR_` tags from Table 17.1). If you pass in 0 as the tag, all property tags are masked as on. The `SetMask` function is defined as

```
void SetMask(AddressCard *pac, HHPRTAG hhProp);
```

After you have set the mask for the available properties, you can finally call the `AddAddressCard()` function to add your new contact. It takes three parameters: a pointer to the new address card, a pointer to a `PEGOID` that will receive the object identifier for the new record, and a pointer that will get the index of the new address card (based on the current sort order).

```
BOOL fAdded = AddAddressCard(AddressCard *pac, PEGOID *poidCard,
```

➥`int *pindex);`

For an example of adding a new contact, look at Listing 17.2. Be sure that the Contacts database is already open before adding a new `AddressCard`.

LISTING 17.2 Creating a New Contact

```
 1: BOOL NewContact(HWND hWndParent)
 2: {
 3:     if(!hWndParent)
 4:         return FALSE;
 5:     if(!OpenContacts(hWndParent))
 6:         return FALSE;
 7:
 8:     AddressCard adrCard;
 9:     PEGOID OID = 0;
10:     int nIndex = 0;
11:     BOOL fAdded = FALSE;
12:
13:     memset(&adrCard, 0, sizeof(AddressCard));
14:
15:     // Build the contact
16:     adrCard.pszGivenName = TEXT("Diane");
17:     adrCard.pszSurname = TEXT("Allerdice");
18:     adrCard.pszEmail = TEXT("diane@nowhere.com");
```

```
19:        adrCard.pszCompany = TEXT("Nowhere Movie Company");
20:        adrCard.pszDepartment = TEXT("Employee Relations");
21:        adrCard.pszWorkPhone = TEXT("(555) 555-1212");
22:        adrCard.pszOfficeAddrStreet = TEXT("1212 Movie Blvd");
23:        adrCard.pszOfficeAddrCity = TEXT("Hollywood");
24:        adrCard.pszOfficeAddrState = TEXT("CA");
25:        adrCard.pszOfficeAddrPostalCode = TEXT("99999");
26:        adrCard.pszOfficeAddrCountry = TEXT("USA");
27:        adrCard.stBirthday.wYear = 1969;
28:        adrCard.stBirthday.wMonth = 11;
29:        adrCard.stBirthday.wDay = 14;
30:
31:        // Apply the appropriate contact masks
32:        SetMask(&adrCard, HHPR_GIVEN_NAME);
33:        SetMask(&adrCard, HHPR_SURNAME);
34:        SetMask(&adrCard, HHPR_EMAIL1_EMAIL_ADDRESS);
35:        SetMask(&adrCard, HHPR_COMPANY_NAME);
36:        SetMask(&adrCard, HHPR_DEPARTMENT_NAME);
37:        SetMask(&adrCard, HHPR_OFFICE_TELEPHONE_NUMBER);
38:        SetMask(&adrCard, HHPR_OFFICE_ADDRESS_STREET);
39:        SetMask(&adrCard, HHPR_OTHER_ADDRESS_CITY);
40:        SetMask(&adrCard, HHPR_OTHER_ADDRESS_STATE);
41:        SetMask(&adrCard, HHPR_OTHER_ADDRESS_POSTAL_CODE);
42:        SetMask(&adrCard, HHPR_OTHER_ADDRESS_COUNTRY);
43:        SetMask(&adrCard, HHPR_BIRTHDAY);
44:
45:        // Add the new contact
46:        fAdded = AddAddressCard(&adrCard, &OID, &nIndex);
47:
48:        CloseAddressBook();
49:        return TRUE;
50: }
```

Modifying an Existing Contact

To modify an existing address card, you must first find and open the card you want to modify. You will have to get the address card's OID in order to modify the card. To search the database for an OID, see the section "Searching the Contacts Database" later in the chapter. If you already know the index of the contact you want to retrieve, you can use the GetAddressCardOid() function. This call takes only one parameter, which is the index of the card for which you want to get the object identifier.

```
PEGOID pOid = GetAddressCardOid(int nIndex);
```

Conversely, if you already know the PEGOID of a particular address card, you can use the GetAddressCardIndex() function to find the index of the particular card. It takes only one parameter, which is the PEGOID of the card for which you want to get the index.

```
int nIndex = GetAddressCardIndex(PEGOID oidCard);
```

17

To use either the `GetAddressCardIndex()` or the `GetAddressCardOid()` function, you must have specified a sort order when opening the Contacts database with `OpenAddressBook`. If you do not specify a sort order, both these calls with fail.

When you know the address card's `OID`, there are two ways to get the current properties on an address card. Both will return to you an `AddressCard` structure with which you can make your modifications.

To retrieve the entire card, you can call the `OpenAddressCard()` function. It is defined as

```
BOOL fOpened = OpenAddressCard(PEGOID oidCard, AddressCard *pac,
➡ULONG uFlags);
```

The function takes three parameters: the `PEGOID` of the card you want to receive, a pointer to an `AddressCard` structure that receives the card's information, and a flag field.

The flags can be set to either `OAC_ALLOCATE`, which will allocate additional memory so that you can modify the card's data, or `0`, which will make the `AddressCard` you received for read-only purposes.

To retrieve only the card properties you are interested in, you can use the `GetAddressCardProperties()` function call. The call takes four parameters: the `PEGOID` of the card you want to get data from, a pointer to an `AddressCard` structure that receives the card information, the number of property tags in the property tag array, and finally, a pointer to an array of property tags (the tags that begin with `HHPR_` in the preceding code snippets) that identify the properties you want to receive.

The function is defined as

```
BOOL fGetProps = GetAddressCardProperties(PEGOID oidCard,
➡AddressCard *pac, int numRequestedProps, HHPRTAG *rghhProp);
```

After you have used one of these methods to get the card's property data, you can then modify the strings in the `AddressCard` structure you received. Next, you must call the `SetMask()` function (as described previously in the section "Adding a New Contact") on each property you have modified.

You can now call the `ModifyAddressCard()` function to store your changes to the address card:

```
BOOL ModifyAddressCard(AddressCard *pac, PEGOID oidCard, int *pindex);
```

The `ModifyAddressCard` function takes three parameters: the pointer to the address card you have modified, the `PEGOID` of the card to modify, and a pointer that will receive the index of the newly modified address card.

When you finish modifying the address card's properties, you will also have to call the FreeAddressCard function to free the memory that the system allocated for the address card when you received it. You only have to pass in the pointer to the AddressCard structure that you received.

```
void FreeAddressCard(AddressCard *pac);
```

For an example of how to modify an address card, look at Listing 17.3.

LISTING 17.3 Modifying an Address Card

```
 1: BOOL ModifyContact(HWND hWndParent)
 2: {
 3:     if(!hWndParent)
 4:         return FALSE;
 5:     if(!OpenContacts(hWndParent))
 6:         return FALSE;
 7:
 8:     // Get the first contact's object identifier
 9:     PEGOID pOid = GetAddressCardOid;
10:     if(pOid == 0) {
11:         CloseAddressBook();
12:         return FALSE;
13:     }
14:
15:     // Get the contact's properties
16:     AddressCard AdrCard;
17:     BOOL fOpened = FALSE;
18:     int nIndex = 0;
19:
20:     memset(&AdrCard, 0, sizeof(AddressCard));
21:     fOpened = OpenAddressCard(pOid, &AdrCard, OAC_ALLOCATE);
22:     if(fOpened) {
23:         // Modify the record
24:         AdrCard.pszDepartment = TEXT("Modified Department");
25:         SetMask(&AdrCard, HHPR_DEPARTMENT_NAME);
26:
27:         // Save the changes back to the database
28:         ModifyAddressCard(&AdrCard, pOid, &nIndex);
29:
30:         // Free the memory allocated to the contact
31:         FreeAddressCard(&AdrCard);
32:     }
33:
34:     CloseAddressBook();
35:     return TRUE;
36: }
```

17

Deleting a Contact

To delete an address card from the Contacts database, you must retrieve the card's OID before you delete. See the previous section on getting an address card's object identifier.

To delete an address card, you only have to call the DeleteAddressCard() function. Its only parameter is the address card's OID to delete:

```
BOOL fDeleted = DeleteAddressCard(PEGOID oidCard);
```

The function will return TRUE or FALSE, depending on whether it was able to successfully delete the entry. This call will fail if the database was not previously opened by calling the OpenAddressBook() function.

Searching the Contacts Database

To search for a particular entry in the Contacts database, you can use the GetMatchingEntry() function call:

```
BOOL fFound = GetMatchingEntry(TCHAR *szMatch, int *pBufSize,
➥ TCHAR *szField, PEGOID *poidMatch, HHPRTAG *phhMatch);
```

The function takes five parameters: a pointer to a buffer with the string to match, the size of the buffer, the name of the property to search for (see the GetPropertyDataStruct() function described in the next section), a pointer to receive the object ID of the record, and a pointer to receive the property tag that contains the string.

If there is more than one result for the search criteria, Windows CE will automatically pop up a dialog that allows the user to choose a contact.

For example, the following code searches the contacts for the name *Lisa* on a P/PC (a P/PC uses the HHPR_FILEAS tag):

```
1: BOOL FindContacts(HWND hWndParent)
2: {
3:      TCHAR tchSearch[64] = TEXT("\0");
4:      PEGOID OID = 0;
5:      HHPRTAG hhMatch = 0;
6:      int nSearchLen = 0;
7:      PropertyDataStruct pds;
8:      BOOL fFound = FALSE;
9:
10:     if(!hWndParent)
11:         return FALSE;
12:     if(!OpenContacts(hWndParent))
13:         return FALSE;
14:
```

```
15:    _tcscpy(tchSearch, TEXT("Lisa"));
16:    nSearchLen = sizeof(tchSearch);
17:
18:    GetPropertyDataStruct(GPDS_PROPERTY, HHPR_FILEAS, &pds);
19:    fFound = GetMatchingEntry(tchSearch, &nSearchLen,
       ➥pds.pszPropertyName, &OID, &hhMatch);
20:
21:    CloseAddressBook();
22:    return TRUE;
23: }
```

Getting Information from the Contacts Database

To obtain the number of contacts in the Contacts database, you can call the
GetNumberOfAddressCards() function. It does not take any parameters and will return
an integer value for the number of records.

```
int nCards = GetNumberOfAddressCards(void);
```

For more detailed information on the individual properties, you can use the
GetPropertyDataStruct() call, which takes the following parameters:

- nFlag specifies how the function should get data. It can be set to the following.

  - GPDS_INDEX[md]To use the property's index to retrieve information

  - GPDS_NAME[md]To use the property's name to retrieve information

  - GPDS_PROPERTY[md]To use one of the property tags to retrieve information

- uValue specifies what to retrieve, depending on what the fFlag field is set to.

- pPds specifies a pointer to a PropertyDataStruct structure, which will receive
  information about the property.

The function is defined as

```
int nPos = GetPropertyDataStruct(int fFlag, ULONG uValue,
➥PropertyDataStruct *ppds);
```

and will return the index of the specified property. You will get a GPDS_ERR return code if
the function fails.

Sorting the Contacts Database

To obtain information about the Contacts database sort order, you can call the
GetSortOrder() function. This will return to you a property tag (an HHPR_ tag) that the

database is sorted under. The call takes a single parameter, a flag (TRUE or FALSE) specifying whether you want to get the actual sort or the user-perceived sort order.

```
HHPRTAG hhprTag = GetSortOrder(BOOL fDatabaseSort);
```

What is a perceived sort order? Well, some properties can't be used to sort the database. For example, HHPR_LAST_FIRST_NAME can't be used to perform the actual sort. The user, however, will see the entry as Last, First Name, while the database is actually sorting on HHPR_SURNAME. A list of user-perceived sort orders appears in Table 17.2.

TABLE 17.2 User-Perceived Sort Orders

User-Perceived Order	Actual Order
HHPR_FIRST_LAST_NAME	HHPR_GIVEN_NAME
HHPR_LAST_FIRST_NAME	HHPR_SURNAME
HHPR_HOME_ADDRESS	HHPR_HOME_ADDRESS_STREET
HHPR_OFFICE_ADDRESS	HHPR_OFFICE_ADDRESS_STREET
HHPR_OTHER_ADDRESS	HHPR_OTHER_ADDRESS_STREET

If you want to set the sort order for the Contacts database, you can call the SetSortOrder() function. This call takes a single parameter, the property tag that you want to sort on. It will return TRUE or FALSE, depending on whether the call was successful.

```
BOOL fSetOrder = SetSortOrder(HHPRTAG hhProp);
```

To find out what columns can be sorted on, you can use the GetColumnProperties() call. This function takes two parameters: a pointer to an array that will get the property tags (the HHPR_ tags) that can be sorted and a pointer to an integer that receives the number of tags copied to the array.

This function is defined as

```
BOOL fSorted = GetColumnProperties(HHPRTAG *propList, int * pColumns);
```

Finally, if you want to change the sorting properties for the Contacts database, you can use the SetColumnProperties() function:

```
BOOL fSorted = SetColumnProperties(HHPRTAG *propList, int nColumns);
```

To call this function, you must provide a pointer to an array of up to four property tags and an integer that specifies the number of property tags in the array. If you pass in NULL for the property list, the database will sort using the default.

Summary

In this hour, you were shown how to use the Contacts database API. When developing applications that require information about people, such as email addresses or contact information, using the Contacts database can provide a nice feeling of integration with the user's Windows CE device. It should be noted that the Windows CE logo specifications require you not to duplicate the functionality of the Contacts database in your own application.

Q&A

Q Will I ever have to create the Contacts database?

A Most likely, no. Unless you accidentally delete the database, it is standard on all devices.

Q When getting a contact's address card, is it better to use `OpenAddressCard` or `GetAddressCardProperties`?

A `GetAddressCardProperties` will use less memory because you specify what properties you want to get.

Workshop

The Workshop is designed to help you anticipate possible questions, review what you've learned, and begin thinking ahead about putting your knowledge into practice. The answers to the quiz are in Appendix A, "Answers."

Quiz

1. How do you go about creating a new Contacts database?
2. What is an address card?
3. What are address card properties?
4. What do you call to add a new contact?
5. When adding a new contact, what do you have to do to your `AddressCard` before adding it?
6. How do you delete a contact?
7. How do you find out how many contacts are in the database?

Exercises

1. Modify Listing 17.3 so that you add a second email address to a contact.

17

Hour **18**

Creating Mail-Enabled Applications

This lesson focuses on how to use the Windows CE Mail API. Windows CE does not use MAPI; it has its own unique API for accessing the email message store.

In this hour, you will learn

- How to open and close the mail message store
- How to read messages from the mail message store
- How to write messages to the mail message store

An Introduction to the Windows CE Mail API

You will be introduced to the Windows CE mail structures and functions in the following sections. They are simple and straightforward, but they are powerful because they allow you to *quickly* mail-enable your Windows CE applications.

> The function pointers for the Mail API that are defined in MSGSTORE.H are
> listed in the following sections. They are helpful because they enable you to
> dynamically load MSGSTORE.DLL at runtime, making your application more
> portable. MSGSTORE.DLL is available on all PC Companion Windows CE
> devices, but is an optional component of the operating system. It may not
> be available on all non–PC Companion Windows CE devices you are
> interested in running your application on. If you statically link with
> MSGSTORE.LIB, your application will fail to start on systems that do not have
> MSGSTORE.DLL. If you dynamically load it at runtime (using the LoadLibrary
> system API), you will be able to run on systems that don't have
> MSGSTORE.DLL, but with your mail-enabled features disabled. This is
> demonstrated in the source code later in this lesson.

Introducing the `MailMsg` Structure

The `MailMsg` structure, in Listing 18.1, is the underlying data structure used by many of
the Windows CE Mail APIs.

LISTING 18.1   The `MailMsg` Structure

```
 1: typedef struct MailMsg_s {
 2:      DWORD      dwMsgId;
 3:      DWORD      dwFlags;
 4:      DWORD      dwMsgLen;
 5:      WORD       wBodyLen;
 6:      FILETIME   ftDate;
 7:      LPWSTR     szSvcId;
 8:      LPWSTR     szSvcNam;
 9:      WCHAR*     pwcHeaders;
10:      LPWSTR     szBody;
11:      CEOID      oid;
12:      HANDLE     hHeap;
13: } MailMsg;
```

The `dwMsgId` member specifies the ID of the message to retrieve. `dwMsgId` is ignored
when storing a message. The `dwFlags` member can contain a combination of three types
of flags: folder flags, message flags, and status flags (examined in more depth in the
following paragraph). `dwMsgLen` contains the length of the complete body of the message
on the server. `wBodyLen` contains the length of the message body in the message store.
`ftDate` contains the time the message was received. `szSvcId` is the service-defined ID.
`szSvcNam` contains the service name. `pwcHeaders` contains the NULL-separated message
header fields. The buffer is double NULL terminated. The `szBody` member contains the

message body. oid is the database object ID, which should not be modified by your program. hHeap is the heap for the message storage.

Folder, Message, and Status Flags

The folder flags specify the folder in which to carry out a requested action (such as locating or storing a message). Only one folder flag should be used at a time (that is, they should not be combined with one another). A folder flag can be combined with message and status flags.

The message flags specify the following:

- How much of the message to retrieve from the message store
- How the message should be handled within the message store

The status flags are used to indicate the status of a message. They can also be used to specify search criteria for the MailFirst and MailNext functions.

Refer to the Microsoft help system at http://msdn.microsoft.com for an in-depth explanation of the various flags available for each of these three categories.

Introducing the Basic Mail APIs

The following are the basic functions necessary for opening the message store, reading and writing messages and folders from it, closing the message store, and retrieving error codes and messages when failures are encountered:

- MailOpen function
- MailPut function
- MailGet function
- MailUpdate function
- MailDelete function
- MailFree function
- MailClose function
- MailError function
- MailErrorMsg function

With the exception of the MailError and MailErrorMsg functions, the mail functions return TRUE if they are successful. If they fail, they return FALSE and set internal error information that can be retrieved using the MailError and MailErrorMsg functions. The following sections discuss all these functions in depth.

18

The `MailOpen` Function

The `MailOpen` function opens the mail message store. It requires two parameters:

- `phMail` is a pointer to the handle that should receive the current mail context.
- `fAllowCreate` specifies whether the message store should be created if it is not already present on the system. If this is `FALSE` and the message store is not present, `MailOpen` will fail. If this is `TRUE` and the message store already exists or the message store was created with its default folders (Inbox, Outbox, and so on), `MailOpen` will succeed.

The predefined function pointer for `MailOpen` is `PMAILOPEN`.

The `MailPut` Function

The `MailPut` function creates a new mail entry in the message store. It requires two parameters:

- `hMail` is a handle to the current mail context.
- `pmn` is a pointer to a `MailMsg` structure, in which `dwMsgID` is ignored.

The predefined function pointer for `MailPut` is `PMAILPUT`.

The `MailGet` Function

The `MailGet` function retrieves a mail message from the message store. It requires two parameters:

- `hMail` is a handle to the current mail context.
- `pmn` is a pointer to a `MailMsg` structure. The `oid` member specifies which message to retrieve. The `dwFlags` member specifies how much of the message to return in the `MailMsg` structure. Any memory allocated by this function should be freed with a call to `MailFree`.

The predefined function pointer for `MailGet` is `PMAILGET`.

The `MailUpdate` Function

The `MailUpdate` function updates the message information in the message store. The mail message being updated must have previously been returned by `MailGet`, `MailFirst`, or `MailNext`. It requires three parameters:

- `hMail` is the handle to the current mail context.
- `pmm` is a pointer to the `MailMsg` structure variable that contains the updated fields.

- fDoAll specifies whether all the fields should be updated. If you only want to save changes to the dwFlags member, this can be set to FALSE; otherwise, it should be set to TRUE.

The predefined function pointer for MailUpdate is PMAILUPDATE.

The MailDelete Function

The MailDelete function deletes the specified message from the message store. It requires two parameters:

- hMail is the mail handle to the current mail context.
- pmm is a pointer to a MailMsg structure variable whose oid member specifies the object identifier of the message to delete.

The predefined function pointer for MailDelete is PMAILDELETE.

The MailFree Function

The MailFree function frees memory allocated by a previous call to MailGet, MailFirst, or MailNext. MailFree has one parameter: pmm specifies the mail message to free.

The predefined function pointer for MailFree is PMAILFREE.

The MailClose Function

The MailClose function frees the handle to the current mail context. It requires one parameter: the handle to the current mail context you want to release.

The predefined function pointer for MailClose is PMAILCLOSE.

The MailError Function

The MailError function returns the error or warning code of the previously called Mail API function. A return value of 0 indicates that no warnings or errors were encountered. If the return value is greater than zero, it indicates that an error was encountered. If the return value is less than zero, it indicates that a warning was encountered.

The mail error value is reset by each Mail API function. To accurately capture an error code, you call MailError after a mail function returns FALSE and before you call in to any other mail functions. This is different from the standard Win32 APIs, which usually only call the SetLastError function (thereby changing the value returned by GetLastError) if an error condition is encountered.

The predefined function pointer for MailError is PMAILERROR.

The MailErrorMsg Function

The MailErrorMsg function returns the last mail error code. It also fills a string buffer with a description of the error and indicates the source code line number on which the error occurred. MailErrorMsg requires four parameters:

- hMail is the handle to the mail context.
- szBuf is the buffer to fill with a description of the error condition.
- iBufLen is the length of the input buffer in number of characters (not number of bytes).
- piSrcLine is a pointer to an integer that receives the number of the line where the error occurred.

The predefined function pointer for MailErrorMsg is PMAILERRORMSG.

Locating Mail Messages: MailFirst and MailNext

The MailFirst and MailNext functions are used to enumerate through mail messages in the message store. The dwFlags member of the MailMsg structure allows you to specify which folder to search or whether all folders should be searched.

Like the MailGet function, both MailFirst and MailNext allow you to specify how much of the message to retrieve by using the dwFlags member of the MailMsg structure. If MAIL_GET_FLAGS is specified, the flags and object identifier of the message is retrieved. If MAIL_GET_BODY is specified, the entire message (flags and body) is retrieved. If neither flag is specified, everything *but* the message body is retrieved.

If you aren't using MAIL_GET_FLAGS (that is, you are either using or not specifying either flag), MailFirst and MailNext will allocate memory for you. You must free this memory when you are done with it by calling the MailFree function.

The MailFirst Function

The MailFirst function retrieves the first message of a certain type from a folder in the message store. This function requires two parameters:

- hMail is the handle to the current mail context.
- pmm is a pointer to a mail message structure. The dwFlags field specifies which folder to look in, what type of messages to look for, and how much of the message to retrieve.

The predefined function pointer for `MailFirst` is `PMAILFIRST`.

The `MailNext` Function

The `MailNext` function retrieves the next message of a certain type from a folder in the message store. This function requires two parameters:

- `hMail` is the handle to the current mail context.
- `pmm` is a pointer to a mail message structure containing the previous mail message that was found.

The predefined function pointer for `MailNext` is `PMAILNEXT`.

Other Important Routines

Some other routines that are important to remember are

- `MailHeaderLen`, `MailGetField`, and `MailSetField`—The functions used to access the mail headers
- `MailPutFolder`—The function that allows you to work with folders

These are available on all versions of Windows CE.

Accessing the Mail Headers

The `MailHeaderLen` function returns the number of characters used in the entire header string. The header string is a collection of message header entries composed of a `name` field separated from its associated `value` field by a `NULL` character. Additionally, the entries are separated from each other by a `NULL` character. The header string is terminated by two `NULL` characters.

The `MailGetField` and `MailSetField` functions are used to read, write, add, and delete fields from the message header of a particular mail message (specified by the `pmm` parameter). The field names are not case sensitive: either `cc` or `CC` will work. Examples of field names include `To`, `From`, and `Subject`. You can use Microsoft's Pocket Inbox to display the names and values of all the message headers. It displays them when you view a message (see Figure 18.1).

18

FIGURE 18.1

Message header field names and values are viewable from within Pocket Inbox.

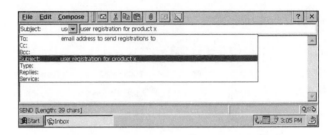

If fGetName is FALSE, MailGetFields returns a pointer to the value stored for this field. If fGetName is TRUE, MailGetFields returns a pointer to the name.

MailSetField sets the field specified by the szName parameter to the value specified by the szVal parameter. If the field doesn't exist in the message header, it will be created. If szVal is NULL and the field exists in the message header, it will be deleted from the message header.

Working with Folders

The MailPutFolder function allows you to add, delete, or rename folders.

> The Inbox, Outbox, and Sent folders are system folders. System folders cannot be modified or deleted.

The MailGetFolderName function allows you to retrieve a folder name based on a folder ID. The MailGetFolderId function retrieves a folder ID, based on the folder name that you provide.

An Overview of Mail APIs Available in Windows CE 2.0 and Above

The APIs I have discussed up to this point are available on all versions of Windows CE. With Windows CE 2.0, some additional functionality has been added, namely, support for attachments and the capability to specify the sort order for MailFirst and MailNext to use.

Table 18.1 provides you with an overview of what functions were added and their purpose.

TABLE 18.1   Mail APIs Added in Windows CE 2.0

Function	What It Does
MailDeleteAttachment	Deletes attachments from the specified message
MailGetAttachment	Gets attachments for the specified message
MailGetSort	Gets the sort order for `MailFirst` and `MailNext`
MailLocalAttachmentLen	Returns the total local storage used to store the attachments
MailPutAttachment	Adds or modifies attachments for the specified message
MailRequestAttachment	Requests the message store to mark an attachment for download, so that it will be downloaded next time the mail client is connected to the server
MailSetSort	Sets the sort order for `MailFirst` and `MailNext`

Writing Mail Messages to the Mail Message Store

The follow example shows how to modify a basic text editor so that it can be used to generate email. The user is given the ability to email the contents of the file being edited to an email address of his or her choosing.

The first step is to ask the user for

- The email address of the desired recipient
- The subject line to use for the email message (see Figure 18.2)

FIGURE 18.2

Asking the user for an email address and a message subject.

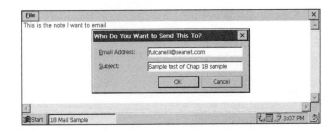

If the user clicks Cancel, the operation is aborted. If the user clicks OK, you want to use the current contents of the edit control to create an outgoing email to the specified recipient. Listing 18.2 shows you how.

LISTING 18.2   Providing a Text Editor with the Capability to Copy the Current
Document into an Outgoing Email Message

```
 1: VOID CreateOutgoingEmail()
 2: {
 3:     TCHAR    *tcBuffer;
 4:     DWORD    dwBufferSize;
 5:
 6:     PMAILOPEN    pMailOpen   = (PMAILOPEN)   GetProcAddress(
         ➥ g_hMailDll, TEXT( "MailOpen" ) );
 7:     PMAILCLOSE   pMailClose  = (PMAILCLOSE)  GetProcAddress(
         ➥ g_hMailDll, TEXT( "MailClose" ) );
 8:     PMAILPUT   pMailPut   = (PMAILPUT)   GetProcAddress(
         ➥g_hMailDll, TEXT( "MailPut" ) );
 9:
10:     PMAILSETFIELD   pMailSetField = (PMAILSETFIELD) GetProcAddress(
         ➥ g_hMailDll, TEXT( "MailSetField" ) );
11:
12:     HANDLE        hMail;
13:     MailMsg       MailMessage;
14:
15:     SHELLEXECUTEINFO    si;
16:
17:
18:     if ( !pMailOpen ¦¦ !pMailClose ¦¦ !pMailPut ¦¦ !pMailSetField ) {
19:         MessageBox( GetFocus(), TEXT( "Could not load mail " )
             ➥TEXT( "function pointers" ),
20:                     szTitle, MB_OK¦MB_ICONEXCLAMATION );
21:         return;
22:     }
23:
24:     if ( pMailOpen( &hMail, TRUE ) ) {
25:
26:         dwBufferSize = GetWindowTextLength( g_hwndText ) + 1;
27:
28:         tcBuffer = (TCHAR*) malloc( dwBufferSize * sizeof(TCHAR) );
29:
30:         if ( tcBuffer ) {
31:
32:             SYSTEMTIME    st;
33:
34:             // initialize the mail message to have the desired TO and
35:             // SUBJECT fields and the correct mail message body.
36:             memset( &MailMessage, 0x00, sizeof( MailMessage ) );
37:             pMailSetField( &MailMessage, TEXT( "To" ),
                 ➥g_tcEmailAddress );
38:             pMailSetField( &MailMessage, TEXT( "Subject" ),
                 ➥g_tcSubjectLine );
39:             GetWindowText( g_hwndText, tcBuffer, dwBufferSize );
40:             MailMessage.szBody = tcBuffer;
```

```
41:
42:                 // we want to place the message in the Outbox,
                     // ready to be sent
43:                 MailMessage.dwFlags = MAIL_FOLDER_OUTBOX |
                     ➥MAIL_STATUS_COMPOSED;
44:
45:                 // properly time/date stamp this email
                     // with the current time
46:                 GetLocalTime( &st );
47:                 SystemTimeToFileTime( &st, &MailMessage.ftDate );
48:
49:                 // add the message to the message store
50:                 if ( !pMailPut( hMail, &MailMessage ) )
                     ➥ShowMailError( hMail );
51:
52:                 // close our handle to the message store
53:                 pMailClose( hMail );
54:
55:                 // free the text buffer
56:                 free( tcBuffer );
57:
58:                 // launch Pocket Mail
59:                 memset( &si, 0x00, sizeof( si ) );
60:                 si.cbSize = sizeof( si );
61:                 si.lpFile = TEXT( "\\windows\\pmail.exe" );
62:                 ShellExecuteEx( &si );
63:
64:             }
65:
66:         }
67:
68: }
```

Note that the Windows CE version of GetProcAddress requires a Unicode string for its second parameter. This is in contrast to the Windows NT version of the function, which requires an ANSI string, even when building Unicode applications.

Reading Mail Messages from the Mail Message Store

The following example shows how to modify a basic text editor to allow your users to import text from email messages. This is done by providing a mechanism for browsing received emails, allowing the user to select one of them, and then importing its contents into the file currently being edited.

The first step is to enable the user to browse the email messages in the Inbox. Figure 18.3 shows how this appears to the user.

FIGURE **18.3**

Allowing the user to select the email message to import.

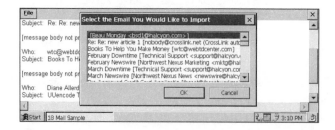

> A List control was chosen for simplicity's sake. If this code was being used in a commercial application, a ListView would be more appropriate.

After the user selects the desired email message, it is imported into the current file at the current location in the edit window. Listing 18.3 shows how DLGPROC implements this.

LISTING 18.3   A DLGPROC to Enable the User to Select an Email Message to Import into an Edit Control

```
 1: LRESULT CALLBACK SelectEmailToImport(
 2:                     HWND hDlg, UINT message,
 3:                     WPARAM wParam, LPARAM lParam )
 4: {
 5:     HANDLE      hMail;
 6:     MailMsg     MailMessage;
 7:     INT         i;
 8:     TCHAR       *tc, tcText[MAX_PATH+1];
 9:
10:     // the choice is to declare these as static OR use GetProcAddress
11:     // twice (once on WM_INITDIALOG and once on IDOK). The assumption
12:     // is that using static would generate less code than additional
13:     // function calls, but you yourself can experiment by doing before
14:     // and after comparisons of the EXE and OBJ file sizes
15:     static HWND         hControl;
16:     static PMAILOPEN    pMailOpen;
17:     static PMAILCLOSE   pMailClose;
18:     static PMAILPUT     pMailGet;
19:     static PMAILPUT     pMailFirst;
20:     static PMAILPUT     pMailNext;
21:     static PMAILFREE    pMailFree;
22:     static PMAILGETFIELD pMailGetField;
```

```
23:
24:        switch (message)
25:        {
26:            case WM_INITDIALOG:
27:
28:                if ( g_hMailDll == NULL ) {
29:                    MessageBox(    hDlg,
30:                                    TEXT( "Function not available because" )
31:                                    ➡TEXT( "MSGSTORE.DLL is not present" ),
                                        szTitle,
32:                                    MB_OK¦MB_ICONEXCLAMATION );
33:                    PostMessage( hDlg, WM_COMMAND, IDCANCEL, 0 );
34:                    break;
35:                }
36:
37:                // list the email messages available to import
38:                {
39:                    pMailOpen    = (PMAILOPEN)     GetProcAddress( g_hMailDll,
                        ➡ TEXT( "MailOpen" ) );
40:                    pMailClose   = (PMAILCLOSE)    GetProcAddress(
                        ➡g_hMailDll, TEXT( "MailClose" ) );
41:                    pMailGet     = (PMAILGET)      GetProcAddress( g_hMailDll,
                        ➡ TEXT( "MailGet" ) );
42:                    pMailFirst   = (PMAILFIRST)    GetProcAddress(
                        ➡g_hMailDll, TEXT( "MailFirst" ) );
43:                    pMailNext    = (PMAILNEXT)     GetProcAddress( g_hMailDll,
                        ➡TEXT( "MailNext" ) );
44:                    pMailFree    = (PMAILFREE)     GetProcAddress( g_hMailDll,
                        ➡ TEXT( "MailFree" ) );
45:                    pMailGetField = (PMAILGETFIELD) GetProcAddress(
                        ➡g_hMailDll, TEXT( "MailGetField" ) );
46:
47:                    hControl = GetDlgItem( hDlg, IDC_EMAILLIST );
48:
49:                    if ( !pMailOpen ¦¦ !pMailClose ¦¦ !pMailGet ¦¦
                        ➡!pMailGetField ) {
50:                        MessageBox( GetFocus(), TEXT( "Could not load mail" )
                                        ➡TEXT( "function pointers" ),
51:                                    szTitle, MB_OK¦MB_ICONEXCLAMATION );
52:                        break;
53:                    }
54:
55:                    if ( pMailOpen( &hMail, TRUE ) ) {
56:
57:                        memset( &MailMessage, 0x00, sizeof( MailMessage ) );
58:                        MailMessage.dwFlags = lParam;
59:
60:                        if ( !pMailFirst( hMail, &MailMessage ) ) {
61:
62:                            ShowMailError( hMail );
63:                            EnableWindow( GetDlgItem( hDlg, IDOK ), FALSE );
```

continues

18

LISTING **18.3**   continued

```
 64:                     return FALSE;
 65:
 66:                 } else {
 67:
 68:                     TCHAR    *ptcSubject;
 69:                     TCHAR    *ptcName;
 70:                     TCHAR    tcString[MAX_PATH];
 71:
 72:                     i = 0;
 73:
 74:                     do {
 75:
 76:                         ptcSubject = pMailGetField( &MailMessage,
                            ➥TEXT( "Subject" ), FALSE );
 77:
 78:                         ptcName = pMailGetField( &MailMessage,
                            ➥TEXT( "From" ), FALSE );
 79:
 80:                         if ( !ptcName ¦¦ ( _tcslen( ptcName ) == 0 ) )
 81:                             ptcName = pMailGetField( &MailMessage,
                                ➥TEXT( "To" ), FALSE );
 82:
 83:                         _tsprintf( tcString, TEXT( "%s [%s]" ),
                            ➥ptcSubject, ptcName );
 84:
 85:                         ListBox_AddString( hControl, tcString );
 86:                         ListBox_SetItemData( hControl, i,
                            ➥(INT)MailMessage.oid );
 87:                         i++;
 88:
 89:                         pMailFree( &MailMessage );
 90:
 91:                         // reset 'dwFlags' to the search flags
 92:                         MailMessage.dwFlags = lParam;
 93:
 94:                     } while( pMailNext( hMail, &MailMessage ) );
 95:
 96:                 }
 97:
 98:                 pMailClose( hMail );
 99:
100:             }
101:
102:             ListBox_SetCurSel( hControl, 0 );
103:         }
104:         return TRUE;
105:         break;
106:
```

```
107:          case WM_COMMAND:
108:
109:              switch( LOWORD( wParam ) ) {
110:
111:                  case IDC_EMAILLIST:
112:
113:                      if ( HIWORD( wParam ) == LBN_DBLCLK )
114:                          PostMessage( hDlg, WM_COMMAND, IDOK, 0 );
115:
116:                      break;
117:
118:                  case IDOK:
119:                      // save the selection
120:                      i = ListBox_GetCurSel( hControl );
121:
122:                      memset( &MailMessage, 0x00, sizeof( MailMessage ) );
123:                      MailMessage.oid = ListBox_GetItemData( hControl, i );
124:                      MailMessage.dwFlags = MAIL_GET_BODY;
125:
126:                      pMailOpen( &hMail, TRUE );
127:
128:                      if ( !pMailGet( hMail, &MailMessage ) ) {
129:
130:                          ShowMailError( hMail );
131:
132:                      } else {
133:
134:                          // insert who this message was from/to
135:                          // in the edit window
136:                          tc = pMailGetField( &MailMessage, TEXT( "From" ),
                                    ➥ FALSE );
137:                          if ( !tc ¦¦ ( _tcslen( tc ) == 0 ) )
138:                              tc = pMailGetField( &MailMessage,
                                      ➥TEXT( "To" ), FALSE );
139:                          _tsprintf( tcText, TEXT( "\r\nWho:      %s\r\n" ),
                                    ➥ tc );
140:                          Edit_ReplaceSel( g_hwndText, tcText );
141:
142:                          // insert the subject line for this message
143:                          // into the edit window
144:                          tc = pMailGetField( &MailMessage,
                                  ➥TEXT( "Subject" ), FALSE );
145:                          _tsprintf( tcText, TEXT( "Subject:  %s\r\n\r\n" ),
                                    ➥ tc );
146:                          Edit_ReplaceSel( g_hwndText, tcText );
147:
148:                          // insert the message body into the edit window
149:                          if ( _tcslen( MailMessage.szBody ) > 0 )
150:                              Edit_ReplaceSel( g_hwndText,
                                      ➥MailMessage.szBody );
151:                          else
```

continues

18

LISTING **18.3**   continued

```
152:                                    Edit_ReplaceSel( g_hwndText,
                                    ➥TEXT("[body not present]\r\n" ) );
153:
154:                    }
155:
156:                    pMailFree( &MailMessage );
157:
158:                    pMailClose( hMail );
159:
160:                    // note: fall through on purpose
161:
162:                case IDCANCEL:
163:                    EndDialog( hDlg, LOWORD(wParam)==IDOK );
164:                    return TRUE;
165:                    break;
166:
167:            }
168:            break;
169:
170:    }
171:    return FALSE;
172: }
```

Summary

In this hour, you were introduced to the Windows CE Mail API. You learned that it is an API specific to Windows CE and that it is not based on MAPI. You then learned about the core functions necessary for accessing the Windows CE message store. You learned how to open it, read from it, write to it, and close it. You learned how to read, write, add, and delete fields from a message header. You also learned how to enumerate through messages in a particular folder, as well as how to add, delete, and rename email folders. You then finished the hour by reviewing code samples for reading messages from the message store, as well as creating new outgoing email messages.

Q&A

Q **We are about to ship our Windows CE mail-enabled application targeting the SH3, MIPS, and StrongARM CPUs. We have a copy of the ETK (Embedded Tool Kit) for Windows CE, which has some additional compilers for the SH4 and PowerPC, but it does not include MSGSTORE.LIB for those targets. Will we have to rebuild and rerelease our application as PC Companions using these as CPUs start appearing on the market?**

A Not if you dynamically load MSGSTORE.DLL at runtime, as the code examples in this lesson (and on the CD-ROM) do. Doing it this way enables you to build for CPUs for which you don't yet have a MSGSTORE.LIB.

Workshop

The Workshop is designed to help you anticipate possible questions, review what you've learned, and begin thinking ahead about putting your knowledge into practice. The answers to the quiz are in Appendix A, "Answers."

Quiz

1. You attempt to use `MailPutFolder` to rename a folder, but it fails. The folder's ID is `0x000000FD`. Why wasn't this successful?

2. What does the mail header field `BCC` do?

Exercises

1. Your company has the capability to receive user registrations via email and automatically parse them into a database of registered users. To your application's About box, add a Register Now button that collects the user's information, formats it, and emails it to your user registration email address.

2. Write an editor program that allows the user to edit a single message that is then mailed to multiple recipients. The recipient email addresses are parsed from an external data file. This file is a text file, with each email address on its own line.

18

HOUR 19

Monitoring Power and System Resources

This lesson instructs you how to utilize the Windows CE APIs related to monitoring power and memory status. Some of these functions are similar to their desktop Win32 counterparts, and some are unique to Windows CE.

In this hour, you will learn

- The Windows CE function for getting the current power status and its associated data structure
- How to tell the battery driver to adjust its "time remaining" values after you have updated the system time
- Various methods and situations for indicating power status to your users
- How to determine the current memory status on a Windows CE device

Introducing Power Monitoring on Windows CE

Power is important on Windows CE devices, as they are primarily operated on battery power while away from the user's desktop computer. Creating your applications so that they are aware of power conditions makes them more user friendly. The basis of Windows CE's power monitoring is rooted in the GetSystemPowerStatusEx function and the SYSTEM_POWER_STATUS_EX structure. After we cover these topics, we will briefly cover the BatteryNotifyOfTimeChange function, which should be used in the rare event that your application needs to modify the system time.

The GetSystemPowerStatusEx Function

GetSystemPowerStatusEx is the function that allows your program to retrieve the current power status of the Windows CE device. This includes

- The remaining life of the main battery
- The remaining life of the backup battery
- Whether the batteries are currently being charged
- Whether the device is running on battery power or AC power

A non-Ex version of this function (that is, GetSystemPowerStatus) exists on Windows 95, Windows 98, and Windows NT, but is not available on Windows CE.

The GetSystemPowerStatusEx function takes two parameters:

- A pointer to a SYSTEM_POWER_STATUS_EX variable (which is discussed in the next section).
- A boolean flag that indicates whether to read power information directly from the device driver or use the power information that was cached the last time the system requested it from the device driver. If this parameter is set to TRUE, it retrieves the latest information from the device driver. If it is set to FALSE, cached information is used. Cached power information may be several seconds old.

This function can also be invoked from the desktop computer to which the Windows CE device is attached. This enables a desktop application (such as a setup program) to check the power status of the Windows CE device. The function to use in the desktop application is the CeGetSystemPowerStatusEx, which can be found in RAPI.H.

The SYSTEM_POWER_STATUS_EX Structure

You can't use GetSystemPowerStatusEx without passing in a pointer to the SYSTEM_POWER_STATUS_EX structure. What does it look like? Listing 19.1 shows how the structure is declared in WINBASE.H and RAPI.H.

LISTING 19.1 The SYSTEM_POWER_STATUS_EX Structure

```
 1: typedef struct _SYSTEM_POWER_STATUS_EX {
 2:     BYTE ACLineStatus;
 3:     BYTE BatteryFlag;
 4:     BYTE BatteryLifePercent;
 5:     BYTE Reserved1;
 6:     DWORD BatteryLifeTime;
 7:     DWORD BatteryFullLifeTime;
 8:     BYTE Reserved2;
 9:     BYTE BackupBatteryFlag;
10:     BYTE BackupBatteryLifePercent;
11:     BYTE Reserved3;
12:     DWORD BackupBatteryLifeTime;
13:     DWORD BackupBatteryFullLifeTime;
14: }   SYSTEM_POWER_STATUS_EX, *PSYSTEM_POWER_STATUS_EX,
        ➡*LPSYSTEM_POWER_STATUS_EX;
```

The following sections explain the important members—ACLineStatus, BatteryFlag, and BackupBatteryFlag—as well as the battery life for the main battery and for the backup battery, and the reserved fields.

19

It is up to the device manufacturer to determine which fields of SYSTEM_POWER_STATUS_EX are supported on their device. What this means to you, the programmer, is that you should not assume that all fields will be supported on all devices. Typically, your program is told that a certain field is not supported by its value being set to an UNKNOWN flag. Some examples are BATTERY_PERCENTAGE_UNKNOWN and BATTERY_LIFE_UNKNOWN.

ACLineStatus

ACLineStatus communicates the AC power status. Table 19.1 explains the meaning of its values.

TABLE 19.1   What Do the Values of ACLineStatus Mean?

Value	Meaning
AC_LINE_OFFLINE	The device is not on AC power.
AC_LINE_ONLINE	The device is on AC power.
AC_LINE_UNKNOWN	The state of AC power is not determinable or is not supported by your device manufacturer.

BatteryFlag and BackupBatteryFlag

BatteryFlag indicates the status of the main battery, and BackupBatteryFlag indicates the status of the backup battery. Table 19.2 explains the meaning of their values.

TABLE 19.2   What Do the Values of BatteryFlag and BackupBatteryFlag Mean?

Value	Meaning
BATTERY_FLAG_HIGH	The battery has a strong charge.
BATTERY_FLAG_LOW	The battery is running low.
BATTERY_FLAG_CRITICAL	The battery is almost out of power.
BATTERY_FLAG_CHARGING	The battery is currently being charged.
BATTERY_FLAG_NO_BATTERY	The battery is not present.
BATTERY_FLAG_UNKNOWN	The battery charge is not determinable or is not supported by your device manufacturer.

The Battery Life for the Main Battery

BatteryLifePercent is the percentage of main battery charge remaining. Its value can be between 0 and 100, or BATTERY_PERCENTAGE_UNKNOWN (255) if the value is not determinable. For example, a value of 50 indicates that 50% of the batter charge is remaining.

BatteryFullLifeTime indicates the number of seconds of battery life when the main battery is at full charge. BatteryLifeTime is the number of seconds of main battery life currently remaining. Either of these fields can be set to BATTERY_LIFE_UNKNOWN if their values are not determinable.

The Battery Life for the Backup Battery

BackupBatteryLifePercent is the percentage of backup battery charge remaining. Its value can be between 0 and 100, or BATTERY_PERCENTAGE_UNKNOWN (255) if the value is not determinable. BackupBatteryFullLifeTime indicates the number of seconds of battery life when the backup battery is at full charge. BackupBatteryLifeTime is the number of seconds of backup battery life currently remaining. Either of these fields can be set to BATTERY_LIFE_UNKNOWN if their values are not determinable.

Initialize Reserved Fields to Zero

SYSTEM_POWER_STATUS_EX contains three reserved BYTE fields named Reserved1, Reserved2, and Reserved3. These should be set to zero.

Windows CE 1.1 and Above: The BatteryNotifyOfTimeChange Function

If your program changes the time on the Windows CE device using the SetSystemTime function, the battery life fields of the SYSTEM_POWER_STATUS_EX structure will not be automatically updated. It is your program's responsibility to explicitly update them by using the BatteryNotifyOfChange function immediately after calling SetSystemTime.

The BatteryNotifyOfTimeChange function requires two parameters:

- fForward is a boolean value that should be set to TRUE if the time has been advanced. If the system time has been turned back, this should be set to FALSE.

- pftDelta is a pointer to a FILETIME structure variable that indicates the amount of the time change.

Putting It into Practice: Examples Using GetSystemPowerStatusEx

The two code examples that follow illustrate how you can use the GetSystemPowerStatusEx function within your own applications. The first example illustrates how to add power information to your application's About box. The second example updates the current power status on the application's status bar every five seconds and alerts the user when the power level falls below a predetermined threshold.

Displaying the Current Power Status

This first code snippet, in Listing 19.2, is an example of how power status could be reported in an application that doesn't have any interaction with external devices. It is a generic program that includes battery power information in its About box (see Figure 19.1). Listing 19.2 is the DLGPROC for this About box.

LISTING 19.2   The DLGPROC for an About Box That Reports Power Status

```
 1: LRESULT CALLBACK About( HWND hDlg, UINT message,
                       ➥ WPARAM wParam, LPARAM lParam)
 2: {
 3:   SYSTEM_POWER_STATUS_EX    Power;
 4:   TCHAR                     tcString[MAX_PATH];
 5:
 6:   switch ( message ) {
 7:
 8:      case WM_INITDIALOG:
 9:
10:         /*******************************************************
11:          * get the current power status
12:          *******************************************************/
13:         if ( GetSystemPowerStatusEx( &Power, FALSE ) ) {
14:
15:            /*******************************************************
16:             * set the power status (AC or DC)
17:             *******************************************************/
18:            switch( Power.ACLineStatus ) {
19:               case AC_LINE_OFFLINE:
20:                  _tcscpy( tcString,
                              ➥TEXT( "AC Power is Off-Line" ) );
21:                  break;
22:               case AC_LINE_ONLINE:
23:                  _tcscpy( tcString,
                              ➥TEXT( "AC Power is On-Line" ) );
24:                  break;
25:               case AC_LINE_BACKUP_POWER:
26:                  _tcscpy( tcString, TEXT( "On Backup Power" ) );
27:                  break;
28:               default:
29:                  _tcscpy( tcString, TEXT( "<unknown>" ) );
30:            }
31:
32:            SetWindowText( GetDlgItem( hDlg, IDC_POWER_STATUS ),
                          ➥tcString );
33:
34:            /*******************************************************
35:             * show the percentage that the main battery is charged
36:             *******************************************************/
37:            if ( Power.BatteryLifePercent ==
                     ➥BATTERY_PERCENTAGE_UNKNOWN )
38:               _tcscpy( tcString, TEXT( "<unknown>" ) );
39:            else
40:               wsprintf( tcString, TEXT( "%d%%" ),
                            ➥Power.BatteryLifePercent );
41:            SetWindowText( GetDlgItem( hDlg,
                           ➥IDC_POWER_PERCENTCHARGED ),
                           ➥tcString );
```

```
42:
43:          /********************************************************
44:           * show how many MINUTES (not seconds) are remaining
45:           * for this battery
46:           ********************************************************/
47:          if ( Power.BatteryLifeTime == BATTERY_LIFE_UNKNOWN )
48:              _tcscpy( tcString, TEXT( "<unknown>" ) );
49:          else
50:              wsprintf( tcString, TEXT( "%d Minutes" ),
                          ➥Power.BatteryLifeTime/60 );
51:          SetWindowText( GetDlgItem( hDlg,
                          ➥IDC_POWER_MINUTESREMAINING ),
                          ➥tcString );
52:
53:      }
54:      return TRUE;
55:
56:  case WM_COMMAND:
57:      if (LOWORD(wParam) == IDOK || LOWORD(wParam) == IDCANCEL) {
58:          EndDialog(hDlg, LOWORD(wParam));
59:          return TRUE;
60:      }
61:      break;
62:
63: }
64:
65: return FALSE;
66: }
```

FIGURE 19.1

An About box that provides useful power information to the user.

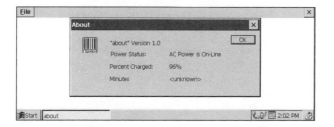

19

"We're Giving Her All We've Got, Captain!"—Keeping Your Users Up-to-Date on Power Status

Consider the scenario where your application interacts with devices that drain a Windows CE device's battery power. This includes applications that spend more than a brief amount of time reading from or writing to the following:

- The external 9-pin serial port
- The built-in infrared port

- The various PC cards supported by Windows CE
- Built-in hardware and/or software modems

If your application's use of these devices could result in the complete draining of your user's battery, your users might appreciate frequent updates on the current battery status. The code in Listing 19.3 updates the current power status on the status bar every five seconds. It assumes that the user is performing long operations with an external device that has to be aborted if the power level falls below a certain threshold (see Figure 19.2). In the example, this threshold is 70%.

LISTING 19.3   Provide Battery Charge Status on the Status Bar, and Abort Any Battery-Draining Activity If the Battery Charge Falls Below 70%

```
 1: case WM_CREATE:
 2:
 3:     /******************************************************************
 4:      * create the command bar
 5:      ******************************************************************/
 6:     g_hwndCB = CommandBar_Create( hInst, hWnd, 1);
 7:     CommandBar_InsertMenubar( g_hwndCB, hInst, IDC_STATUSBAR, 0);
 8:     CommandBar_AddAdornments( g_hwndCB, 0, 0);
 9:
10:     InitCommonControls();
11:
12:     GetClientRect( hWnd, &rc );
13:     g_hStatus = CreateWindow(    STATUSCLASSNAME, TEXT( "" ),
                      ➥WS_CHILD ¦ WS_VISIBLE,
14:                   0, rc.bottom-rc.top-25, rc.right-rc.left,
15:                   25, hWnd, NULL, hInst, NULL );
16:
17:     SetTimer( hWnd, 1, 5000, NULL );
18:     g_AbortPowerDrainingActivity = FALSE;
19:     // ask it to update the status bar ASAP
20:     PostMessage( hWnd, WM_TIMER, 0, 0 );
21:
22:     return TRUE;
23:     break;
24:
25: case WM_TIMER:
26:     {
27:         SYSTEM_POWER_STATUS_EX    Power;
28:         TCHAR    tcStatusBarText[MAX_PATH];
29:
30:         if ( GetSystemPowerStatusEx( &Power, TRUE ) ) {
31:
32:             if ( Power.BatteryLifePercent !=
                    ➥ BATTERY_PERCENTAGE_UNKNOWN ) {
33:
```

```
34:                        if ( Power.BatteryLifePercent < 70 ) {
35:
36:                            g_AbortPowerDrainingActivity = TRUE;
37:                            KillTimer( hWnd, 1 );
38:                            MessageBox(     hWnd,
39:                                    TEXT( "Battery charge has fallen " )
                                    ➥TEXT( "below 70%!" ),
40:                                    TEXT( "Cannot Continue" ),
41:                                    MB_OK ¦ MB_ICONEXCLAMATION );
42:
43:                            _tcscpy( tcStatusBarText,
                                    ➥ TEXT( "Status: Offline" ) );
44:
45:                        } else {
46:
47:                            wsprintf( tcStatusBarText, TEXT( "Power: %d%%" ),
                                    ➥ Power.BatteryLifePercent );
48:
49:                        }
50:
51:                    } else {
52:
53:                        _tcscpy( tcStatusBarText,
                                ➥ TEXT( "Power: <unknown>" ) );
54:
55:                    }
56:
57:                    SetWindowText( g_hStatus, tcStatusBarText );
58:
59:                }
60:
61:            }
62:
63:    break;
```

While the battery charge remains at 70% or above, the code in Listing 19.3 will display the current battery charge in the application's status bar. When the battery charge falls below 70%, the user is notified. Figure 19.2 shows this code in operation.

FIGURE 19.2

Alerting the user when the battery charge drops below a threshold.

How do you select your "we don't have enough power" threshold? It depends on your application and how a typical user interacts with it.

For example, some of the early versions of bFAX Pro that came prebundled on Windows CE devices would warn the user if he or she attempted to send a fax on battery power *and* the battery level was less than 80%. This value was determined experimentally by sending three-page faxes with a wide variety of PC card modems while running on battery power. It was experimentally observed that if the battery level on this particular device was at least 80%, the fax would be successfully sent without the device shutting off because of lack of power. A three-page fax was chosen because the average fax length is two pages.

Checking Memory Status

Windows CE supports the same `GlobalMemoryStatus` function and `MEMORYSTATUS` structure that you may be familiar with from your desktop Win32 programming experience. If your Windows CE program requires a large amount of memory to perform an operation it can use `GlobalMemoryStatus` to check if enough memory is available before starting the operation.

Using the `GlobalMemoryStatus` Function

The `GlobalMemoryStatus` function is used to retrieve information about the current status of virtual and physical memory on the system. It requires a `MEMORYSTATUS` structure as its only parameter. The `MEMORYSTATUS` structure is discussed in the next session.

This function can also be invoked from the desktop computer to which the Windows CE device is attached. The API to use in a desktop application is the `CeGlobalMemoryStatus` RAPI function, which can be found in RAPI.H.

The `MEMORYSTATUS` Structure

The current memory status is returned via the `MEMORYSTATUS` structure. The following table explains what each of its members represents.

TABLE 19.3 The `MEMORYSTATUS` Structure

Member	Meaning
dwLength	The length of the structure
dwMemoryLoad	A rough percentage of "memory currently in use"
dwTotalPhys	The total number of bytes of physical memory

Member	Meaning
dwAvailPhys	The number of bytes of available physical memory
dwTotalPageFile	The total bytes that can be stored in the paging file
dwAvailPageFile	The number of bytes available in the paging file
dwTotalVirtual	The total bytes of virtual memory available
dwAvailVirtual	The number of uncommitted bytes in virtual memory

Summary

In this hour, you learned how to use the GetSystemPowerStatusEx function to make your Windows CE applications power-aware. You learned how to notify the batter driver to update its timers after you change the system clock. You also learned how to utilize the GlobalMemoryStatus function to monitor the current status of physical and virtual memory on a Windows CE device.

Q&A

Q What does the GetSystemPowerStatusEx function do under the Windows CE emulator running on my desktop Windows NT machine?

A The help system indicates that GetSystemPowerStatusEx is not implemented for the emulation environment. This doesn't mean that your program will fail to link for the emulation environment because this function cannot be found at link time. It does mean that the function will not return accurate power information for your desktop NT machine. If you have to test different power-related code paths under the emulator, it is recommended that you #ifdef your code to provide hard-coded initialization values when running under emulation—for example:

```
    SYSTEM_POWER_STATUS_EX    Power;
    GetSystemPowerStatusEx( &Power, FALSE );

#ifdef _WIN32_WCE_EMULATION
    // note: testing failure code path
    Power.ACLineStatus != AC_LINE_OFFLINE;
#endif

    if ( Power.ACLineStatus != AC_LINE_ONLINE ) {
        MessageBox( GetFocus(),
                    TEXT( "AC Power not available, " )
                    TEXT( "cannot open pod bay doors" ),
                    TEXT( "HAL:" ), MB_OK );
    }
```

19

Q The `GlobalMemoryStatus` function indicates that I have plenty of memory available, but my application fails to create a new bitmap because of lack of memory. What is going on?

A GDI objects are allocated from the GDI heap, not the global heap. Most likely, your application is running out of GDI memory because it (or another program on the device) is not freeing GDI objects. Make sure that your application frees all GDI objects allocated by using the `DeleteObject` function.

Workshop

The Workshop is designed to help you anticipate possible questions, review what you've learned, and begin thinking ahead about putting your knowledge into practice. The answers to the quiz are in Appendix A, "Answers."

Quiz

1. The GetSystemPowerStatusEx function allows you to get cached power information rather than retrieve it directly from the device driver. What is the advantage of this?

2. What is the remote API version of GlobalMemoryStatus and which header file is it in?

3. What is the total size of the Windows CE virtual address space?

Exercise

1. Is the speed hit between using noncached power information and cached power information significant? Write a program that times how long it takes to call the `GetSystemPowerStatusEx` function 1,000 times each way, and compare the results.

Hour **20**

Communicating with the Desktop

Windows CE devices are frequently marketed as "desktop companions," which means that one of their main goals in life is to transfer information to and from a PC running Windows NT, 95, or 98. To make this transfer as smooth as possible, Windows CE provides software to connect the two and a standard set of Remote API (RAPI) calls to perform just about any type of operation that you would need. If the standard RAPI functions don't cut it, an escape hatch lets you roll your own custom methods.

In this hour, you will learn

- UnderstandingWindows CE Services
- Overview of the Remote API (RAPI)
- Using RAPI.DLL and RAPI system status functions
- How to put CeRapiInvoke to work

Windows CE Services

Windows CE Services is the connectivity software that allows Windows CE devices to have conversations with desktop PCs. It provides an Explorer-like interface of the device's file system that enables you to perform most of the same actions as the desktop Explorer (for example, drag-and-drop files, and so on).

The connection works over either a serial port or an ethernet network connection. Although an ethernet connection requires more hardware and setup, it is much faster than the serial connection. It's worth the extra setup and cost, especially if you use it over an existing LAN. Chris De Herrera's Ethernet Connectivity FAQ at http://www.cewindows.net/wce/20/ethernet.htm is a great resource for details on getting everything up and running.

In Hour 23, "Debugging Windows CE Applications with Visual C++," you will see how to use the Windows CE Services ethernet connection to significantly improve the performance of the debugger.

Keeping files and information consistent between your PC and your device is another big feature that Windows CE Services provides. ActiveSync provides an easy way to customize this process and allows you to convert between desktop and Windows CE file formats as well. ActiveSync is covered in detail next in Hour 21, "Creating ActiveSync Modules." The Remote API (RAPI) is the plumbing on which Windows CE Services Explorer and ActiveSync are built. It provides a standard way of manipulating files on the device, as well as many other features. In the rest of this hour, I will drill down and show everything of which RAPI is capable.

An Overview of the Remote API

As shown in Table 20.1, Remote API (RAPI) consists of 67 functions loosely organized into eight distinct groups.

TABLE 20.1 The Breakdown of RAPI Functions

Startup and Shutdown	
HRESULT	CeRapiInitEx(RAPIINIT*);
HRESULT	CeRapiInit();
HRESULT	CeRapiUninit();
Object Store Databases Manipulation	
CEOID	CeCreateDatabase(LPWSTR, DWORD, WORD, SORTORDERSPEC*);
BOOL	CeDeleteDatabase(CEOID);

```
BOOL      CeDeleteRecord(HANDLE, CEOID);

HANDLE    CeFindFirstDatabase(DWORD);

CEOID     CeFindNextDatabase(HANDLE);

HANDLE    CeOpenDatabase(PCEOID, LPWSTR, CEPROPID, DWORD, HWND);

CEOID     CeReadRecordProps(HANDLE, DWORD, LPWORD, CEPROPID*, LPBYTE*, LPDWORD);

CEOID     CeSeekDatabase(HANDLE, DWORD, LONG, LPDWORD);

BOOL      CeSetDatabaseInfo(CEOID, CEDBASEINFO*);

CEOID     CeWriteRecordProps(HANDLE, CEOID, WORD, CEPROPVAL*);

BOOL      CeOidGetInfo(CEOID, CEOIDINFO*);

BOOL      CeFindAllDatabases(DWORD, WORD, LPWORD, LPLPCEDB_FIND_DATA);
```

Object Store File Manipulation

```
HANDLE    CeFindFirstFile(LPCWSTR, LPCE_FIND_DATA);

BOOL      CeFindNextFile(HANDLE, LPCE_FIND_DATA);

BOOL      CeFindClose(HANDLE);

DWOR      CeGetFileAttributes(LPCWSTR);

BOOL      CeSetFileAttributes(LPCWSTR, DWORD);

HANDLE    CeCreateFile(LPCWSTR, DWORD, DWORD, LPSECURITY_ATTRIBUTES, DWORD, DWORD,
          HANDLE);

BOOL      CeReadFile(HANDLE, LPVOID, DWORD, LPDWORD, LPOVERLAPPED);

BOOL      CeWriteFile(HANDLE, LPCVOID, DWORD, LPDWORD, LPOVERLAPPED);

BOOL      CeCloseHandle(HANDLE);

BOOL      CeFindAllFiles(LPCWSTR, DWORD, LPDWORD, LPLPCE_FIND_DATA);

DWORD     CeSetFilePointer(HANDLE, LONG, PLONG, DWORD);

BOOL      CeSetEndOfFile(HANDLE);

BOOL      CeCreateDirectory(LPCWSTR, LPSECURITY_ATTRIBUTES);

BOOL      CeRemoveDirectory(LPCWSTR);

BOOL      CeMoveFile(LPCWSTR, LPCWSTR);

BOOL      CeCopyFile(LPCWSTR, LPCWSTR, BOOL);

BOOL      CeDeleteFile(LPCWSTR);

DWORD     CeGetFileSize(HANDLE, LPDWORD);

BOOL      CeGetFileTime(HANDLE, LPFILETIME, LPFILETIME, LPFILETIME);

BOOL      CeSetFileTime(HANDLE, LPFILETIME, LPFILETIME, LPFILETIME);
```

20

continues

TABLE 20.1   continued

Process Creation

DWORD	CeGetLastError(void);
BOOL	CeCreateProcess(LPCWSTR, LPCWSTR, LPSECURITY_ATTRIBUTES, LPSECURITY_ATTRIBUTES, BOOL, DWORD, LPVOID, LPWSTR, LPSTARTUPINFO, LPPROCESS_INFORMATION);

Registry Manipulation

LONG	CeRegOpenKeyEx(HKEY, LPCWSTR, DWORD, REGSAM, PHKEY);
LONG	CeRegEnumKeyEx(HKEY, DWORD, LPWSTR, LPDWORD, LPDWORD, LPWSTR, LPDWORD, PFILETIME);
LONG	CeRegCreateKeyEx(HKEY, LPCWSTR, DWORD, LPWSTR, DWORD, REGSAM, LPSECURITY_ATTRIBUTES, PHKEY, LPDWORD);
LONG	CeRegCloseKey(HKEY);
LONG	CeRegDeleteKey(HKEY, LPCWSTR);
LONG	CeRegEnumValue(HKEY, DWORD, LPWSTR, LPDWORD, LPDWORD, LPDWORD, LPBYTE, LPDWORD);
LONG	CeRegDeleteValue(HKEY, LPCWSTR);
LONG	CeRegQueryInfoKey(HKEY, LPWSTR, LPDWORD, LPDWORD, LPDWORD, LPDWORD, LPDWORD, LPDWORD, LPDWORD, LPDWORD, LPDWORD, PFILETIME);
LONG	CeRegQueryValueEx(HKEY, LPCWSTR, LPDWORD, LPDWORD, LPBYTE, LPDWORD);
LONG	CeRegSetValueEx(HKEY, LPCWSTR, DWORD, DWORD, LPBYTE, DWORD);

System Information and Status

BOOL	CeGetStoreInformation(LPSTORE_INFORMATION);
INT	CeGetSystemMetrics(INT);
INT	CeGetDesktopDeviceCaps(INT);
VOID	CeGetSystemInfo(LPSYSTEM_INFO);
DWORD	CeSHCreateShortcut(LPWSTR, LPWSTR);
BOOL	CeSHGetShortcutTarget(LPWSTR, LPWSTR, INT);
BOOL	CeCheckPassword(LPWSTR);
BOOL	CeGetVersionEx(LPCEOSVERSIONINFO);
VOID	CeGlobalMemoryStatus (LPMEMORYSTATUS);
BOOL	CeGetSystemPowerStatusEx(PSYSTEM_POWER_STATUS_EX, BOOL);
DWORD	CeGetTempPath(DWORD, LPWSTR);
DWORD	CeGetSpecialFolderPath(int, DWORD, LPWSTR);

Window Information

HWND	CeGetWindow(HWND, UINT);
LONG	CeGetWindowLong(HWND, int);
int	CeGetWindowText(HWND, LPWSTR, int);
int	CeGetClassName(HWND, LPWSTR, int);

Simple Remote Procedure Call

HRESULT	CeRapiInvoke(LPCWSTR, LPCWSTR,DWORD,BYTE *, DWORD *,BYTE **, IRAPIStream **,DWORD);
HRESULT	CeRapiGetError(void);
HRESULT	CeRapiFreeBuffer(LPVOID);

The startup and shutdown functions initialize the connection with the device and are necessary before any other RAPI function is called. I'll go over these in detail in this lesson's section titled "RAPI Startup and Shutdown."

The next four groups provide remote implementations of standard Windows CE APIs. For example, to get the list of files on the remote device, Windows CE Services Explorer uses CeFindFirstFile, CeFindNextFile, and CeFindClose. Because you already learned about the file and Registry functions in Hour 9, "The Object Store: Files and Registry," the database functions in Hour 10, " Advanced Object Store: The Database API," and process creation in Hour 11, "Threads and Processes," I won't go over these functions again here.

The sixth group, System Information and Status, allows you to query the device for information such as the operating system version number, microprocessor architecture, and memory usage. I'll go over these functions in detail and use them in a sample application in this hour's section titled "RAPI System Status Functions."

The seventh group, Window Information, is an odd set of functions that mirror a few of the Windows CE APIs for using window handles. Generally, they're not very helpful, so I won't discuss them any further this hour.

The last group, Simple RPC, is probably the most useful RAPI feature. CeRapiInvoke allows you to call a function in an arbitrary DLL on the device and pass results back to the desktop. This enables you to add custom functions and extend RAPI to provide functionality that isn't available in the standard set of APIs. I'll cover CeRapiInvoke in detail in this hour's section titled "Putting CeRapiInvoke to Work."

20

When you're using RAPI in your application, it is good to keep in mind how RAPI is implemented. Although it might seem more complicated, RAPI is nothing more than a process on the desktop and the device communicating via Winsock, much like the remote debugging process described in Hour 23, "Debugging Windows CE Applications with Visual C++." For example, when you call CeWriteFile, RAPI just transfers the parameters to the device, uses them to call the WriteFile API, and then ships the return value back to you. No smoke and mirrors—just straightforward network programming.

Using RAPI.DLL

The desktop side of RAPI is implemented in the single file RAPI.DLL, which is installed with Windows CE Services. If you have Visual C++ installed, Windows CE Services also puts the header file RAPI.H and the import library RAPI.LIB in the standard include and lib directory, respectively.

Because RAPI.DLL is not built in to the operating system and can't really be distributed with your application, it's usually good practice to not statically link to RAPI.DLL with the import library. If you do and users do not have Windows CE Services installed, they will not be able to run your application at all because the operating system will try to load the file at runtime. The best approach is to dynamically link to the DLL with the LoadLibrary and GetProcAddress APIs and just disable features if it is not available. You can do that by using the code in Listing 20.1.

LISTING 20.1   Implicitly Linking to RAPI.DLL

```
 1: typedef HRESULT (WINAPI *PFN_RAPIINIT)();
 2:
 3: PFN_RAPIINIT    pfnRapiInit = NULL;
 4: HMODULE         hRapiLib = LoadLibrary("rapi.dll");
 5:
 6: if ( hRapiLib )
 7: {
 8:     pfnRapiInit = (PFN_RAPIINIT)GetProcAddress(hRapiLib, "CeRapiInit");
 9:
10:     if ( pfnRapiInit )
11:     {
12:         // successfully loaded…
13:     }
14:
15:     FreeLibrary(hRapiLib);
16: }
```

This code tries to load RAPI.DLL and get a pointer to the `CeRapiInit` function. If this works, you know that RAPI is available, and you can use it in your application.

Notice one subtle point about dynamically linking to RAPI.DLL. In the `typedef` for your function pointer, you use

```
typedef HRESULT (WINAPI *PFN_RAPIINIT)();
```

instead of

```
typedef HRESULT (*PFN_RAPIINIT)();
```

to specify that this function uses the same calling convention as the Win32 APIs. This is absolutely necessary to successfully call RAPI functions via dynamic linking. If you don't specify a calling convention, the compiler will use the default one, which is wrong in this case (__cdecl instead of __stdcall, for those curious about the details). If you leave the default off, you might be able to get by with calling functions with no parameters. However, if any arguments exist, the stack will be incorrect after the function returns, and havoc will undoubtedly ensue. The /GZ switch for the Visual C++ compiler will catch this problem, as well as other common mistakes such as uninitialized local variables. I highly recommend you use it for debug builds of your product.

RAPI Startup and Shutdown

RAPI provides two functions for initializing a connection: `CeRapiInit` and `CeRapiInitEx`. The difference between the two is very simple.

`CeRapiInit` blocks the calling thread and will not return until the connection is successfully initiated. Although this might be acceptable for some limited situations, too many things can go wrong for this to be a good general solution. What if the user forgets to plug in the cable first? What if there is no underlying Windows CE Services connection? You get the idea.

`CeRapiInitEx` solves this problem by providing the user a Win32 event handle that is signaled when the connection is completed or fails. This allows you to wait for a period of time and then abandon the connection if it is taking too long. The event and status are returned through a `RAPIINIT` structure that is passed as a parameter to `CeRapiInitEx`, as shown in Listing 20.2.

20

LISTING 20.2   Calling CeRapiInitEx

```
 1: RAPIINIT ri = { sizeof(ri) };
 2: HRESULT hr = CeRapiInitEx(&ri);
 3:
 4: if ( SUCCEEDED(hr) )
 5: {
 6:     DWORD dwRet = WaitForSingleObject(ri.heRapiInit, 5000);
 7:
 8:     if ( (dwRet == WAIT_OBJECT_0) && SUCCEEDED(ri.hrRapiInit) )
 9:     {
10:         // connection SUCCEEDED…
11:     }
12:     else
13:     {
14:         // connection failed…
15:     }
16:
17:     CeRapiUninit();
18: }
19: else
20: {
21:     // CeRapiInitEx failed...
22: }
```

After initializing a RAPIINIT structure and making sure that the call was successful, you wait 5 seconds for the system to signal the event. If the wait times out or returns a failure code via the hrRapiInit member of RAPIINIT, you know that the connection didn't succeed in the time allowed. Notice that, in either case, you must call CeRapiUninit to either tear down the existing connection or tell the system that you are no longer waiting and it can stop trying to connect.

RAPI System Status Functions

The RAPI system status functions allow you to query the device about the processor, the operating system version, and other information. They are all remote versions of local functions that can be directly called on the device.

Figure 20.1 shows a screen shot of the CEStatus sample application that uses some of the RAPI functions to gather and display useful information about the device. Full source code to CEStatus is available on the CD-ROM.

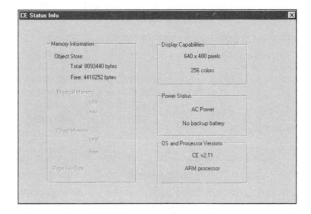

FIGURE 20.1
The CEStatus application.

You might notice that the page file and physical and virtual memory information is disabled. This is because CeGlobalMemoryStatus is broken and returns garbage information. The device implementation works perfectly well when you call it from a Windows CE application. However, somewhere in the round trip between the desktop and the device, CeGlobalMemoryStatus becomes confused and doesn't return the right information. If you need this information in your application, you can use CeRapiInvoke, discussed in depth in the next section, to work around the problem.

Putting CeRapiInvoke to Work

Suppose that you are writing a Windows NT application that has to display the list of all the DLLs loaded on your Windows CE device. How would you go about doing this? One way would be to launch a program on the device that writes to a file or the Registry and then read that data via RAPI. This approach is problematic because it is almost impossible to determine when all the data has been written.

Another possibility is to have a program on the device create a socket connection through which to pipe the data. This would work, but for this small transaction, it requires a lot of overhead. CeRapiInvoke solves this dilemma by providing a way to call a function in a DLL on the device and have it pass back a block of data or a pointer to an IRAPIStream COM object that allows bidirectional communication.

20

The prototype for `CeRapiInvoke` looks like this:

```
HRESULT STDAPICALLTYPE CeRapiInvoke(LPCWSTR      lpwszDll,
                                    LPCWSTR      lpwszFunc,
                                    DWORD        dwInputCount,
                                    LPBYTE       pcbIn,
                                    WORD         pcbOutput,
                                    LPBYTE       ppbOutput,
                                    IRAPIStream  ppStream,
                                    DWORD        dwReserved)
```

The name of a DLL in the Windows directory on the device is `lpwszDll`, and `lpwszFunc` is the name of a function exported from the DLL you want to call. The next two parameters, `dwInputCount` and `pcbIn`, specify the data you want to pass to the remote function. These parameters are optional, but if one contains valid data, they both must.

The output parameters, `pcbOutput` and `ppbOutput`, allow the remote function to return a buffer to the caller. The `ppStream` parameter provides the COM interface for sending and receiving data and determines the mode that this call to `CeRapiInvoke` is using. The last parameter is reserved for future use and should be set to zero.

`CeRapiInvoke` can be used in either block or stream mode. In block mode, the `ppStream` parameter must be `NULL`; the remote function is called synchronously; and data is passed back through the `pcbOutput` and `ppbOutput` parameters. By *synchronously*, I mean that the call to `CeRapiInvoke` will not return until the remote function has completed.

When `ppStream` is not `NULL`, the remote function is called asynchronously; `CeRapiInvoke` returns without waiting for `lpwszFunc` to complete; and `ppStream` points to an initialized `IRAPIStream` object that is connected to the corresponding stream on the device. Data can now be sent back and forth until the stream is closed on both ends. Even though `pcbOutput` and `ppbOutput` are used only for block mode, they must both be non-`NULL`, or `CeRapiInvoke` will return `E_FAIL` with a last error value of `ERROR_INVALID_PARAMETER`.

Although the name of the remote function can be that of any export, RAPI requires the prototype to be

```
HRESULT STDAPICALLTYPE RemoteFunc(DWORD        cbInput,
                                  BYTE         pbInput,
                                  DWORD        pcbOutput
                                  BYTE         ppbOutput,
                                  IRAPIStream  pStream)
```

The first two parameters are copies of the input parameters from `CeRapiInvoke`. The next two parameters, `pcbOutput` and `ppbOutput`, are filled in by `RemoteFunc` and passed back to the caller of `CeRapiInvoke` in block mode. RAPI requires that the memory for ppbOutput be allocated with LocalAlloc to ensure that it is freed correctly. The last parameter is a pointer to an IRAPIStream that RAPI has allocated if the ppStream parameter in the call to CeRapiInvoke was non-NULL.

That last point about IRAPIStream is an important one: RAPI allocates and frees the object for you. In other words, to call CeRapiInvoke in stream mode, the ppStream parameter should be the address of a pointer to an IRAPIStream object that is initialized to NULL.

RAPI does not allow the use of an object you allocate, and attempting to do so will result in a memory leak. When both sides are finished with the stream, they just have to call Release to decrement the reference count and allow the object to be freed.

IRAPIStream is derived from the standard COM IStream interface and provides two additional functions:

```
HRESULT SetRapiStat(RAPISTREAMFLAG Flag, DWORD dwValue)
HRESULT GetRapiStat(RAPISTREAMFLAG Flag, DWORD *pdwValue)
```

Currently, only one flag is supported: STREAM_TIMEOUT_READ. The online documentation for STREAM_TIMEOUT_READ states that it "allows setting timeouts for the IStream::Read method," but never states what units are expected (that is, seconds, milliseconds, and so on). When GetRapiStat is called with a non-NULL pdwValue parameter, it returns the Win32 code ERROR_INVALID_PARAMETER (which is not a valid HRESULT). Calling it with a NULL parameter results in an access violation exception. Conversely, calling SetRapiStat with any nonzero value in dwValue did not cause Read to time out in any way that I could tell. Additionally, the declaration of IRAPIStream is not included in the Windows CE 2.0 headers and must be retrieved from the Windows NT RAPI.H include file. For these reasons, I suggest that you stick with just the IStream-level features and not use any IRAPIStream specifics. CeRapiInvoke's stream mode also has another more serious problem, which I'll discuss at the end of this section.

Similar to GetRapiStat with a non-NULL second parameter, that the return value from CeRapiInvoke is an HRESULT is deceiving. In reality, it can be an HRESULT, the return code from lpwszFunc, or a Win32 error code indicating that the DLL did not exist on the device, the function requested was not exported from the DLL, or the remote function caused an exception. The effect of this is that you must do something similar to the code in Listing 20.3 where you explicitly check for the non-HRESULT values before using the SUCCEEDED macro.

20

LISTING 20.3   Testing the Return Value of `CeRapiInvoke`

```
 1: /*
 2:     This handles the overloaded return value from
 3:     CeRapiInvoke.
 4: */
 5:
 6: BOOL CRI_Success(HRESULT hr)
 7: {
 8:
 9:     BOOL bOK = TRUE;
10:
11:     if ( hr == ERROR_FILE_NOT_FOUND          ||
12:           hr == ERROR_CALL_NOT_IMPLEMENTED   ||
13:           hr == ERROR_EXCEPTION_IN_SERVICE )
14:     {
15:         bOK = FALSE;
16:     }
17:     else
18:         bOK = (SUCCEEDED(hr));
19:
20:     return bOK;
21: }
```

There is still a problem, however. In block mode, the return value from `CeRapiInvoke` will be the return value from `lpwszFunc` if no errors occurred. This means that if `lpwszFunc` innocuously returns the same value as one of the Win32 error codes, there is no way to discern whether an error occurred. To avoid this situation, I recommend that you return `S_OK` or `S_FALSE` only from the remote function. This problem does not occur in stream mode for the reason that, because of the asynchronous nature of the call, there is no way to retrieve the return value from the remote function.

Now that I've covered how to use `CeRapiInvoke`, take a look at some code that solves the original problem presented (getting a list of all DLLs loaded on the device) and provides a simple dialog-based chat example. The first part uses `CeRapiInvoke` in block mode, and the second uses stream mode. The full source for the example is on the CD-ROM.

The examples are organized into two Windows NT executables, `CRIBlock` and `CRIStream`, and one Windows CE DLL, `CRIDLL`, which provides the remote functions.

The source for `CRIBlock` is a straightforward Win32 dialog application. Listing 20.4 shows the application's `WinMain`. After initializing RAPI, we then call the `GetLoadedModules` routine in `CRIDLL` using `CeRapiInvoke` and test for success using the code in Listing 20.3. If the call succeeds, you then use the Win32 `DialogBoxParam` API to display the module list passed back through the output parameters of `CeRapiInvoke`.

When the user closes the dialog box, DialogBoxParam will return, and you then free the module list using CeRapiFreeBuffer.

LISTING 20.4 CRIBlock's WinMain

```
 1: int WINAPI WinMain (HINSTANCE hInstance,
 2:                HINSTANCE hPrevInstance,
 3:                LPSTR lpCmdLine,
 4:                int nCmdShow)
 5: {
 6:     RAPIINIT ri = { sizeof(RAPIINIT) };
 7:     if ( SUCCEEDED(CeRapiInitEx(&ri)) )
 8:     // wait for 15 seconds for the connection...
 9:     if ( (WaitForSingleObject(ri.heRapiInit, 15000)
10: ➥== WAIT_OBJECT_0) &&
11: ➥SUCCEEDED(ri.hrRapiInit) )
12:        {
13:            HRESULT hr;
14:            DWORD   dwBuf;
15:            BYTE    *pbuf;
16:
            hr = CeRapiInvoke(_T("cridll.dll"),
17:                            _T("GetLoadedModules"),
18:                            0,
19:                            NULL,
20:                            &dwBuf,
21:                            &pbuf,
22:                            NULL,
23:                            0);
24:        if ( CRI_Success(hr) )
25:        {
26:            if ( pbuf == NULL )
27:            {
28:                MessageBox(NULL, _
29:               ➥T("Loaded Module List"), _
30:               ➥T("No loaded modules found on device"), MB_OK);
31:            }
32:            else
33:            {
34:                // display the dialog
35:                // and pass the pointer to the module list
36:                DialogBoxParam(hInstance,
37:                                MAKEINTRESOURCE(IDD_BLOCKDLG),
38:                                NULL,
39:                                (DLGPROC)ModuleDlgProc,
40:                                (LPARAM)pbuf);
41:            }
42:            // free the memory allocated
43:            // by the call to CeRapiInvoke
```

continues

20

LISTING 20.4   continued

```
44:                    CeRapiFreeBuffer(pbuf);
45:                }
46:            else
47:                {
48:                        MessageBox(NULL,
49:                        L"CeRapiInvoke failed",
50:                        L"CeRapiInvoke failed",
51:                        MB_OK);
52:                }
53:            }
54:        else
55:            {
56:                    MessageBox(NULL, _
57:                    T("CeRapiInitEx failed"), _
58:                    T("CeRapiInitEx failed"),
59:                    MB_OK);
60:            }
61:        // have to call uninit even if the
62:        // connection did not succeed
63:        CeRapiUninit();
64:    }
65:    else
66:    {
67:        MessageBox(NULL, _
68:                T("CeRapiInitEx failed"), _
69:                T("CeRapiInitEx failed"),
70:                MB_OK);
71:    }
72:    return 0;
73: }
```

The dialog box on the host side is boring. In the WM_INITDIALOG handler, you parse the newline-delimited module list using the C runtime routine _tcstok and add the strings to a list box. The WM_COMMAND handler takes care of closing the dialog when the user clicks the OK or Cancel buttons. All the real action takes place in the CRIDLL routine GetLoadedModules, presented in Listing 20.5.

LISTING 20.5   The DLL Called by CeRapiInvoke

```
1: STDAPI GetLoadedModules(
2:     DWORD cbInput,
3:     BYTE  *pInput,
4:     DWORD *pcbOutput,
5:     BYTE  **ppOutput,
6:     IRAPIStream *pIRAPIStream )
7: {
8:     HANDLE          hSnap;
```

```
 9:     MODULEENTRY32    me = { sizeof(MODULEENTRY32) };
10:     LPWSTR           lpwszMods = NULL;
11:     DWORD            dwCurSize = 0;
12:     // init output variables
13:     *ppOutput = NULL;
14:     *pcbOutput = 0;
15:     // get module list
16:     hSnap = CreateToolhelp32Snapshot(
17:  ➥TH32CS_SNAPMODULE ¦ TH32CS_GETALLMODS, 0);
18:     if ( hSnap == (HANDLE)-1 )
19:     {
20:         return S_FALSE;
21:     }
22:         BOOL bFound = Module32First(hSnap, &me);
23:         while ( bFound == TRUE )
24:         {
25:         // package up modules as CRLF delimited list
26:         dwCurSize += (wcslen(me.szModule)*sizeof(TCHAR))
27:  ➥+ (sizeof(TCHAR)*2);
28:         if ( lpwszMods == NULL )
29:         lpwszMods = (LPWSTR)LocalAlloc(LPTR, dwCurSize);
30:         else
31:         lpwszMods = (LPWSTR)LocalReAlloc((HLOCAL)lpwszMods,
32:                                     dwCurSize, LMEM_MOVEABLE);
33:         if ( lpwszMods == NULL )
34:         {
35:          dwCurSize = 0;
36:          break;
37:         }
38:         wcscat(lpwszMods, me.szModule);
39:         wcscat(lpwszMods, L"\n");
40:         bFound = Module32Next(hSnap, &me);
41:     }
42:     CloseToolhelp32Snapshot(hSnap);
43:     // fill in output vars
44:     *ppOutput = (PBYTE)lpwszMods;
45:     *pcbOutput = dwCurSize;
46:     return S_OK;
47: }
48: BOOL CALLBACK DlgProc(HWND hwndDlg,
49:                       UINT uMsg,
50:                       WPARAM wParam,
51:                       LPARAM lParam);
52:
53: STDAPI DlgStreamTest(
54:     DWORD cbInput,
55:     BYTE  *pInput,
56:     DWORD *pcbOutput,
57:     BYTE  **ppOutput,
58:     IRAPIStream *pIRAPIStream )
59: {
```

20

continues

LISTING 20.5 continued

```
60:       // init output variables
61:       *pcbOutput = 0;
62:       *ppOutput = NULL;
63:       // display the dialog, passing the stream in lParam
64:       DialogBoxParam(g_hInstance,
65:                       MAKEINTRESOURCE(IDD_MAINDLG),
66:                       NULL,
67:                       (DLGPROC)DlgProc,
68:                       (LPARAM)pIRAPIStream);
69:       return S_OK;
70: }
71:
72: // simple struct to pass to thread function
73: struct ReceiveData
74: {
75:       HWND hwnd;
76:       IRAPIStream *pStream;
77: };

78: DWORD WINAPI ReceiveThread(PVOID pv)
79: {
80:       DWORD       cbOut, cbRead;
81:       HRESULT     hr;
82:       ReceiveData  *prd = (ReceiveData*)pv;
83:       TCHAR       chBuf[TEXT_MAX];
84:       if ( prd == NULL ¦¦ prd->pStream == NULL ¦¦ !IsWindow(prd->hwnd) )
85:       {
86:           OutputDebugString(L"ERROR: invalid
87:
              ➥parameter to ReceiveThread\n");
88:           // release the stream if we can
89:           if ( prd && prd->pStream )
90:               prd->pStream->Release();
91:           return 0;
92:       }
93:       while ( TRUE )
94:       {
95:           hr = prd->pStream->Read( &cbOut, sizeof ( cbOut ), &cbRead );
96:           if ( SUCCEEDED(hr) )
97:           {
98:               hr = prd->pStream->Read( (PBYTE)chBuf, cbOut , &cbRead );
99:               if ( SUCCEEDED(hr) )
100:              {
101:                  if ( wcscmp(chBuf, L"\x01¦done¦\x02") == 0 )
102:                      break;
103:                  SetWindowText(GetDlgItem(prd->hwnd, IDC_TEXT), chBuf);
104:              }
105:              else
106:              {
```

```
107:                     OutputDebugString(_T("ERROR: read size failed...\n"));
108:                     break;
109:             }
110:         }
111:         else
112:         {
113:             OutputDebugString(_T("ERROR: read data failed...\n"));
114:             break;
115:         }
116:     }
117:     // Post a message back to the dialog to let it know that we are
       ➥finished
118:     // DO NOT change this to send because the dialog waits for the
119:     // thread to exit
120:     PostMessage(prd->hwnd, WM_COMMAND, MAKELONG(IDC_FINISHED,BN_CLICKED),
       ➥NULL);
121: 199:    // release the stream interface
122:     prd->pStream->Release();
123: 202:    return 0;
124: }
125:
126: BOOL CALLBACK DlgProc(HWND hwndDlg,
127:                       UINT uMsg,
128:                       WPARAM wParam,
129:                       LPARAM lParam)
130: {
131:         BOOL    bRet = FALSE;
132:         static ReceiveData rd;
133:     static HANDLE hReceiveThread = NULL;
134:
135:     switch( uMsg )
136:     {
137:         case WM_INITDIALOG:
138:             {
139:                 // limit the text box to MAX_CHARS
140:                 SendMessage(GetDlgItem(hwndDlg, IDC_TEXT),
141:                         EM_LIMITTEXT, MAX_CHARS, 0);
142:                 // start the receive thread
143:                 rd.hwnd = hwndDlg;
144:                 rd.pStream = (IRAPIStream*)lParam;
145:                 DWORD dwTID;
146:                 hReceiveThread = CreateThread(NULL, 0,
147:                                                 ReceiveThread,
148:                                                 &rd, 0, &dwTID);
149:                 if ( hReceiveThread == NULL )
150:                 {
151:                     OutputDebugString(_T("ERROR: could not
152:                     ➥create ReceiveThread...\n"));
153:                     rd.pStream->Release();
154:                 }
155:                 else
```

continues

20

LISTING 20.5 continued

```
156:                   {
157:                           // make sure that the window is visible
158:                           SetForegroundWindow(hwndDlg);
159:                   }
160:                   bRet = TRUE;
161:               }
162:           break;
163:       case WM_COMMAND:
164:           {
165:               int     nID = LOWORD(wParam);
166:               int     wNotify = HIWORD(wParam);
167:               // end the dialog if we received an
168:               // IDC_FINISHED notification
169:               if ( wNotify == BN_CLICKED && nID == IDC_FINISHED )
170:               {
171:                   // wait for ReceiveThread to exit and kill the dialog
172:                   if ( hReceiveThread )
173:                   {
174:                       WaitForSingleObject(hReceiveThread, INFINITE);
175:                       hReceiveThread = NULL;
176:                   }
177:                   EndDialog(hwndDlg, IDC_FINISHED);
178:                   bRet = TRUE;
179:               }
180:           }
181:           break;
182:       }
183:       return bRet;
184: }
```

GetLoadedModules uses the Windows CE ToolHelp routines to retrieve the list of currently loaded DLLs. I discussed the ToolHelp functions previously in Hour 11, "Threads and Processes." The call to CreateToolhelp32Snapshot uses the TH32CS_SNAPMODULE and TH32CS_GETALLMODS flags to accomplish this. If you've used ToolHelp before on Windows 95, you will notice that the TH32CS_GETALLMODS flag is not provided there and is specific to Windows CE. If you didn't include it, you would retrieve the names of the modules loaded for the current process instead of the entire operating system. The code then builds up the module list using the Module32First and Module32Next functions, allocating memory along the way with LocalAlloc and LocalReAlloc as required by RAPI. When Module32Next returns FALSE, you drop out of the loop, close the ToolHelp handle, and set the ppOutput and pcbOutput parameters.

Using LocalAlloc and LocalReAlloc in this manner exposed a quirk in the Windows CE implementation. In the past, when I used them in a loop such as this on Windows NT, I used LPTR as the flag to LocalReAlloc, which enabled me to allocate up to nearly 512KB. On Windows CE, this same scenario never allocates more than 1KB! This size limitation is too small, even for the process list. Changing the LocalReAlloc flag to LMEM_MOVEABLE works on both Windows NT and CE and allows memory up to the size of the biggest free block to be allocated, because the location can be moved after the call to LocalAlloc rather than be expanded in place.

The source for the second example, CRIStream, appears in Listing 20.6. WinMain calls CeRapiInitEx just like CRIBlock and then displays the dialog shown in Figure 20.2.

FIGURE 20.2
CRIStream.

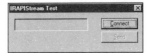

When the dialog is first displayed, the edit box and Send button are disabled. After the user clicks the Connect button, a dialog box is created on the Windows CE device; the edit box and Send button are enabled; and the Connect button changes to Disconnect. Clicking the Send button sends the text in the edit box to the device, which is then displayed on the device dialog in a read-only edit box. The dialog box on the device does not accept any user input and is destroyed automatically when the user clicks the Disconnect button. The connection can be created and destroyed as many times as the user likes, and clicking the close icon in the upper-right corner or pressing Esc on the keyboard will close the dialog box.

LISTING 20.6   Using CeRapiInvoke's Stream Mode

20

```
 1: #include <windows.h>
 2: #include <tchar.h>
 3: #include <rapi.h>
 4:
 5: #include "..\common.h"
 6:
 7: // max size for text box in dialog
 8: const int MAX_CHARS = 32;
 9: const int TEXT_MAX = MAX_CHARS+1;
10:
11: BOOL CALLBACK DlgProc(HWND hwndDlg,
```

continues

LISTING 20.6 continued

```
12:                            UINT uMsg,
13:                            WPARAM wParam,
14:                            LPARAM lParam);
15:
16:
17: HRESULT DoCRI();
18: void SendText(HWND hwnd);
19: BOOL Connect(HWND hwnd);
20: BOOL Disconnect(HWND hwnd);
21:
22: IRAPIStream *g_pStream = NULL;
23:
24:
25: int WINAPI WinMain (HINSTANCE hInstance,
26:                     HINSTANCE hPrevInstance,
27:                     LPSTR lpCmdLine,
28:                     int nCmdShow)
29: {
30:     RAPIINIT ri = { sizeof(RAPIINIT) };
31:
32:     if ( SUCCEEDED(CeRapiInitEx(&ri)) )
33:     {
34:         // wait for 15 seconds for the connection...
35:         if ( (WaitForSingleObject(ri.heRapiInit, 15000)
           ➥== WAIT_OBJECT_0) &&
36:              SUCCEEDED(ri.hrRapiInit) )
37:         {
38:             DialogBox(hInstance,
39:                       MAKEINTRESOURCE(IDD_MAINDLG),
40:                       NULL,
41:                       (DLGPROC)DlgProc);
42:         }
43:         else
44:         {
45:             MessageBox(NULL, _T("CeRapiInitEx failed"),
               ➥_T("CeRapiInitEx failed"), MB_OK);
46:         }
47:
48:         // have to call uninit even if the connection did not succeed
49:         CeRapiUninit();
50:     }
51:     else
52:     {
53:         MessageBox(NULL, _T("CeRapiInitEx failed"), _
           ➥T("CeRapiInitEx failed"), MB_OK);
54:     }
55:
56:     return 0;
57: }
```

```
58:
59:
60: BOOL CALLBACK DlgProc(HWND hwndDlg,
61:                       UINT uMsg,
62:                       WPARAM wParam,
63:                       LPARAM lParam)
64: {
65:     BOOL    bRet = FALSE;
66:
67:     switch( uMsg )
68:     {
69:         case WM_INITDIALOG:
70:             SendMessage(GetDlgItem(hwndDlg, IDC_TEXT),
                ➥EM_LIMITTEXT, MAX_CHARS, 0);
71:             EnableWindow(GetDlgItem(hwndDlg, IDC_CONNECT), TRUE);
72:             EnableWindow(GetDlgItem(hwndDlg, IDC_TEXT), FALSE);
73:             EnableWindow(GetDlgItem(hwndDlg, IDC_SEND), FALSE);
74:             break;
75:
76:         case WM_COMMAND:
77:         {
78:             int     nID = LOWORD(wParam);
79:             int     wNotify = HIWORD(wParam);
80:             HWND    hwndCtl = (HWND)lParam;
81:
82:             // handle a click on the send, connect, or cancel buttons
83:             if ( wNotify == BN_CLICKED )
84:             {
85:               switch( nID )
86:                 {
87:                   case IDCANCEL:
88:                       Disconnect(hwndDlg);
89:                       EndDialog(hwndDlg, IDCANCEL);
90:                       bRet = TRUE;
91:                       break;
92:
93:                   case IDC_CONNECT:
94:                       if ( g_pStream )
95:                           Disconnect(hwndDlg);
96:                       else
97:                           Connect(hwndDlg);
98:                       bRet = TRUE;
99:                       break;
100:
101:                   case IDC_SEND:
102:                       SendText(hwndDlg);
103:                       bRet = TRUE;
104:                       break;
105:                 }
106:             }
107:         }
```

20

continues

LISTING 20.6   continued

```
108:            break;
109:        }
110:
111:    return bRet;
112: }
113:
114:
115: BOOL Connect(HWND hwnd)
116: {
117:     HRESULT hr = DoCRI();
118:
119:     if ( CRI_Success(hr) )
120:     {
121:         // enable UI to show connectivity
122:         EnableWindow(GetDlgItem(hwnd, IDC_TEXT), TRUE);
123:         EnableWindow(GetDlgItem(hwnd, IDC_SEND), TRUE);
124:
125:         SetWindowText(GetDlgItem(hwnd, IDC_CONNECT),
             ➥_T("&Disconnect"));
126:
127:     }
128:     else
129:     {
130:         // notify w/ a messagebox
131:         MessageBox(hwnd, _T("Could not connect"), _T("Error"), MB_OK);
132:     }
133:
134:     return CRI_Success(hr);
135:
136: }
137:
138: BOOL Disconnect(HWND hwnd)
139: {
140:     DWORD   cbWritten, cb;
141:     TCHAR chBuf[TEXT_MAX];
142:
143:     if ( g_pStream )
144:     {
145:         wcscpy(chBuf, L"\x01¦done¦\x02");
146:         cb = (wcslen(chBuf)*sizeof(TCHAR)) + sizeof(TCHAR);
147:
148:         g_pStream->Write(&cb, sizeof cb, &cbWritten);
149:         g_pStream->Write(chBuf, cb, &cbWritten);
150:
151:         g_pStream->Release();
152:         g_pStream = NULL;
153:     }
154:
155:     // enable UI to show connectivity
```

```
156:        EnableWindow(GetDlgItem(hwnd, IDC_TEXT), FALSE);
157:        EnableWindow(GetDlgItem(hwnd, IDC_SEND), FALSE);
158:
159:        SetWindowText(GetDlgItem(hwnd, IDC_CONNECT), _T("&Connect"));
160:
161:        return TRUE;
162:
163: }
164:
165:
166:
167: HRESULT DoCRI()
168: {
169:        HRESULT hr;
170:
171:        DWORD cb = 0;
172:        PBYTE pbuf = NULL;
173:
174:
175:        hr = CeRapiInvoke(_T("cridll.dll"),
176:                          _T("DlgStreamTest"),
177:                          0,
178:                          NULL,
179:                          &cb,
180:                          &pbuf,
181:                          &g_pStream,
182:                          0);
183:
184:        // free any allocated output buffer
185:        if ( pbuf )
186:            CeRapiFreeBuffer(pbuf);
187:
188:        return hr;
189: }
190:
191:
192: void SendText(HWND hwndDlg)
193: {
194:        DWORD   cbWritten, cb;
195:        TCHAR chBuf[TEXT_MAX];
196:
197:
198:        if ( g_pStream )
199:        {
200:            GetWindowText(GetDlgItem(hwndDlg, IDC_TEXT),
201:                                     chBuf,
202:                                     TEXT_MAX);
203:
204:            cb = (wcslen(chBuf)*sizeof(TCHAR)) + sizeof(TCHAR);
205:
206:            g_pStream->Write(&cb, sizeof cb, &cbWritten);
```

20

continues

LISTING 20.6   continued

```
207:            g_pStream->Write(chBuf, cb, &cbWritten);
208:        }
209: }
```

The WM_INITDIALOG handler in DlgProc takes care of initially disabling the edit box and Connect buttons, as well as limiting the edit box to the maximum number of characters the user is allowed to input. The WM_COMMAND case handles all the user input. IDCANCEL simply calls EndDialog after calling Disconnect to make sure that you don't close the dialog while still connected to the device. The case for IDC_CONNECT checks whether you are currently connected and then calls the appropriate Connect or Disconnect routine.

The Connect routine uses DoCRI to call CeRapiInvoke in stream mode, passing a pointer to the global g_pStream that is initialized to NULL. If the call to CeRapiInvoke succeeds, the user interface is updated to the connected state. The Disconnect routine writes a "magic string" to the stream, telling the device that it is disconnecting (this is explained more in the following paragraph), and then updates the user interface to the disconnected state. The final user input that WM_COMMAND handles is IDC_SEND, which just gets the data from the edit box and sends it over g_pStream by writing first the number of bytes being sent and then the bytes themselves. Now, refer to Listing 20.3 at the CRIDLL routine DlgStreamTest, which takes care of things on the device side.

DlgStreamTest just initializes the output variables to NULL and then displays a dialog with DialogBoxParam, passing the pointer to the IRAPIStream in the DlgProc's LPARAM. After limiting the edit box to the maximum number of characters, the WM_INITDIALOG handler starts a separate thread to receive the text, passing the dialog's hWnd and the IRAPIStream pointer in a structure through the thread function's formal parameter. If you were successful in starting the thread, you call SetForegroundWindow with the dialog box's hWnd to make sure that it is not hidden behind some other window.

The thread function ReceiveText then takes over and, after validating its parameters, sits in an endless loop waiting for data from the IRAPIStream. If you are able to read both the size of the data and the data itself, you then check whether you received the magic string indicating that the user wants to disconnect. If not, you just use SetWindowText to display the text in the edit box. Otherwise, you break out of the loop, post an IDC_FINISHED notification to the dialog box, and call Release on the stream pointer. When DlgProc receives the IDC_FINISHED notification, it waits for the thread to finish executing and then kills itself with a call to EndDialog.

> The shutdown sequence for this dialog—although it might seem like overkill—is very important. When I first wrote this example, I had ReceiveThread call SendMessage, and DlgProc did not wait for the secondary thread to exit. This allowed the dialog to close and DlgStreamTest to return before ReceiveThread had completed. The result was that any subsequent connections after the first one would cause intermittent access violation exceptions and crash the Windows CE RAPI component. Changing to the current method solved this problem.
>
> This serves as just another example of how important it is to be careful when doing multithreaded programming—it is very easy to go wrong in even a situation as simple as this.

CeRapiInvoke has a few other quirks. It cannot handle long filenames for the device-side DLL, limiting it to a DOS-style 8.3 filename.

A more serious issue has to do with the stream mode of CeRapiInvoke. During the lifetime of a stream mode connection with the device, calls to other RAPI functions will block and will not return to the caller until the connection is closed. The reason for this is that the stream actually takes over the connection that RAPI uses for communication with the device. Therefore, other functions that want to use it have to wait for it to be available.

Even with its quirks and limitations, CeRapiInvoke is a valuable technique that can be a big help in many situations.

Summary

This hour you've learned the basics of how to carry on a meaningful conversation between a desktop PC and a Windows CE device. I talked about how to use RAPI.DLL, initialize a connection, obtain information about the connected device, and use the infamous CeRapiInvoke.

20

Q&A

Q I dynamically link to RAPI.DLL, and after a few function calls, my process crashes intermittently. How come?

A Make sure that you are specifying WINAPI in your function pointer declarations. If you don't, the wrong calling convention will be used, and the call stack will be corrupted.

Q `CeGlobalMemoryStatus` **is returning garbage values. What am I doing wrong?**

A Nothing, `CeGlobalMemoryStatus` is broken. The easiest solution is to use `CeRapiInvoke` in block mode to implement a workaround.

Workshop

The Workshop is designed to help you anticipate possible questions, review what you've learned, and begin thinking ahead about putting your knowledge into practice. The answers to the quiz are in Appendix A, "Answers."

Quiz

1. What is the difference between `CeRapiInvoke` stream and block modes?

2. What is the difference between `CeRapiInit` and `CeRapiInitEx`?

3. Why should you use `LoadLibrary` and `GetProcAddress` with RAPI.DLL instead of static linking?

4. How can I get information about the files in a specific directory on the device?

5. What is the correct function pointer definition for `CeRapiInit`?

6. The return type of `CeRapiInitEx` is an `HRESULT`. Why can't it be tested with the `SUCCESS` or `FAILURE` macros?

Exercises

1. Modify the `CRIStream` sample to allow text to be sent in either direction.

2. Use `CERapiInvoke` to write a version of `CeGlobalMemoryStatus` that works correctly.

HOUR 21

Creating ActiveSync Modules

This hour will introduce you to what ActiveSync is and how to use it to synchronize your application's data between desktop computers and Windows CE devices.

In this hour, you will learn

- An overview of what ActiveSync is
- How to implement and register the desktop module of an ActiveSync service provider
- How to implement and register the Windows CE device-side module of an ActiveSync service provider
- How to interact with the ActiveSync manager

What Is ActiveSync?

ActiveSync is a framework that enables bidirectional synchronization of data between the desktop computer and Windows CE devices. Synchronization is different from simple data transfer in that modifications to data on one system are automatically transferred to the other system. If specific data has been changed on both systems, ActiveSync has a mechanism to bring the conflict to the user's attention so that he or she can resolve the issue.

ActiveSync service providers are necessary for each type of data you want to synchronize. Table 21.1 lists the default ActiveSync service providers in a typical Windows CE installation.

TABLE 21.1 Default ActiveSync Service Providers

Data Synchronized	Service Providers
Files	cefstore.dll on the desktop and cefobj.dll on the device
Mobile Channels	aafstore.dll on the desktop and aafobj.dll on the device
Outlook	outstore.dll on the desktop and pegobj.dll on the device
SchedulePlus	scdstore.dll on the desktop and pegobj.dll on the device

If you want to synchronize your application's data between desktop computers and Windows CE devices, you must implement an ActiveSync service provider. The next section is an introduction to implementing an ActiveSync service provider.

How Do I Write an ActiveSync Module?

An ActiveSync service provider consists of a desktop component and Windows CE device resident component. The desktop component is a DLL that implements the `IReplObjHandler` and `IReplStore` COM interfaces. The Windows CE resident component is a DLL that implements the `IReplObjHandler` COM interface and the following functions: `InitObjType`, `GetObjTypeInfo`, and `ObjectNotify`. If necessary, you can implement the optional `ReportStatus` function. Two additional functions, `FindObjects` and `SyncData`, are not utilized in versions of Windows CE before version 2.1. These functions and COM interfaces are discussed in more detail in the following sections.

The `ReplObjHandler` Interface

The desktop and Windows CE resident modules both implement the `ReplObjHandler` interface, so we will examine it first. `ReplObjHandler` is essentially the interface used to transfer the synchronization objects between the desktop computer and the Windows CE device and to delete objects when requested. Table 21.2 lists and briefly explains the five methods in the `ReplObjHandler` interface.

TABLE 21.2   The `IReplObjHandler` Interface Methods

Methods	Purpose
DeleteObject	Deletes the object specified by the ActiveSync manager
GetPacket	Converts an object into packets of bytes
Reset	Frees all resources used to transmit and receive packets
SetPacket	Converts packets of bytes into an object
Setup	Initializes the ActiveSync service provider so that it is ready to send and receive packets

The following code listings illustrate how to implement the `IReplObjHandler` methods.

When the ActiveSync manager wishes to initialize your service provider it will invoke your `IReplObjHandler::Setup` method. Your implementation of this method should perform any initializations required for your service provider to send or receive data packets. Listing 21.1 shows how to implement `IReplObjHandler::Setup` for a sample ActiveSync service provider. `CDataHandler` is a class derived from `IReplObjHandler`. `m_pReadSetup` and `m_pWriteSetup` are pointers to a REPLSETUP structure (defined in CESYNC.H) which you may wish to access in other methods.

LISTING 21.1   A Sample `IReplObjHandler::Setup` Implementation

```
 1: STDMETHODIMP CDataHandler::Setup ( PREPLSETUP pSetup )
 2: {
 3:     // we could be reading and writing at the same time,
 4:     // so need to save the pointer to set up struct differently
 5:     if ( pSetup->fRead ) {
 6:         m_pReadSetup = pSetup;
 7:     } else {
 8:         m_pWriteSetup = pSetup;
 9:     }
10:
11:     return NOERROR;
12: }
```

When the ActiveSync manager wishes to receive data from your service provider it will invoke your `IReplObjHandler::GetPacket` method. Listing 21.2 shows how to implement `IReplObjHandler::GetPacket` for the sample ActiveSync service provider, which retrieves the data from a file.

21

LISTING 21.2   A Sample `IReplObjHandler::GetPacket` Implementation

```
1: STDMETHODIMP CDataHandler::GetPacket( LPBYTE *lppbPacket,
              ➡DWORD *pcbPacket, DWORD cbRecommend )
2: {
3:     if (m_pbPacket == NULL)
4:         return RERR_BAD_OBJECT;
5:
6:     HANDLE hFile = CreateFile( tcDataFile, GENERIC_READ,
                            ➡FILE_SHARE_READ, NULL,
7:                             OPEN_EXISTING, 0, NULL );
8:
9:     if (hFile == INVALID_HANDLE_VALUE)
10:         return HRESULT_FROM_WIN32( ERROR_FILE_NOT_FOUND );
11:
12:     memset(m_pbPacket, 0, POCKET_SIZE);
13:
14:     DWORD dwBytes;
15:
16:     // read data from file in a loop
17:     if ( !ReadFile( hFile, m_pbPacket, POCKET_SIZE, &dwBytes, NULL ) ) {
18:         CloseHandle( hFile );
19:         return RERR_BAD_OBJECT;
20:     }
21:
22:     CloseHandle( hFile );
23:
24:     *pcbPacket = dwBytes;
25:     *lppbPacket = m_pbPacket;
26:
27:     return RWRN_LAST_PACKET;
28: }
```

When a packet of data is available to your service provider, the ActiveSync manager will
invoke your service provider's `IReplObjHandler::SetPacket` method. Listing 21.3
shows how to implement `IReplObjHandler::SetPacket` for the sample ActiveSync service provider, which saves the data to a file.

LISTING 21.3   A Sample `IReplObjHandler::SetPacket` Implementation

```
1: STDMETHODIMP CDataHandler::SetPacket( LPBYTE lpbPacket, DWORD cbPacket )
2: {
3:     static UINT s_uItemID = 1;
4:
5:     if (m_pWriteSetup->hItem)
```

```
 6:            PITEM p = (PITEM)m_pWriteSetup->hItem;
 7:
 8:        // append data in a loop
 9:        HANDLE hFile = CreateFile( tcDataFile, GENERIC_WRITE|
10:                             GENERIC_READ, 0, NULL, CREATE_ALWAYS,
                            ➥FILE_ATTRIBUTE_NORMAL, NULL );
11:
12:        if (hFile == INVALID_HANDLE_VALUE)
13:            return HRESULT_FROM_WIN32( ERROR_FILE_NOT_FOUND );
14:
15:        DWORD dwByte;
16:        WriteFile( hFile, lpbPacket, cbPacket, &dwByte, NULL );
17:        CloseHandle( hFile );
18:
19:        PITEM pItem = new CItem;
20:        if ( !pItem )
21:            return E_OUTOFMEMORY;
22:
23:        pItem->m_uid = s_uItemID++;
24:        GetLocalFileTime(&pItem->m_ftModified);
25:
26:        m_pWriteSetup->hItem = (HREPLITEM)pItem;
27:
28:        return NOERROR;
29: }
```

The ActiveSync manager will invoke your service provider's
IReplObjHandler::DeleteObj method when it determines that an object should be
deleted. Listing 21.4 shows how to implement IReplObjHandler::DeleteObj for the
sample ActiveSync service provider. This listing assumes that the object you are synchronizing is a file.

LISTING 21.4 A Sample IReplObjHandler::DeleteObj Implementation

```
1: STDMETHODIMP CDataHandler::DeleteObj( PREPLSETUP  pSetup )
2: {
3:     DeleteFile(tcDataFile);
4:     return NOERROR;
5: }
```

Listing 21.5 shows how to implement IReplObjHandler::Reset for the sample
ActiveSync service provider.

21

LISTING 21.5   A Sample `IReplObjHandler::Reset` Implementation

```
1: STDMETHODIMP CDataHandler::Reset( PREPLSETUP pSetup )
2: {
3:     return NOERROR;
4: }
```

Next, I will discuss how to implement the `IReplStore` interface that is specific to the desktop portion of an ActiveSync service provider.

Implementing the Desktop Module of the ActiveSync Service Provider

The `IReplStore` portion of a desktop ActiveSync service provider is responsible for managing the synchronization objects in the desktop store. It enumerates objects in the desktop store, detects if items have changed or are duplicated, and enables the user to manually resolve conflicts and set the ActiveSync options for the service provider.

The `IReplStore` interface has 22 methods. They are prototyped in the CESYNC.H header file and can be divided into the following: user interface methods, object methods, store methods, handle methods, folder methods, and the `ReportStatus` method.

`IReplStore`: User Interface Methods

The `IReplStore` interface has four user interface–related methods: `ActivateDialog`, `GetConflictInfo`, `GetObjTypeUIData`, and `RemoveDuplicates`.

- `ActivateDialog` enables your ActiveSync service provider to implement a configuration dialog that is accessible to your users from within the ActiveSync manager program. If you do not want to implement this for your service provider, you should return `E_NOTIMPL`.

- `GetConflictInfo` enables your ActiveSync service provider to provide information about two conflicting objects. This is accomplished by populating the fields of the `CONFINFO` structure pointer parameter. You should provide sufficient information in the `szLocalDesc` and `szRemoteDesc` fields to enable your users to resolve the conflict with confidence. If you determine that no real conflict exists, you can signal this programmatically by returning `RERR_IGNORE`.

- `GetObjTypeUIData` enables you to describe how you would like your service provider to appear from within the desktop ActiveSync Status application. This is achieved by populating the fields in the `OBJUIDATA` structure pointer parameter. The information includes the large and small icons to use in the ActiveSync Status application's main window, as well as the text string to use to describe your data.

- `RemoveDuplicates` is invoked by the ActiveSync manager when it would like your service provider to scan its store for duplicate objects and remove them. If you do not want to implement this for your service provider, you should return `E_NOTIMPL`.

`IReplStore`: Object Methods

The `IReplStore` interface has seven object-related methods used for enumerating objects, detecting when objects have been changed or replicated, and comparing objects:

- `CompareItem` compares two handle objects returned by `FindFirstItem` or `FindNextItem`. If the two handles reference the same object, `CompareItem` returns `0`. Otherwise, it returns `1` if the first object is larger or `-1` if the first object is smaller.

- `FindFirstItem` creates a `HREPLITEM` handle for the first item in the specified folder. If there are no items in the folder, the `BOOL` to which the `pfExist` parameter points will be set to `FALSE`.

- `FindItemClose` is invoked when item enumeration is completed in a folder. The ActiveSync service provider should free all memory and resources that were allocated over the course of executing the preceding `FindFirstItem` and `FindNextItem` methods.

- `FindNextItem` creates a `HREPLITEM` handle for the next item in the specified folder.

- `IsItemChanged` returns `TRUE` if it determines that the specified item has changed. The determination is made by comparing the data referenced by the two object handles.

- `IsItemReplicated` returns `TRUE` if it determines that the specified item should be replicated. This method is where the service provider has the opportunity to implement rules for which items should be replicated. If all items should be replicated, this method should always return `TRUE`.

- `UpdateItem` updates the object's information, such as the change number or time stamp.

Although `FindFirstItem` and `FindNextItem` are used to enumerate objects in the folder, your service provider should prevent other threads from modifying data in the store (such as deleting objects in the store). You can achieve this through the use of critical sections.

`IReplStore`: Store-Related Methods

The `IReplStore` interface has three store manipulation methods for initializing, retrieving and comparing store information:

21

- `CompareStoreIDs` is called when the ActiveSync manager has to know whether the current store differs from the last store. This should return `0` if they are equal, `1` if the current store is bigger, and `-1` if the current store is smaller than the last store.
- `GetStoreInfo` returns information about the current store through the use of the `STOREINFO` pointer parameter. If the `lpbStoreId` member is set to `NULL`, the ActiveSync manager is requesting that the size of the store identifier be returned in the `cbStoreId` member so that it can allocate the required memory.
- `Initialize` is called by the ActiveSync manager to initialize your ActiveSync service provider. If the `uFlags` parameter is set to `ISF_REMOTE_CONNECTED`, the user is synchronizing remotely, and your service provider should run without displaying any user interface.

`IReplStore`: Handle-Related Methods

The `IReplStore` interface has five methods to manipulate objects, including the ability to copy them, free them, check their validity, and convert them to and from an array of bytes:

- `BytesToObject` converts an array of bytes to an `HREPLOBJ` object. It can be used for items (`HREPLITEM`) and folders (`HREPLFLD`).
- `CopyObject` copies the contents of one `HREPLITEM` or `HREPLFLD` handle to another. This is called when the ActiveSync manager detects that an object has been changed since the last replication.
- `FreeObject` is invoked when the specified object should be destroyed. All memory allocated for the object should be freed.
- `ObjectToBytes` converts an object to an array of bytes. It works on both items (`HREPLITEM`) and folders (`HREPLFLD`).
- `IsValidObject` determines whether the folder and item handles specified are valid. It should return `NOERROR` if the handles are valid, `RERR_CORRUPT` if corrupted data is detected for the specified handles, and `RERR_OBJECT_DELETED` if the objects specified by the handles have been deleted and are no longer available in the store.

`IReplStore`: Folder-Related Methods

The `IReplStore` interface has two methods for detecting when folders have changed and retrieving information about them:

- `GetFolderInfo` is used to retrieve a folder handle for the specified object type. If the `phFolder` parameter is `NULL`, the ActiveSync manager is relying on your service provider to create a new handle for the specified folder.

- IsFolderChanged informs the ActiveSync manager if any object in the folder has changed since the last time this method was invoked.

IReplStore: The ReportStatus Method

The ActiveSync manager uses the ReportStatus method to report status to your service provider. This includes such items of interest as

- Synchronization is about to start or end.
- A failure occurred while writing or delete an object on the device.
- The ActiveSync manager is about to interrupt the current operations (such as when the user attempts to shut down the desktop system).
- Synchronization is being performed remotely (and the service provider should not require any user interaction to successfully complete the synchronization).
- The user has changed the system date.

If your service provider is not interested in these items, it can always return NOERROR.

Now that we have finished examining IReplStore's interfaces, we will turn out attention to the IReplNotify interfaces that are available to your desktop ActiveSync service provider.

Making Use of the IReplNotify Interface

Your ActiveSync service provider is able to query the ActiveSync manager through the IReplNotify interface. Table 21.3 briefly explains the four methods your service provider can use.

TABLE 21.3 The IReplNotify Interfaces

Method	Purpose
GetWindow	Retrieves the parent window to use for your dialogs
OnItemNotify	Indicates that an item has been added, changed, or deleted
SetStatusText	Sets the text displayed in the Explorer's status window
QueryDevice	Requests a DEVINFO or HKEY corresponding to a Windows CE device

This concludes the overview of the IReplStore interface that must be implemented in the desktop portion of an ActiveSync service provider. Next, you will turn your attention to the functions that have to be implemented in the Windows CE portion of an ActiveSync service provider.

21

Implementing the Device-Side Module of the ActiveSync Service Provider

Your device-side ActiveSync service provider must implement the ReplObjHandler methods and export several additional functions. The ReplObjHandler methods that are necessary to support were discussed earlier this hour when we examined the implementation of the desktop ActiveSync service provider module. The additional functions needed are listed in Table 21.4. They are specific to the Windows CE module.

TABLE 21.4 Exported Functions Required in the Device-Side Module

Function	Purpose
InitObjType	Used to initialize or terminate the service provider
GetObjTypeInfo	Specifies whether you are connected to the first or second partner computer (ActiveSync supports synchronizing with two desktop computers, such as your home computer and your work computer)
ObjectNotify	Used to determine whether an enumerated object is to be handled by this particular ActiveSync service provider

Additionally, you have the option of implementing three more functions, listed in Table 21.5.

TABLE 21.5 Additional Exported Functions in the Device-Side Module

Function	Purpose
FindObjects	Enables you to enumerate all objects to be synchronized within a database volume (in either RAM or on a storage card)
ReportStatus	Called by the server to retrieve synchronization status
SyncData	A more flexible method for transmitting and receiving data to/from the desktop server

The ReportStatus function is optional in all versions of Windows CE, but the FindObjects and SyncData functions are used only in version 2.1 of Windows CE and above.

Registering Your ActiveSync Service Provider

For the ActiveSync manager to know about your ActiveSync service provider and start using it, you must properly register it on both the desktop computer and the Windows CE device. This is accomplished via Registry entries on both computers. How do you register a desktop module?

The desktop ActiveSync service provider is registered by creating Registry entries under HKEY_CLASSES_ROOT and HKEY_LOCAL_MACHINE.

Table 21.6 lists the entries that have to be created under HKEY_CLASSES_ROOT.

TABLE 21.6 Desktop HKEY_CLASSES_ROOT Registry Entries Required for Your ActiveSync Service Provider

Entry	Value
Clsid\<class id>\InProcServer32	The full path to your service provider DLL
Clsid\<class id>\ProgID	Your ProgID key
<ProgID>\CLSID	The class ID for COM to use

Every ActiveSync service provider should have a unique class identifier (CLSID). Do not worry if you have never generated a CLSID before. You can use the GUIDGEN.EXE tool included with Visual C++ to generate one for you. Figure 21.1 shows GUIDGEN.EXE in action.

FIGURE 21.1

Using the GUIDGEN.EXE tool to create a unique class identifier (CLSID).

Table 21.7 lists the entries that have to be created under HKEY_LOCAL_MACHINE\ Software\Microsoft\Windows CE Services\Services\Synchronization\Objects\ MyApp to complete the desktop registration of your service provider.

21

TABLE 21.7 Desktop HKEY_LOCAL_MACHINE Registry Entries Required for Your ActiveSync Service Provider

Entry	Value
[Default]	The name of the object being synchronized (for example, MyApp)
Disabled	Specifies whether the service provider should be disabled by default (for example, 0)
Display Name	The string to be used in user feedback for a single object (for example, MyApp's Object)
Plural Name	The string to be used in user feedback for multiple objects (for example, MyApp's Objects)
Store	The ProgID of your service provider (for example, MyApp.WinCE.Application)

A quick way to check whether you have properly registered your desktop ActiveSync service provider is to verify that it is accessible from within the ActiveSync Status application. You can launch this by clicking on the Mobile Devices icon in the task tray and selecting ActiveSync Status from the pop-up menu, or you can launch the Mobile Devices application and select ActiveSync Options from the Tools menu. If your service provider is registered correctly, you will see it in the Synchronization Services list. When you select it within the list and press Options, it will display the options dialog, shown in Figure 21.2, that you implemented in your IReplStore::ActivateDialog method.

FIGURE 21.2

Accessing your service provider's options dialog from within the ActiveSync Options application.

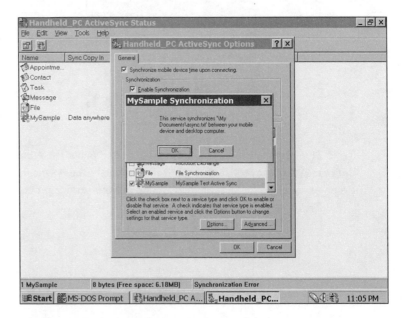

After you have verified that the desktop module is correctly registered, you are ready to register the device-side module.

The Windows CE ActiveSync service provider is registered by creating two entries under the HKEY_LOCAL_MACHINE\Windows CE Services\Synchronization\Objects\MyApp Registry key. Table 21.8 lists these entries.

TABLE 21.8   Device-Side HKEY_LOCAL_MACHINE Registry Entries Required for Your ActiveSync Service Provider

Entry	Value
Store	The name of your device-side service provider DLL (for example, myapp.dll)
Display Name	The same string that is configured for Display Name under HKEY_LOCAL_MACHINE in the desktop Registry (for example, MyApp's Object)

Now that you have built and registered your service providers, you are ready to begin debugging them.

Debugging Your ActiveSync Service Provider on the Desktop

Debugging your desktop ActiveSync service provider DLL is similar to debugging any other DLL on the desktop—you have to tell the Visual C++ integrated development environment which program you would like to run that will load your DLL. In the case of your service provider, that program is SYNCMGR.EXE, which is usually installed in the \Program Files\Windows CE Services directory on your desktop computer. Figure 21.3 shows you how to configure this within the Visual C++ integrated development environment.

21

FIGURE 21.3

Configuring SYNCMGR.EXE as the executable to run when debugging an ActiveSync service provider.

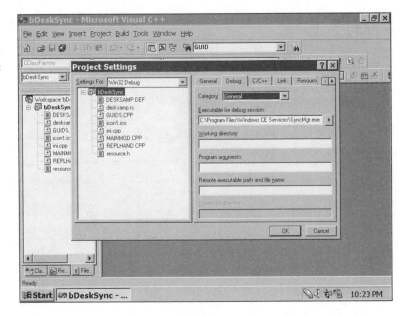

While you are implementing and debugging your ActiveSync service provider DLLs, you will have to rebuild them multiple times. If the ActiveSync manager has your service providers loaded, you will not be able to successfully complete the build process because the output file is still being used. Your desktop module will fail to link. Your Windows CE module will link, but will fail to download to the device. This is easily resolved by forcing the ActiveSync manager to unload the service provider DLLs that it has loaded.

There are several ways to force the ActiveSync manager to unload your service provider. The most time and effort intensive method is to physically disconnect the Windows CE device from the desktop computer. The more efficient method is to use the ActiveSync manager's /quit command line option. Running syncmgr.exe /quit will cause the ActiveSync manager to unload your DLL without interfering with the connection to the Windows CE device. If the ActiveSync manager appears to be in an indeterminate state, or the /quit command-line option does not appear to have worked, using

```
syncmgr.exe /show
```

followed by

```
syncmgr.exe /quit
```

should do the trick. If you encounter this scenario often, you can create a simple batch file that will save you from having to retype these commands.

Summary

In this hour, you learned what ActiveSync is, how to interact with the ActiveSync manager, and how to implement your ActiveSync service provider. In addition to creating both the desktop computer and Windows CE portions of your ActiveSync service provider, you also learned how to register them on both systems so that they can be found and used by the ActiveSync manager.

Q&A

Q Will my ActiveSync service provider be used by the ActiveSync manager only when a Windows CE device is connected to the desktop computer?

A No, the ActiveSync manager may call the following methods in your ActiveSync service provider when there is no connection to a Windows CE device: `ActivateDialog`, `BytesToObject`, `GetFolderInfo`, `GetObjTypeUIData`, `GetStoreInfo`, `ObjectToBytes`, and `ReportStatus`. You should ensure that these will work properly when `Initialize` is not invoked first.

Q Where can I find some samples for implementing an ActiveSync service provider?

A You can find a sample stock portfolio ActiveSync module (including source code) at `http://msdn.microsoft.com/library/techart/activesync.htm`.

Workshop

The Workshop is designed to help you anticipate possible questions, review what you've learned, and begin thinking ahead about putting your knowledge into practice. The answers to the quiz are in Appendix A, "Answers."

Quiz

1. How do you create a CLSID?

2. Every time you rebuild your desktop ActiveSync service provider, you are disconnecting your Windows CE device from your desktop computer so that the ActiveSync manager will release the preceding build of your module. What is a quicker and more efficient way to do this?

3. Which two interfaces must be implemented in the desktop portion of an ActiveSync service provider?

4. Which device-side ActiveSync service provider functions are called only in Windows CE 2.1 and above?

21

Exercise

Create an ActiveSync module that continuously keeps a text file synchronized between the desktop computer and the Windows CE device. On the desktop computer, the file will be c:\temp\ActiveSync.txt; on the Windows CE device, it will be \My Documents\ActiveSync.txt. If the file is modified on either computer, the change will automatically be propagated to the user computer within 5 seconds.

Hour **22**

The Cure for the Common Crash

In this hour, I will give you tips on how to isolate and resolve common Windows CE application problems. The focus is on problems that are more likely to manifest on Windows CE devices than on your desktop computer.

In this hour, you will learn

- Why preexisting problems with your code might not surface until you run on an actual Windows CE device
- Strategies for isolating and resolving memory overwrites and memory alignment issues
- Stack size issues that might arise because of differences between Windows CE and desktop Windows
- Resource issues that might lead to execution problems on Windows CE
- How to implement and use asserts in your code to make your application more bulletproof

When an application behaves differently on Windows CE than on the desktop, a developer's first inclination is usually to blame the operating system or the development tools. The majority of the time, it turns out to be a problem with the application itself that didn't manifest until it was run on Windows CE. Why is this? Some items to take into consideration are

- The desktop emulator is implemented on top of the desktop Win32 APIs. The Windows CE APIs are implemented from a different code base.

- The desktop emulator runs on x86. Currently, all commercially available Windows CE PC-Companion devices use an SH3, an SH4, a MIPS, or a StrongARM processor. Building for various CPUs results in variables being organized differently in memory. The memory overwrite that went unnoticed on the desktop might now be trampling over another important memory buffer when the application is rebuilt and run on a different CPU.

One of the first Windows CE crashes that I helped someone solve involved something similar to the following code:

```
void foo()
{
    char c, s[256];

    while( c = 0; c < 255, c++ ) s[c] = c;
}
```

The developer was using the character array as a look-up table, and because there were only 256 slots, he used a char as the index for the character array. What made the code crash was that, by default, char is signed under Visual C++, giving it a range of values from -128 to 127. When c is 127 and incremented by 1, it wraps around to -128, and then you are writing to memory before the start of your buffer. Whether or not the memory trash manifests itself to the users of your program depends on how your variables and data buffers are organized in memory. This can vary based on the compiler and the compiler options you are using to build with.

Memory Issues

When an application behaves oddly on Windows CE, one of the first issues that come to mind is the possibility of a memory overwrite. Some scenarios that can lead to a memory overwrite include

- The application allocates only enough memory for single byte strings, not Unicode strings.

- The application is writing past the end of a block of memory (this includes not allocating enough memory for strings to include the null terminating character, which is two bytes for a Unicode string).

- The application is writing before the start of a block of memory.

- The application is using `memset` or `memcpy` to set or copy the wrong number of bytes.

- The application is not checking return values (that is, assuming that memory has been successfully allocated when it hasn't, and so on).

- The application is reading from uninitialized memory or writing to memory that has already been freed.

Strategies for tracking down memory overwrites include

- Using desktop debugging tools, such as BoundsChecker or SoftICE, to monitor your program while running under the desktop emulation environment. You can learn more about BoundsChecker and SoftICE at `http://www.numega.com`.

- Creating and maintaining a desktop Win32 version of your product. You cannot mix desktop Win32 configurations with Windows CE within a single Visual C++ project file so you will need to create a separate Visual C++ project for your desktop build. Debugging a Win32 native application on the desktop enables some debugging tools to detect problems that they do not detect while running under the emulator.

- Reviewing the code in the areas where the memory overwrite manifests.

- If the values of particular global variables are being overwritten over the course of program execution, using the `ASSERT` macro (discussed later in this hour) in the main message-processing loop to alert you immediately when the memory overwrite has happened. For example, if you have a global variable, `g_tcAppName`, that is initialized to `TEXT( "My App" )` but is being overwritten during program execution, you can add

```
ASSERT( (_tcscmp( g_tcAppName, TEXT( "My App" ) ) ) == 0 );
```

  to the application's main message-processing loop so that the assert is evaluated for each message received while the program is run. When the value of `g_tcAppName` is changed, the assert will be hit for the next message the program receives.

- Creating your own wrapper functions for common memory-manipulation functions. These functions implement additional levels of corruption detection, explained in greater detail in the following section.

Creating Your Own Memory Wrapper Functions

If you or your team are encountering recurring problems with memory overwritten on Windows CE, you might invest some time in creating your own memory wrapper functions. Through the magic of macros, these functions can insert themselves between your code and the system memory functions so that you can perform additional error checking. The following is a brief example of how to go about doing this.

You will have to add a header file to your project that is included by all your source files. The purpose of this header file is to remap calls to the system memory functions to your memory functions, which is accomplished by the following:

```
// welcome to mymemory.h
#ifndef DO_NOT_TRACK_MEMORY
#undef malloc
#undef free
// the following are implemented in mymemory.c
#define malloc  my_malloc
#define free    my_free
#endif
```

Note that you can use the DO_NOT_TRACK_MEMORY define to remove the memory wrapper functions from your shipping code.

The next step is to create wrappers for the memory functions. For this version of malloc, you will initialize the memory to 0xAA and within your free, you will set the memory to 0xBB. This helps you because if you are debugging a memory problem and notice that the buffer is set to 0xAA, you know that you are likely dealing with uninitialized memory. Similarly, if the buffer you are working with is set to 0xBB, you are likely working with a buffer that has already been freed elsewhere in your application. This is easily implemented, as you see in Listing 22.1.

LISTING 22.1 Implementing Wrapper Functions for Malloc and Free

```
 1: // welcome to mymemory.c
 2: // we don't want to have mymemory.h remap the memory functions
 3: // we need to call
 4: #include <windows.h>
 5: #include <malloc.h>
 6:
 7: void *my_malloc( size_t size )
 8: {
 9:     // allocate the buffer requested by the calling routine
10:     void *buffer = malloc( size );
11:
12:     // if we were successful, initialize it to 0xAA
```

```
13:     if ( buffer != NULL )
14:         memset( buffer, 0xAA, size );
15:
16:     // return the buffer pointer to the calling routine
17:     return buffer;
18: }
19:
20: void my_free( void *memblock )
21: {
22:     // if the memory pointer is not null, set its buffer
23:     // contents to be 0xBB
24:     if ( memblock != NULL )
25:         memset( memblock, 0xBB, _msize(memblock ) );
26:
27:     // free the memory as requested
28:     free( memblock );
29: }
```

You can improve this code to allocate and initialize "guard" bytes before and after the buffer that is requested in `malloc`. When the memory is freed, the `free` routine can check to make sure that the guard bytes have the same value with which they were initialized. If they don't, it is conclusive that the memory being freed has been overwritten somewhere within your program.

Misaligned Memory

If you have always programmed on Intel x86 processors, you might not be familiar with memory alignment issues that can lead to problems on Windows NT and Windows CE systems that use RISC processors. Memory is considered unaligned if you are accessing it outside of the natural boundary.

If you have a variable that is not guaranteed to be on a properly aligned boundary, you should let the compiler know so that it can generate the proper code to prevent a runtime misalignment error from occurring. You notify the compiler that a variable might be unaligned by using the __unaligned qualifier when you declare the variable.

This is how the __unaligned qualifier is used:

```
__unaligned int *pi;
```

This will not compile for x86 because the __unaligned keyword is not applicable to the x86 compiler. The recommended way in which to declare a variable as unaligned is to the use the UNALIGNED macro provided by the system header files:

```
UNALIGNED int *pi;
```

This macro will resolve to __unaligned int *pi; if you are building for a CPU that requires it; otherwise, it will resolve to int *pi;.

Listing 22.2 is an example that illustrates a misaligned memory problem. The first case attempts to set a DWORD pointer to aligned memory. This will work fine on all CPU architectures. The second test case attempts to set a DWORD pointer to unaligned memory. This will fail on RISC processors. The third case shows you how to fix the second case, by using an unaligned DWORD pointer to access unaligned memory.

LISTING 22.2   Incorrect and Correct Methods to Access Unaligned Memory

```
 1: BYTE bGlobalArray[20] = {    0, 0, 0, 0, 0,
 2:                 0, 0, 0, 0, 0,
 3:                 0, 0, 0, 0, 0,
 4:                 0, 0, 0, 0,
 5:                 };
 6:
 7: #define TELL_USER MessageBox(hWnd,TEXT,TEXT("Status:"),MB_OK)
 8:
 9: LRESULT CALLBACK WndProc(HWND hWnd, UINT message, WPARAM wParam,
                        ➡LPARAM lParam)
10: {
11:     int    wmId, wmEvent;
12:     DWORD    *lpdwValue;
13:     UNALIGNED DWORD    *lpdwUnaligned;
14:
15:     switch (message) {
16:        case WM_COMMAND:
17:            wmId    = LOWORD(wParam);
18:            wmEvent = HIWORD(wParam);
19:
20:            // Parse the menu selections:
21:            switch( wmId ) {
22:
23:                case ID_FILE_TEST1:
24:                    TELL_USER( "access aligned memory" );
25:                    lpdwValue = (LPDWORD)&bGlobalArray[0];
26:                    *lpdwValue = 0;
27:                    TELL_USER( "We succeeded." );
28:                    break;
29:
30:                case ID_FILE_TEST2:
31:                    TELL_USER( "access unaligned memory" );
32:                    lpdwValue = (LPDWORD)&bGlobalArray[1];
33:                    *lpdwValue = 0;
34:                    TELL_USER( "We succeeded." );
35:                    break;
36:
```

22

```
37:                case ID_FILE_TEST3:
38:                    TELL_USER( "use an unaligned pointer." );
39:                    lpdwUnaligned = (LPDWORD)&bGlobalArray[1];
40:                    *lpdwUnaligned = 0;
41:                    TELL_USER( "We succeeded." );
42:                    break;
43:
44:                case IDM_FILE_EXIT:
45:                    DestroyWindow(hWnd);
46:                    break;
47:
48:                default:
49:                    return DefWindowProc(hWnd, message, wParam, lParam);
50:            }
51:            break;
52:
53:        case WM_CREATE:
54:            hwndCB = CommandBar_Create(hInst, hWnd, 1);
55:            CommandBar_InsertMenubar(hwndCB, hInst, IDM_MENU, 0);
56:            CommandBar_AddAdornments(hwndCB, 0, 0);
57:            break;
58:
59:        case WM_DESTROY:
60:            CommandBar_Destroy(hwndCB);
61:            PostQuitMessage;
62:            break;
63:
64:        default:
65:            return DefWindowProc(hWnd, message, wParam, lParam);
66:    }
67:    return 0;
68: }
69:
```

Help! My Application Hangs on `FindWindow()`

Perhaps you want your users to be able to run only one instance of your program at a time. To achieve this, you write start-up code that looks something like Listing 22.3.

LISTING 22.3 Using FindWindow to Determine Whether Your Application Is Already Running

```
1: TCHAR    g_tcAppName[]     = TEXT( "MyApp" );
2: TCHAR    g_tcClassName[]   = TEXT( "MyClass" );
3:
4: int WINAPI WinMain(    HINSTANCE hInstance,
5:                        HINSTANCE hPrevInstance,
6:                        LPTSTR    lpCmdLine,
```

continues

LISTING 22.3   continued

```
 7:                 int       nCmdShow )
 8: {
 9:     HWND    hPrevious;
10:
11:     hPrevious = FindWindow( NULL, g_tcAppName );
12:     if ( hPrevious != NULL ) {
13:         // if our application is already running, set it to the
14:         // foreground before shutting this instance down
15:         SetForegroundWindow( hPrevious );
16:         return 0;
17:     }
18:
19:     // if we made it here, there are no other instances
20:     // of our application running. We should go ahead
21:     // and initialize our application  as we normally would…
22: }
23:
```

If an instance of your program is already running, the current instance will find it and set it to be the foreground window before shutting itself down. If no other instances of your program are running, the current instance will continue to start up normally.

The problem is that if your users are running certain third-party programs at the same time, your application may not return from the call to FindWindow() until the other application is closed by the user. In the meantime, this leaves your user with the impression that your application has locked up, when it actually hasn't.

Why this happens is not clear because the source code for programs that cause this to happen is not publicly available. However, a simple workaround exists. The problem happens only when you search for your window based on window title (the second parameter), not when you search for your window class (the first parameter).

If you change your code from

```
hPrevious = FindWindow( NULL, g_tcAppName );
```

to

```
hPrevious = FindWindow( g_tcClassName, NULL );
```

your program will start without problem, no matter what other programs your users might be running concurrently.

Stack Size Issues

A coworker encountered the following scenario when implementing a recursive function that enumerated through all the files on a Windows CE device. The program always crashed after the same number of iterations. When built as a native Windows NT application, the application ran fine on the desktop. We examined the code for memory overwritten, but we did not find any. What was the problem?

The function had several local variables, some of which were quite large. After consulting all available documentation, we discovered that the maximum stack size for a thread on Windows CE is 58KB (the actual stack size is 60KB, the remaining 2KB are reserved for stack overflow control). This means that any program that has to use more than 58KB on the stack will generate a stack overflow exception at runtime. After the routine was optimized to reduce the number and size of local variables on the stack, it ran as perfectly on Windows CE as it did on the desktop.

Listing 22.4 is a sample that illustrates the problem. Each time the recursive function is called, an additional 2KB is stored on the stack.

LISTING 22.4 A Recursive Function Designed to Waste Stack Space

```
 1: VOID TestRecursion( INT iTimesToRecurse )
 2: {
 3:     CHAR     szDummyBuffer[2048];
 4:
 5:     // use szDummyBuffer to make sure that the compiler
 6:     // doesn't optimize it away
 7:     szDummyBuffer[ iTimesToRecurse ] = iTimesToRecurse;
 8:
 9:     if ( iTimesToRecurse > 0 )
10:         TestRecursion( —iTimesToRecurse );
11: }
12:
```

If you recurse 20 levels deep, there are no problems:

```
case ID_FILE_RECURSE20TIMES:
    MessageBox( hWnd, TEXT( "Starting Recursion" ),
              TEXT( "Recursion" ), MB_OK );
    TestRecursion( 20 );
    MessageBox( hWnd, TEXT( "Ending Recursion" ),
              TEXT( " Recursion " ), MB_OK );
    break;
```

If you attempt to recurse 50 levels deep, you run into a crashing problem on Windows CE.

```
case ID_FILE_RECURSE50TIMES:
    MessageBox( hWnd, TEXT( "Starting Recursion" ),
                TEXT( " Recursion " ), MB_OK );
    TestRecursion( 50 );
    // note: we never make it to the following line
    MessageBox( hWnd, TEXT( "Ending Recursion" ),
                TEXT( " Recursion " ), MB_OK );
    break;
```

If a native desktop application runs out of stack space, the user is presented with an error dialog containing a brief description of the problem. When the 50-level–deep recursion sample runs out of space on Windows CE, the user is not notified, but the application freezes, with the Starting Recursion pop-up message still displayed on the screen.

The cure for this crash is to revisit the product requirements to determine the maximum number of times this routine will have to recurse and then make sure your program is designed to handle it without generating a stack overflow. If your application really requires a large amount of memory while recursing, consider using heap space instead of stack space.

Application Hangs When Attempting to Display a Dialog

Two issues relating to your application's resource section can cause it to hang when attempting to display a dialog. The first issue is present in Visual C++ 5.0, but fixed in Visual C++ 6. The second is still present in Visual C++ 6, but easily avoidable. The first issue relates to the use of DIALOGEX in your RC file, and the second issue is caused by directly editing your EXE's resource section with Visual C++. First, we will examine the DIALOGEX issue.

DIALOGEX in Your RC File

Failing to display a dialog that is defined using the DIALOGEX keyword (instead of DIALOG) has been fixed in Visual C++ 6, but I briefly mention it here in case you or anyone you work with might be using previous versions of the development tools.

Inserting a dialog into your application typically generates an entry in the RC file that looks like this:

```
IDD_ABOUTBOX DIALOG DISCARDABLE 0, 0, 110,
```

Sometimes, when you modify your dialog within the resource editor, it might automatically change DIALOG DISCARDABLE to DIALOGEX in your RC file:

```
IDD_ABOUTBOX DIALOGEX 0, 0, 110,
```

22

When you build with tools prior to Visual C++ 6, this would cause your application to hang at runtime when the user attempts to view this particular dialog. Opening the RC file as a text file within Visual C++ and editing it to replace DIALOGEX with DIALOG solves the problem.

Directly Editing the Resource Section of a Windows CE EXE File

The Visual C++ integrated development environment has a neat feature that allows you to open an executable and directly modify and save changes to its resources (such as menus, dialogs, strings, and so on). In addition, you are also allowed to drag and drop new resources from RC files, RES files, and other EXE files directly into your EXE file and save them. This enables you to produce an English build of your product and then replace the English user interface with a German or French user interface without having to rebuild your product.

How would you do this? From within Visual C++, you would select File, Open and then specify the name of the EXE file you are interested in modifying. Before clicking the Open button on the Open dialog, make sure that you set the Open As combo box to Resources. When you click the Open button, you are then able to directly edit the resources (dialogs, menus, strings, and so on) contained within the executable. You commit your changes back to the executable file by selecting File and Save.

This feature does not work for Windows CE EXE files. You are able to open, edit, and save the resource sections of the Windows CE EXE file, but when attempting to display a modified dialog on a Windows CE device, your application might hang.

If the capability to easily support multiple language builds is important for your application, I recommend that you separate your user interface into a separate DLL from the main program. Producing a German build is then as easy as taking a previously and fully tested English build and providing the German user interface DLL with it.

Presumably, this is what Microsoft has done with Pocket Word and Pocket Excel. If you examine your \WINDOWS folder, you will note that Pocket Word consists of at least pword.exe and pwd_res.dll and that Pocket Excel consists of at least pxl.exe and pxl_res.dll. The DLLs with res in their names are likely to contain the user interface resources for the associated EXE.

> To view DLL files, you must make sure that your Explorer is configured within its View->Options dialog to show all files and not to hide file extensions.

Defensive Programming: Be Assertive

The ASSERT macro enables you to check your assumptions within debug builds and lets you (and your testers) know immediately whether any of your assumptions are not correct. The ASSERT macro is written so that it performs checking only in debug builds. It is absent from release builds, so your released program does not grow in size because of them. This is why you never want to place code you need in the released build of your product (such as a function call) inside an ASSERT. If you do place a function inside an ASSERT, it will be stripped from the release build at compile time. If you want to track function call return values in this manner, you can use the VERIFY macro.

For example, code such as

```
ASSERT( CloseHandle( hFile ) == TRUE );
```

should be rewritten as

```
VERIFY( CloseHandle( hFile ) == TRUE );
```

or hFile will be closed only in debug builds of your product. The VERIFY macro is very similar to ASSERT, except that the code it "wraps" is still executed in release builds of your product.

Still not convinced? Which bug report do you think would help you track down and fix a problem more quickly (assuming that your testing department is testing the debug build of your application):

```
Application sometimes hangs when performing X, but only on processor Y
```

or

```
When performing X, we hit assertion 'x < 0' on line 20 of main.cpp
```

Most of the time required to fix a bug is spent isolating where the problem occurs, not actually fixing the problem. Using the ASSERT and VERIFY macros will help you pinpoint problems more quickly.

If you are still not convinced, perhaps reading *Writing Solid Code* by Steve Maguire or *Code Complete* by Steve McConnell might help change your mind.

You have started using the ASSERT and VERIFY macros in your Windows CE code, but now it no longer builds. What kind of trouble have you stumbled onto now? Not to despair—the issue is that these macros are not provided in the Windows CE header files. You can easily get around this by implementing your own versions of ASSERT and VERIFY.

The ASSERT macro should check to make sure that its parameter is TRUE. If it is not, the macro should tell the user what its parameter is and from which file and line of source code it was called. This is achieved by the following:

```
#undef ASSERT

#if defined( DEBUG ) || defined( _DEBUG )
VOID my_assert( CHAR *szAssertion, CHAR *szFile, INT iLineNumber );
#define  ASSERT  { if (!) my_assert(#a,__FILE__,__LINE__); }
#else
#define  ASSERT
#endif
```

The my_assert() function is implemented next.

The VERIFY macro works like the ASSERT macro, except that its parameter is not removed from nondebug builds of your product:

```
#undef VERIFY

#ifdef DEBUG
#define    VERIFY    ASSERT
#else
#define    VERIFY    a
#endif
```

When creating a debug build, the ASSERT and VERIFY macros expand into function calls to the my_assert() function call. This function is implemented in Listing 22.5.

LISTING 22.5   Implementing an Assert Function

```
 1: #if defined( DEBUG ) || defined( _DEBUG )
 2:
 3: VOID my_assert( CHAR *szAssertion, CHAR *szFile, INT iLineNumber )
 4: {
 5:     TCHAR     tcMessage[1024];
 6:     TCHAR     tcFile[MAX_PATH];
 7:     TCHAR     tcAssertion[1024];
 8:
 9:     // convert from single-byte to double-byte char strings
10:     mbstowcs( tcFile, szFile, strlen( szFile ) + 1 );
11:     mbstowcs( tcAssertion, szAssertion, strlen( szAssertion ) + 1 );
12:
13:     wsprintf( tcMessage,
14:             TEXT( "Failed: %s, Line: %d\n\nExpression: %s\n\n" )
15:             TEXT( "GetLastError() returns: %d" ),
16:             tcFile, iLineNumber, tcAssertion, GetLastError() );
17:
```

continues

LISTING 22.5　continued

```
18:     MessageBox( GetFocus(), tcMessage,
19:             TEXT( "Assertion Failed!" ),
20:             MB_OK¦MB_ICONEXCLAMATION¦MB_SETFOREGROUND );
21:
22: }
23:
24: #endif     // DEBUG or _DEBUG
25:
```

Listing 22.6 shows you how to use the ASSERT and VERIFY macros in your program. It attempts to create a file with a name that contains wildcards (an impossible filename). The value returned to the file handle is tested using the ASSERT macro. The attempt to close the file handle is tested using the VERIFY macro. The VERIFY macro is used so that the call to CloseHandle()is present in both debug and retail builds.

LISTING 22.6　Code to Purposefully Trigger an Assertion

```
 1: HANDLE    hFile;
 2:
 3: #ifndef DEBUG
 4: MessageBox(    hWnd,
 5:             TEXT( "This is a retail build. You will only see " )
 6:             TEXT( "the assert in DEBUG builds." ),
 7:             TEXT( "Note:" ), MB_OK );
 8: #endif
 9:
10: // Try to create a file with an impossible name
11: hFile = CreateFile( TEXT( "\\dummy*.txt" ),
12:             GENERIC_WRITE, 0,
13:             NULL, CREATE_ALWAYS, 0, NULL );
14:
15: // In debug build, this assert will bring the
16: // failure to your attention
17: ASSERT( hFile != INVALID_HANDLE_VALUE );
18:
19: if ( hFile != INVALID_HANDLE_VALUE ) {
20:
21:     // The following line will be executed in both debug
22:     // and release builds. If it fails, it will
23:     // be brought to your attention only in debug builds.
24:     VERIFY( CloseHandle( hFile ) );
25:
26: }
27:
```

Figure 22.1 shows what it looks like when you run a debug build of this application.

FIGURE 22.1

This ASSERT is hit when you attempt to create a file with an invalid filename.

22

The assert message in Figure 22.1 indicates that GetLastError() returns 123. What does this mean? To find the answer, you can either look up the error number within the winerror.h header file or use the Error Lookup tool provided on the Tools menu within the Visual C++ IDE. Either method will indicate that the error is The filename, directory name, or volume label syntax is incorrect.

A Brief Word About Uninitialized Variables

A discussion of bugs and crashes would not be complete without mentioning uninitialized variables. You can protect yourself and your product from this risk in the following three ways:

- Adjust your coding style so that all variables used are always initialized. You run a small risk of performing some unnecessary initializations that might cause the compiler to generate some extra code. A related option is to make sure that you don't declare a variable in your source code until you are about to use it. A larger drawback is that if you are working with other people on the same code base, you have no guarantee of their being as careful.

- Periodically, run a tool that detects uninitialized variables in your sources, such as PC-Lint. The drawback here is that someone has to remember to periodically run the tool and review the issues it uncovers. In the swirl of shipping a product, this is likely one of the first things to be neglected.

- Modify your build process to prevent your product from building successfully if there are any uninitialized variables. You can do this by building your project at warning level 4 (the most sensitive warning level) and then using #pragma warning to disable warnings you don't care about. The drawback to this is that if you are building with [nd]WX (treat all warnings as errors), you have to disable some warnings within the Visual C++ header files in order for them to build.

You can learn more about PC-Lint at http://www.gimpel.com. You can configure Lint to examine code based on settings stored in an LNT file. The following LNT file (CE.LNT) works well for processing Windows CE source code:

```
co-msc50.lnt
options.lnt  -si4 -sp4 -e18 -e15 -e49 -e64 -e534 -e539 -e18
  ➡-e783 -e537 -e525 -e744 -e760 -D_ULONGLONG_ -D_WIN32
  ➡-DUNICODE -D_WIN32_WCE=200 -I<path to your includes folder>
```

The co-msc50.lnt and options.lnt files referenced are default files created by the PC-Lint installation process.

Summary

In this hour, you learned tips and techniques for addressing application issues that are likely to manifest on Windows CE systems. I covered some of the basics about why you might get different behavior on Windows CE than on desktop Windows. You also learned about issues relating to memory overwrites, memory alignment, stack overflow conditions, and resource section problems. You ended the hour by learning how to implement asserts in Windows CE applications, making it easier to pinpoint the location of failures in your debug builds.

Q&A

Q How do I use a bug detection tool such as BoundsChecker when running under the desktop emulation environment?

A You use it the same as you would with a native desktop Win32 application. The main difference is that many errors may be reported that are not directly related to your application. You can create your own error suppression library within BoundsChecker to filter out the warnings and errors your application is not generating.

Q **I want to debug my Windows CE application as a native Windows NT application. How do I build my Windows CE application to target desktop Windows operating systems?**

A The Visual C++ 6.0 Toolkits for Windows CE do not support combining Windows CE and desktop Windows build targets in the same project files, so you have to create a separate project file to target desktop Windows. After you have created the project files, you must add each of the source files used in the Windows CE version of the product. You will have to #ifdef any Windows CE–specific code that will not compile for the desktop in order to build successfully.

22

Workshop

The Workshop is designed to help you anticipate possible questions, review what you've learned, and begin thinking ahead about putting your knowledge into practice. The answers to the quiz are in Appendix A, "Answers."

Quiz

1. How many bytes do you need to allocate the Unicode representation of Hello?

2. How much of a thread's stack space is reserved for stack overflow control?

3. Why use UNALIGNED instead of the __unaligned qualifier?

4. The FindWindow function is not returning when you search based on a window title. How do you address this?

5. Is it advisable to place a function call inside an ASSERT?

6. You have implemented the memory wrapper functions discussed at the beginning of this hour. When debugging your program, you notice that your application is displaying garbage characters in the title of your pop-up MessageBox messages. You are using a global TCHAR pointer to store the title. If you don't use the memory wrapper functions, it displays the title correctly. What is most likely going wrong?

7. How many bugs are in the following code, and what are they?

```
 1: // This function returns the WCHAR representation of the
 2: // ascii string that is passed to it. It allocates the
 3: // buffer for the WCHAR version of the string.
 4: WCHAR *AsciiToWCHAR( CHAR *szOriginal )
 5: {
 6:     WCHAR    *wcReturn, *wc;
 7:     CHAR     *c;
 8:     DWORD    dwLength;
 9:
10:     ASSERT( szOriginal );
```

```
11:       ASSERT( ( dwLength = strlen( szOriginal ) ) > 0 );
12:
13:       // allocate the WCHAR buffer
14:       wcReturn = (WCHAR*) malloc( dwLength*sizeof(WCHAR) + 1 );
15:
16:       // use a string and WCHAR pointer to walk the two buffers,
17:       // transferring values from the ascii buffer to the WCHAR buffer
18:       // (note: in the real world this should really be done
19:       // with mbstowcs())
20:       c = szOriginal;
21:       wc = wcReturn;
22:       while( *c ) {
23:           *wc = (WCHAR)*c;
24:           wc++;
25:           c++;
26:       }
27:
28:       // return a pointer to the WCHAR buffer
29:       return wcReturn;
30: }
```

Exercises

1. Update the `my_assert` function listed earlier in this hour to provide the user with the option to hit a hard-coded break point (that is, a call to `DebugBreak`. This makes it easier for you, the developer, to break into the debugger when a problem is encountered.

2. Improve the `malloc` and `free` wrapper functions covered earlier in this hour to detect whether the start or end of the memory buffer has been overwritten. Do this by implementing a guard `DWORD` immediately before and after the buffer, as described in the section "Creating Your Own Memory Wrapper Functions."

HOUR **23**

Debugging Windows CE Applications with Visual C++

If you've been around the industry a while, you know that one of the biggest misconceptions is that developers spend most of their time writing code. The reality is that debugging comprises the majority of the software development life cycle.

Unfortunately, programming for Windows CE is no different in this respect. Bugs still rear their ugly heads and have to be hunted down and squashed. This hour, I will talk about how debugging code targeted for Windows CE is different from the desktop and discuss some strategies for getting the most from the Visual C++ Toolkit for Windows CE (VCCE) debugger.

In this hour, you will learn

- Missing features for Windows CE
- An introduction to remote debugging

- Speed and efficiency considerations
- Breakpoint and single-stepping issues
- DLL issues
- Alternative debugging strategies

Features Missing from Windows CE

Just as the Win32 API on Windows CE is a subset of its cousins on the desktop, the Windows CE Toolkit lacks some features from the desktop version—most because of sound technical reasons that make these features difficult-to-impossible to implement and some strictly for reasons of size.

The largest notably missing feature from VCCE 6 is Edit and Continue. First introduced with Visual C++ 6, Edit and Continue allows you to make certain types of changes while you are debugging and has your running program reflect those changes without being recompiled. Because of the large amount of writes to the debuggee's address space, it is inefficient to do this under Windows CE. The reasons become more apparent in the next section, which introduces remote debugging.

NEW TERM   A *debuggee* is the process that is being controlled and manipulated by a debugger.

Another notably absent feature from VCCE is the capability to attach to and debug a running process. Although this feature is available in the preceding version, it was dropped for this one. The reasons for this are purely technical: Windows CE has problems suspending threads that are currently executing a system call. This makes attaching by calling the `DebugActiveProcess` API a hit-or-miss action instead of a guaranteed success—not exactly the desired behavior for reliable debugging. The thread suspension issue is discussed in Hour 11, "Threads and Processes," and I'll touch on it again later this hour in the section "Breakpoint and Single-Stepping Issues."

A related fallout from the lack of Attach to Process support is the lack of capability to provide JIT debugging. Although the operating system hooks necessary for JIT have been available since v2.0, without proper `DebugActiveProcess` support, they can't be utilized.

NEW TERM   *JIT debugging* is an operating system feature that enables you to attach to and debug a process that has crashed.

The last debugging feature missing from VCCE is C runtime library (RTL) support. Recent versions of the desktop Visual C++ RTL have provided significant new functionality to catch memory allocation, leak, and overwrite problems, as well as a configurable ASSERT facility with the capability to redirect output. Additionally, because the RTL source code is provided on the Visual C++ CD-ROM, you can step through problematic RTL routines to see exactly what's happening.

Windows CE, on the other hand, does not provide source code and implements the RTL as a DLL that is built in to the operating system's ROM image, omitting the memory diagnostic features. The drawback of the DLL approach is that you cannot step into RTL routines because they now reside in ROM. The benefit is that the RTL takes up less space on the device because all executables (including user-downloaded applications) just link to a single DLL, rather than each include its own separate copy. Debugging code stored in ROM is discussed further in this hour's section titled "Breakpoint and Single-Stepping Issues."

The lack of memory diagnostic services in the Windows CE RTL, however, is independent of whether the library is statically or dynamically linked (although one could argue that the features were left out for reasons of size). It is hoped that the Windows CE RTL will catch up with the desktop diagnostic features in some future version.

An Introduction to Remote Debugging

If you've ever used Visual C++'s MSVCMON to debug another desktop Windows NT or Windows 95 machine, as is common for DirectX developers, you are probably familiar with remote debugging already, and you can skip to the next section on improving remote debugging performance on Windows CE.

Imagine having to do all your Windows CE debugging on the device itself. That undersized keyboard and little screen would quickly wear down your patience, and you'd soon be yearning for the vast real estate of your desktop Windows NT or Windows 95 machine. Luckily, you don't have to go through this painful process. Instead, VCCE allows you to talk with the device over a communication medium and utilize the comfort of your desktop machine.

The magic that allows this to happen is called *remote debugging*, and it has some significant differences from the normal scenario of the debugger and the debuggee running on the same machine. All the differences stem from your no longer being able to directly reach into the debuggee's address space. Instead, you have to send a command to a stub running on the remote machine, asking it to reach into the debuggee on your behalf. With VCCE, CEMON is the remote stub that does the desktop debugger's bidding.

The most visible result of this change in strategy is speed. Remote debugging is inherently slower than local debugging. The process of sending a command across a link, executing it, and sending a reply takes more overhead (and thus, more time) than the equivalent on a single machine. In the next section, I'll discuss ways to make remote debugging as fast as possible.

Another issue that crops up with remote debugging is the fact that two executable files are involved: the one running on the target machine and the one residing on the host machine. It is very important that these two files be the exact same version. If they are not, the tables that map memory addresses to source code line numbers will be incorrect, and single stepping will not work correctly. Because the host version of the executable is used for line number maps, symbolic debugging information, and other things, remote debugging also causes problems trying to debug a DLL when you don't have the corresponding executable that utilizes it (for example, Control Panel applets). I'll come back to DLL debugging problems later in this hour.

Speed and Efficiency Considerations

As mentioned before, the main problem with remote debugging is that it tends to be slower because of the necessary communication overhead. When the communication is done over an inherently slow serial link, the performance can degrade to an almost unusable level. Previous versions of VCCE provide the serial port as the only option and thus have developed a bad reputation for being inherently slow.

Fortunately, VCCE 6.0 has rectified this situation. A new feature named Platform Manager enables you to communicate over a fast ethernet link that brings remote debugging up to almost the speed of desktop performance. A 10Mbps ethernet connection is more than 85 times faster than a 115KB baud serial connection. This increase doesn't result in debugging that is 85 times faster, but it is significantly better than using a serial connection.

The ethernet connection between your desktop and a Windows CE device is managed by Windows CE services. You will also need a PCMCIA ethernet card for your device (unless you're using a desktop Windows CE platform such as CEPC). The best source of information for getting everything up and running is Chris De Herrera's Windows CE Web site at http://cewindows.net. He maintains an up-to-date frequently asked questions (FAQ) list on ethernet, as well as many other Windows CE-related topics. Also, be sure to check that the PCMCIA card you are using is on his list of Windows CE-supported ethernet adapters.

When you have a Windows CE Services partnership and ethernet connection, you can configure Platform Manager to start taking advantage of it. Selecting the Configure Platform Manager item in the VCCE 6.0 tools menu will display a dialog that looks something like Figure 23.1.

FIGURE 23.1

The Platform Manager dialog box.

If you have SDKs installed other than the default H/PC and P/PC that comes with VCCE, you will see an entry here for each of those platforms. The Properties dialog for each platform will tell you the operating system version and CPUs it supports.

The next level of the tree control displays each device for that platform. The default is an entry for a real device and its emulation, but you can add as many devices as you like. If you display the properties for the default device entry, you will get a dialog similar to Figure 23.2, allowing you to select the communication mechanism, or "transport," you would like to use.

FIGURE 23.2

The PPP transport corresponds to the serial port, whereas the TCP/IP transport corresponds to the ethernet connection.

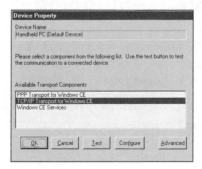

These transports are poorly named. Don't feel bad if they leave you confused. Actually, they both use TCP/IP. The difference is just in their use of the Point-to-Point Protocol (PPP) or ethernet for the underlying data transfer. PPP allows you to use a normal serial port, whereas ethernet requires a special adapter card.

The remaining transport, Windows CE Services, is the default and supports communication over both ethernet and PPP. The drawback is that it does not allow you to configure a timeout value or any other option, whereas the other two options do. After you select a transport, you can click the Test button to verify the connection or the Configure button to change the default settings.

Switching to ethernet solves the vast majority of VCCE's remote debugging performance problems, but there is one other area you should watch out for—memory breakpoints.

NEW TERM A *memory breakpoint* is a breakpoint that stops a debuggee when a specified memory address changes or contains a certain value.

Memory breakpoints are set on the Data tab of VCCE's Breakpoint dialog box. The problem with using them under Windows CE is that they cause a major performance decrease, essentially checking the breakpoint expression after every CPU instruction. Because desktop operating systems are mostly concerned with only x86 microprocessors, they can take advantage of this to implement this feature much more efficiently. Windows CE does not have this luxury and thus defaults to a portable, and much slower, strategy.

Breakpoint and Single-Stepping Issues

Single stepping through source code or assembly language instructions is understandably the most important feature of any interactive debugger, and VCCE is no different in this regard. The majority of the time, stepping around is identical to the desktop environment, but at times Windows CE takes a separate path.

The most notable exception is that you cannot step through the source or assembly for code that is in ROM. This is equally true for both operating system modules and applications that happen to be included in the operating system image. The reason for this is that the debugger must write a series of breakpoint instructions into the debuggee to execute the single step, and by definition, ROM is unwritable. This can rear its head in ugly ways because sometimes the debugger cannot write any breakpoints for the step command and ends up executing a Go instead, stopping at a seemingly unrelated breakpoint far down the line.

Another stepping scenario that causes problems in Windows CE is when multiple threads are executing the same routine (the MFC MTGDI sample provided with the P/PC and H/PC SDKs is a good example of this). If you set a breakpoint in the routine, it will not always fire for every thread in the debuggee. The reason for this is that Windows CE cannot suspend a thread that is currently executing a system call. By *system call*, I mean any exported Win32 API function or internal operating-system function. This means that the Windows CE debug APIs cannot always suspend every thread when a breakpoint is hit, and thus, some threads will continue to run. Luckily, this happens only while debugging heavily multithreaded applications.

Another issue that affects stepping through code under Windows CE is the operating system's PSL (Protected Server Library) architecture. A PSL is a hybrid between a DLL and a standalone process. The main reason that PSLs are used is to minimize the time required for an application to call any function exported by the operating system kernel (that is, Win32 APIs). For a more in-depth discussion of PSLs, see Hour 3 of *Inside Windows CE* by Microsoft Press.

PSLs affect stepping when the operating system makes a callback into a user-provided function indirectly (via a window message procedure) or directly (via EnumWindows, EnumFontFamilies, and so on). When you hit a breakpoint in the callback procedure, the trace shown in the debugger's Call Stack window ends at the PSL's address (see Figure 23.3), instead of showing the full history, as Visual C++ does for NT (see Figure 23.4).

FIGURE 23.3

The EnumWindows *stack trace on Windows CE.*

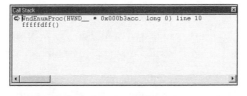

FIGURE 23.4

The EnumWindows *stack trace on Windows NT.*

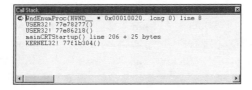

The problem is that the process of using a PSL to simulate a kernel call purposely results in the return address of the callback being an invalid address. Because the address is invalid, the debugger cannot unwind the call stack any further and thus stops as soon as it bumps into the PSL.

This also causes problems when you try to step out of the callback routine via a single step or return step. Because the return address is invalid, the step cannot be executed, and the step is instead turned into a Go command; the program runs until it hits another breakpoint or completes execution.

DLL Issues

As mentioned in the introduction to remote debugging, debugging DLLs on Windows CE involves several difficulties. Because the debugger needs a copy of the executable file on the host machine, debugging a DLL is impossible unless you have the file that uses that DLL. For example, you can't debug a Control Panel applet with VCCE because you don't have a host-side copy of CTLPNL.EXE for the debugger to play with. Other examples of this scenario include device drivers and Pocket Mail transports.

An obvious solution is to copy the file from the object store of the device to the desktop. Unfortunately, this will not work because you cannot treat executable images stored in ROM as regular files. See Hour 9, "The Object Store: Files and the Registry," for details on why. The only remedy to this situation is to buy Platform Builder and use the WinDbg kernel debugger with a CEPC or another reference platform. See the Platform Builder online help for details on setting up and using WinDbg.

NEW TERM *Platform Builder* is the Microsoft product used to build Windows CE OS configurations, roll custom SDKs, and provide kernel debugger capability. See http://www.microsoft.com/windowsce/Embedded/resources/pb.asp for details.

NEW TERM *CEPC* is a specialized version of Windows CE provided with Platform Builder and tailored to run on normal desktop PC hardware.

Another debugging issue has to do with hitting a breakpoint set in a DLL's entry point. Commonly named DllMain, the entry point is called when a process loads or unloads a DLL and when a thread is created or destroyed. The second parameter to DllMain, dwReason, is set to DLL_PROCESS_ATTACH, DLL_PROCESS_DETACH, DLL_THREAD_ATTACH, and DLL_THREAD_DETACH, respectively, to indicate these events. The problem is that the Windows CE debug APIs must call DllMain with DLL_PROCESS_ATTACH as part of the loading process, but the debugger must be notified of the DLL load before DllMain is called, so that the code can be debugged. This is a classic bootstrapping problem, and the end result is that you cannot step through the code for the DLL_PROCESS_ATTACH event. Windows NT and Windows 95/98 do not have this problem, and it is hoped that Windows CE will be updated with a fix in some future version. Because you can't step through the code, you have to resort to less useful debugging strategies to find problems in your DLL_PROCESS_ATTACH code. See the "Alternative Debugging Strategies" section at the end of this lesson for some options.

> Even though DllMain's lpReserved parameter is documented as being unused, on desktop Win32 platforms, it is always zero if the DLL is explicitly loaded via LoadLibrary and non-zero if it is implicitly loaded via an import library. Unfortunately, this undocumented behavior is not maintained on Windows CE—lpReserved is always non-zero.

23

One of the new features of VCCE 6 is the capability to directly debug a DLL project. Previous versions of the toolkit have problems determining the executable to launch and force you to create a dummy EXE project to debug your DLL. To set up a DLL project for debugging, you must add the name and location of the executable to the project settings and the location of the DLL to the Additional DLLs section of the project settings. When you're done, the dialog boxes should look something like Figures 23.5 and 23.6.

FIGURE 23.5

Debug tab General settings for DLL debugging.

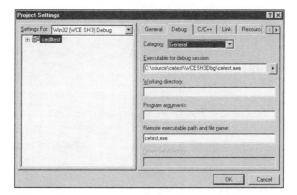

FIGURE 23.6

Debug tab Additional DLL settings for DLL debugging.

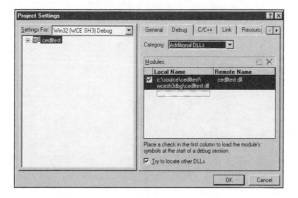

If you forget to add these settings before you debug the DLL for the first time, the debugger will prompt you for the information with a series of dialog boxes.

Alternative Debugging Strategies

Sometimes stepping through code is not the right approach for finding a nasty bug. When working with multiple threads or "headless" applications that don't have a user interface, it's very useful to have a simple "debugging by printf" facility to track calling sequences and variable values. In the case of DllMain's DLL_PROCESS_ATTACH event, it's the only way to see what's happening.

The Win32 OutputDebugString API provides some help here, but it's not a silver bullet. Although it does enable you to display a text string in the debugger's output window, the overhead of having to run the process under the debugger is overkill and, for situations such as Control Panel applets, impossible.

The remedy is to override the operating system's implementation of OutputDebugString and display the text in a viewer running on the device rather than on the desktop.

DBWinCE is a utility that does exactly this. You simply add the file dbwclient.c to your project, recompile, and run DBWinCE. No other modifications are necessary. Whenever your application calls OutputDebugString, the text will show up in the DBWinCE client window.

The source code for dbwclient.c appears in Listing 23.1 and is very straightforward. It simply locates the DBWinCE window by its classname and then sends the text with the WM_COPYDATA message. WM_COPYDATA is covered in depth in Hour 12, "Controlling Interprocess Communication."

LISTING 23.1   Client Code for the DBWinCE Utility

```
/*
    Override the WinCE ODS function and send the text to
    DBWinCE
*/

#define STRICT
#include <windows.h>

void WINAPI OutputDebugStringW(LPCTSTR pcsz)
{
        COPYDATASTRUCT cds;
```

```
HWND hwnd = FindWindow(_T("DBWinCE"), NULL);

if ( hwnd )
{
        cds.cbData = (_tcslen(pcsz) + 1) * sizeof(TCHAR);
        cds.lpData = (PVOID)pcsz;

        SendMessage(hwnd, WM_COPYDATA, 0, (LPARAM)&cds);
}
}
```

23

DBWinCE runs on any Windows CE device, including the P/PC and the H/PC Pro. The full source code is available on the CD-ROM.

Summary

This lesson introduces you to the Windows CE remote debugger and provides you with some strategies for getting the best possible performance out of it. You also learned about some Windows CE-specific debugger issues and how to work around them.

Q&A

Q Debugging is too slow. How can I speed it up?

A Use an ethernet connection instead of a serial link, and avoid the use of memory breakpoints as much as possible.

Q How can I debug the DLL_PROCESS_ATTACH event in my DllMain under Windows CE?

A Unfortunately, the Windows CE debug APIs have a bug that doesn't let you hit breakpoints or step through the code for the DLL_PROCESS_ATTACH event. You have to use OutputDebugString with the VCCE debugger or DBWinCE to see what's happening.

Workshop

The Workshop is designed to help you anticipate possible questions, review what you've learned, and begin thinking ahead about putting your knowledge into practice. The answers to the quiz are in Appendix A, "Answers."

Quiz

1. How is remote debugging different from debugging on a single machine?

2. Why was Attach to Process debugging removed from VCCE 6?

3. Why can't I step through the assembler instructions for a Windows CE system call in the debugger?

4. When I hit a breakpoint in a window message handler routine, my call stack doesn't show the full history. Why?

5. Why can't I debug Control Panel applets or Pocket Mail transports with VCCE 6?

6. What is a PSL?

7. Does the C runtime library track memory leaks on Windows CE?

8. Why are memory breakpoints slow on Windows CE?

9. Is the new Visual C++ 6 Edit and Continue debugger feature available in VCCE?

10. What is Platform Manager?

Exercise

Steal the code for saving a text file from TestEdit, and integrate it into DBWinCE. Add support for displaying the sending process's ID with the text in.

Hour 24

Advanced Topics: MFC, ATL, and POOM

Now is your opportunity to study how to use the Microsoft Foundation Classes (MFC), the Active Template Library (ATL), and the Pocket Outlook Object Model (POOM). MFC and ATL for Windows CE are similar to their desktop counterparts, but POOM is specific to Windows CE. POOM allows you to adapt your Windows CE applications to interact with the standard Microsoft PIM applications included in ROM on Windows CE devices.

In this hour, you will learn

- What's new, different, and absent in MFC for Windows CE
- What's new, different, and absent in ATL for Windows CE
- What POOM is and how to make use of it from within your own applications

MFC on Windows CE

MFC for Windows CE supports many of the classes and global functions you have learned to use with standard MFC. The following sections explain what is new, what is different from standard MFC, what is absent in MFC for Windows CE, and how to get started creating new MFC projects.

MFC for Windows CE support (headers, libraries, and sources) is included in the Handheld PC (H/PC), Palm-size PC (PsPC), and Handheld PC Professional Edition toolkits.

First, you will look at what is new with MFC for Windows CE 2.10.

What's New in MFC for Windows CE

In addition to support for the latest processors, MFC for Windows CE now includes several Windows CE–specific classes:

- The CCeCommandBar class is used to create and manage command bars that contain menus, buttons, combo boxes, and adornments.
- The CCeDBDatabase class provides an interface to manipulate Windows CE databases, including adding and deleting records and creating and destroying databases.
- The CCeDBRecord class allows you to modify the properties for a database record.
- The CCeDBProp class is used to retrieve and modify values for a record's properties.
- The CCeDBEnum class is used to enumerate the databases on the Windows CE device.

The following standard MFC classes were added with Windows CE 2.10:

CColorDialog	CHttpFile	CInternetSession
CControlBar	CImageList	CMonthCalCtrl
CDateTimeCtrl	CInternetConnection	CPalette
CDialogBar	CInternetException	CPrintDialog
CHttpConnection	CInternetFile	CPrintInfo

What's Different in MFC for Windows CE

The CCeSocket class was created to simulate asynchronous behavior. You use the Windows CE–specific WM_SOCKET_NOTIFY message to notify a sockets window that a socket event has happened. Use the global AfxGetCeSocketWindow MFC function to obtain the handle to the invisible window to which you should send socket notification messages.

Your Windows CE MFC applications should act on the WM_HIBERNATE message generated when the system is low on resources. This is done by creating a handler for the WM_HIBERNATE message in a class derived from the CApp class.

The following MFC classes differ from standard MFC:

CAsyncSocket	CFrameWnd	CReBarCtrl
CBitmap	CGdiObject	CRectTracker
CBrush	CHttpConnection	CRgn
CButton	CImageList	CSocket
CComboBox	CInternetConnection	CSpinButtonCtrl
CCommandLineInfo	CInternetFile	CSplitterWnd
CCommonDialog	CInternetSession	CStatic
CDC	CListBox	CStatusBarCtrl
CDialog	CListCtrl	CStdioFile
CDocTemplate	CMenu	CString
CDocument	COleDateTime	CSyncObject
CEdit	COleDateTimeSpan	CTabCtrl
CEditView	COleObjectFactory	CTime
CEvent	CPalette	CToolBarCtrl
CFile	CPen	CView
CFileDialog	CPrintDialog	CWinApp
CFont	CPropertyPage	CWinThread
CFontHolder	CPropertySheet	CWnd

24

The following MFC classes differ from standard MFC, as well as previous versions of MFC on Windows CE (before Windows CE 2.10):

CBrush	CFrameWnd	CView
CDC	COleControl	CWinApp
CDocTemplate	CRectTracker	CWnd
CEditView	CTime	

If any of these directly affect the applications you are interested in writing or porting, the online help system can provide you with the details of how they differ.

MFC for Windows CE disables some Windows CE functions that would prevent MFC from functioning correctly on Windows CE. Table 24.1 lists the functions that are disabled by MFC and the Win32 APIs you should use in their place.

TABLE 24.1   Win32 APIs Disabled by MFC and Their Replacements

Disabled Function	Replacement Function
DrawIcon	DrawIconEx
GetDlgItemText	GetWindowText
LoadCursor	LoadImage
SendDlgItemMessage	SendMessage
SetDlgItemText	SetWindowText
TrackPopupMenu	TrackPopupMenuEx

What's Absent from MFC for Windows CE

The following common dialog MFC classes are not supported:

CFontDialog	CPageSetupDialog

The following common control MFC classes are not supported:

CAnimateCtrl	CDragListBox	CMiniFrameWnd
CCheckListBox	CHotKeyCtrl	CToolTipCtrl

The following DAO MFC classes are not supported:

CDaoDatabase	CDaoQueryDef	CDaoTableDef
CDaoException	CDaoRecordset	CDaoWorkspace
CDaoFieldExchange	CDaoRecordView	

The following MFC Internet classes are not on Windows CE:

CFtpConnection	CGopherFileFind	CHttpFilterContext
CFtpFileFind	CGopherLocator	CHttpServer
CGopherConnection	CHtmlStream	CHttpServerContext
CGopherFile	CHttpFilter	

The following MFC MDI classes are not supported on Windows CE:

CMDIChildWnd	CMDIFrameWnd	CMultiDocTemplate

The following MFC ODBC classes are not available on Windows CE:

CDatabase	CDBVariant	CRecordset
DBException	CFieldExchange	CRecordView

These MFC OLE classes are not supported on Windows CE:

CAsyncMonikerFile	COleClientItem	COleIPFrameWnd
CCachedDataPathProperty	COleCmdUI	COleLinkingDoc
CDataPathProperty	COleDataObject	COleMessageFilter
CDocItem	COleDataSource	COleServerDoc
CDocObjectServer	COleDocument	COleServerItem
CDocObjectServerItem	COleDropSource	COleStreamFile
CMonikerFile	COleDropTarget	COleTemplateServer

24

The Rich Edit control is not available on Windows CE, so the MFC Rich Edit control classes are not implemented:

CRichEditCntrl	CRichEditDoc
CRichEditCntrlItem	CRichEditView

The following MFC synchronization classes are not available on Windows CE:

CMutex	CMultiLock	CSemaphore

The following MFC classes are also not supported on Windows CE:

CDockState	CMetaFileDC	CSharedFile
CFileFind	CPictureHolder	

The following global MFC functions are not supported on Windows CE:

AfxDaoInit	AfxOleLockApp
AfxDaoTerm	AfxOleLockControl
AfxDbInit	AfxOleParseURL
AfxDbInitModule	AfxOleSetEditMenu
AfxGetInternetHandleType	AfxOleSetUserCtrl
AfxInitRichEdit	AfxOleTypeMatchGuid
AfxNetInitModule	AfxOleUnlockApp
AfxOleCanExitApp	AfxOleUnlockControl
AfxOleGetMessageFilter	AfxThrowDaoException
AfxOleGetUserCtrl	AfxThrowDBException

The following standard MFC structures are not supported on Windows CE:

ABC	COMPAREITEMSTRUCT
ABCFLOAT	DEVNAMES
CDaoDatabaseInfo	EXTENSION_CONTROL_BLOCK
CDaoErrorInfo	HSE_VERSION_INFO
CDaoFieldInfo	HTTP_FILTER_AUTHENT
CDaoIndexInfo	HTTP_FILTER_CONTEXT
CDaoIndexFieldInfo	HTTP_FILTER_CONTEXT
CDaoParameterInfo	HTTP_FILTER_LOG

CDaoQueryDefInfo	HTTP_FILTER_RAW_DATA
CDaoRelationInfo	HTTP_FILTER_URL_MAP
CDaoRelationFieldInfo	HTTP_FILTER_VERSION
CDaoTableDefInfo	LINGER
CDaoWorkspaceInfo	MINMAXINFO
HTTP_FILTER_PREPROC_HEADERS	NCCALCSIZE_PARAMS
CODBCFieldInfo	WINDOWPLACEMENT
COLORADJUSTMENT	XFORM

Now that you have the background information about what is available and what isn't, you can begin creating a Windows CE MFC application.

Creating a New MFC Project Targeting Windows CE

Creating a new Windows CE MFC project is easy using the Visual C++ IDE wizards. Figure 24.1 shows how to specify that an MFC project should be created.

24

FIGURE 24.1

Creating a new Windows CE MFC project.

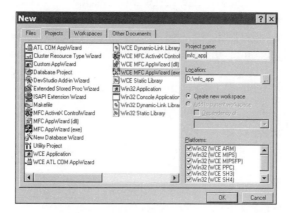

As shown in Figure 24.1, you have the option of creating an MFC application (EXE) or dynamic link library (DLL). After you select one or the other, you are lead through an MFC application wizard that is similar to the wizard used to create desktop MFC applications.

If you choose to create an MFC application, you are presented with a four-page wizard that allows you to specify

- Whether you would like to create a single-document application or a dialog-based application (multiple-document interface [MDI] applications are not supported on Windows CE)

- Whether document/view architecture support is included
- In what language you would like the resources
- Whether support for the following is included: Windows CE sockets, printing (available in MFC for Windows CE 2.1 and above), Windows help, and ActiveX controls
- What type of control bar you would like included in your application
- How many files you would like on your Recent File List
- Whether you would like source code comments included in the generated source code
- Whether you want to statically link to the MFC library or use the shared MFC DLL
- The classnames for the classes it will create for you

If you are creating an MFC DLL, you are presented with a one-page wizard that allows you to specify

- Whether you want to create a regular DLL statically linked to the MFC LIB, a regular DLL that uses the shared MFC DLL, or an MFC extension DLL that uses the shared MFC DLL. Using the shared MFC DLL decreases your program size greatly but requires that the MFC DLL be installed on the user's Windows CE device (it is included in CD-ROM on the newer devices, and you can redistribute a ROM-able version of the DLL with your application).
- Whether you would like automation or Windows CE socket support included in your DLL.
- Whether you would like source code comments included in the generated source code.

Now that you know how to create new Windows CE MFC applications, take a look at the samples included with the Windows CE toolkits.

MFC Samples Included with the Windows CE Toolkits

When you installed the Windows CE toolkits for Visual C++, MFC sample code was installed with the H/PC, PsPC, and H/PC Professional Edition toolkits. The samples for the H/PC were installed under the \Windows CE Tools\Wce200\MS HPC\Samples\MFC directory. The PsPC samples were installed under \Windows CE Tools\Wce201\MS Palm Size PC\Samples\MFC. The H/PC Professional Edition samples were installed under \Windows CE Tools\Wce211\MS HPC Pro\Samples\MFC.

Table 24.2 lists the MFC samples included with the Windows CE toolkits and describes what they can teach you.

TABLE 24.2   MFC Samples Included with Windows CE Toolkits

Sample	Demonstrates
CBARTEST	How to create a command bar using `CCeCommandBar`.
CHATSRVR/CHATTER	Socket communication using `CCeSocket`.
CHKBOOK	How to provide multiple views without MDI support.
CMNCTRLS	How to use `CListCtrl`, `CProgressCtrl`, `CSliderCtrl`, `CSpinButtonCtrl`, and `CTreeCtrl`.
COLLECT	The various collection classes available.
CTRLTEST	How to implement custom controls.
DYNAMENU	How to dynamically update menus.
ETCHA	Capturing what the user has drawn with the stylus.
GENERIC	Basic drawing and message processing.
HELLO	A generic "Hello World" MFC application.
HELLOAPP	A minimalist version of "HELLO."
HTTP	How to use the `CHttpConnection`, `CHttpFile`, `CInternetFile`, and `CInternetSession` classes to download HTML text from a user-specified Web site.
MATHS	How to embed ActiveX controls that you have created within an MFC ActiveX container. This sample includes the source code in MATHS, MATHS1, MATHS2, and MATHS3.
MODELESS	How to use `CDialog` to create a modeless dialog.
MTGDI	How to share GDI resources among several threads.
NPP	A simple Notepad application.
PALETTE	How to use the `CPalette` class to paint higher quality bitmaps.
PROPDLG	How to use `CPropertyPage` and `CPropertySheet` to implement property sheets.
SMILEY/SMILEYDG	How to create an ActiveX control and invoke methods, handle events, and change properties.
STASPLIT	How to implement dynamic and static splitter windows.
WCEDBTST	How to use `CCeDBDatabase`, `CCeDBEnum`, `CCeDBProp`, and `CCeDBRecord` classes to access and modify Windows CE databases.

24

If you have installed the H/PC Professional Edition toolkit, you will have a few more samples at your disposal. Specifically, the BANNER sample will show you how to use the CBannerMatrix and CPrintDialog classes to implement printing support, and the COLOR sample reveals how to use the CColorDialog class to add color to an application. Additionally, the standard CHATTER and CHATSRVR samples included with the H/PC Professional Edition toolkit were modified to use the Windows CE–specific CCeSocket class.

ATL on Windows CE

ATL for Windows CE 2.10 supports many classes, global functions, and macros you have learned to use with standard ATL. The following sections explain what is new, what is different from standard ATL, what is absent in ATL for Windows CE, and how to get started creating new ATL projects.

ATL for Windows CE support (headers, libraries, and sources) is included in the H/PC and H/PC Professional Edition toolkits, but is absent from the current P/PC toolkit.

First, you will see what is new with ATL for Windows CE 2.10.

What's New in ATL for Windows CE

ATL for Windows CE 2.10 now supports composite controls. A *composite control* is an ActiveX control that can contain other controls. These *other* controls can be standard Windows controls (such as an edit control) or other ActiveX controls. The COMPCTRL and COMPCNTR samples mentioned later this hour illustrate how to use composite controls.

Additionally, several standard ATL classes are now available in Windows CE 2.10:

1. The CAxDialogImpl class implements a dialog box that hosts ActiveX controls.

2. The CAxWindow class manipulates a window that hosts ActiveX controls. CAxWindow wraps the AxWin class, which provides the hosting.

3. The CComAutoCriticalSection class exposes methods for obtaining and releasing ownership of critical section objects. Critical section objects are automatically initialized in the constructor and automatically deleted in the destructor.

4. Classes derived from the CComCompositeControl class can host traditional Windows controls and ActiveX controls.

5. CComSimpleThreadAllocator::GetThread cycles through threads by selecting the next thread in the sequence. It is called by CComAutoThreadModule::CreateInstance.

6. The `CSimpleDialog` class implements a simple modal dialog box.

7. The `CWinTraits` class enables you to specify the standard and extended styles for an ATL window object.

8. The `CWinTraitsOR` class is similar to the `CWinTraits` class, except that it adds the specified standard and extended styles (effectively logically OR'd) to the values provided when the ATL window object was created.

The following ATL classes do not do anything in Windows CE 2.10, but are included so that future versions of ATL for Windows CE will be backward compatible: `CComApartment`, `CComAutoThreadModule`, and `CComClassFactoryAutoThread`.

What's Different in ATL for Windows CE

The following ATL classes differ from the standard ATL library provided on desktop Windows:

CComApartment	CWindowImpl
CComControl	CWinTraits
CComGlobalsThreadModel	CWinTraitsOR
CComModule	CWndClassInfo
CComObjectThreadModel	IdataObjectImpl
CContainedWindow	IoleObjectImpl
CStockPropImpl	IpropertyPageImpl
CWindow	

If any of these directly affect the applications you are interested in writing or porting, the online help system can provide you with the details of how they differ.

What's Absent from ATL for Windows CE

ATL for Windows CE is a lean version of the standard ATL library design for the Windows CE environment. To achieve this, some features of standard ATL are not currently included in ATL for Windows CE. The more noteworthy missing features are

- The apartment threading model
- Asynchronous monikers
- Out-of-process servers
- Snap-in objects
- Safety maps

Because of these differences, ATL for Windows CE does not support the following standard ATL classes:

CBindStatusCallback   IObjectSafetyImpl

CSnapInItemImpl   IServiceProviderInfo

CSnapInPropertyPageImpl

Additionally, some ATL classes implemented for Windows CE do not support all the methods that are supported in the standard ATL library. Consult the Windows CE Toolkit documentation for further information on any classes in which you are particularly interested.

Next, I will show you how to create a new Windows CE ATL project.

Creating a New ATL Project Targeting Windows CE

Creating a new Windows CE ATL project is straightforward when using the Visual C++ IDE wizards. Figure 24.2 shows how to begin creating a new Windows CE ATL project.

FIGURE 24.2

Creating a new Windows CE ATL project.

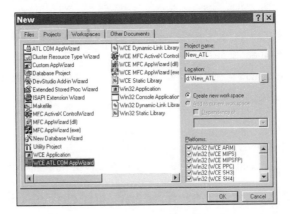

Completing this step creates a skeleton ATL project that implements DllCanUnloadNow, DllGetClassObject, DllRegisterServer, and DllUnregisterServer and contains a single instance of CComModule. At this point, the ATL project does not contain any COM objects. COM objects can easily be inserted into your project by using the ATL Object Wizard, displayed in Figure 24.3.

FIGURE 24.3

Using the ATL Object Wizard.

This wizard is invoked by selecting New ATL Object from the Insert menu. The ATL Object Wizard takes care of automatically creating the COM interface map entries, the IDL definitions, and the header files for the component you select.

Next, you will briefly review the ATL for Windows CE samples included with the Windows CE Toolkit.

ATL Samples Included with the Windows CE Toolkit

When you installed the Windows CE Toolkit for Visual C++, three ATL for Windows CE samples were also installed on your desktop computer. The samples for the H/PC were installed under the \Windows CE Tools\Wce200\MS HPC\Samples\ATL directory. If you also installed the H/PC Professional Edition toolkit, these samples (and a fourth sample) were installed under the \Windows CE Tools\Wce211\MS HPC PRO\Samples\ATL folder.

The following describes what samples were installed and what they can teach you. The COUNT and COUNTCNT samples demonstrate how to use containment in an ATL control. The POLYGON and POLYCNTR samples demonstrate how to implement custom properties, events, and a property page for an ATL control. The SKETCH and SKETCNTR samples demonstrate how to capture mouse messages from the touch screen and use them to draw on the display.

CNT or *CNTR* in the sample name indicates that it is a container.

If you also installed the H/PC Professional Edition toolkit for Windows CE, you have a fourth sample on your system. The COMPCTRL and COMPCNT samples demonstrate how to use composite controls, which is a new feature available in Windows CE 2.10 and above.

24

Next, you will examine the Pocket Outlook Object Model to learn what it is and how you can use it within your own applications.

An Introduction to POOM

POOM allows you to adapt your Windows CE applications to interact with the standard Microsoft Pocket Outlook applications included in ROM on Windows CE devices. Even though Microsoft provides an extensive API to work with the Contacts Database (see Hour 17, "Working with the Contacts Database API"), it does not help when you want to interface with the other Pocket Outlook applications. To solve this issue, Microsoft has released a freely downloadable software development kit (at `http://msdn.microsoft.com/cetools/platform/poomsdk.asp`). POOM is a set of COM interfaces that enable you to manipulate Contact, Calendar, and Task data.

Extending Calendar, Tasks, and Contacts Through Plug-Ins

The Calendar, Tasks, and Contacts applications all allow you to extend their basic functionality by adding a registered DLL. After this external plug-in has been configured, it will appear as a menu item in the appropriate application's Tools menu. When the user selects the item, a predefined callback routine inside your DLL is called with information about the application that is calling you.

To register a plug-in DLL, you must create a Registry key under the following Registry path:

- To create an entry for the Contacts application,
  `HKEY_LOCAL_MACHINE\Software\Microsoft\PimApps\PimExtensions\Contacts\AddIns`

- To create an entry for the Calendar application,
  `HKEY_LOCAL_MACHINE\Software\Microsoft\PimApps\PimExtensions\Calendar\AddIns`

- To create an entry for the Tasks application,
  `HKEY_LOCAL_MACHINE\Software\Microsoft\PimApps\PimExtensions\Tasks\AddIns`

The key name you register should be the name of your plug-in extension. For example, if you wanted to create a plug-in that attaches a voice memo to a contact, you would register the key `HKEY_LOCAL_MACHINE\Software\Microsoft\PimApps\PimExtensions\Contacts\AddIns\VoiceMenu`.

After you create the Registry key, you must create two additional Registry entries, described in Table 24.3, underneath the new key in order to complete the DLL's registration.

TABLE 24.3 Registry Values for Outlook Integration

Registry Value	Description
DLL	This value has the filename of your plug-in (for example, voicememo.dll).
Menu	This value has the name that you would want to appear in the Tools menu (for example, Voice Memo).

After you register the DLL, you must export the function `CePimCommand()` from your plug-in DLL.

```
1: void __cdecl CePimCommand(HWND hWnd, PIMTYPE ptData,
2: ➥ UINT uDataCount, HANDLE *rghData, void *pReserved);
```

The `CePimCommand()` function takes the following parameters:

- `HWND hWnd` is the handle to the application calling your function.

- `PIMTYPE ptData` is dependent on which version of Windows CE is calling your function. If it is a P/PC version 1.2, then `PT_CONTACT = 0`, `PT_CALENDAR = 1`, and `PT_TASKS = 2`. If any other version of Windows CE calls `PT_CALENDAR = 0`, then `PT_TASKS = 1` and `PT_CONTACT = 2`.

- `UINT uDataCount` is the number of items in the array `rghData`.

- `HANDLE *rghData` points to an array of OIDs (object identifiers) indicating which items are selected.

- `void *pReserved` is not used and will be `NULL`.

What does this all mean? Listing 24.1 shows an example of the callback function inside your registered DLL. This will just pop up a message box when your menu item is selected:

LISTING 24.1 The Plug-In Callback Function

```
1: #ifdef __cplusplus
2: #define EXPORT extern "C" __declspec (dllexport)
3: #else
4: #define EXPORT __declspec (dllexport)
5: #endif
6:
7: EXPORT void CePimCommand(HWND hWnd, PIMTYPE ptData, UINT uDataCount,
8: ➥HANDLE *rghData, void *pReserved)
```

continues

24

LISTING 24.1   continued

```
 9: {
10:     MessageBox(hWnd, TEXT("Inside the callback"),
11:     ➡TEXT("POOM Plug-in"), MB_OK);
12: }
```

From here, you could create your own windows, dialogs, or application support routines that directly interact with the Outlook applications.

The POOM Interfaces

POOM consists of several COM interfaces that enable you to manipulate items in the Pocket Outlook databases.

The main interface to POOM is IPOutlookApp. This is the only interface you have to create in order to derive all the other POOM objects. After the interface is created, you only have to log on to the application object for access to the various folder objects.

Essentially, each folder is a collection of items. A folder, in this instance, can be Contacts, Tasks, Calendar, and so on. Inside each folder are the individual items that make up the database. For example, the Calendar folder would contain appointment objects.

A detailed examination of each interface would take an hour by itself and is beyond the scope of this introduction to POOM. However, Table 24.4 gives a brief look at the POOM interfaces.

TABLE 24.4   The POOM Interfaces

Interface	Description
IPOutlookApp	This is the main application object that you create by using CoCreateInstance(). After you create this, you can log on and retrieve other folders.
IFolder	Each folder contains a collection of items. There are five folder types: Calendar, Contacts, Tasks, Cities, and Infrared.
IPOutlookItemCollection	Used to add or retrieve items from outlook databases.
ICity	City information, including longitude and latitude data. Typically, only a read-only interface because most cities are in ROM. However, you can access user-defined cities through this interface.
IContact	Contact information.
ITask	Task information.

Interface	Description
IAppointment	Calendar information.
ITimeZone	A read-only object that allows you to view time zone information.
IRecurrencePattern	Information about the recurrence of a task or appointment.
IExceptions	A read-only collection object that has a list of exceptions to a recurring appointment.
IException	A read-only object that has information about a particular exception to a recurring appointment.
IRecipients	A collection of recipients for a meeting request appointment.
IRecipient	Information about an individual member of a recipient collection.

Summary

In this hour, you learned about the Microsoft Foundation Classes, the Active Template Library, and the Pocket Outlook Object Model for Windows CE. You learned how MFC and ATL differ from their standard desktop implementations. You also learned what is new in the latest Windows CE version, as well as what features are currently absent. You ended the hour by learning what the Pocket Outlook Object Model is and how to begin using it within your own applications.

Q&A

Q How do I register COM objects on my Windows CE device?

A Use the REGSVRCE.EXE tool to register it "by hand." You do this by copying REGSVRCE.EXE to your Windows CE device and then invoking it with the name of your DLL as its solitary parameter. REGSVRCE.EXE is located in the target\<cpu> directory under a platform SDK installation (for example, the SH3 H/PC version is located in the \Windows CE Tools\Wce200\MS HPC\Target\SH3 directory).

When you are packaging your components into a CAB file for distribution, you can have the CAB file extraction engine automatically register them for you using [CESelfRegister] in the [DefaultInstall] section of the .INF file used to create the CAB file.

Workshop

The Workshop is designed to help you anticipate possible questions, review what you've learned, and begin thinking ahead about putting your knowledge into practice. The answers to the quiz are in Appendix A, "Answers."

Quiz

1. How do you subclass a control using MFC on Windows CE?
2. How do you handle a WM_HIBERNATE message within your MFC application?
3. What is the name of the main interface to POOM?
4. What are the four MFC classes specifically designed for working with Windows CE databases, and what do they do?
5. When using the CCeSocket class, how do you determine the invisible window to which you should send WM_SOCKET_NOTIFY?

Exercises

1. Create a single-document MFC application that displays Hello World in the document view.
2. Create a dialog box MFC application that displays Hello when you select its Hello button.

PART V
Appendixes

Hour

APPENDIX **A**

Answers

Hour 1, "Getting Started with Visual C++ for Windows CE"

Quiz

1. How do you create a screen capture of your application running on a Windows CE device?

   Use the Remote Zoomin tool to perform screen captures.

2. How do you manually edit the Registry on a Windows CE device?

   Use the Remote Registry Editor to view and modify the Windows CE Registry.

3. How do you reset the emulation environment to its initial state?

   Replace the corresponding OBS file on your hard drive with the original OBS file from the installation CD-ROM.

4. How do you determine which type of CPU your Windows CE device uses?

The System Control Panel applet (on the Windows CE device) will tell you what CPU the device uses.

5. What function will convert Unicode text to ASCII text?

   wcstombs. To help you remember this, you can read this as *wcs* (wide character string) *to mbs* (multibyte string).

6. How do you perform a clean reinstallation of the Visual C++ for Windows CE toolkits?

   Use the Add/Remove Programs Control Panel applet to uninstall the Windows CE toolkits and Visual C++. Next, remove all Registry entries under HKEY_CURRENT_USER\Software\Microsoft\DevStudio and HKEY_LOCAL_MACHINE\Software\Microsoft\DevStudio, reinstall Visual C++, run it once, and then install the Visual C++ for Windows CE toolkits.

Exercises

1. Create a simple text viewer that loads a text file into an edit control window for viewing. (*Hint*: Edit controls under Windows CE require Unicode text strings.)

   This is achieved by modifying the Hello World! application in the following manner:

   - Remove the WM_PAINT code for displaying Hello World!.
   - Use CreateWindow to create a read-only multiline edit control child window of the main window on startup.
   - Add a menu item (Open) to allow users to select a text file to load. When users select that menu item, use the GetOpenFileName common dialog to enable them to select the text file they want to load. When they have chosen a text file, use the code in Listing 1.2 to load the code into the edit control.

     The source code to do this is provided in the HOUR01\EXER01 directory on the CD-ROM.

2. Add the capability to edit and save text files to the text viewer you created in exercise 1.

   This is accomplished by modifying the code in exercise 1.

   - Not restricting the edit control to being read-only
   - Adding another menu item (Save) to enable the user to save the current contents of the edit control. When the user selects this menu item, the application should allow the user to select the name of the file to which he or she wants to save the edit control contents. When the file is chosen, the program should retrieve the contents of the edit control, use the wcstombs function to

convert it from Unicode to a multibyte text string, and then save it to the specified file.

The source code to do this is provided in the HOUR01\EXER02 directory on the CD-ROM.

Hour 2, "What's Different About Windows CE?"

Quiz

1. Do `mbstowcs` return the same value on Windows 95 and Windows CE?

   No, Windows CE includes the null character in `count` and returns the number of bytes instead of the number of wide characters.

2. Does Windows CE support MAPI?

   No, Windows CE has its own proprietary API for handling email.

3. What ANSI standard C function can be used to emulate the behavior of the missing `atof` function?

   `sscanf`

4. Are INI files supported on Windows CE?

   No, you must use the Registry instead.

5. What is COREDLL.LIB?

   The import library that merges the functionality in Kernel, User, and GDI. Linking against this file resolves almost all the Win32 API calls.

6. What is the difference between ANSI, Unicode, and multibyte strings?

   The number of bytes in a character is 1 in ANSI, 2 in Unicode, and variable length in multibyte.

7. What WinInet protocols are supported on Windows CE?

   HTTP and FTP.

8. How do you implement resizable windows on Windows CE?

   This is a trick question—you can't. Windows are either maximized or minimized and cannot be resized.

9. How does structured exception handling (SEH) differ on Windows 95 and Windows CE?

   SEH on Windows CE does not fire destructors and cannot handle a return in a `__finally` block.

A

10. What Win32 API function can you use to play WAV files on both Windows 95 and Windows CE?

    sndPlaySound

Exercises

1. Try porting the Visual C++ 6.0 GENERIC sample to Windows CE.

   (No answer required)

2. Translate the following code to TCHAR style rather than directly use char:

```
char *strdup(const char *pcsz)
{
    char *psz = malloc(strlen(pcsz)+1);
    strcpy(psz, pcsz);
    return psz;
```

   The code should look something like the following:

```
LPTSTR strdup(LPCTSTR pcsz)
{
    int iSize = _tcslen(pcsz);
    LPTSTR psz = malloc((iSize+1) * sizeof(TCHAR));
    _tcscpy(psz, pcsz);
    return psz;
}
```

Hour 3, "Building User Interfaces—Command Bars and Bands"

Quiz

1. What is the purpose of a command bar?

   Command bars are used to consolidate both menus and toolbars into a single control to give more room on the screen for your application.

2. How do I add items to a command bar?

   To add a menu, use the CommandBar_InsertMenuBar() function. To add buttons, use the CommandBar_InsertButtons() function.

3. How do I handle command bar menu notifications for drop-down buttons?

   WM_NOTIFY will be sent with the TBM_DROPDOWN notification.

4. Why is it beneficial to use a command band instead of a command bar?

   Command bands allow the user to resize and change the layout. You can also add more items because bands can be minimized and maximized.

5. How do I handle a command band resize notification?

WM_NOTIFY will be sent a RBN_LAYOUTCHANGE notification message.

6. How do I restore a command band to a preset state?

Before closing your application, call the CommandBands_GetRestoreInformation() function to obtain the state information for the band. When your application reopens, use that data to create your bands.

7. What is the image flag used for in REBARBANDINFO?

The image flag is used when command bands are minimized. The band shows the icon representing the band.

8. How do I add ToolTips to command bar buttons?

Use the CommandBar_AddTooltips() function.

9. How do you enable and disable command bar buttons?

The same way you would on a normal toolbar. Use the TB_ENABLEBUTTON function to enable and disable buttons.

10. How do I insert a separator into a command bar?

Use the TBSTYLE_SEP style when adding a TBBUTTON.

Exercises

1. Modify the example of inserting command bands to add a bitmap to the band background.

Modify the code to

```
rbbs[1].cbSize = sizeof(REBARBANDINFO);
rbbs[1].fMask = RBBIM_ID | RBBIM_SIZE | RBBIM_BACKGROUND;
rbbs[1].wID = ID_TOOLSBAND;
rbbs[1].cx = 100;

HBITMAP hBitMap = (HBITMAP)LoadBitmap(ghInstance,
➥ MAKEINTRESOURCE(IDB_BITMAP));
rbbs[1].hbmBack = hBitMap;
```

You should also make sure that the buttons in the TBBUTTON structure have the TBSTYLE_TRANSPARENT style bit set as well.

2. Add ToolTips to the command band rather than to the Command Bar example.

To add ToolTips to the command band, just get the handle of the command bar from the band, and use the same function call, CommandBar_AddToolTips(), to add the ToolTips.

A

Hour 4, "Using the HTML Viewer"

Quiz

1. What is the classname for the HTML View control?

   `DISPLAYCLASS`

2. What is the difference between `DTM_ADDTEXT` and `DTM_ADDTEXTW`?

   `DTM_ADDTEXT` is used to send straight ASCII text to the HTML View control, whereas `DTM_ADDTEXTW` is used to send Unicode data.

3. How do I clear the HTML View control?

   You must send the control a `WM_SETTEXT` message with a blank for the text. For example,

   `SendMessage(ghHTML, WM_SETTEXT, 01, (LPARAM)TEXT(""));`

4. What notification will I receive when the user clicks on a hyperlink?

   You will receive a `NM_HOTSPOT` notification when a user clicks a hyperlink.

5. What is an anchor?

   An *anchor* is a link to another document. This can include a bookmark or an entire page.

6. What are some uses for the `<META>` tag?

   The `<META>` tag is designed so that additional information can be sent along with the current HTML page. Internet rating systems have been using the tag to describe adult content. Push HTML pages also have been using `<META>` tags to describe incoming documents.

7. How can I make sure that images will be shrunk to fit the window?

   Send the control the `DTM_ENABLESHRINK` message.

8. How do I get the title for an HTML document?

   You will be sent the `NM_TITLE` notification message if the document has a title in it. Typically, you will want to set the status bar text or the window title to the title of the document.

9. How do I loop a sound file that is specified as `INFINITE`?

   When calling the `PlaySound` API call, you will want to use the flags `SND_LOOP` and `SND_ASYNC`.

10. How do I fail an image load request?

    Send the control a `DTM_IMAGEFAIL` message. Make sure that you include the cookie number sent to you in the initial `NM_INLINE_IMAGE` notification request.

Exercises

1. Modify the sample to search for bookmarks.

   You will have to search the URL string for the # character. If this is found, you have a bookmark in your link request. For example,

   ```
   if(strchr(nmHTML->szTarget, '#')) {
       SendMessage(ghHTMLView, DTM_ANCHOR, 0L, (LPARAM)nmHTML->szTarget);
       return TRUE;
   }
   ```

2. Try experimenting with the DTM_ENABLESHRINK message to see how it changes the images.

   (No answer required)

Hour 5, "Working with Standard Controls"

Quiz

1. What makes a control a Standard Control?

   Standard Controls send notifications as WM_COMMAND messages.

2. What are the various types of button controls?

   Push buttons, group boxes, check boxes, and radio buttons.

3. How do I get my current selection from a list box?

   Send the LB_GETCURSEL message to the list control.

4. How do I set text in an edit control?

   Use the WM_SETTEXT message.

5. Does Windows CE support any memory enhancements for combo boxes?

   Yes, use the CBS_EX_CONSTSTRINGDATA style. This will force Windows CE to store only the pointer of the null-terminated string passed to it, rather than create a copy of it.

6. Can static controls send me notifications when they are clicked?

   Yes, set the SS_NOTIFY style to receive notifications from the control. You will receive a STN_CLICKED notification message.

7. What does the BS_AUTORADIOBUTTON style do?

   BS_AUTORADIOBUTTON clears all other buttons in the group of radio buttons when this button is selected.

A

Exercise

Modify the sample given for owner draw push buttons to draw an icon in the button.

Adding support for images in buttons is easy when you receive the WM_DRAWITEM message. To draw an icon (IDI_BUTTON_ICON) in the center of your button, use the following code:

```
 1: case WM_DRAWITEM: {
 2: LPDRAWITEMSTRUCT lpdis = (LPDRAWITEMSTRUCT)lParam;
 3: if(lpdis->CtlType == ODT_BUTTON) {
 4:         RECT rct;
 5:         SetRectEmpty(&rct);
 6:         GetClientRect(GetDlgItem(hDlg, (UINT)wParam), &rct);
 7:         if(lpdis->itemState & ODS_SELECTED)
 8:                 DrawFrameControl(lpdis->hDC, &rct, DFC_BUTTON,
 9:                 ➥DFCS_BUTTONPUSH | DFCS_PUSHED);
10:         else
11:                 DrawFrameControl(lpdis->hDC, &rct, DFC_BUTTON,
                    DFCS_BUTTONPUSH);
12:         // Find center of the rect for a 16x16 icon
13:         rct.top+= ((rct.bottom - rct.top)/2) - 8;
14:         rct.left+= ((rct.right - rct.left)/2) - 8;
15:         // Draw the image on the button
16:         DrawIcon(lpdis->hDC, rct.left, rct.top,
17:         ➥LoadIcon(_hInstance, MAKEINTRESOURCE(IDI_BUTTON_ICON)));
18: }
```

Hour 6, "Incorporating Common Controls"

Quiz

1. What is the major difference between Standard and Common Controls?

   The Common Controls use WM_NOTIFY to send messages, whereas the Standard Controls use WM_COMMAND.

2. How do I set full row selection in a list view?

   Use the function SetExtendedListViewStyle() using the LVS_EX_FULLROWSELECT flag.

3. For what are tree view controls used?

   Primarily for showing data in a hierarchy (with a parent-child relationship).

4. What is a buddy control?

   A buddy control is an up/down control that has attached itself to an edit control.

5. What controls support the custom draw service?

   Tree view, list view, header, trackbar, and command band controls all support the custom draw service.

6. How can I display a progress bar vertically?

   By using the PBS_VERTICAL style.

7. How do I set a list view to be virtual?

   To make a list view control into a virtual control, you use the LVS_OWNERDATA style.

Exercise

Modify the example for the virtual list view control to use the custom draw service. Make every other list view item display in red instead of black.

To implement custom draw services, all you have to do is process the NM_CUSTOMDRAW notification message. To make every other item red, just take the item number and check the remainder when you divide by 2. If 0, it's an even number; otherwise, it will be odd. For example:

```
 1: case NM_CUSTOMDRAW: {
 2:     NMLVCUSTOMDRAW *lpNMCustomDraw = (NMLVCUSTOMDRAW *)lParam;
 3:     if(lpNMCustomDraw->nmcd.dwDrawStage == CDDS_PREPAINT)
 4:             return CDRF_NOTIFYITEMDRAW;
 5:     if(lpNMCustomDraw->nmcd.dwDrawStage == CDDS_ITEMPREPAINT) {
 6:             // If there's a remainder when dividing by 2, then red
 7: if(lpNMCustomDraw->nmcd.dwItemSpec % 2)
 8:                     lpNMCustomDraw->clrText = RGB(255, 0, 0);
 9:             return CDRF_DODEFAULT;
10:     }
11:     return CDRF_DODEFAULT;
12: }
13: break;
```

Hour 7, "Activating the Common Dialogs"

Quiz

1. Can I hook or template the File Open or File Save dialog?

   No, dialog hooks and templates are available only for the Color and Print dialogs.

2. Are the Print and Color dialogs supported on the P/PC platform?

   No, currently only the File Save and File Open dialogs are on the Palm-size platform.

3. On the H/PC Professional Edition, should I use PrintDlg to print?

   Even though it is supported, you should be using PageSetupDlg on H/PC Professional Edition platforms because PageSetupDlg is used only for backwards compatibility.

A

4. On the File Open or File Save common dialog, how can I change the dialog title?

You have to modify the lpcstrTitle member of the OPENFILENAME structure.

5. How do I get error information for my common dialogs?

You have to call the CommDlgExtendedError() function.

6. How do I get the color the user selected in the Color dialog?

When the dialog returns, you can get the selected color from the rgbResult member of the CHOOSECOLOR structure.

7. What does the CC_SOLIDCOLOR flag do in the CHOOSECOLOR structure?

It specifies that the dialog should display only solid colors.

Exercises

1. Modify the sample code so that the File Save dialog will not prompt for overwrite errors.

You have to remove the OFN_OVERWRITEPROMPT flag from the Flags member of the OPENFILENAME structure.

2. Create a PrintDlg common dialog that has default margins of 1 1/2 inches and a minimum margin of 1/2 inch.

You have to initialize the margin structures to do this:

```
PRINTDLG pDlg;
memset(&pDlg, 0, sizeof(PRINTDLG));

pDlg.cbStruct = sizeof(PRINTDLG);
pDlg.hwndOwner = hParent;
SetRect(&pDlg.rcMargin, 1500, 1500, 1500, 1000);
SetRect(&pDlg.rcMinMargin, 500, 500, 500, 500);
pDlg.dwFlags = PD_SELECTALLPAGES ¦ PD_SELECTPORTRAIT
➡¦ PD_MARGINS ¦ PD_MINMARGINS;
PrintDlg(&pDlg);
```

Hour 8, "Working with Graphics Devices"

Quiz

1. What does the term *2bp* mean?

2bp means *two bits per pixel*. This is a bitmap format that represents four colors (such as white, black, light gray, and dark gray). Windows CE is the only version of Windows that supports this type of bitmap.

2. Your program eventually fails to create a GDI object because of lack of memory. Shutting down the program and restarting it does not help. The only way you and

your users can get it to start working again is to reset the Windows CE device. What is the likely culprit?

Most likely, your program is not deleting GDI objects after it is done with them. In general, any memory that your program does not free will be freed when your application is shut down. However, any GDI objects created by your program are created on the GDI heap and are not automatically freed when your program is terminated. This is why restarting your program does not solve the symptom, but resetting the device does. Review your source code to make sure that all GDI objects created are also freed after they are no longer needed.

3. My desktop Win32 code will not compile for Windows CE because `MoveTo` and `LineTo` are unrecognized. How do I fix this?

Rewrite your code to use the `PolyLine` function.

4. Which bit block transfer function is only available on Windows CE?

`TransparentImage`

5. What function do you use to create a compressed bitmap on Windows CE?

Windows CE does not include native support for compressed bitmaps.

6. My desktop Win32 code uses `TextOut`, but doesn't compile for Windows CE. How do I fix this?

Rewrite your code to use the `TextOutEx` function.

7. When `EnumFontFamilies` invokes your callback function, how do you determine whether you have received a pointer to a raster font or a TrueType font?

You can determine this by examining the third parameter to your callback function. If the `RASTER_FONTTYPE` bit is set, it is a raster font; if the `TRUETYPE_FONTTYPE` bit is set, it is a TrueType font.

Exercises

1. Create a simple text editor that enables the user to select the font used in the edit window, using the font selection dialog sample code covered in this lesson.

The program should be changed to create a multiline edit child window on startup. When the user selects a new font, the `WM_SETFONT` message should be sent to the edit control so that it can switch to using the selected font.

2. Modify the screen capture utility in this lesson to create black-and-white screen captures.

The bmi structure should be changed from

```
static struct {
        BITMAPINFOHEADER bmih;
        RGBQUAD rgq[16];
} bmi;
```

to

```
static struct {
        BITMAPINFOHEADER bmih;
        RGBQUAD rgq[2];
} bmi;
```

and the code specifying the bit depth should be changed from

```
    bmi.bmih.biBitCount = 4;
```

to

```
    bmi.bmih.biBitCount = 1;
```

Finally, the color values can be set with just the following code:

```
    // set the 2 color values
    bmi.rgq[0].rgbRed     = 0;
    bmi.rgq[0].rgbGreen   = 0;
    bmi.rgq[0].rgbBlue    = 0;
    bmi.rgq[1].rgbRed     = 255;
    bmi.rgq[1].rgbGreen   = 255;
    bmi.rgq[1].rgbBlue    = 255;
```

Hour 9, "The Object Store: Files and the Registry"

Quiz

1. What is the object store?

   The object store is RAM-based storage used to store your files, databases, and the Registry. It is like your Windows CE device hard drive.

2. What flags do you use to create a new file?

   When using the CreateFile function, you can use either the CREATE_NEW or CREATE_ALWAYS flags.

3. If there were four mounted devices on your Windows CE device, what would their device names be?

   \Storage Card 1, \Storage Card 2, \Storage Card 3, and \Storage Card 4.

4. How do you set the file pointer?

   Use the SetFilePointer function call.

5. How do you delete a directory?

Use the `RemoveDirectory()` function call. You must make sure that the directory is empty before removing it; otherwise, the function will fail.

6. What is an OID?

An OID is an object identifier. Every file, directory, database, and database record has a unique OID that associates it inside the object store.

7. What are the types of Registry values?

The Registry can contain values that are of type `REG_NONE`, `REG_SZ`, `REG_EXPAND_SZ`, `REG_BINARY`, `REG_DWORD`, `REG_DWORD_LITTLE_ENDIAN`, `REG_DWORD_BIG_ENDIAN`, `REG_LINK`, `REG_MULTI_SZ`, and `REG_RESOURCE_LIST`.

8. What is the largest file you can have on a Windows CE device?

On a Windows CE 2.0 device, 4MB is the largest size file you can have. This has increased to 16MB on Windows CE 2.11.

Exercise

Modify Listing 9.4 to automatically create the Registry key if it does not already exist.

The only modification necessary is to use the `RegCreateKeyEx` function instead of the `RegOpenKeyEx`, as previously described.

Hour 10, "Advanced Object Store: The Database API"

Quiz

1. Can you lock a database?

No, database locking is not supported on Windows CE. However, you can receive notifications when database events occur.

2. What is the maximum number of sort indices?

A maximum of four sort indices is supported.

3. What are database properties?

Each record contains properties. A property is a data type and a value for that property. For example, a property might be called `Name`, be of a string type, and contain the name `Randy Santossio`.

A

4. What are the new property types under Windows CE 2.1?

   Windows CE 2.1 and later support the `CEVT_BOOL` and `CEVT_R8` data types.

5. How can I seek a database for a particular index?

   The easiest way is to use the `CEDB_SEEK_BEGINNING` flag when calling `CeSeekDatabase` and specify the index of the record in the `dwValue` field.

6. What is the major difference between databases on Windows CE 2.0 and on Windows CE 2.1?

   The major difference is that database volumes can now exist outside the object store. External devices, such as flash cards, can contain databases. If mounted volumes are used, you should call the Ex versions of the Database API calls.

7. How do I delete a database record?

   Use the `CeDeleteRecord()` function call.

Exercise

Write a function to delete a database, based on its OID. Make sure that the function prompts the user to continue, providing the database name.

```
 1: BOOL DeleteDB(CEOID ceOID)
 2: {
 3:     CEOIDINFO ceOIDInf;
 4:     TCHAR tchString[255] = TEXT("\0");
 5:
 6:     // Get the information about the OID
 7:     memset(&ceOIDInf, 0, sizeof(CEOIDINFO));
 8:     if(!CeOidGetInfo((CEOID)ceOID, &ceOIDInf))
 9:         return FALSE;
10:
11:     // Put up a warning
12:     wsprintf(tchString, TEXT("Are you sure you want to
        ➥delete the database '%s'?"),
        ➥ceOIDInf.infDatabase.szDbaseName);
13:     if(MessageBox(ghWnd, tchString, TEXT("DB Manager"),
        ➥MB_YESNO) == IDNO)
14:         return FALSE;
15:
16:     // Delete the database
17:     CeDeleteDatabase(ceOID);
18:
19:     return TRUE;
20: }
```

Hour 11, "Threads and Processes"

Quiz

1. How many thread priorities are available on Windows CE?

   Eight levels.

2. How many concurrent processes can run on Windows CE?

   Up to 32 processes.

3. Why do you need thread safety to do a simple integer increment (such as `InterlockedIncrement`)?

   Thread safety is necessary because the increment is implemented with multiple CPU instructions. To behave properly, the instructions must execute together as an atomic operation.

4. What is the difference between dynamic and static TLS? Which one should you use on Windows CE?

   Dynamic TLS is done at runtime with the `TlsAlloc`, `TlsFree`, `TlsSetValue`, and `TlsGetValue` APIs, whereas static TLS is specified at compile time with the `__declspec(thread)` variable declaration attribute. You should always use dynamic TLS on Windows CE because static TLS is not supported.

5. What is the difference between a mutex and a critical section?

   A mutex is a kernel object that can be shared across multiple processes, whereas a critical section can be used only in a single process. A mutex is also much less efficient than a critical section.

6. Are kernel object names case-sensitive?

   Yes, an object named `VICTORIA` is distinct from one named `victoria`.

7. How much virtual memory space does each process have on Windows CE?

   32MB

8. Can `WaitForMultipleObjects` be used to wait for more than one handle to be signaled?

   No, the `bWaitForAll` flag must be false, or the API will immediately return with a `GetLastError` value of `ERROR_INVALID_PARAMETER`.

9. How is the scope of kernel object handles different on Windows CE than on Windows NT or 95? Should you make use of it in your applications?

   Whereas kernel object handles on Windows NT and Windows 95 are valid only in a single process, Windows CE allows them to be used in any process. It is a bad

A

idea to take advantage of this "feature" because a handle shared in this manner does not have its reference count incremented, which can result in the object being destroyed prematurely.

10. What's the best way to implement thread suspension on Windows CE?

    The most reliable method is to add an event to your thread routine and have another thread reset the event when it wants to suspend it. This works around the problem that SuspendThread has with threads that are executing system calls.

Exercises

1. Implement a completely thread-safe OpenEvent function using the CreateEvent API.

```
HANDLE WINAPI OpenEvent(DWORD dwDesiredAccess,
                        BOOL bInheritHandle,
                        LPCTSTR lpName)
{
    HANDLE hEvent = NULL;

    if ( lpName == NULL )
        return NULL;

    // use a mutex to ensure thread safety across all processes
    HANDLE hMutex = CreateMutex(NULL, FALSE, _T("OPEN_EVENT_MUTEX"));

    if ( hMutex &&
        (WaitForSingleObject(hMutex, INFINITE) == WAIT_OBJECT_0) )
    {
        hEvent = CreateEvent(NULL, FALSE, FALSE, lpName);

        // close it if we didn't open an existing object
        if ( hEvent && (GetLastError() != ERROR_ALREADY_EXISTS) )
        {
            CloseHandle(hEvent);
            hEvent = NULL;
        }


        ReleaseMutex(hMutex);
    }

    if ( hMutex )
        CloseHandle(hMutex);

    return hEvent;
}
```

2. Describe what priority inversion is and how Windows CE solves it.

   Priority inversion occurs when a lower priority thread owns a resource that a higher priority thread needs to continue running. Windows CE deals with this situation by temporarily raising the priority thread that owns the resource to the priority of the waiting thread so that the resource will be released and the higher priority can continue running.

Hour 12, "Controlling Interprocess Communication"

Quiz

1. How are the Clipboard APIs different on Windows CE?

   Only a subset of the built-in Clipboard types are supported, and the Clipboard view functions are not provided. Additionally, OpenClipboard requires an HWND that was created in the calling process in order for SetClipboardData to work correctly.

2. How do I avoid problems with WM_COPYDATA on Windows CE?

   Make sure that the COPYDATASTRUCT used is a local variable. Using global, static, or dynamically allocated memory will cause the receiver to get garbage instead of the real data.

3. How do I simulate DDE on Windows CE?

   For most DDE applications, a memory-mapped file and an event to signal changes will provide the same functionality.

4. What is a Remote Procedure Call (RPC)?

   The process of calling a function whose code is in another process or resides on another machine. Windows CE doesn't have a generic RPC feature, but one can be simulated with Winsock.

Exercise

Listing 12.2 is not thread-safe because OpenMMF, TransferMMFToEditBox, and so on, use shared data without a mutex. Change the code so that it is thread-safe.

A named mutex should be used inside OpenMMF, CloseMMF, TransferMMFToEditBox, and TransferEditBoxToMMF.

A

Hour 13, "WinSock and Serial Communications"

Quiz

1. How can I work around Windows CE's lack of the `WSAAsync` WinSock APIs?

   You have two options. The first is to use `ioctlsocket` to make a socket nonblocking and use `select` to wait for data to arrive. The second option is to do all blocking socket I/O in separate threads so that your user interface is consistently updated.

2. How can I work around Windows CE's lack of support for the `SetCommConfig` API?

   Use `SetCommState` instead.

3. How can I force a thread to return from a call to `WaitCommEvent`?

   Call `SetCommMask` on the port handle with a mask value of 0.

4. How can I set a serial port to raw IR mode?

   Use the `EscapeCommFunction` API with the `SETIR` status code.

5. How can I set a socket to be nonblocking?

   Use the `ioctlsocket` API like this:
   ```
   u_long fOn = TRUE;
   iotclsocket(sock, FIONBIO, &fOn);
   ```

Exercises

1. Change the socket test example to use nonblocking sockets rather than rely on the blocking properties of `recv` and `send`.

   (No answer required)

2. Modify CETTY to support the IR serial port via IrComm.

   (No answer required)

Hour 14, "Printing"

Quiz

1. How do you get a valid printer DC?

   Call the `PrintDlg` function, and use the value returned in the *hdc* member of the `PRINTDLG` parameter.

2. PrintDlg() returns FALSE no matter what values you specify for the *dwFlags* member of the PRINTDLG structure. CommDlgExtendedError returns 4100. What is going wrong?

Error 4100 is PDERR_CREATEDCFAILURE, which means that the PrintDlg function was unable to get the printer DC. The usual culprit in this scenario is the lack of an actual connection to the printer on the port selected by the user (from within the PrintDlg dialog).

3. Which members are the same in the PRINTDLG structure used on desktop Win32 and the version used on Windows CE?

lCustData is the only member that is exactly the same data type and the same spelling. Six other members (hdc, cbStruct, dwFlags, hinst, pszPrintTemplateName, and pfnPrintHook) are functionally similar to their desktop counterparts, but are spelled differently.

4. What are the four main functions used for actually printing a document?

StartDoc, StartPage, EndPage and EndDoc are the functions used for actually printing a document. The PrintDlg function is used to get the printer's device context, and the AbortDoc and SetAbortProc functions are necessary to implement the capability to cancel a print job.

5. How do you print on Windows CE 1.0?

Printing support is not included in the Windows CE 1.0 operating system, so you must either write directly to the printer within your application or use a third-party application (such as bPRINT) that writes directly to the printer.

6. From the user's perspective, what is different between the desktop Win32 version of the PrintDlg function and the Windows CE version?

The following are not supported on the Windows CE version:

- Specifying a range of pages to print
- Specifying the number of copies to print
- Viewing the printer name
- Viewing the printer status
- Adjusting printer properties
- Printing to a file

7. How do you spool a print job on Windows CE?

Print spooling support is not currently included in the Windows CE operating system. Third-party printing applications (such as bPRINT) enable you to spool print jobs.

A

Exercises

1. Create a simple text editor that prints out the contents of its edit control window. (See the companion CD-ROM.)

2. Change the program in exercise 1 to include a working Cancel dialog. (See the companion CD-ROM.)

Hour 15, "Targeting the Palm-Size PC"

Quiz

1. How many Palm-size PC–specific issues are there with the application in Figure 15.4?

FIGURE 15.4

How many issues are there with this application?

This is essentially a Handheld PC application running on a Palm-size PC. The menus should not contain shortcut keys. The ToolTips should not contain hotkeys (Ctrl+O). The tab control (Source and HTML) should be horizontal across the top of the edit window, not vertical down the left side of the edit window. The text on the tab control is not visible. The edit window has the current focus, but the program has not automatically activated the SIP.

2. How does an application know when to resize itself after the user has hidden the SIP?

The application receives a WM_SETTINGCHANGE message whose WPARAM parameter is set to SPI_SETINFO.

3. What are the two types of controls that can have ToolTips?

Text and button controls.

4. How do you launch the Voice Recorder control to automatically start playing a WAV file?

   Create the control with the VRS_PLAY_MODE style flag.

Exercises

1. Create a program that uses the Voice Recorder control to record and play WAV files.

   (See the companion CD-ROM.)

2. Add a dialog to the program that you created in the preceding step. This dialog should contain a CAPEDIT control for the name of the WAV file, and a TTBUTTON control to browse for WAV files. The Browse button should include ToolTip text.

   (See the companion CD-ROM.)

Hour 16, "Using AppInstall to Redistribute Your Programs"

Quiz

1. Your application is failing to install because it shares a DLL with another product of yours that is already installed and running on the device. For your install to complete successfully, the other application using the DLL must be shut down so that the CAB file extraction engine can successfully examine the DLL and overwrite it with the version within your CAB file if necessary. How do you do this programmatically from within the setup?

   You could write your Install_Init function (which you provide in your setup.dll) to check whether the DLL file in question is already on the device. If it is, there are several ways to determine whether it is currently in use (for example, by using FindWindow() to see whether other applications known to use it are currently running or by attempting to temporarily rename it).

2. You have a file TEST.DLL that you would like to install as MYAPP.DLL in the \WINDOWS folder on the Windows CE device. You do not want to install this file if a newer version of MYAPP.DLL is already installed. You also want to reference-count this shared component. What line would you add to your INF file's [CopyFiles] section to achieve this?

The follow INF file entries implement this for an SH3 install. You should repeat this logic for each CPU you intend to support.

```
[DestinationDirs]
Files.SH3=0,%CE2% ; CE2 is \WINDOWS
[DefaultInstall.SH3]
CopyFiles= Files.SH3
 [Files.SH3]
; rename 'myapp.exe' to 'My App.exe'
MyApp.dll,test.exe,,0xA0000000
```

3. How do you install a file to the My Documents directory on the Windows CE device?

   Use the %CE5% variable for the desired file in the [DestinationDirs] section.

4. What is the difference between the Load_PegCpuType function and the Load_PegGetPlatformName function?

   Load_PegCpuType tells you whether you are installing on an SH3 or a MIPS device. The Load_PegGetPlatformName function returns more information about the CPU, such as whether it is a MIPS R3910 or MIPS R4100 CPU.

Exercises

1. Create a CAB file that installs your application (or one of the sample programs).

   (No answer required)

2. Modify the CAB file in exercise #1 to display a pop-up Hello message to the user before installing.

   This is implemented by

   1. Adding the following line to the [DefaultInstall] section of the INF file:
      ```
      CESetupDLL = Setup.dll
      ```

   2. Adding setup.dll to the [SourceDisksFiles] section.

   3. Adding a MessageBox function call to the Install_Init callback function in the CAB file's SETUP.DLL. This is implemented as follows:
      ```
      __declspec(dllexport) codeINSTALL_INIT
      Install_Init( HWND hwndParent, BOOL fFirstCall,
                    BOOL fPreviouslyInstalled, LPCTSTR pszInstallDir )
      {
          MessageBox( hwndParent, TEXT( "Hello from Install_Init" ),
                      TEXT( "BUGBUG" ), MB_OK );
          return codeINSTALL_INIT_CONTINUE;
      }
      ```

Hour 17, "Working with the Contacts Database API"

Quiz

1. How do you go about creating a new Contacts database?

   If you are unable to open the Contacts database, you can call the CreateAddressBook function to build a new one.

2. What is an address card?

   Each record in the Contacts database is stored as an address card.

3. What are address card properties?

   Every address card has several address card properties that define the address card. Some examples are contact name, address, email, and so on.

4. What do you call to add a new contact?

   You must call the AddAddressCard function to add a new record.

5. When adding a new contact, what do you have to do to your AddressCard before adding it?

   When filling out the AddressCard structure, you must call SetMask on each property you are adding.

6. How do you delete a contact?

   Call the DeleteAddressCard function to delete a contact after getting its object identifier.

7. How do you find out how many contacts are in the database?

   By calling the GetNumberOfAddressCards function.

Exercise

Modify Listing 17.3 so that you add a second email address to a contact.

To add a second email address, after you have received the AddressCard structure to modify, you must add the following code:

```
AdrCard.pszEmail2 = TEXT("SecondEmail@nowhere.com");
SetMask(&AdrCard, HHPR_EMAIL2_EMAIL_ADDRESS);

// Save the changes back to the database
ModifyAddressCard(&AdrCard, pOid, &nIndex);
```

A

Hour 18, "Creating Mail-Enabled Applications"

Quiz

1. You attempt to use `MailPutFolder` to rename a folder, but it fails. The folder's ID is `0x000000FD`. Why wasn't this successful?

   The value for `MAIL_FOLDER_OUTBOX` is `0x000000FD`. You were attempting to rename the Outbox, which cannot be renamed or deleted.

2. What does the mail header field `BCC` do?

   `BCC` stands for *blind cc*. Any email addresses you place in this field will be cc'd on the email, but the other recipients (in the `To` and `Cc` fields) will not be aware of it.

Exercises

1. Your company has the capability to receive user registrations via email and automatically parse them into a database of registered users. To your application's About box, add a Register Now button that collects the user's information, formats it, and emails it to your user registration email address.

   (See the companion CD-ROM.)

2. Write an editor program that allows the user to edit a single message that is then mailed to multiple recipients. The recipient email addresses are parsed from an external data file. This file is text file, with each email address on its own line.

   (See the companion CD-ROM.)

Hour 19, "Monitoring Power and System Resources"

Quiz

1. The `GetSystemPowerStatusEx` function allows you to get cached power information rather than retrieve it directly from the device driver. What is the advantage of this?

   Using cached information is quicker than using noncached information.

2. What is the remote API version of `GlobalMemoryStatus`, and in which header file is it?

   The `CeGlobalMemoryStatus` function is found in RAPI.H.

3. What is the total size of the Windows CE virtual address space?

4GB.

Exercise

Is the speed hit between using noncached power information and cached power information significant? Write a program that times how long it takes to call the GetSystemPowerStatusEx function 1,000 times each way, and compare the results.

(See the companion CD-ROM.) For 1,000 function calls, it's a difference of ~100 milliseconds, depending on the device used. This difference is not significant for most applications.

Hour 20, "Communicating with the Desktop"

Quiz

1. What is the difference between CeRapiInvoke stream and block modes?

   Stream mode allows you to continuously send information to and from the device until the connection is closed, whereas block mode is a one-time data transfer.

2. What is the difference between CeRapiInit and CeRapiInitEx?

   CeRapiInitEx allows you to time out and cancel the connection. CeRapiInit, on the other hand, will block until the connection succeeds or fails.

3. Why should you use LoadLibrary and GetProcAddress with RAPI.DLL instead of static linking?

   Customers might not have installed Windows CE Services before they run your software. If you statically link and RAPI.DLL is not available, they will be unable to load your application.

4. How can I get information about the files in a specific directory on the device?

   You can use a series of calls to CeFindFirstFile and CeFindNextFile, but it is usually more efficient to use CeFindAllFiles.

5. What is the correct function pointer definition for CeRapiInit?

   ```
   typedef HRESULT (WINAPI *PFN_RAPIINIT)();
   ```

   The most common mistake is to forget the WINAPI specification that uses the __stdcall calling convention. If you use the /GZ switch to compile your code, these types of errors will be caught automatically at runtime.

6. The return type of CeRapiInitEx is an HRESULT. Why can't it be tested with the SUCCESS or FAILURE macros?

A

The reason is that the return value doesn't always conform to the HRESULT standard format. Sometimes Win32 error codes such as ERROR_FILE_NOT_FOUND are returned, and those values will not work correctly with SUCCESS or FAILURE. To catch all real error codes, use CRI_Success as shown in Listing 20.3.

Exercises

1. Modify the CRIStream sample to allow text to be sent either direction.

   (No answer required)

2. Use CERapiInvoke to write a version of CeGlobalMemoryStatus that works correctly.

   (No answer required)

Hour 21, "Creating ActiveSync Modules"

Quiz

1. How do you create a CLSID?

   Use the GUIDGEN.EXE tool provided with Visual C++.

2. Every time you rebuild your desktop ActiveSync service provider, you are disconnecting your Windows CE device from your desktop computer so that the ActiveSync manager will release the preceding build of your module. What is a quicker and more efficient way to do this?

   It would be quicker for you to use the syncmgr.exe /quit command to force the ActiveSync manager to unload the service provider DLLs.

3. Which two interfaces must be implemented in the desktop portion of an ActiveSync service provider?

   The desktop ActiveSync service provider module has to implement a IReplStore interface and a IReplObjHandler interface.

4. Which device-side ActiveSync service provider functions are called only in Windows CE 2.1 and above?

   The FindObjects and SyncData functions are not used before Windows CE 2.1.

Exercise

Create an ActiveSync module that continuously keeps a text file synchronized between the desktop computer and the Windows CE device. On the desktop computer, the file will be c:\temp\ActiveSync.txt; on the Windows CE device, it will be

\My Documents\ActiveSync.txt. If the file is modified on either computer, the change will automatically be propagated to the user computer within 5 seconds.

(See the companion CD-ROM.)

Hour 22, "The Cure for the Common Crash"

Quiz

1. How many bytes do you need to allocate the Unicode representation of `Hello`?

   Twelve bytes are needed: ten bytes are required to hold the Unicode string characters, and two bytes are needed to hold the null terminator character.

2. How much of a thread's stack space is reserved for stack overflow control?

   2KB

3. Why use `UNALIGNED` instead of the `__unaligned` qualifier?

   `__unaligned` is not required or supported on all CPUs. The `UNALIGNED` macro takes this into account when building for a specific CPU. You will not be able to build your source code for X86 unless it uses `UNALIGNED` instead of `__unaligned`.

4. The `FindWindow` function is not returning when you search based on a window title. How do you address this?

   Change your code to search for the window based on the name of the window class (the first parameter to `FindWindow`), not the name of the window title (the second parameter to `FindWindow`).

5. Is it advisable to place a function call inside an `ASSERT`?

   Not if you want the function to be invoked in the release build of your application. The `VERIFY` macro should be used in place of `ASSERT` if you want the function call to remain in your release build.

6. You have implemented the memory wrapper functions discussed at the beginning of this hour. When debugging your program, you notice that your application is displaying garbage characters in the title of your pop-up `MessageBox` messages. You are using a global `TCHAR` pointer to store the title. If you don't use the memory wrapper functions, it displays the title correctly. What is most likely going wrong?

   The error is that the global `TCHAR` buffer that stores the title string is being freed before it is used in the `MessageBox` calls. The garbage characters in the title are due to the `free` wrapper function setting the buffer to `0xBB` before freeing it. The source code for the solution to exercise 2 provides you with hands-on experience with this.

A

7. How many bugs are in the following code, and what are they?

Three. Each one is explained in a BUGBUG comment in the source code.

```
 1: // This function returns the WCHAR representation of the
 2: // ascii string that is passed to it. It allocates the
 3: // buffer for the WCHAR version of the string.
 4: WCHAR *AsciiToWCHAR( CHAR *szOriginal )
 5: {
 6:     WCHAR      *wcReturn, *wc;
 7:     CHAR       *c;
 8:     DWORD      dwLength;
 9:
10:     ASSERT( szOriginal );
11:      /*
12:         BUGBUG - there is a bug in the following line of code. It
13:         is okay to use "ASSERT( strlen( szOriginal ) > 0 )", but the
14:         problem is that a value is being assigned to "dwLength"
15:         inside the assert. This means that "dwLength" will not
16:         be initialized properly in non-debug builds when asserts
17:         are stripped out. Use VERIFY here instead.
18:      */
19:     ASSERT( ( dwLength = strlen( szOriginal ) ) > 0 );
20:
21:     // allocate the WCHAR buffer
22:      /*
23:         BUGBUG - the bug in the following line of code is that the
24:         "+1" for the null terminating character is not being
25:         multiplied by the size of WCHAR, meaning that the buffer
26:         allocated will be 1 byte too small to hold the desired
27:         string. A proper parameter to "malloc" would be
28:         "( dwLength + 1 ) * sizeof( WCHAR )".
29:      */
30:     wcReturn = (WCHAR*) malloc( dwLength*sizeof(WCHAR) + 1 );
31:
32:     // use a string and WCHAR pointer to walk the two buffers,
33:     // transferring values from the ascii buffer to the WCHAR buffer
34:     // (note: in the real world, this should really be done
35:     //   with mbstowcs()
36:
37:      /*
38:         BUGBUG - the following code fails to copy the null
39:         terminating character to the WCHAR string after it is
40:         reached in the ascii string.
41:      */
42:
43:     c = szOriginal;
44:     wc = wcReturn;
45:     while( *c ) {
46:         *wc = (WCHAR)*c;
47:         wc++;
48:         c++;
```

```
49:    }
50:
51:    // return a pointer to the WCHAR buffer
52:    return wcReturn;
53: }
```

Exercises

1. Update the my_assert function listed earlier in this hour to provide the user with the option to hit a hard-coded break point (that is, a call to DebugBreak. This makes it easier for you the developer to break into the debugger when a problem is encountered.

```
 1: #if defined( DEBUG ) || defined( _DEBUG )
 2:
 3: VOID my_assert( CHAR *szAssertion, CHAR *szFile, INT iLineNumber )
 4: {
 5:     TCHAR    tcMessage[1024];
 6:     TCHAR    tcFile[MAX_PATH];
 7:     TCHAR    tcAssertion[1024];
 8:
 9:     // convert from single-byte to double-byte char strings
10:     mbstowcs( tcFile, szFile, strlen( szFile ) + 1 );
11:     mbstowcs( tcAssertion, szAssertion, strlen( szAssertion ) + 1 );
12:
13:     /****************************************************************
14:      * this version also provides the option for the developer to hit
15:      * a hardcoded break point
16:      ****************************************************************/
17:
18:     _tsprintf(    tcMessage,
19:                 TEXT( "Failed: %s, Line: %d\n\nExpression: %s\n\n" )
20:                 TEXT( "GetLastError() returns: %d\n\n" )
21:                 TEXT( "Would you like to hit a hardcoded " )
22:                  TEXT( "break point?" ),
23:                 tcFile, iLineNumber, tcAssertion, GetLastError() );
24:
25:     if ( IDYES == MessageBox(    GetFocus(), tcMessage,
26:                     TEXT( "Assertion Failed!" ),
27:                     MB_YESNO|MB_ICONEXCLAMATION|
28:                     MB_SETFOREGROUND ) ) {
29:
30:         DebugBreak();
31:
32:     }
33:
34: #endif
35:
36: }
37:
```

A

```
38: #endif    // DEBUG or _DEBUG
39:
```

2. Improve the `malloc` and `free` wrapper functions covered earlier in this hour to detect whether the start or end of the memory buffer has been overwritten. Do this by implementing a guard `DWORD` immediately before and after the buffer, as described in the section "Creating Your Own Memory Wrapper Functions."

```
 1: void *my_malloc( size_t size )
 2: {
 3:     DWORD    dwGuard = 0xABABABAB;
 4:     BYTE     bOffset = 4;
 5:
 6:     // allocate the buffer requested by the calling routine
 7:     // plus room for a guard DWORD at the start and end
 8:     void *buffer = malloc( size + 8 );
 9:
10:     // if we were successful, initialize it to 0xAA
11:     if ( buffer != NULL ) {
12:
13:         // buffer might be slightly larger than what was
14:         // requested; adjust 'size' accordingly
15:         size = _msize( buffer ) - 8;
16:
17:         memset( ((BYTE*)buffer)+4, 0xAA, size );
18:         memcpy( buffer, &dwGuard, 4 );
19:         memcpy( ((BYTE*)buffer)+size+4, &dwGuard, 4 );
20:     }
21:
22:     // return the buffer pointer to the calling routine
23:     // The "+4" returns the pointer to the buffer after
24:     // the guard DWORD at the start of the buffer
25:      return ( ((BYTE*)buffer) + bOffset );
26: }
27:
28: void my_free( void *memblock )
29: {
30:     BOOL     fMemoryTrash = FALSE;
31:     DWORD    dwBufferSize = _msize( ((BYTE*)memblock)-4 ) - 8;
32:     DWORD    dwGuard = 0xABABABAB;
33:
34:     // if the memory pointer is not null, check whether it is
35:     // healthy; then set its buffer contents to be 0xBB
36:     if ( memblock != NULL ) {
37:
38:         fMemoryTrash = ( memcmp( ((BYTE*)memblock)-4,
39:                         &dwGuard, 4 ) != 0 );
40:         fMemoryTrash |= ( memcmp( ((BYTE*)memblock)+
41:                         dwBufferSize, &dwGuard, 4 ) != 0 );
42:
```

```
43:         memset( memblock, 0xBB, dwBufferSize );
44:     }
45:
46:     // free the memory as requested (-4 is to free the entire block).
47:     free( ((BYTE*)memblock) - 4 );
48:
49:     MessageBox(    GetFocus(),
50:             fMemoryTrash ? TEXT( "Overwrite!" ) :
51:             TEXT( "NO Overwrite" ),
52:             TEXT( "Freeing Memory" ), MB_OK );
53:
54: }
53:
```

Note that this code depends on _msize returning the correct size of the buffer. This may not happen if the memory overwritten is too severe. A better implementation is to create a linked list of allocated memory and independently keep track of the size of each memory block allocated.

The following code will generate a memory overwrite if 16 bytes are allocated to store an 18-byte string (8 Unicode characters, plus the null termination). The memory overwrite goes away if the 18 bytes are allocated.

```
 1: TCHAR    *g_tcWindowClass, *g_tcTitle;
 2:
 3: #if
 4:
 5:     // use this code to generate a memory overwrite
 6:
 7:     g_tcWindowClass   = (TCHAR*)malloc( 16 );
 8:     g_tcTitle         = (TCHAR*)malloc( 16 );
 9:
10: #else
11:
12:     // use this code to avoid a memory overwrite, but we are still
13:     // accessing freed memory when handling the
14:     //   ID_FILE_VIEWMESSAGEBOXWITHFREEDMEMORYUSEDASTITLE
15:     // message below
16:     g_tcWindowClass   = (TCHAR*)malloc( 18 );
17:     g_tcTitle         = (TCHAR*)malloc( 18 );
18:
19: #endif
20:
21:     _tcscpy( g_tcTitle, TEXT( "My Title" ) );
22:     _tcscpy( g_tcWindowClass, TEXT( "My Class" ) );
23:
24:     // Initialize global strings
25:     MyRegisterClass(hInstance, g_tcWindowClass );
26:
27:     hWnd = CreateWindow( g_tcWindowClass, g_tcTitle, WS_VISIBLE,
```

A

```
28:          0, 0, CW_USEDEFAULT, CW_USEDEFAULT, NULL, NULL,
29:          hInstance, NULL);
30:
31:    free( g_tcWindowClass );
32:    free( g_tcTitle     );
33:
34:
```

Hour 23, "Debugging Windows CE Applications with Visual C++"

Quiz

1. How is remote debugging different from debugging on a single machine?

   Remote debugging requires a communication transport mechanism and a stub program running on the target device to manipulate the debuggee process.

2. Why was Attach to Process debugging removed from VCCE 6?

   Because the underlying thread suspension mechanism that Attach to Process relies on does not always work on Windows CE, the feature was unreliable.

3. Why can't I step through the assembler instructions for a Windows CE system call in the debugger?

   Single stepping requires a series of break points to be written, and because the operating system kernel implementation is in ROM, this is not possible.

4. When I hit a break point in a window message handler routine, my call stack doesn't show the full history. Why?

   Because the callback is via a PSL, the return address is invalid, so the stack trace stops earlier than its desktop equivalent.

5. Why can't I debug Control Panel applets or Pocket Mail transports with VCCE 6?

   The applet or transport is a DLL and is utilized by an executable stored in ROM. Because the necessary executable does not reside on the desktop machine, it cannot be launched by the debugger. Thus, the dependent DLL cannot be debugged.

6. What is a PSL?

   PSL stands for Protected Server Library. According to the *Microsoft Press Book*, it is "a hybrid between a DLL and a standalone process." It is used to minimize the time necessary for system calls on Windows CE.

7. Does the C runtime library track memory leaks on Windows CE?

No, the memory leak tracking facilities available in the desktop C runtime library are not implemented on Windows CE.

8. Why are memory break points slow on Windows CE?

Because Windows CE targets multiple microprocessors, a portable implementation is used that requires checking the break point expression after each CPU instruction.

9. Is the new Visual C++ 6 Edit and Continue debugger feature available in VCCE?

No, Edit and Continue was dropped from VCCE for performance reasons.

10. What is Platform Manager?

Platform Manager is a new feature of VCCE 6 that enables you to configure Windows CE devices to use the serial port or ethernet as a communications medium.

Hour 24, "Advanced Topics: MFC, ATL, and POOM"

A

Quiz

1. How do you subclass a control using MFC on Windows CE?

Subclassing is not supported on MFC for Windows CE.

2. How do you handle a WM_HIBERNATE message within your MFC application?

Implement a handler for the WM_HIBERNATE message in a class derived from CWnd.

3. What is the name of the main interface to POOM?

IPOutlookApp

4. What are the four MFC classes specifically designed for working with Windows CE databases, and what do they do?

The CCeDBEnum class is used for enumerating the databases. The CCeDBDatabase class is used for manipulating databases. The CCeDBRecord class is used for manipulating records within a database. The CCeDBProp class is used for manipulating a database record's properties.

5. When using the CCeSocket class, how do you determine the invisible window to which you should send WM_SOCKET_NOTIFY?

The global AfxGetCeSocketWindow function will return the window handle to the invisible socket window.

Exercises

1. Create a single document MFC application that displays Hello World in the document view.

   This is achieved by creating a new single document MFC application and then updating the OnDraw method of the view class to display Hello World.

   ```
   void CHelloView::OnDraw(CDC* pDC)
   {
       TCHAR    tcHello[] = TEXT( "Hello!" );
       RECT     rt;
       GetClientRect( &rt );
       DrawText( pDC->m_hDC, tcHello, _tcslen(tcHello), &rt, DT_CENTER );
   }
   ```

2. Create a dialog box MFC application that displays Hello when you select its Hello button.

   This is achieved by creating a dialog box MFC application and adding a Hello button to it in the Visual C++ resource editor. Double-clicking the button opens the Add Member Function dialog. Clicking OK creates the following code within your project:

   ```
   void CHelloDlg::OnButtonHello()
   {
       // TODO: Add your control notification handler code here

   }
   ```

   Now it is just a matter of adding

   ```
   MessageBox( TEXT( "Hello!" ), TEXT( "Exercise" ), MB_OK );
   ```

   to the body of CHelloDlg::OnButtonHello().

APPENDIX **B**

What's on the CD-ROM

The companion CD-ROM contains the authors' source code for the examples, as well as 30-day evaluation copies of bSQUARE's bUSEFUL and bPRODUCTIVE application suites.

The bUSEFUL Utilities Pak

Twelve applications, described here, are included in the bUSEFUL Utilities Pak.

bUSEFUL Backup Plus

Avoid potential data loss by backing up all data or portions of data on a device in less than a minute! This is helpful for backing up various device configurations (for example, a contacts database with 4,000 entries) so that you can quickly re-create different testing scenarios.

bUSEFUL Analyzer

Analyze and benchmark every portion of a PC Companion system: CPU information, power management, memory, video, and more. How does your PC Companion stand up?

bUSEFUL FindSpace

Speed device performance by identifying and deleting unnecessary items.

bUSEFUL Script

Automate routine tasks such as logging on to an ISP, retrieving email, and more. Create scripts to automatically put your own application through its paces.

bUSEFUL List Plus

Easily track all your projects and tasks.

bUSEFUL Launch

Save time by creating a customized start menu for the fast launching of items used the most: folders, programs, files, Web sites, and more.

bUSEFUL Notepad

Create and edit text files the quick and easy way.

bTASK

BSQUARE's popular software for navigating applications, closing applications, and viewing device information, including storage and battery status.

bUSEFUL HTML Editor

Create, edit, and save HTML files (.HTM and .HTML)—as well as Windows CE help files (.HTC and .HTP)—remotely on a PC Companion.

bUSEFUL UUEncode

Convert files to a uuencoded format to enable larger email transmissions from a PC Companion.

bFIND

Never lose track of information again with this global search utility that searches for files, file contents, databases, contacts, and more.

bUSEFUL MoonPhase

With 11 serious applications, a little lightheartedness is in store with this fun utility for tracking the phases of the moon and more.

The bPRODUCTIVE Essentials Pak

The new bPRODUCTIVE Essentials Pak includes full versions of the BSQUARE applications described here.

bFAX Pro (H/PC) or bFAX Express (PsPC)

The industry standard in faxing software for PC Companions.

bPRINT

Print to more printers, queue jobs for batch printing, and more. This is the only commercial print application available for Palm-size PCs (PSPCs). Export data from your own application to a supported file format, and then queue that file within bPRINT by launching bPRINT with a command line of the exported file's name within double quotes.

bTRACK

The most comprehensive way to track your time and expenses.

bREADY Viewer

View your important information in electronic books.

bMOBILE News

Read and respond to Internet newsgroups—anywhere, anytime.

bTASK (PSPC)

Easily navigate and close applications on your P/PC.

B

INDEX

Q

QueryDevice method, 345
Quinn, Bob, 216

R

radio buttons, 80-81
RAM, object store, 140
RAPI (Remote API), 311-321
    calling DLL functions, 319-321,
        323-335
    CeRapiInvoke function, 319-321,
        323-335
    DLL, 316-317, 335
    header file, 316
    import library, 316
    initializing connection, 315
    linking, 316-317, 335
    memory leaks, 321
    object store database functions, 312
    object store file functions, 313
    process creation functions, 314
    registry functions, 314
    simple remote procedure call, 315
    startup/shutdown functions, 312, 315,
        317-318
    system functions, 314-315, 318-319
    window information functions, 315
    WinSock, 316
RAS (Remote Access Services), 28
raw mode, 212
ReadFile() function, 142, 208
reading
    database records, 169-171
    files, 142
ReadProcessMemory API, 194

rebar controls, 47
REBARBANDINFO structure, 49-50
Record button, 236
records, 160
    deleting, 172
    reading, 169-170
    searching for, 168-169
    writing, 171
RecountCards() function, 269
rectangles, 124, 136
recursion, 362
RegCloseKey() function, 157
RegCreateKeyEx() function, 151
RegDeleteValue() function, 153
RegEnumKeyEx() function, 154
RegEnumValue() function, 154
registration, 399
Registry, 150
    ActiveSync, 346, 348-349
    closing, 157
    creating keys, 151
    data types, 152
    deleting keys, 153
    editing, 9
    initialize settings, 9
    installing entries, 254-255
    key parameters, 155
    keys, 150, 396
    list keys, 154-155
    list values, 156-157
    modifying, 20
    opening keys, 152
    RAPI functions, 314
    reading, 152
    root keys, 151
    root-level entries, 158
    uninstalling, 9
    values, 153
    writing to, 153

Other Related Titles

**Sams Teach Yourself
Visual C++ 6 in 24
Hours**
0-672-31303-0
Mickey Williams
$24.99 USA / $35.95 CAN

**Sams Teach Yourself
C++ in 24 Hours, Second
Edition**
0-672-31516-5
Jesse Liberty
$19.99 USA / $28.95 CAN

**Sams Teach Yourself
Outlook 2000
Programming in 24
Hours**
0-672-31651-X
Sue Mosher
$19.99 USA / $28.95 CAN

**Sams Teach Yourself
Word 2000 Automation
in 24 Hours**
0-672-31652-8
Pam Palmer
$19.99 USA / $28.95 CAN

**Sams Teach Yourself
Microsoft FrontPage
2000 in 24 Hours**
0-672-31500-9
Dick Oliver and
Rogers Cadenhead
$19.99 USA / $28.95 CAN

**Sams Teach Yourself
Visual C++ 6 in 21 Days:
Complete Compiler
Edition**
0-672-31403-7
Davis Chapman
$49.99 USA / $71.95 CAN

**Sams Teach Yourself
UML in 24 Hours**
0-672-31636-6
Joseph Schmuller
$24.99 USA / $37.95 CAN

**Sams Teach Yourself
Palm Programming in 24
Hours**
0-672-31611-0
Gavin Maxwell
$24.99 USA / $37.95 CAN

Palm Programming
0-672-31493-2
Glenn Bachmann
$29.99 USA / $44.95 CAN

**Sams Teach Yourself
Visual C++ 6 in 21 Days**
0-672-31240-9
Davis Chapman
$34.99 USA / $50.95 CAN

**Sams Teach Yourself
MFC in 24 Hours**
0-672-31553-X
Michael Morrison
$24.99 USA / $35.95 CAN

SAMS

www.samspublishing.com

All prices are subject to change.

Make the most of your Handheld PC

This conveniently assembled collection of the latest Windows® CE applications is designed to save you time and simplify your information management.

- **Financial Consultant 2.0** - Make financial decisions quickly
- **Pocket Finance 2.0** - Enter your transactions as you make them
- **bTASK™** - Navigate applications from one program
- **Print-to-bFAX™** - fax from any program that supports printing
- **PhoneTone™ Generator & Speed Dialer** - Generate TouchTone™ sounds from your Handheld PC.
- **Casino Royal 1.01** - Save some time to play!

Macmillan PlusPack for Windows® CE

ISBN: 1-57595-259-9 $39.95 US / $49.95 CAN

Available at software retailers or online at: www.macmillansoftware.com

SOFTWARE LICENSE INFORMATION

The accompanying CD-ROM contains two groups of software programs. Software programs are used pursuant to end user license agreements that describe the terms of use. These do not apply to the CD-ROM itself, but to the software stored on it.

The first group of programs consists of 30-day evaluation copies of certain BSQUARE software programs, bUSEFUL and bPRODUCTIVE (that comes in a version for a hand-held and for palm-sized PCs). Each of these evaluation copies has an end user license agreement ("EULA") that governs its use. You must agree to this EULA in order to use the software. The 30 days begins when you install the software. At the end of the 30 days, the programs will no longer work. If you wish to purchase a non-expiring copy then follow the instructions provided in the program.

The second group of software programs are certain sample programs as described in this book. These programs are found in directories that are related to chapters in the book. For these sample programs, which will not have an accompanying EULA, the following end user license applies. Please note that it is very different from the EULAs for the first group of programs.

BSQUARE END USER LICENSE AGREEMENT

IMPORTANT-READ CAREFULLY: This End User License Agreement ("EULA") is a legal agreement between you (either an individual or a single entity) and BSQUARE CORPORATION ("Manufacturer") the manufacturer of the sample programs provided on the accompanying CD-ROM ("SAMPLE SOFTWARE"). The SAMPLE SOFTWARE includes computer software. By installing, copying or otherwise using the SOFTWARE, you agree to be bound by the terms of this EULA. If you do not agree to the terms of this EULA, the Manufacturer is unwilling to license the SOFTWARE to you. In such event, you may not use or copy the SOFTWARE and you should contact the Manufacturer.

SOFTWARE LICENSE.

The SAMPLE SOFTWARE is protected by copyright laws and international copyright treaties, as well as other intellectual property laws and treaties. The SAMPLE SOFT-WARE is licensed, not sold.

GRANT OF LICENSE. This EULA grants you the following rights:

- Usage. This SAMPLE SOFTWARE is provided for educational purposes only and not as a consumer product. It is designed and provided to illustrate certain techniques described in the accompanying book. The SAMPLE SOFTWARE may not be used in any other way.

- Back-up Copy. You may make a single copy of the SOFTWARE for use solely for archival purposes with the System.

DESCRIPTION OF OTHER RIGHTS AND LIMITATIONS.

- Rental. You may not rent or lease the SAMPLE SOFTWARE.

- Software Transfer. You may permanently transfer all of your rights under this EULA only as part of a sale or transfer provided you retain no copies, you transfer all of the SAMPLE SOFTWARE (including all component parts, the media, any upgrades or backup copies, and this EULA), and the recipient agrees to the terms of this EULA.

- Termination. Without prejudice to any other rights, Manufacturer may terminate this EULA if you fail to comply with the terms and conditions of this EULA. In such event, you must destroy all copies of the SAMPLE SOFTWARE and all of its component parts.

COPYRIGHT.

All title and copyrights in and to the SAMPLE SOFTWARE and any copies of the SAMPLE SOFTWARE, are owned by BSQUARE CORPORATION or its suppliers. All rights not specifically granted under this EULA are reserved by BSQUARE CORPORATION.

- **NO WARRANTIES**. THE SAMPLE SOFTWARE IS PROVIDED TO THE END USER "AS IS" WITHOUT WARRANTY OF ANY KIND, EITHER EXPRESSED OR IMPLIED, INCLUDING, BUT NOT LIMITED TO, WARRANTIES OF NON-INFRINGEMENT, MERCHANTABILITY, AND/OR FITNESS FOR A PARTICULAR PURPOSE. THE ENTIRE RISK OF THE QUALITY AND PERFORMANCE OF THE SAMPLE SOFTWARE IS WITH YOU. IF YOU LIVE IN A STATE THAT DOES NOT ALLOW THE EXCLUSION OF IMPLIED WARRANTIES, ANY IMPLIED WARRANTIES ARE LIMITED TO NINETY DAYS FROM LOADING THE SAMPLE SOFTWARE ONTO YOUR SYSTEM.

- **No Liability for Consequential Damages**. NEITHER MANUFACTURER NOR MANUFACTURER'S SUPPLIERS SHALL BE HELD TO ANY LIABILITY FOR ANY DAMAGES SUFFERED OR INCURRED BY THE END USER (INCLUDING, BUT NOT LIMITED TO, GENERAL, SPECIAL, CONSEQUENTIAL OR INCIDENTAL DAMAGES INCLUDING DAMAGES FOR LOSS OF BUSINESS PROFITS, BUSINESS INTERRUPTION, LOSS OF BUSINESS INFORMATION AND THE LIKE), ARISING FROM OR IN CONNECTION WITH THE DELIVERY, USE OR PERFORMANCE OF THE SAMPLE SOFTWARE. SOME STATES/JURISDICTIONS DO NOT ALLOW THE EXCLUSION OR LIMITATION OF INCIDENTAL OR CONSEQUENTIAL DAMAGES, SO

THE ABOVE LIMITATION OR EXCLUSION MAY NOT APPLY TO YOU.

U.S. GOVERNMENT RESTRICTED RIGHTS.

The SAMPLE SOFTWARE and documentation are provided with RESTRICTED RIGHTS. Use, duplication, or disclosure by the Government is subject to restrictions as set forth in subparagraph (c)(1)(ii) of the Rights in Technical Data and Computer Software clause at DFARS 252.227-7013 or subparagraphs (c)(1) and (2) of the Commercial Computer Software-Restricted Rights at 48 CFR 52.227-19, as applicable. Manufacturer is BSQUARE CORPORATION /3633 - 136th Place SE, Suite 100/Bellevue WA 98006.

This EULA is governed by the laws of the State of Washington, United States of America.

This warranty gives you specific legal rights, and you may also have other rights which vary from state to state or jurisdiction to jurisdiction.

Should you have any questions concerning this EULA, please contact the Manufacturer.